Jürgen Rothlauf
A Global View on Intercultural Management

Jürgen Rothlauf

A Global View on Intercultural Management

Challenges in a Globalized World

DE GRUYTER
OLDENBOURG

ISBN 978-3-11-040062-5
e-ISBN (PDF) 978-3-11-037628-9
e-ISBN (EPUB) 978-3-11-039790-1

Library of Congress Cataloging-in-Publication Data
A CIP catalog record for this book has been applied for at the Library of Congress.

Bibliographic information published by the Deutsche Nationalbibliothek
The Deutsche Nationalbibliothek lists this publication in the Deutsche Nationalbibliografie;
detailed bibliographic data are available on the Internet at http://dnb.dnb.de.

© 2014 Walter de Gruyter GmbH, Berlin/Munich/Boston
Cover illustration: Robert Churchill/iStock/Thinkstock
Printing and Binding: CPI books GmbH, Leck
♾ Printed on acid-free paper
Printed in Germany

www.degruyter.com

Preface

The world becomes more and more global. Managers around the world are, or soon will be, involved to some degree in international business. The escalating level of international involvement and competition in today's business areas requires that managers develop and improve their skills necessary for effective cross-national interactions and daily operations in foreign subsidiaries. Feedback from companies operating abroad reveals that expatriate failure is often caused by the ineffective management of intercultural relations, so the fate of expatriate missions depends at least in part on the international managers' cultural skills and sensitivity.

The questions related to the right intercultural understanding and behavior are vital in order to be successful in an ongoing worldwide competition. The companies have to develop a strategy that is supportive in their efforts to work effectively and efficiently across borders. Today's manager increasingly has to work in international and cross cultural environments. In addition to the normal pressures, managers are now required to cope with challenges, friction and misunderstandings emanating from cross cultural differences. Effective management in the modern environment demands cross cultural competency in order to make the best out of a multicultural team. Therefore a holistic approach that takes all intercultural aspects into consideration is absolutely necessary.

The aim of this book is to provide an excellent multicultural overview of the challenges we face today in the demanding arena of global business interactions. The book is a value-added primer for readers who need an orientation to varied business cultures. It allows readers to achieve a higher level of awareness of the requirements imposed by different cultural situations. Moreover this volume is geared to students of International Management as well as responsible practitioners of the same. Above all, however, it is aimed at management staff in the process of preparing for international assignments either for a private enterprise or in development-aid institutions.

A Comprehensive View on Intercultural Management – Challenges in a Globalized World is presented in nine chapters. Chapter 10 should enable readers to test their intercultural skills. A globality check, a test for global management skills and a crossword puzzle are waiting to get the right intercultural answers.
The opening chapter 1 explores business challenges encountered in global management and tries to underline the importance of Intercultural Management nowadays.
Chapter 2 deals with all facets of culture. Moreover a various cultural models are presented trying to provide a conceptual framework that enables companies and managers to assess relevant cultural variables and develop cultural profiles of different countries.

Chapter 3 focuses on corporate cultures and describes the seven cultural integration drivers that are helpful to become a successful player in an internationally challenging environment.

Moreover a look at Mergers & Acquisition aims at providing the reader to get a deeper insight into all important aspects that are relevant for doing business in a globalized world.

The ability to deal constructively on an interpersonal level with cultural diversity and the multitude of attitudes and values will become a key qualification. Chapter 4 tries to give an answer how cultural business values differ and in which way values do influence multicultural organizations.

Everything we do across national and cultural borders, or within diverse societies, needs to take cultural differences into account. Chapter 5 is dedicated to present intercultural skills and attitudes that all belong to the wide field of intercultural competence.

Effective business communications are critical to the growth of every organization. Chapter 6 provides some good examples of how business introductions, telephone calls, presentations, and written communication can lead to an operation's success or failure.

It is crucial for international managers to understand the influence of culture on decision-making styles and processes. Whenever somebody has to guide a team the relevant leadership qualifications are asked for. And there is no one single leadership style that fits to all intercultural challenges. How to behave properly is shown in chapter 7.

The ability to develop effective multicultural teams is essential in light of the increasing proliferation of foreign subsidiaries, joint venture, and other transnational alliances. Working in a multicultural team requires a set of skills that are quite different compared to a local team. Chapter 8 presents how a positive climate can be established and what sort of intercultural challenges are demanded in this context.

Chapter 9 focuses on intercultural preparation and reintegration. It centres on the necessity of training for cross-cultural interactions and discusses what global players can learn from our survey that was conducted in 2009 and which role the family has to play in the preparation for an international assignment.

Each chapter is accompanied by a case study and/or a role play. Moreover, students and other interculturally involved persons have asked experts about their opinions on different topics related to the intercultural world. Both, the questions and the answers conclude each chapter.

I do hope that the scope and the richness of the book, as well as the depth of its specific practical business situations, will help the reader to get a better intercultural understanding. Moreover, I would feel honored if some of my ideas will help readers to acquire the poise and confidence they need to be truly effective in doing business across cultures – both at home and abroad.

Acknowledgments

I would like to acknowledge those who have helped to make this book a reality. Special thanks go to my students of the international study courses "Leisure and Tourism Management" and "Baltic Management Studies" at the University of Applied Sciences in Stralsund and to my students at the Université de Haute-Alsace in Mulhouse/Colmar, who have given me many ideas by taking a deeper look into their assignments. Some of the results of their surveys are to be found in this book.

I would like to give special recognition to my former English teacher at the Bayernkolleg Schweinfurt, Gerald Jansche, and former lecturer at the University of Applied Sciences Schweinfurt/Würzburg for his initial support in reading some parts of the book.

Also, I owe a special debt for the encouragement from the De Gruyter Oldenbourg Publishing Company and to Dr. Stefan Giesen for the fruitful co-operation.

Finally, I am more than grateful to Elisabeth Guth, my former student and now a Bachelor graduate from my university. I appreciate her stimulation, advice, and support over all stages of this project.

Prof. Dr. Jürgen Rothlauf

Table of Contents

List of Figures

List of Tables

1   Globalization and Intercultural Management

1.0   Statement of the problem

Globalization and Business issues
(Julia Serdyuk)

Globalization eliminates the boundaries between the countries and provides new opportunities for business: want to open a subsidiary in Egypt? Go ahead! Want to sell your shoes of high quality in Kazakhstan? You can try! However, as the reality shows, it is not that simple and in many cases cultural differences, including differences in management style, can prevent the success of a joint venture.

In spite of all the differences between business cultures, we cannot neglect certain common grounds that constitute business in general. For example, each business deals with profit-orientation, professional development of staff, etc. And, thanks to globalization, today various countries can share and learn from each other in order to adopt new elements in their own operation. For example, Japanese companies now seem to be picking up lessons from American management to become more flexible and less avoiding uncertainty; American companies are learning best practices from their counterparts in other parts of the world, especially from Japan.

Having been off the market for many years, and under the pressure of "command" authority, Russia had difficulties to enter the world market. While globalization was already involving all other countries, it did not "touch" Russian business and management style until the 90's, when the country started reforming its own business style. Now, Russia constitutes a part of the business world and is interconnected with the world system. Russia adopted some well-known management models as well as developed its own business strategies. What model of business style has Russia chosen? It is hard to define the model itself, as it is still being developed, but we can characterize Russian management style as more autocratic than democratic. Although the tendency in management here is to get more people-oriented, less "power-oriented", employees get more and more appreciation for their knowledge, experience, and creativity. They are also given more choices and responsibilities at the workplace. I think, this indicates the development of a new management style, which has more similarities with American and European ones.

To summarize, globalization provides many opportunities as well as challenges in business. In order to better utilize the opportunities for different countries to operate successfully, under the conditions of cultural diversity, we need to go beyond our cultural stereotypes. Curiosity, openness and striving to reach mutual understanding should become good features for intercultural management. We can learn a lot from each other, but we need to learn to be tolerant and respectful to all the differences we face, when we do business together.

In: Cross-Cultural Blog: management style and globalization, in web: http://web.stanford.edu/group/ccr/blog/2009/02/globalization_and_business_iss.html, accessed 23/06/2014

1.1   "The Global Challenge"

Every day we hear it on the news, read it in the papers, overhear people talking about it, and in every single instance the word "globalization" seems to have a different meaning. So, what is globalization?

At the political and economic level, globalization is the process of denationalization of markets, politics and legal systems; it is the rise of global economy. At the business level, the process of globalization is when companies decide to take part in the emerging global economy and establish themselves in foreign markets. They adapt their products or services to the linguistic and cultural requirements of different nations. Then, they might take advantage of the Internet revolution and establish a virtual presence on the international marketplace. E-commerce has changed traditional business practices by providing direct international access to information and products.

Whatever their industry or country of origin, all companies are facing the same challenge to a greater or lesser degree: globalization. It is becoming more and more evident that companies need to plan ahead and anticipate coming developments if they are to be successful in the future. Ecological matters have gained in importance at the turn of the century. Climate change is perceived as the biggest challenge to mankind and affects all industries and societies alike (Stern, 2008, p. 1).

In the past, it was primarily reductions in tariff and trade barriers that stimulated global trade and encouraged the integration of international business. Today, however, the key factor is the global networking that has been made possible by new communication technologies. Increasingly intense international competition is accelerating structural change throughout the world. More and more, industries that only "yesterday" limited their production to the United States, Europe or Japan are feeling the influence of threshold countries. Moreover, jobs that seemed guaranteed for life some years ago are moving into these low-wage countries. No longer are they limited to the production of simple toys for children – today companies in threshold countries are producing luxury consumer goods, consumer electronics and highly sophisticated machines and vehicles, and with dizzying success (Lippisch/Köppel, 2007, p. 3).

In order to be economically successful in the global market, it is not only the hard facts that count – such as the general economic and commercial settings, product quality or innovative products and services. "Soft" competencies, especially social competence and excellent communication skills, become more and more important. Thus, a balanced consideration of hard facts and "soft" competencies is increasingly becoming a prerequisite for global success. Only companies and organizations with a multicultural structure will succeed beyond the regional level and will continue to be successful on a global scale. In the future, mono-structures and mono-cultures will be limited to regional importance. However, multicultural organizations will not prosper automatically, just because they are multicultural. On the contrary, if managed badly, they may function worse than mono-cultural organizations. Thus, the skills to lead a multicultural organization have to be in the focus and are paramount for the success in the global market.

These consequences of global competition are putting pressure on companies in the developed Western countries. Companies from Central and Western Europe are faced with the question of how to respond in order to remain competitive. Market isolation is a strategy that no longer works in today's globalized world, and it is likely to do more harm than good.

Instead, today it is crucial to establish a solid competitive position in the global arena and to defend that position by continually adapting to meet the needs of the market. There is no doubt that a corporate culture that is open to innovation and shaped by global thinking plays a key role in this context, a culture in which representatives of different countries and cultures can come together, while giving due regard to the developments and conditions that influence a company's actions (Lippisch/Köppel, 2007, p. 3). International business and professional activity demand movement beyond one particular cultural conditioning into a transcultural arena.

The technological environment surrounding businesses today is characterized by a soaring speed of change and innovation. Revolutionizing innovations in the fields such as microelectronic, robotic and generic engineering can be perceived as a threat or chance to the enterprise's competition (Welge/Al-Laham, 2008, p. 295).

If globalization refers to the transmission of ideas, meanings and values across world space the intercultural aspect is obvious. In the contemporary period, and from the beginning of the twentieth century, this process is marked by the common consumption of cultures that have been diffused by the Internet, popular culture media, and international travel. This has added to processes of commodity exchange and colonization which have a longer history of carrying cultural meaning across the globe. The circulation of cultures enables individuals to partake in extended social relations that cross national and regional borders. The creation and expansion of such social relations is not merely observed on a material level. Cultural globalization involves the formation of shared norms and knowledge with which people associate their individual and collective cultural identities. It brings increasing interconnectedness among different populations and cultures (Steger/James, 2010, p. 12).

As far as global challenges are concerned, the current developments can be split into four main categories (Rothlauf, 2004, pp. 25ff), namely:

- new technologies
- new markets
- new environmental drivers
- new global players

Within this framework, an intercultural answer has to be given, which includes:
- new corporate culture
- new skills
- new management and working styles
- new company structures

Both, challenges and the intercultural answers will be presented in the following and are also illustrated in Fig. 1.1.

1.1.1   Global challenges

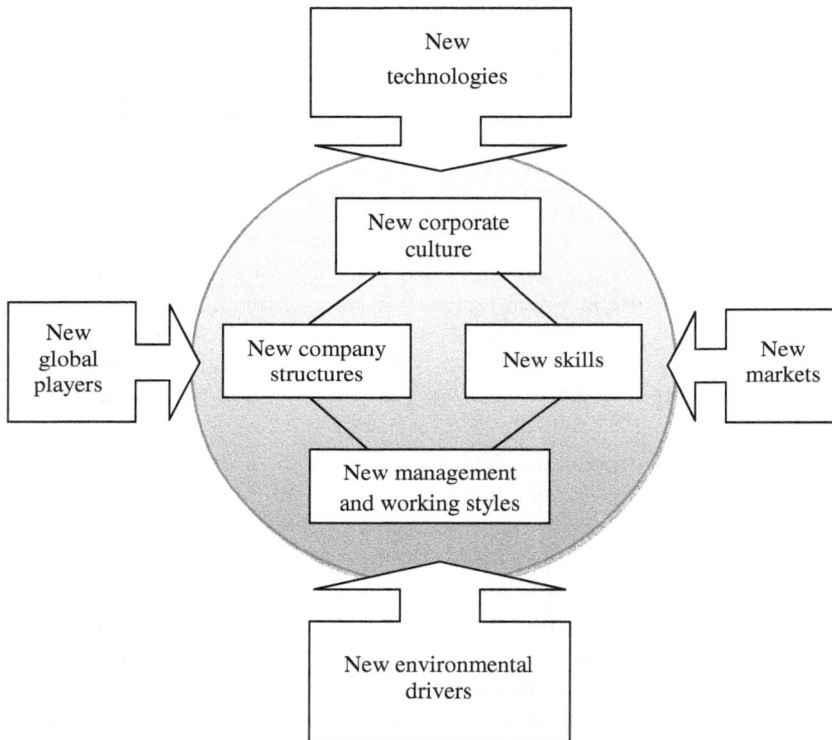

Fig. 1.1:   Challenges and solutions in the global context
Source: Own illustration

New technologies

New information and communication technologies, such as the internet, are ubiquitous and cheap; they control the markets, permit worldwide access to information, foster global trends and reach the most distant corner of the world.

Moreover, an emerging technology as distinguished from a conventional technology is a field of technology that broaches new territory in some significant way with new technological developments. Examples of currently emerging technologies include educational technology, nanotechnology, biotechnology, cognitive science, robotics, and artificial intelligence.

New markets

Business is always changing and to maximize the relevant business options one have to explore new markets and to expand the current buiness activities. As resources become scarcer and scarcer and domestic markets are reaching the saturation point, it is becoming increasingly important to open up new sales, resource and labor markets. A successful search for geographic or technical alternatives is part of a company's international strategy. Moving into new territories and categories is a radical strategy that can create major potential for incremental business growth. To succeed it requires a precise understanding of market dynamics, consumer behaviour and the competitive landscape of the specific markets.

New global players

Companies from threshold countries are developing at a breathtaking speed. They have the benefit of a plentiful supply of cheap, motivated and well-qualified workers. They are developing an increasingly accurate sense of where the demand is, and their ability to offer high-quality products at a reasonable price is growing as well.

A good example for those new global players is BRICS, an acronym for an association of five major emerging national economies: Brazil, Russia, India, China and South Africa. The BRICS members are all developing or nearly industrialised countries, but they are distinguished by their large, fast-growing economies. Moreover more and more developing countries are now entering the international stage and will play a larger role in the future.

New environmental drivers

Climate change and energy supply concerns are the primary drivers in the present debate. It has now been scientifically proven that climate change is triggered off by the emission of anthropogenic greenhouse gases; first and foremost CO_2. In order to find adequate solutions to meet the manifold environmental need an urgent global response is demanded. The growing pollution all around the world has to be taken into account and the focus of all business activities should move to a higher environmental commitment of all parties involved in this context. In the long run, only those enterprises will survive that have the right answer in this very challenging field and can offer environmentally friendly products and services.

The Global Toothbrush
(Ralf Hoppe)

How many employees does it take to manufacture a toothbrush? Forty-five-hundred employees, 10 countries, five time zones.

Philips and its suppliers produce the electronic toothbrush "Sonicare Elite 7000" and its sister models at 12 locations and in five time zones. Once or twice a week, some 100,000 fully-functioning circuit boards leave the Manila factory. From Manila's cargo airport they are flown via Tokyo to Seattle. A half day's delay can wreak havoc in the entire system with a minimum of inventory and extremely tight timelines.

The toothbrush is essentially comprised of 38 components. The parts of the energy cell, a rechargeable nickel-cadmium battery, are supplied by Japan, France and China. The circuit board, its electronic heart, comes pre-etched from Zhuhai in the Pearl River delta of south eastern China. The copper coils originate from the Chinese industrial city of Shenzhen, not far from Zhuhai. They are wound by armies of women with bandaged fingers. Globalization is largely a female phenomenon.

The 49 components on the board – transistors and resistors at the size of match heads – hail from Malaysia. They are soldered and tested in Manila. Then they are flown to Snoqualmie on the West Coast of the U.S., the site of the parent plant. Meanwhile, back in Europe, the more complicated plastic parts are trucked from Klagenfurt in Austria to Bremerhaven in Germany. Klagenfurt also supplies blades made of special steel produced in Sandviken, Sweden. A freighter from Bremerhaven takes the half-finished brushes across the Atlantic to Port Elizabeth, New Jersey. From there they cross the continental United States by train. And in Snoqualmie, a 40 minute drive from Seattle, the final product is assembled and packaged.

Philips is a Netherlands corporation. But there are only two Dutch citizens among the 120 on this carousel of cultures and continents. The foreman in Snoqualmie comes from Gambia. Bernard Lim Nam Onn, the boss in Zhuhai, is Chinese, but was born in Malaysia and raised in Singapore. There are Irish, Ukrainians, Indians, Cambodians, Vietnamese, Thai. Globalization is carving out new biographies and cross-referencing them around the world.

In: Spiegel Special – International Edition, Nr. 7/2005, pp. 130ff

1.1.2   The intercultural answer

Given the variety of challenges, the solution must vary as well. Apart from technological solutions, a specific view on the so-called soft factors enables us to get a better understanding of how the problems can be solved in the future (Lippisch/Köppel, 2007, p. 8).

New company structures

Among the ways in which companies seek enhanced flexibility to meet the challenges of increasingly volatile markets are the outsourcing of certain services that were not marketable in the past. This market-driven increase in flexibility needs to be applied at the operational level; corporate structures as well as management methods need to be adapted to meet the needs of the future.

New management and working styles

The push towards increasing flexibility, accompanied by an increasing acceptance of personal responsibility continues in processes at the human level: decentralization, fluid company borders, globally organized added value and constant change require alterations in management and work models as well. The relevant demands must be taken into account in employment relationships, work-hour arrangements, incentive systems and further training programs, especially intercultural training programs.

Global managers work with people who have very different ideas about how business gets done. They must understand and adapt to country differences in unions, corporate governance, political legislation, investment policies etc. that can have an impact on business.

Moreover, global managers have to be fully aware of the complexity of norms, beliefs, values and attitudes that distinguish one cultural group from another. Working globally, managers must address multiple and differing expectations about how people (employees, colleagues, customers, suppliers, distributors, etc.) should behave, and how work should get done. Given the cultural diversity of our world, this is an extremely challenging task and requires a new thinking as far as the relevant working style is concerned. Today's leaders need to adapt to leading and managing people of different cultures. Cultural differences impact everything from inter-personnel communication to health and safety procedures to project management. In short, no corner of any business escapes.

New skills

In globally active companies it is becoming more and more important that each employee shows personal initiative; they also need to be able to adapt their tasks to the changing demands within and outside the company, in order to meet the challenges of global business. Economically-driven diversity management is one way of ensuring that the various available human resources are used and combined in a manner appropriate to the specific situation.

As with all businesses success depends upon effective cooperation and communication within a company, particularly within multicultural teams. Therefore, business structures have to be radically transformed in the given context. Changes in areas such as communication and information technology and shifts towards global interdependence are obvious and having resulted in companies that are becoming increasingly international and as a logical consequence more and more intercultural.

New corporate culture

A global mindset and an innovative spirit should be made an integral part of the company and its corporate culture. Executives and employees, who understand global contexts and the need for innovation as well as its consequences for their own behavior, are crucial for establishing such a corporate culture. Furthermore, a company's leadership has a responsibility to encourage, communicate and implement a continuously developing corporate culture with a specific focus on newly formed multicultural teams. Establishing and implementing ethical principles constitutes a major challenge in this context – all the more so because such principles need to be internationally applicable, binding and interculturally accepted.

*"The magic in the globalization of the last years
is the mixture of different cultures."*
(Matthew Emmens)

Wolfsburg's Gateway to Asia
(Martin Posth)

We were slowly getting to know our Chinese partners in exciting discussions concerning special topics and were developing perspectives for Shanghai VWs together. When we were taking a look at the largely automated body-shell manufacture in Sao Paulo, it quickly dawned on us all that we would not need all that many robots in the production process. In China, where there was no limit to a very cheap workforce, robots were only supposed to be employed where the precision of the human hand and the human eye did not meet the demands for the quality to be safeguarded that we aspired to.

In our Mexican plant in Puebla, which we visited afterwards, everything worked out a bit differently than in Brazil on account of conditions typical of each particular country. Thus our Chinese fellow travellers got the impression of a capability of adaptation on the part of our concern to the different cultural and social conditions prevailing in each country concerned.

Then we headed for Tennessee, whereto the Japanese had succeeded in exporting their kind of car production to the USA. One of the first "transplants" – that was the term given to these manufacturing plants – was the subsidiary of Nissan in Smyrna, a small town near Nashville. Here, the Japanese had managed to adapt their legendary production system – cost-effectively, swiftly and quality-consciously – to US conditions and, at the same time, to establish a totally different cultural constellation successfully. We realised that in the factory halls of Shanghai Volkswagen two cultures would come together. Will we succeed in mediating constructively and productively between cultures, something that experts term as "Cross Cultural Management" nowadays?

In: 1000 Tage in Shanghai, 2006, p. 25 (own translation)

1.2   Intercultural management

The economic globalisation, the technological progress and the revolution of the information and communication technology sector have facilitated the communication among people around the world. While the psychology and sociology have reacted by studying the relations deriving from cultural exchanges, the economy developed a new discipline in the 1970s – the intercultural management – aimed at adapting the marketing rules to the specific cultural characteristics of a target market. Since then, the scope and object of study have been expanded to include the management at the level of organisations operating in a multi-cultural environment, especially for companies operating branches outside the country of origin. Consequently, the intercultural management has rapidly developed the notions of mother-culture versus enterprise-culture. The first element is specific for the country from which the company originates, while the second is specific for the country in which the company opens its branch. In order to avoid possible cultural conflicts, the intercultural management uses specific tools and methods that mediate between two or more cultures.

1.2.1   Definition of intercultural management

Intercultural Management can be described as a combination of knowledge, insights and skills which are necessary for adequately dealing with national and regional cultures and differences between cultures at several management levels within and between organisations (Burggraaf, 1998). It is not a separate subject but an integral part of general and international management.

Fig. 1.2:   Management interrelations
Source: Own illustration

Intercultural Management interleaves with international management as some similarities occur. It might therefore be relevant to depict those features of international management that are effective. These features are:

- Teams consist of internationally representative managers
- Structural forms such as organic modes exist
- Leadership includes varied skills appropriate for the global context
- Motivation is appropriate for diversity
- Organisational cultures such as those characterising learning organisations exist
- Communication methods and systems are available and applicable
- Human resource management systems and practices that reflect the dynamic of operating in the global context are used (Jacob, 2003)

As part of the term intercultural management the expression management is ubiquitous. Management is the on-going professional composition, steering and development of (complex) structures and processes in order to achieve the goals of the organisations. (Koch, Speiser, 2008)

For a definition of intercultural management the general management definition needs to be extended by the cultural component. Therefore, intercultural management can mean to achieve goals with professional means by persons of other or different cultural influence. It is the composition, steering and development of structures and processes in order to achieve the goals of an organisation in a context that is shaped by the coincidence of at least two different cultures. (Koch/Speiser, 2008)

1.2.2   The importance of intercultural management

If you agree with Elashmawi/Harris (1993, p. 1), who say that *"the new world market will not only be international, but intensely intercultural"*, it will become obvious that the international management of the future will also – or even particularly – make the inclusion of intercultural management an absolute necessity. Hambrick/Snow (1989, pp. 84ff) arrive at a similar conclusion and say:

> *"Integration and human resource management are dependent upon one another to the degree that structuring a firm's global activities involves the deployment and use of human capital and other human aspects."*

The need for a specific intercultural discipline in the management field comes from the fact that speaking a foreign language is not enough for a sufficient communication between people belonging to different cultures. The surface of a process is much more complex than the simple understanding of what the other says. This is because the communication is not linear, which means that the transmission of a message is never neutral; the spoken message transmits words and notions, but also norms and values and some of these norms and values may not be fully shared by the dialogue partner. (Meunier/Zaman, n.y.)

Consequently, managers have to be aware not only of the different language of the business partner but their diverging attitude, time perception, behaviours, traditions and further aspects related to a different culture. At this point, intercultural management provides the opportunity to be aware of it and deal with such cultural aspects. Failures in one's behavior while doing business or misunderstandings of the business partners' actions can lead to severe problems and even a termination of the partnership.

Intercultural Management in China

In a study dealing with intercultural management in China conducted by students of the University of Applied Sciences in Stralsund, 37 companies from China and Germany participated filled in the survey. The results show that the majority of companies consider intercultural management as very important for their German-Chinese business relations.

Question: Do you think intercultural management in China plays a crucial role in doing your business successfully? If yes, why?

(extract)

- *Different cultures implement different working styles which should be taken into consideration*
- *Intercultural management can bridge the different understanding and thinking between people in China and Germany or Europe.*
- *Proper understanding of local culture is essential for conducting business here. Otherwise, there will be certainly problems with communication.*

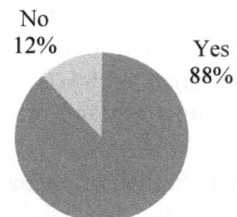

No 12%   Yes 88%

In: Golz/Kerwin/Rimaite, Written Assignment, 2013 (unpublished)

In recent years, the intercultural management has become particularly important as the phe-nomena of globalisation has been accompanied by increasing migration flows, enlargement of the European Union, economic openness of many countries around the world, the emer-gence of new economies like China and the expansion of economic partnerships between countries disposing of different economic systems. The cooperation between these different economic systems, which are based on significant cultural differences, requires a new – in-tercultural – approach.

Another possibility of integrating intercultural thinking and acting into the existing curricu-lum can be seen in the job enlargement of international personnel management. Especially in Anglosaxon literature (Black/Mendenhall, 1990; Phatak, 1997; Teagarden/Gordon, 1994; Tung, 1981), strong reference is to be found. The authors share the opinion that

"these new roles include international extensions of more traditional human resource management support functions such as providing country-specific knowledge of union and labour policies, legal and regulatory requirements, compensation, and benefit practises. They include preparing people for international assignments, and re-entry after those assignments are completed." (Teagarden/Glinow, 1997, p. 8)

30 TIPS ON HOW TO LEARN ACROSS CULTURES (1-2)
(Andre Laurent)

1. Be aware of your own very special culture as a unique peculiarity. When working across cultures you will often be the "stranger" – perceived by others as being "strange".

2. The culture that you ignore most – in terms of its shaping power on yourself – is obvi-ously your own culture. It is very difficult to look at oneself from the outside. We can make interesting observations and comments about other cultures. But we often re-main blind to our own.

In: SIETAR (Hrsg.), Keynote-Speech, Kongress 2000, Ludwigshafen

For companies, this approach means that the consideration of the intercultural issues of all cross-border activities must no longer be neglected. Far more than before, these issues have to explicitly find their way into the respective activity's intercultural orientation. (Perlmutter, 1965, p. 153)

Those who want to succeed on international markets have to deal with unprecedented prob-lems, which result due to the mere fact that there is contact with foreign countries, cultures as well as economic and social structures. However, an explicit implication of those factors does not happen in most cases. At this point, intercultural management comes into place.

At the University of Applied Sciences Stralsund, a study was conducted by the four students Carolin Boden, Elisabeth Guth, Nelly Heinze and Sarah Lang, who questioned 22 consulting companies and experts about the influence of cultural aspects on the failure of mergers and acquisitions (M&A). The results underline the importance of intercultural management and training during the M&A process, but can be transferred to other fields as well.

Please rate the importance of intercultural management in case of international Mergers and Acquisitions.

(very important) 6	███████████████████████████ 59%
5	████████ 14%
4	█████████ 18%
3	0%
2	██ 5%
(very unimportant) 1	██ 5%

Average rating: 5.09

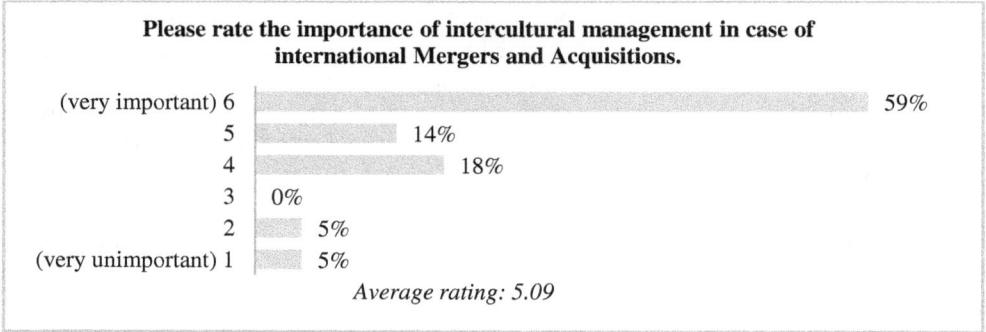

Fig. 1.3:   Importance of intercultural training for international M&A
Source: Boden/Guth/Heinze/Lang, 2011, p. 81

1.2.3   The tasks of intercultural management

The discussion, whether the topic of management has to be seen in a "culture-bound" (hypothesis by culturalist respectively cultural relativists) or "culture-free" context (hyphothesis by universalists), has shown that the majority – according to Hofstede (1993) – considers management as a culture-bound phenomenon. Hence, a particular sensibilization for cultural phenomena is required. (Kumar, 1988, pp. 389ff, Kiechl, 1997, p. 16)

While a few scientists (Thomas, 1996; Kiechl, 1990) have pointed out a global convergence and have consequently ruled out a connection between ethnoculture and corporate culture, the majority of scientific studies (Adler, 1983; Perlmutter, 1965; Hofstede, 1993) verify that undertakings in different nations reveal different corporate cultures, which can be traced back to the respective ethnocultures. At internationally active companies, the ethnocultural influence on the corporate culture, which depends on the nature of the relationships between the subsidiaries and the parent company and between the different subsidiaries, can be monitored and to a certain degree even steered (Kiechl, 1997, p. 14).

Race
(Barack Obama)

As the child of a black man and a white woman, someone who was born in the racial melting pot of Hawaii, with a sister who's half Indonesian but who's usually mistaken for Mexican or Puerto Rican, and a brother-in-law and niece of Chinese descent, with some blood relatives who resemble Margaret Thatcher and others who could pass for Bernie Mac, so that family get-togethers over Christmas take on the appearance of a UN General Assembly meeting, I've never had the option of restricting my loyalties on the basis of race, or measuring my worth on the basis of tribe. Moreover, I believe that part of America's genius has always been its ability to absorb newcomers, to forge a national identity out of the disparate lot that arrived on our shores.

In: The Audacity of Hope, New York 2006, p. 231

One can conclude that the task of intercultural management includes the concrete design of functional, structural and personnel management processes. Its aim is to facilitate a successful overcoming of management problems by providing adequate approaches for efficient international actions. (Perlitz, 1995, p. 318) Therefore, professionals and executives of internationally operating companies do not only need legal, technical and economic expertise and speak foreign languages but also have to adjust their behavior to intercultural standards which enable them to work effectively in a foreign environment.

Whoever wants to remain internationally successful has to be able to assess anticipatorily the impacts of cultural differences on management practices, individual work attitudes, communication, the conduct of negotiations etc. (Weidmann, 1995, p. 41) However, this way of thinking may not be seen as a one-way street. The necessity to observe and apply intercultural principles and behavior is not only vital for external business relations but also for internal business processes.

In future, one can assume that the number of business meetings where participants come from different cultural backgrounds will increase (Mauritz, 1996, p. 1). For German companies, this development means that they will have to integrate more employees from other cultures into the company – regardless whether they work at the corporate head office or at foreign subsidiaries. The new questions and solution approaches involved are also part of intercultural management.

Connecting Intercultural Communication and Management
(Gary R. Weaver)

The workplace of the new millennium will be multicultural and global. With greater intercultural interaction, the differences are not simple going to disappear. We will not link arms in the office, sing "We are the World", and find that we can easily overcome the communication breakdowns or conflicts. As long as we remain within our own culture, we take it for granted. However, when we leave it and interact with people from other backgrounds, we become more consciously aware of our own culture, and it becomes more important to us.

In: Intercultural Management Institute, Washington, DC, Nr. 9, 2001, S. 3

1.2.4   Challenges in the field of intercultural management

Similarities of social habits, tastes and exposure might make managers across nations more homogeneous, but there are still differences coming from cultures that have to be considered. Quite a bit of intercultural management today deals with the construction of mechanisms for integration.

Today there is an increasing preoccupation about the leadership and management styles, which are appropriate for intercultural management. Another important point regarding the repertoire of abilities needed by global managers is to feel comfortable in culturally diverse teams. Cultural orientations are learnt behaviours. Therefore, managers can develop the flexibility and openness which is necessary to transit from one cultural context to another. This is part of the challenge when working for professionally managed and high performance companies. (Jacob, 2003)

Some of these challenges have been described by Nardon/Sanchez-Runde/Steers (2010, pp. 16ff):

"This evolution from a principally bicultural business environment to a more multicultural or global environment presents managers with at least three new challenges in attempting to adapt quickly to the new realities on the ground:

1. *It is sometimes unclear to which culture we should adapt. Suppose that your company has asked you to join a global project team to work on a six-month R&D project. The team includes one Mexican, one German, one Chinese, and one Russian. Every member of the team has a permanent appointment in their home country but is temporarily assigned to work at company headquarters in Switzerland for this project. Which culture should team members adapt to? In this case, there is no dominant cultural group to dictate the rules. Considering the multiple cultures involved, and the little exposure each manager has likely had with the other cultures, the traditional approach to adaptation is unlikely to be successful. Nevertheless, the group must be able to work together quickly and effectively to produce results (and protect their careers), despite their differences. What would you do?*

2. *Many intercultural encounters happen on short notice, leaving little time to learn about the other culture. Imagine that you just returned from a week's stay in India where you were negotiating an outsourcing agreement. As you arrive in your home office, you learn that an incredible acquisition opportunity just turned up in South Africa and that you are supposed to leave in a week to explore the matter further. You have never been to South Africa, nor do you know somebody from there. What do you do?*

3. *Intercultural meetings increasingly occur virtually by way of computers or video conferencing instead of through more traditional face-to-face interactions. Suppose you were asked to build a partnership with a Korean partner that you have never met and you know little about Korean culture. Suppose further that this task is to be completed online, without any face-to-face communication or interactions. Your boss is in a hurry for results. What would you do?*

Taken together, these three challenges illustrate just how difficult it can be to work or manage across cultures in today's rapidly changing business environment. The old ways of communicating, negotiating, leading, and doing business are simply less effective than they were in the past."

"Seven social sins:
politics without principles, wealth without work,
pleasure without conscience, knowledge without character,
commerce without morality, science without humanity,
and worship without sacrifice."

(Mahatma Gandhi)

The Rise of Generation Global – Seizing opportunity in a world economy that ignores borders
(Roger Cohen)

My son Daniel is working in Vietnam marketing Budweiser beer, an American on. Budweiser may be as American as you can get, but it's now owned by Anheuser-Busch InBev, a Belgium-based company. InBev itself was created a few years ago by the merger of a Brazilian company, Ambev, with Interbrew of Belgium.

That's a lot of info to crowd into the top of a column, forgive me, but the modern world is a little like that: a tangled web of cross-border holdings where national icons are not really that national at all. Daniel, 27, is heading to Brazil for a month to train with Brazilian marketers on how to sell an American beer to the 80 million citizens of fast-growing Vietnam. He's part of Generation Global (GG).

The existence of GG is a hopeful thing. Never before have so many young people been so aware of the shared challenges facing the globe, so determined to get "out there" to learn about it, or so intent on making a contribution to a more equitable world. The borderless cyber-communities of social networking have a powerful effect on their views. My son's Vietnamese-Brazilian connection is interesting. That's where the growth is. He's American-educated, but if he'd stayed in the United States after completing his M.B.A. he might well have found himself joining the long line of twenty-somethings without a job. The growth that has helped avert economic meltdown since 2008 has come overwhelmingly from next-wave countries like China, Vietnam, India, Russia, Brazil, Indonesia and South Africa. These are the places on which multinational corporations are focused.

Now I'm for a more multipolar world because the United States simply does not have the resources to assume ad infinitum its current pivotal role in global security. But I'm also mindful that the worlds of 1914 and 1939 were multipolar – and produced cataclysm. Careful what you wish for is a useful maxim when radical power shifts, of the sort occurring today, are in progress.

The emergent powers represent a hodgepodge of systems and values, which is one reason their voices are indistinct, along with the fact that they are for now intensely focused on their own development. You have the authoritarian systems (in their different forms) of China, Vietnam and Russia; and the sprawling democracies (one old, one middle-aged, one newish, one new) of India, Brazil, South Africa and Indonesia. All, in varying degrees, have misgivings about the western-dominated world whose time is coming to an end.

Another thing they have in common is their burning desire to grow. Many of these nations know much from their own histories of the struggle for freedom (ongoing in Iran), for peace (ongoing in Israel-Palestine), for a national reconciliation (Afghanistan), for an end totalitarian misery (North Korea). How emergent powers assume the responsibility growth brings seems to me critical.

For now, they lag the corporations that knit the world closer and have landed my son in a Brazilian-Belgian-American-Vietnamese web. I'll raise a glass to that particular exotic brew.

In: New York Times, 22nd February 2010, p. 2

1.2.5   The European Union and intercultural dialogue

Even the European Union has recognised the importance of questions related to intercultural management, which was reflected by the decision of the European Parliament and the European Council to designate the year 2008 as the European Year of Intercultural Dialogue. This year recognises that Europe's great cultural diversity represents a unique advantage. It encourages all those living in Europe to explore the benefits of its rich cultural heritage and opportunities to learn from different cultural traditions (interculturaldialogue 2008.eu.406.0.html).

European Year of 2008
Intercultural Dialogue

The overall objectives of the European Year of Intercultural Dialogue aim to contribute to (Official Journal of the European Union, 30/12/2006):

• promoting intercultural dialogue as a process in which all those living in the EU can improve their ability to deal with a more open, but also more complex, cultural environment, where, in different Member States as well as within each Member State, different cultural identities and beliefs coexist,
• highlighting intercultural dialogue as an opportunity to contribute to and benefit from a diverse and dynamic society, not only in Europe but also in the world,
• raising the awareness of all those living in the EU, in particular young people, of the importance of developing an active European citizenship which is open to the world, respects cultural diversity and is based on common values in the EU as laid down in Article 6 of the EU Treaty and the Charter of Fundamental Rights of the European Union,
• highlighting the contribution of different cultures and expressions of cultural diversity to the heritage and ways of life of the Member States.

The specific objectives of the European Year of Intercultural Dialogue shall be to:

• seek to raise the awareness of all those living in the EU, in particular young people, of the importance of engaging in intercultural dialogue in their daily lives,
• work to identify, share and give a visible European recognition to best practices in promoting intercultural dialogue throughout the EU, especially among young people and children,
• foster the role of education as an important medium for teaching about diversity, increase the understanding of other cultures and developing skills and best social practices, and highlight the central role of the media in promoting the principle of equality and mutual understanding,
• raise the profile, increase the coherence of and promote all Community programmes and actions contributing to intercultural dialogue and ensure their continuity,

- contribute to exploring new approaches to intercultural dialogue involving cooperation between a wide range of stakeholders from different sectors.

1.2.6 Intercultural management vs. cross-cultural-management

Some research approaches differentiate between an "intercultural" and a "cross-cultural" point of view. Intercultural studies concentrate on cross-border contacts and relationships, whereas "cross-cultural" studies compare certain phenomena in different cultural surroundings. (Koester/Wiseman/Sanders, 1993, p. 5)

On the one hand, works in culturally comparative psychology have e.g. proved that cultural factors have a big influence on psychological processes such as perception, motivation, cognition and emotion. Moreover, the results show that some psychological laws hold across cultural borders but also that such generalizations are not possible without restrictions. (Thomas, 1993, p. 387) Consequently, the "cross-cultural" perspective always generates comparative assertations, which means that the focus is on the cultural comparison.

Three Levels of cultural studies

(William B. Hart)

Cultural studies are done at three levels: Monocultural studies, cross-cultural studies, and intercultural studies. Monocultural or single culture studies are common in anthropology and sociology. Cross-cultural studies are studies that compare the characteristics of two or more cultures. Intercultural studies are studies that focus on the interaction of two or more cultures and answer the main question of what happens when two or more cultures interact (at the interpersonal level, group level or international level). The focus of intercultural relations is with the intercultural studies. Monocultural and cross-cultural studies cannot be ignored, however, because they serve as necessary precursors to intercultural studies.

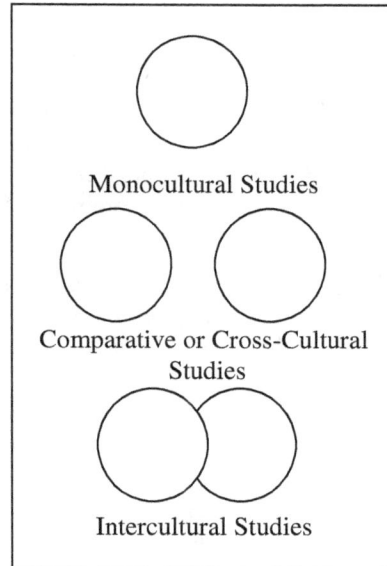

Monocultural Studies

Comparative or Cross-Cultural Studies

Intercultural Studies

In: The E-Journal of Intercultural Relations, Nr. 6, 1998, S. 1

On the other hand, the prefix "inter" is mainly used to describe connections between individual units, especially in the context of border crossing. International encounters reach across national borders and intercultural contacts across cultural barriers. The relationships between social organizations are always of an intercultural nature, since every organization is by definition a specific culture which distinguishes itself from the culture of other organizations. If one however assumes that the use of the prefix "inter" – as is to be found e.g. in the words "inter"-cultural or "inter"-national management (Mauritz, 1996, p. 74) – implies an isolated view on cultures or nations, then this definition fails the holistic approach connected to cross-border interactions. Intercultural considerations can never be completely independent from comparative statements but need them as a basis in order to gain qualitatively distinguishable results. The actions of expatriate managers are influenced by their own as well as foreign moral concepts.

1.3   The expert's view: Interview with Dr. Thomas Zenetti

Dr. Thomas Zenetti is the Head of the international Master program "Intercultural Management" at the Université de Haute-Alsace Mulhouse-Colmar (recorded 25/07/2014).

Rothlauf: *In general, what are the reasons today to deal with questions related to intercultural issues?*

Zenetti: In my understanding, it is all about the way you communicate with people from another culture. It is not enough to understand the language of your partner. Somebody from Great Britain thinks and behaves differently compared to a U.S. citizen, although they both speak English. I myself have made the experience that our neighbors from the German speaking part of Switzerland react completely different than we Germans. Related to our Master program, it is obvious that such an exchange between students from different cultures can only function if the peculiarities of each culture are taken into consideration. As relevant studies have clearly proven, the neglect of those intercultural issues will not only cause problems in private life but moreover in business life you will lose a lot of money.

Rothlauf: *What were your fundamental ideas behind offering your students an international Master program entitled "Intercultural Management" and which kind of initial difficulties did you have to overcome?*

Zenetti: Here, several factors play a role and come together: On the one hand, we have a literature and linguistics program in applied foreign languages on a bachelor level with a strong focus on business administration, on which we can build on. On the other hand, our university, located in the Upper Rhine region, has a pioneering role in cross-border programs, especially as far as interculturally designed working programs are concerned. As a logical consequence of all these facts, a Master degree program in intercultural management was the best answer. Still, it was not that easy to start with this program. It took a lot of hard work to get the support from the faculty, because the so-called "soft factors" of this program did not correlate with the ideas of classical business programs and the linguistics colleagues had to be convinced that we are not in concurrence to their existing programs but look for an interdisciplinary co-operation. In the end, we succeeded in bridging the gap, a really intercultural task.

Rothlauf: *Where do you see the special feature of this course and what makes this program unique compared to other international programs, especially those that are offered in France?*

Zenetti: First of all, it is the language program in combination with management courses. About half of the offered language courses are in French, at least 30 per cent in English and about 20 percent – depending on the selected elective courses – in German or Spanish. But if the students are interested in learning more languages, we give them the opportunity to learn, for example, the Chinese, the Japanese or the Russian language as well. This variety of languages we do offer is relatively rare in France, particularly at small universities. For such a program, we do not only need students with a good command of economics, an interest in learning three foreign languages, but also faculty members who are capable of transferring our ideas into reality.

Rothlauf: *Who are the students that are enrolled in your Master program and what different nationalities are represented in this course?*

Zenetti: It is clear that Mulhouse has not the same appeal as Paris or Lyon, but there is a steadily growing demand for this program that allows us to select our students accordingly. About 25 percent of all students are coming from outside France. So, we are happy to have not only students from the neighboring countries like Germany and Switzerland but also from Russia, China and from South America.

Rothlauf: *How do the students work and live together? Different religious affiliations, different language levels, different notions of time and so on can cause a variety of problems. How do you cope with all those challenges?*

Zenetti: We always analyze the situation and, in a joint effort, we are looking for a solution, sometimes with the help from members of the group itself, sometimes we offer support from our university. Let me give you an example: A female Russian student had been elected as the leader of a group and had distributed different tasks among the members of the group. She then got angry as the Chinese student did not stick to the deadlines. The problem was caused by an intercultural misunderstanding: A simple "niet" is not in line with the Chinese culture, where everybody tries to be in harmony, which means that the students tried to avoid to say "no". At the end, however, they finished the project in a very successful manner.

Rothlauf: *Are there any first reactions from the labor market and is it difficult for your graduates to find a job?*

Zenetti: Ninety to ninety-five percent of our graduates get a job in the first three months after finishing this program. More than half of the students receive a job offer at the end of their six-month internship. Especially in a country like France with an unfortunately high rate of youth unemployment, we are proud to publish those figures. Moreover, the companies tell us that our concept is in line with their perception: instead of focusing on selected issues such as human resource management or project management, the variety of courses makes the difference. The linkage of intercultural aspects with language courses and a holistic approach to questions that are essential in business administration generate a program that is pretty well accepted by the companies.

Rothlauf: *What are your personal experiences in this context?*

Zenetti: As a German who has now lived for three and a half decades in France, I have got to know all the different stages of the acculturation process, without becoming a 100 percent Frenchman. It is very interesting to see how the theories of Hofstede, Hall and others are in line with my own experiences. Moreover, it is a wonderful opportunity for me to see the differences as well as similarities among our students coming from all around the world. To help them to get a more differentiated intercultural view is a challenging task and I am proud to be part of this program.

---

30 TIPS ON HOW TO LEARN ACROSS CULTURES (3–4)
(Andre Laurent)

3. Intercultural situations offer the unique opportunity to reduce our blind spot. Other cultures act as privileged mirrors in which we can see more of our own cultural make-up as a result of being confronted and challenged by other cultural models. This leads to greater understanding of the peculiarities of our own culture.

4. Don't expect others to think and act as you do. Your culture – and therefore your own preferred way of getting things done – is just one among many. Expect others to think and act differently. Recognize that your way can be the exception rather than the norm.

In: SIETAR (Hrsg.), Keynote-Speech, Kongress 2000, Ludwigshafen

---

1.4 Case Study: Interviewing costumers in Asia – The impact of culture

1. Language issues

The choice of the interview language is a very important aspect for cross-cultural research studies and it needs to be taken into account already in the pre-interview stage.

Relying on English as the only language in a global research limits the access to respondents. Furthermore, it might also result in the fact that data is collected from respondents who are fluent in English, but whose attitudes and behavior differ tremendously from the non-English speaking population.

Even between English-speaking countries, significant linguistical differences may occur. When interviewing Indian respondents, for example, it becomes clear that some words have a completely different meaning than in the UK. The word "sincere" which in England signifies "honest" and "true" and which refers to someone who "is honest and says what he really feels or believes", is used in India to indicate someone who accepted responsibility. As the meaning of words is shared only by members of the same culture, people from different cultural background have a different understanding of the same word. Researchers, therefore, have to be aware of the fact that there exist many "Englishes" instead of the one English language. Consequently, when doing cross-cultural studies, it is crucial to compare equivalent expressions in all relevant languages in order to be able to identify the most appropriate term to fit into the respective context.

2. Individual interviews or focus groups

In many Asian countries, and especially in China, the predominant Confucian philosophy emphasizes the importance of the group. As a consequence, the unit of analysis of a qualitative research conducted in Asia might be the group itself and not the individual. This means that focus groups rather than the usual one-to-one interviews need to be carried out as almost all believes, attitudes and values of the respondents are a result of in-group interaction. By interviewing Chinese participants in groups, researchers can gain much deeper insights into their way of thinking than in individual interviews as people feel much more comfortable in a group setting which enables them to interprete and evaluate things collectively. It is, however, of great importance that the group under investigation is not randomly formed, but consists of members of the same peer group. In interdependent cultures, such as China, respondents will only express openly their opinion when the participants of the focus group are placed in the same position in hierarchy. Otherwise they feel obliged to agree with people from higher hierarchical positions and change their point of view.

Conducting focus groups in Japan bears some challenges. Compared to other countries, focus groups in Japan seem to be more structured. While some subjects with which respondents can easily identify themselves can generate lively discussions, other topics require a considerable amount of involvement on the part of the moderator in order to make participants talk. Japanese interviewees sometimes hesitate to share their thoughts and opinions if they feel that they are not in line with the group. This is due to the innate Japanese desire to maintain harmony. In case that the respondents' opinions actually are in opposition to those of the group, they might even answer contrary to their own feelings and attitudes. The Japanese culture is a rather neutral culture in which people do not show their true feelings and desires openly; instead emotions are kept hidden as they may conflict with what society expects from the individual. "Tatemae", literally meaning façade, is the behavior which is shown in public and which accounts for the fact that Japanese feel the obligation not to express their opinion freely if this could endanger the social harmony. For Western cultures which are more individualistic, this seems to be hard to understand since people are used to be very independent and do not have to render account to anybody for their behavior. In order to overcome the barriers which make conducting groups in Japan quite difficult, the number of participants in the group should be reduced to a minimum. This is necessary as the size of the group increases the pressure of conformity to group opinion enormously. Consequently, it is sometimes even advisable to conduct triads, a group consisting of only three people.

Source: Dahm, F./Schüle, U., in: UPDATE 12, SS 2011, p. 5–7

Review and Discussion Questions:

1. What is the general message of this article?

2. You are a European manager and currently working in Asia. Are there any significant hints you have to take into your consideration when doing business in this region?

3. How would you transfer ideas from this article into your everyday business life with a specific view on working together with Japanese managers?

4. Which kind of cultural information can you gain by taking a look at this article and compare the relevant information with your home country views!

2 Cultural Reflection as a Starting Point for Intercultural Management

2.0 Statement of the problem

Entering the Market: Culture and Context
(Zubko/Sahay)

Your bags are packed and you have a boarding ticket in hand. A few months earlier, you received word that you would be going to India on business, maybe for your first time or your fifth time. Visas have been arranged. Language lessons may have moved to the top of your MP's playlist. In addition to putting together any presentations and plans, a running list of do's and don'ts runs through your head haphazardly, beginning to jump together. Besides wondering if the project will go smoothly, and thinking through any areas to troubleshoot, you also may be concerned about the food and water, the heat, and whether you will by mistake cross some unknown cultural taboo and offend your Indian colleagues. Friends and coworkers offer advice, both solicited and unsolicited. The company may have handed you a manual on things to know about life in India, or brought you a few books. As you sit there in the airport, you may be asking yourself: What do I really need to know to be able to adapt to any business situation in India? Do I have the tools I need for a successful trip?

The two most overlooked strategic tools that foreign managers often forget to pack are inseparable: *culture* and *context*. Accurate and practical facts about the culture within which you will be working are essential. And yet this key information can become trivial unless you know when, where, and how to use your knowledge of culture within and across appropriate contexts. If you do not include these two indivisible tools in your toolbox, getting things done efficiently and successfully is statistically harder to do and more costly.

In: Inside the Indian Business Mind, 2011, p. xxi

2.1 Acting in a different cultural setting

With the increasing internationalization of business practices and the interchangeability of products, intercultural understanding is of major importance.

From the point of view of international business management, it has become obvious that the intercultural management has the task to prepare people who are confronted with intercultural encounters, so that they are able to identify the effective features of the respective other culture and integrate them into their own course of action. Thus, they can fulfill their specific management tasks under unfamiliar cultural conditions and in interaction with partners from a different cultural background. (Holzmüller, 1997, p. 790)

Intercultural management implies an analysis of the diversity of the respective countries, regions or subcultures and the establishment of general codes of conduct. Cultural concepts provide the framework for action. However, before a deeper understanding of cultural phenomena and dimensions and their background factors is created, it is necessary to deal with the differences of cultures. Here, one of the first questions is: what is actually defined as culture and what contribution can it make to enable us to understand patterns of cultural behavior?

Connecting Intercultural Communication and Management
(Gary R. Weaver)

We cannot be experts on every culture. However, we can develop the flexibility to put ourselves in the psychological and cultural shoes of those who are different. We can begin to appreciate the reality that there are numerous ways of solving a problem and that our way is in large part a result of growing up in our culture. Intercultural awareness and understanding begin with knowing your own culture first. Often this can only come through interaction with those who are different.

In: Intercultural Management Institute, Washington, DC, Nr. 9, 2001, S. 2

2.2 The term "culture" from a scientific-anthropological point of view

Human history is the history of cultures. It extends over many epochs of cultures, from the old Sumerian and Egyptian, the Classic and Mesoamerican through to the Western and Islamic cultures, accompanied by a range of Sinic and Hindu ones (Huntington, 1996, p. 49).

The observation of people and the depiction of differences between people from a scientific and humanistic point of view is the cultural anthropologists' and cultural sociologists' field of work. The phenomenon of culture and the description of what is to be understood by the term "culture" are accompanied by many different definitions. This is especially the case because culture is included in a number of fields of research, which lead to strongly divergent conceptions. In the beginning of the 1950's, Kroeber and Kluckholm compiled 154 different interpretations of "culture" (Kroeber/Kluckhohn, 1952, pp. 43f). However, different definitions of the term can also be found in comparative management studies (Krober-Riehl, 1996; Dülfer, 1996; Staehle, 1991).

If one scientifically-anthropologically deals with culture and its differences regarding individual nations, one has to assume that no homogenous assertions about cultural differences may be expected if the nation(s) combine(s) different ethnical cultures (Scholz, 1995, pp. 7f). Therefore, culture does not take national borders or an entire people into account, but establishes itself where history and certain characteristics indicate mutual behavioral patterns.

Only by this is it possible to explain why Bavarians and Austrians or Frisians (Friesländer) and Danes have more mutual cultural criteria than Bavarians and Frisians, who may live in one state but only belong together because of artificial borders and not because of their cultural history. Likewise, it might be difficult to make statements about the USA's national culture, as the strategy of the melting pot of ethnic groups as well as the one of maintaining group identity are pursued here.

First, we draw back on E.B. Tylor's definition, who understood in the wider ethnographical sense of the word that

> *"Culture [...] is that complex whole which includes knowledge, belief, art, morals, law, custom, and any other capabilities and habits acquired by a man as a member of society." (Tylor, London 1871, p. 1)*

In the subsequent time, the concept of culture has been subject to content-related changes and has been newly interpreted in very different ways. The term "culture", which is also used in the everyday language in various contexts, generally remains vague and only becomes more precise if one tries to conceive its meaning and to substantiate it (Büschges/Abraham/ Funk, 1996, p. 57).

Widely Travelled Visitors

In most cases, Germany is a remote and sometimes alien country for the majority of people in the world. What do visitors think of Germany?

Agnelegan Zigah, Ghana:

Favourite Prejudice and First Thought:
"Among us, people are of the opinion that Germans are not really friendly. Discipline ranks higher with the Germans than enjoyment of life/joie de vivre. Over and above, I am thinking of the complex red tape/ bureaucracy in Germany."

What I would change and take along?
"I would take along quite a number of things: discipline in traffic, traffic regulations, or the equality of treatment by the authorities. There is no corruption, bribery at the grass-roots level in Germany."

Antony Luxmann, Sri Lanka

Favourite Prejudice and First Thought:
"You only have to look at people at an airport. Germans are constantly under stress, as if they escaped from themselves. I take the view they are not really capable of relaxing and find no inner peace and quiet."

What I would change and take along?
"The immigration law! People visit this country in order to do business or to visit families, not to conquer it."

2.3   The Iceberg-Model

One instrument explaining the term culture is the so-called iceberg model. Many people question what culture is. How can it be defined? There are more than 200 different definitions of culture. In a way, the iceberg model can be helpful to gain a better understanding (Rocher, 1969, p. 12).

The iceberg has a visible tip. These are areas of culture that we can see. Such visible elements include things like music, dress, dance, architecture, language, food, gestures, greetings, behaviors, devotional practices, art and more. In addition, it can also relate to clearly apparent behaviors such as people ignoring red traffic lights, spitting on the floor, smoking in public or queuing for a bus.

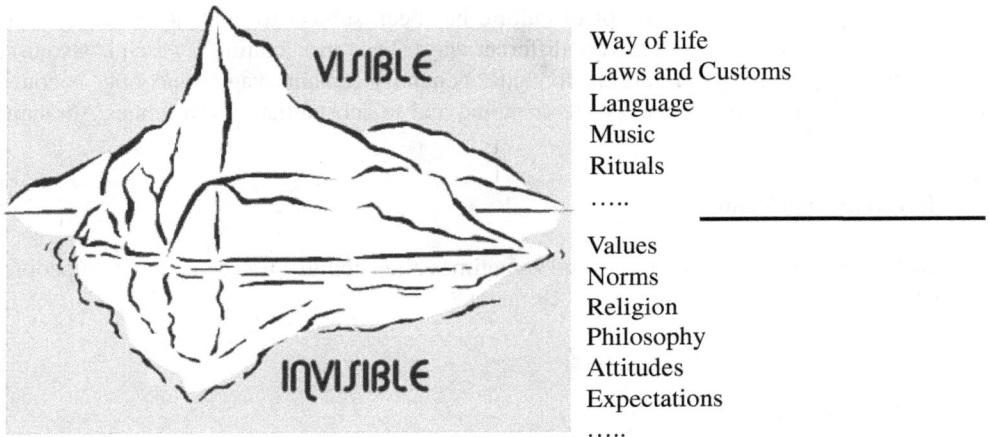

Way of life
Laws and Customs
Language
Music
Rituals
…..

Values
Norms
Religion
Philosophy
Attitudes
Expectations
…..

Fig. 2.1:   Iceberg Model of Culture
Source: Hall, 1976

But none of the visible elements can ever make real sense without understanding the drivers behind them; and these are hidden on the bottom side of the iceberg, the invisible side. So, when thinking about culture, the bottom side of the iceberg will include things such as religious beliefs, worldviews, rules of relationships, the approach to the family, motivations, tolerance for change, attitudes to rules, communication styles, modes of thinking, comfort with risk, the difference between public and private.

For example, why do the English queue for everything? This relates to their approach to fairness, justice, order and rights. The rationale behind the queue is that those that arriving first should by rights be served first or get on a bus first. Many other cultures simply do not queue in this manner, as it is not part of their cultural programming. It is for the reasons of clarity that the iceberg model has become so popular.

Intercultural exercise:
Develop the iceberg model for your own national culture and picture it in a flip chart.
Hint: The participants are required to be concrete in describing their culture, and must not limit themselves to abstract terms.

Mind the gap: Culture in pictures
(Westcombe, J./Boye, S.)

Think of a tree in a wood. The tree stands alone, but is also part of
the forest in which it lives and grows. In a similar way, each of us is
an individual, with our own personality, habits, emotions and experiences. But we all have feelings of belonging and identity that have to
do with the cultures in which we live or grew up.

Another image that is often used to describe culture is that of an iceberg: the parts you can
see above the water are noticeable things, such as food, clothing, language, festivals, music and art. Under the surface, however, are many
more things that are not so obvious: attitudes, values
and beliefs, such as what it means to be polite, or what
makes a friendship. It is beneath the surface where
icebergs are likely to come into contact with one another. When you talk to someone from another culture,
"under-the-surface" factors may play a role without
your realizing it.

A third picture that intercultural trainers like to use is that
of a pair of glasses. Each of us wears cultural glasses. The
world that we see is one that fits our own cultural view.
But we must not forget that other people wear their own
cultural glasses, too.

It is easy to think only in terms of national cultures, but there are many expressions of
culture – in football fans, teenage girls, orchestral musicians or the workers of a particular
company, for example.

In: Spotlight 5/2012, p. 31

"Culture is like dancing;
you cannot join the dance without a sufficient knowledge
of the steps that need to be taken.
In particular, you cannot be the leading partner.
Thus, it is of eminent significance to first watch and
observe the steps of others with a broader empirical knowledge."
(Frick, M./Thomas, G)

2.4   Approaching a systematization of different cultural concepts

Different cultural concepts have attempted to master the complexity of "culture". Those concentrating on the different mental programming of people in terms of the spatial, temporal, human and nature-related orientation have become widely disseminated (cf. Hall, 1959; Kluckhohn/Strodtbeck, 1961; Lane/DiStefano, 1988). The focus here is predominantly on the affective and cognitive determinants of a cultural orientation system which characterize people from specific cultural environments. From the wide range of cultural concepts, the perceptions of Keller, Luthans and Kluckholm, who have tried to specify their ideas by an enumeration of characteristic features, have been singled out in the following.

Other cultures follow their own logic
Interview with Susann Hoppe, Coach at the Carl Duisberg Centre – Excerpt

Zeck: *Why are cultures partly so different?*

Hoppe: Societies have developed various survival strategies on account of geographical changes and as a consequence of war and expulsion over millennia. Those may be moulded differently even within one single culture, e.g. with rural and urban populations. Only since the age of enlightenment has equality been a political and social ideal. The reality prevailing nowadays is more complicated.

Adapted from: FAZ, 10/11.03.2012, p. C2

2.4.1   Keller's cultural concept

For his definition of "culture", Keller assumes the following characteristics (Keller, 1982, pp. 114):

- *"Culture has been created by human beings. It is a product of collective social thinking and the acting of individual people.*
- *Culture is supra-individual and a social phenomenon outlasting the individual.*
- *Culture is learned and communicated with the help of symbols.*
- *Culture controls the behavior by means of norms, rules and codes of conduct.*
- *Culture strives for inner consistence and integration.*
- *Culture is an instrument for adapting to the environment.*
- *Culture is adaptively versatile in the long term."*

2.4.2   Luthans' cultural concept

Aspects of the social culture structuring the life between people can also be found at Luthans, who defines the term "culture" as (Luthans, 1997, p. 96):

- *"Learned. Culture is not inherited or biologically based; it is acquired by learning and experience.*

- *Shared. People as members of a group organization, or society share culture; it is not specific to single individuals.*
- *Transgenerational. Culture is cumulative, passed down from one generation to the next.*
- *Symbolic. Culture is based on the human capacity to symbolize or use one thing to represent another.*
- *Patterned. Culture has structure and is integrated; a change in one part will bring changes in another.*
- *Adaptive. Culture is based on the human capacity to change or adapt, as opposed to the more genetically driven adaptive process of animals."*

2.4.3 Kluckhohn's cultural concept

Kluckhohn, who understood culture as the all-encompassing cohesion of human behavior, arrived at a similar definition. By enumerating the following features, he tried to specify his cultural concept (Kluckhohn, 1951, p. 87):

- *"Culture is learned.*
- *Culture is structured.*
- *Culture derives from the biological, environmental, psychological and historical components of human existence.*
- *Culture is divided into aspects.*
- *Culture is dynamic.*
- *Culture is variable.*
- *Culture exhibits regularities that permit its analysis by the methods of science.*
- *Culture is the instrument whereby the individual adjusts to his total setting, and gains the means for creative expression."*

Hitherto, the listed definitions have made clear that the term "culture" can be defined from different perspectives. The common goal is to give an orientation system and a frame of reference to the individual, in which one can classify one's own experience and behavioral patterns which underlie all attempted explanations. Consequently, the cultural framework sets standards for the perception, thinking, judging and acting (Perlitz, 1995, S. 303).

2.4.4 Schein's Model: Three Levels of Culture

A profound cultural concept covering the entirety of life forms, moral values, beliefs, socio-moral central themes as well as life conditions shaped by human activities in their complexity is recognizable in Schein's "Three Levels of Culture" (Schein, 1984, p. 4).

According to Schein, a culture's basis consists of a set of fundamental patterns of orientation and conception ("ideologies") guiding perception and acting. Usually, there are these self-evident reference points of organizational activities which are tracked without even thinking about them, or often even without knowing them at all.

At the second level, this world view is expressed by specified moral concepts and behavior standards. These are converted into maxims, unwritten codes of conduct, prohibitions, etc. which all members of the organization share to a more or less great extent.

These partly unconscious and invisible assumptions and standards are finally reflected in the third level of symbols and signs. They have the task to perpetuate, to extend and – what is particularly important – to communicate this elusive, hardly deliberate complex of assumptions, patterns of interpretation and moral concepts to new members. Here, the signs and symbols represent the visible part, which, however, is only comprehensible in connection with the underlying moral concepts.

Tab. 2.1:   Schein's Three Levels of Culture
Source: Schein, 1984, p. 4

1st LEVEL Basic Assumptions	2nd LEVEL Norms and Standards	3rd LEVEL Systems of Symbols
Basic assumptions about nature, man and his social relationships; invisible and usually subconscious	Maxims, "ideologies", common values, codes of conduct, prohibitions; partly visible, partly subconscious	Creations of culture (technology, art, behavioral patterns, clothes, language, rituals, manners); visible but in need for interpretation

In literature, there are a vast number of cultural elements which can be basically divided into four main criteria, namely symbols, heroes, rituals and value systems (Weidmann, 1995, p. 43).

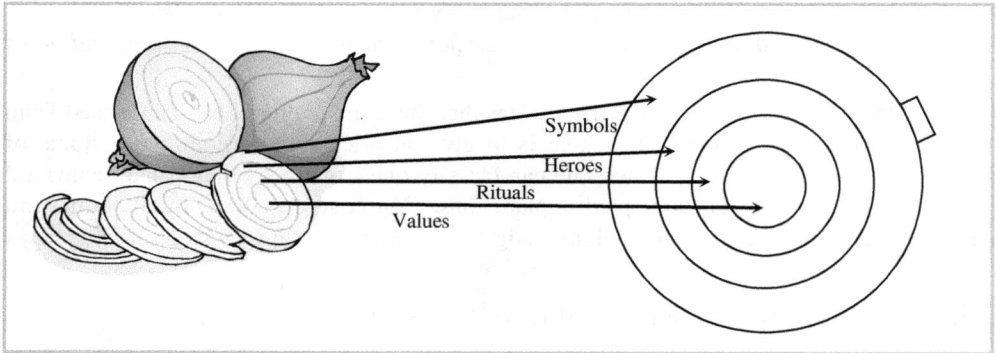

Fig. 2.2:   The "Onion" Model: Manifestation of Culture
Source: Own illustration based on Meier/Roehr, 2004, p. 258 and Hofstede, 2005, p. 7

2.4.5   Symbols

For symbols, the passing on and conveyance of cultural phenomena takes place via words, gestures, images and objects of a certain meaning, which can only be understood by those people belonging to the same culture and are generally based on conversations. On the level of national cultures, symbols also comprise the areas of language and communication. Concerning the culture of an organization, symbols are e.g. abbreviations, terminologies, forms of address (formal or informal), signs, dress regulations, seating arrangements and status symbols mainly to be only recognized and acknowledged by insiders.

2.4.6 Heroes

Real or fictitious, historic or contemporary persons who act as carriers of culture and role models within a culture can be considered as heroes. Nations have their national paragons and folk heroes, generations their role models, whereas in organizations, the selection and recruitment are often based on the vision of the "ideal employee" or the "ideal manager". The founders of organizations are often seen and adored as mystic heroes (Weidmann, 1995, p. 43).

2.4.7 Rituals

Similar to the already mentioned myths like symbols and heroes, rituals are also expressive actions, which cannot only be considered as mere cultural assets but which are also expected to fulfill a practical function (Gussmann/Breit, 1997, p. 117).

> *"Rituals and ceremonies are as important to organization and societies as they are to individuals. They serve four major functions: to socialize, to stabilize, to reduce anxieties and ambiguities, and to convey message to external constituencies."*
> *(Bolman/Deal, 1984, p. 154)*

Rituals are collective activities which might often be technically superfluous but are essential in a certain culture for social reasons. When two Japanese meet and bow, this is as much a national ritual as the greeting behavior of two Germans shaking hands. Moreover, also various formal activities belong to the recurring processes which are defended for apparently rational reasons: meetings, the writing of memos as well as the informal way of organizing formal activities: "Who sits where at a meeting and who talks with whom, how, etc." are expressions of ritual manners. After all, organizational forms in the society, the state and companies are likewise to be allocated to rituals. No matter if it is an official reception or a stock corporation's general meeting, without relation to the respectively accustomed rituals, one would not be able to meet the expectations.

2.4.8 Value systems

Value systems reflect the deepest level of a culture. They represent widespread emotions of which one is often not aware and unable to speak about. Religious beliefs belong to these not easily reflected value systems. They decide on the meaning of good or bad/clean or dirty/beautiful or ugly/natural or unnatural/moral or immoral. These feelings are predominantly found with members of one culture and intensified with people acting as opinion leaders. Since there are interactions between a culture's different elements, symbols, heroes and rituals clearly reflect values, whereas value systems are – however, to a far lesser degree – influenced by interdependencies. (Weidmann, 1995, p. 44) For more information about the World Values Survey, please see chapter 4.

2.5   Insights into five cultural models

A number of authors have tried to identify cultural dimensions in order to illustrate similarities and differences of national cultures. Below, the five best-known cultural models shall be presented.

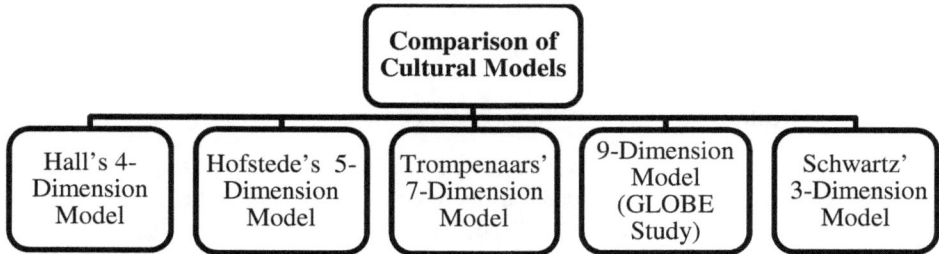

```
                        ┌─────────────────┐
                        │  Comparison of  │
                        │ Cultural Models │
                        └─────────────────┘
```

| Hall's 4-Dimension Model | Hofstede's 5-Dimension Model | Trompenaars' 7-Dimension Model | 9-Dimension Model (GLOBE Study) | Schwartz' 3-Dimension Model |

Fig. 2.3:   Studies on national cultures
Source: Own illustration

2.5.1   Hall's Cultural Model

During his studies, Hall detected four cultural dimensions as particularly important, which he called:

- Context
- Space
- Time
- Information Flow

Context

Hall's first dimension indicates that a certain amount of information has to be transmitted in communication situations, so that the receiver also understands the sender's message. Ideal-typically, Hall identifies so-called high-context cultures and low-context cultures. Asian, Arabian and Mediterranean cultures are characterized by Hall as high-context cultures, whereas US-Americans as well as Central and North Europeans are rather classified as members of low-context cultures.

Hall/Hall (1990, p. 9) describe context orientation as

"High-context people are apt to become impatient and irritated when low-context people insist on giving them information they don't need. Conversely, low-context people are at a loss when high-context people do not provide enough information."

*"The single greatest barrier to business success
is the one erected by culture."*
(E.T. Hall/M.R. Hall)

The following figure shows the range from cultures with a low-context orientation to those with a high-context orientation.

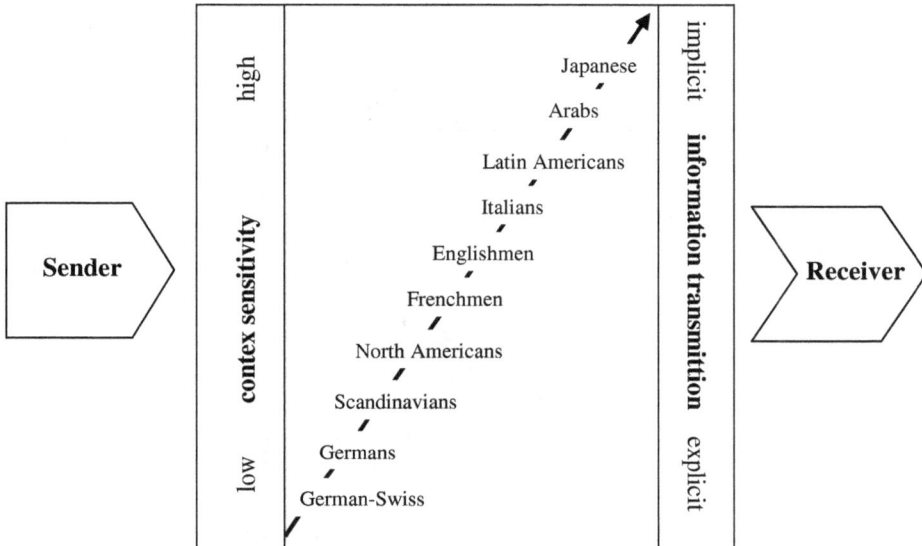

Fig. 2.4:   Low-context- and high-context-cultures
Source: Based on Rösch/Segler, 1987, p. 60

Low context	High context
Business relationships are complicated. Therefore, communication needs to be frank, explicit and direct.	Business relationships are complicated. Therefore, communication needs to be diplomatic, implicit and indirect.

50	40	30	20	10	0	10	20	30	40	50

Fig. 2.5:   Self-evaluation for low and high context orientation
Source: Carté/Fox, 2004, p. 18

Further examples that demonstrate how to use certain questions in this context for an interview or a questionnaire are as follows (Carte/Fox, 2004, pp 147–164):

Time: Monochronic	Time: Polychronic
I prefer to deal with one task at the time in a structural fashion.	I prefer to have many tasks running at the same time.

50	40	30	20	10	0	10	20	30	40	50

Short-Term						Long-Term				
I prefer to focus on the here and now.						I need to see beyond the horizon and plan accordingly.				
50	40	30	20	10	0	10	20	30	40	50

Fixed Truth						Relative Truth				
There are clear rights and wrongs.						What is right and wrong depends on the circumstances.				
50	40	30	20	10	0	10	20	30	40	50

Analytical						Intuitive				
What I value most is a logical, comprehensive and consistent argument. Even if I instinctively feel a proposal is right, I need to test every step of the argument before I can commit myself.						What I value most are creative and intriguing ideas that appeal to the emotions. If I instinctively feel a proposal is right, I don't need to test every step of the argument before I commit myself.				
50	40	30	20	10	0	10	20	30	40	50

Individualistic Relationships						Group-Oriented Relationships				
My first duty should be to myself.						My first duty should be to the group I belong to.				
50	40	30	20	10	0	10	20	30	40	50

Flat Hierachy						Vertical Hierachy				
Leaders should share the power.						Leaders should hold the power.				
50	40	30	20	10	0	10	20	30	40	50

Space

For the second dimension, Hall distinguishes between the so-called personal space and the territory. One the one hand, the personal space is the invisible "circle" surrounding everyone and which may not be entered by another person without permission. On the other hand, the territory is defined as all places and things which a person considers as personal property –

regardless of the legal definition – because they are owned by the person or are used by him/her.

Hall/Hall (1990, p. 11) characterize "space" as

> *"Each person has around him an invisible bubble of space which expands and contracts depending on a number of things: In Northern Europe, the bubbles are quite and people keep their distance. In Southern France, Italy, Greece, and Spain, the bubbles get smaller so that the distance that is perceived as intimate in the North overlaps normal conversational distance in the South."*

Time

Time orientation plays a big role in all cultural models. Hall differentiates between monochronic and polychronic time orientation. An overview can be found in the figure below:

Tab. 2.2:   Monochronic versus polychronic time orientation
Source: Hall/Hall, 1990, p. 15

Monochronic people	Polychronic people
• do one thing at a time	• do many things at once
• concentrate on the job	• are highly distractible and subject to interruptions
• view time commitments as critical	• view time commitments as objectives
• are low context and need information	• are high context and already have information
• are committed to the job	• are committed to people and human relationships
• adhere rigidly to plans	• change plans often and easily
• emphasize promptness	• base promtness on the importance and significance of the relationship
• are accustomed to short-term relationships	• have a strong tendency to build lifetime relationships

In cultures with a monochronic time orientation, time is linearly looked upon, which means that activities are scheduled in order to be managed successively and sequentially. In cultures with a polychronic time orientation, different time frames become indistinct. Time is not a linear but a circular concept, which means that several activities are run simultaneously. According to Hall, the United States and many Central European cultures (Germanic and Scandinavian cultures) are monochronic, whereas Latin American, Arabian and Mediterranean cultures can be considered as rather polychronic.

Information Flow

With his fourth dimension, Hall addresses the different speeds in which information is coded and decoded in communication situations. What is meant with the speed of the information flow in different cultures, Hall/Hall (1990, p. 12) expressed as:

> *"In the United States it is not too difficult to get to know people quickly in a relatively superficial way, which is all that most Americans want. Conversely, in Europe personal relationships and friendships are highly valued and tend to take a long time to solidify."*

Critical review of Hall's study

Hall raises no claim that his four dimensions cover all cultural differences. His cultural dimensions are rather to be understood as a general orientation. Often, Hall's work is only presented in a condensed form and occasionally, only one dimension, mainly context orientation is mentioned; sometimes his work is reduced to two dimensions, namely context and time (Kutschker/Schmid, 2002, p. 701).

Hall himself points out that apart from cultural differences also individual ones exist. Moreover, the dimensions are not independent from one another. Thus, a low-context orientation often comes along not only with a polychronic time orientation but also with a preference for a quick information flow and a comparatively high significance of the personal space.

2.5.2   Hofstede's 5-Dimension Model

In international management, the probably best known study on cultural research is connected with the name of Prof. Dr. Geert Hofstede. He conducted his survey at the American computer company IBM, where he questioned 116,000 employees in 60 countries. The questionnaire was translated into twenty national languages. The initial study (1969–1973) concerning the four dimensions of Power Distance, Uncertainty Avoidance, Individualism/Collectivism and Masculinity/Femininity was extended by the fifth dimension of Long-Term-/Short-Term Orientation in a follow-up study in 1987 (Kutscher/Schmid, 2002, pp. 702f). In 2010, the sixth dimension Indulgence/Restraint was added – based on data of the World Values Survey.

Power Distance

The first dimension determined by Hofstede (1983, p. 419) was the so-called Power Distance Index. He defined it as

"The extent to which less powerful members of institutions and organizations accept that power is distributed unequally."

Tab. 2.3:   Examples of different values for Power Distance
Source: Weidmann, 1995, p. 45

Societies with Low Power Distance Index	Societies with High Power Distance Index
At the workplace	
• Hierarchy implies inequality of roles for functional reasons	• Hierarchy implies existential inequality
• Employees expect to be involved in the decision making process	• Employees expect instructions and regulations
• Tendency towards the delegation of tasks and responsibility	• Tendency towards a centralization of decisions and responsibility
• The ideal boss is a capable democrat	• The ideal boss is a sympathetic autocrat (a good father)
• Co-determination	• Autocracy
• Power is based on knowledge, professional standing and the ability to reward others	• Power is based on family, friends, charisma and the ability to use power as form of pressure
• Religion and philosophical ideas emphasize equality	• Religion and philosophical ideas emphasize division into social classes

• Management theories focus on the role of the employee	• Management theories focus on the role of the leader
• Managers are expected to be modest about privileges and status symbols	• Managers are expected to demonstrate privileges and status symbols

Societies with a high power index are those in which people blindly follow their superiors' instructions, employees are more passive and less actively involved in the decision making process and an autocratic leadership style is predominant. Most of the African, Asian and Latin American countries as well as France, Belgium, Italy and Spain are assigned to that group. A low power distance index is associated with a decentralized organization, a lower share of supervisory personnel and highly qualified staff, who are also involved in the decision making process. A rather partner-like leadership style prevails. America, the United Kingdom, the Scandinavian countries and Germany, among others, are countries with a low power distance.

Individualism versus Collectivism

On the one hand, individualism is expressed by people especially caring for themselves and their immediate environment.

> *"Individualism is the tendency of people to look after themselves and their immediate family only." (Hofstede, 1980, p. 419)*

Collectivism, on the other hand, is linked to people with a sense of belonging to a group or a collective and who attend to the members' needs. In individualistic societies, the pursuit of realizing one's own goals dominates, while the achievement of group's objectives based on a sense of belonging characterizes collectivistic societies.

Tab. 2.4:   Examples of different values for Collectivism/Individualism
Source: Weidmann, 1995, p. 46

Collectivistic Societies	Individualistic Societies
At the workplace	
• Different benchmarks for members of in- groups and out-groups	• Equal treatment of all employees
• People are judged by their group affiliation	• People are judged by their capabilities
• Interpersonal relationships are more important than tasks (harmony)	• Tasks are more important than interpersonal relationships (performance/success)
• Favored recruitment and promotion of members of the in-group	• The relationship between employer and employee is purpose-related and on a contractual basis (labor market)
• Management stands for the leadership of groups	• Management stands for the leadership of individuals
• Aims of the groups dominate personnel planning	• Career planning dominates personnel development

Thus, the different degrees of intensity of individualism vary from one culture to another and can be measured by the so-called Individualism Index. Countries with a very distinct individuality also reflect a high acceptance of a rather Protestant work ethic. They include, among others, all Anglo-American countries, Sweden, Denmark and Germany. Just as in the case of the power distance index, the point scores represent the relative position of the particular country. The lower the score, the more collectivistic and the higher the score, the more individualistic the country is.

Masculinity versus Femininity

Masculinity is defined by Hofstede (1980, pp. 420) as

   "a situation in which the dominant values in society are success, money, and things",

while he describes femininity as

   "a situation in which the dominant values in society are caring for others and the quality of life".

Thus, a country can be described as masculine if it is performance-based, and if its individuals are success-oriented and behave self-confidently. Whereas a feminine culture is characterized by more attention to interpersonal relationships, the preservation of the environment and the quality of life and regards compromises as well as cooperation as a way of accomplishing its goals.

Tab. 2.5:   Examples of different values for Masculinity/Femininity
Source: Weidmann, 1995, p. 48

Feminine Societies	Masculine Societies
At the workplace	
• Self-confident behavior is ridiculed	• Self-confident behavior is acknowledged
• Readiness to assimilate	• Assertiveness
• One sells oneself short	• One exaggerates one's own merits
• Quality of life plays an important role	• Career plays an important role
• Empathy	• Achievement orientation
• "Work to live"	• "Live to work"
• Cooperation, willingness to compromise	• Competition, preparedness for conflict
• Intuition	• Aggression

Uncertainty Avoidance

Hofstede defines (1980, p. 418) Uncertainty Avoidance as

   "the extent to which people feel threatened by ambiguous situations".

Every culture has developed procedures in order to cope with this uncertainty. A society with a strong tendency towards uncertainty avoidance tries to control the future or at least to influence it with the help of regulations, laws and rules of conduct. Less motivated employees and risk-averse managers also belong to this group. Cultures with a low degree of uncertainty avoidance guide their members to more tolerance towards other opinions. Fewer laws and controls, a more distinct readiness for taking risks instead of being passive as well as a higher degree of motivation are also characteristics of this category. Countries with a low uncertainty avoidance show lower values of uncertainty avoidance and vice versa.

Tab. 2.6:   Examples of different values for Uncertainty Avoidance
Source: Weidmann, 1995, p. 49

Societies with Low Uncertainty Avoidance	Societies with High Uncertainty Avoidance
At the workplace	
• Reluctance towards written or oral rules and regulations	• Emotional need for written rules and regulations
• Flat hierarchies, few differences in status	• Strict hierarchies, thinking in terms of status
• High significance of "all-rounders" & common sense	• High significance of "experts & specialists"
• Spontaneous vertical & horizontal communication	• Official channels
• Flexible organization & job design	• Formalization & standardization
• Contracts can be renegotiated (framework conditions, details, etc.)	• Contracts have to be abided by (detailed contracts, providing for all contingencies)
• Readiness for innovation	• Resistance to change

Short-Term versus Long-Term Orientation

The fifth dimension in Hofstede's model deals with moral values connected to a "long-term orientation". It describes the degree to which a society has a pragmatic future-oriented basic attitude in contrast to a dogmatic present-oriented perspective.

Tab. 2.7:   Examples of different values for Long-Term Orientation
Source: Weidmann, 1995, p. 50

Feminine Societies	Masculine Societies
At the workplace	
• Tendency to the absolute truth	• Many "truths" (depending on time, place and circumstances)
• Normativism	• Pragmatism
• Impatience, short-term successes	• Persistence, long-term goal tracking
• Domination of own goals, aversion to heteronomy	• Willingness to bow to a collectivistic goal
• High investments for a fast development (indebtedness)	• Budgeting for the future (savings)

Positively as well as negatively connoted moral concepts of this dimension are reminiscent of Confucius teachings and have also been called "Confucian dynamism" in the context of cultural theory, since their existence was first shown in the Chinese Value Survey (Bond, 1986). However, this dimension is also applicable to countries without a Confucian past. The cultural effects of this dimension's differences are presently researched, so that a detailed table backed by sufficient scientific evidence of the differences at the workplace cannot yet be completely prepared (Weidmann, 1995, p. 50).

Sixth dimension: Indulgence versus Restraint

Hofstede's 5-Dimension Model has become a worldwide respected cultural model. Not only teachers in schools or universities, but even trainers have worked with this model. In the third edition of his book "Cultures and Organizations: Software of the Mind"

(Hofstede/Hofstede/Minkov, 2010) he added a sixth dimension for the first time and he has called it "Indulgence versus Restraint". Hofstede also talked about the sixth dimension in an interview with a group of French students, which you can find on pp. 61ff.

Critical review of Hofstede's study

Hofstede's study did not remain uncriticized. Here some critical voices can be found:

- It is often criticized that his research wants to measure influences of national cultures, but the results could be skewed due to influences of the corporate culture. This criticism seems to be justified, especially against the background of IBM's strong corporate culture, which involves certain recruitment practices and a pressure towards a certain uniformity on the employees.
- Moreover, it is said that the initial study was shaped by the Western culture. According to his critics, Hofstede asked questions which are particular interesting from a Western point of view but might have a different or even no meaning at all in other cultures.
- In the eyes of many authors, the identified dimensions are problematic and he is especially criticized for an insufficient selectivity of the dimensions.

Despite this criticism, Hofstede deserves special acknowledgement for the following points (Kutschker/Schmid, 2002, p. 717):

- Even though Hofstede's study was conducted some time ago, there has not yet been another study which can boast an only approximately similar extent – concerning the number of considered countries and the number of respondents.
- In spite of the problems concerning the dimensions, the study makes a classification of countries based on different criteria possible. Thereby, the study went beyond the works of others, in which only statements concerning one single country or culture-specific aspect were made.
- Hofstede's study does not only allow for a classification but also for a comparison of countries.

Country-specific point scores of the 5-D-Model

Hofstede's 5-Dimension Model can be used as a basis for a comparison of other countries' cultures by the means of selected parameters. The following table shows the five dimensions' index values for 50 selected countries and three regions. For the Long Term Orientation based on the data collected for 23 countries by Bond, not all priorly mentioned countries could be included in the comparison. This table is then supplemented by 32 other countries, which had not been initially taken into account.

Concerning the interpretation of the two tables, all point scores only display the countries' relative and not their absolute positions. From the respective point score, it can be read off to what extent the countries differ from each other. For example regarding masculinity, a high index means that the Philippines with a determined score of 94 belong to the countries with a high degree of masculinity. Conversely, one can conclude that strongly feminine countries, e.g. Norway with an index value of 8, have a low Masculinity Index.

If you try to draw a general conclusion from these two tables, it strikes that the point values for the Power Distance Index (PDI) for Latin-American, Asian and African countries are relatively high, whereas the values are fairly lower for the majority of European and North American countries.

Concerning the Individualism Index (IDV), there are high values for the industrialized countries, including North America, whereas collectivism dominates in the rest of the world.

The Masculinity Index (MAS) is very distinct in Japan as well as in some European countries, among others Germany, Austria and Switzerland. In the Nordic and a number of Romanic and Asian countries the respective values are relatively low.

The Uncertainty Avoidance Index (UAI) is more distinct in the Romanic countries, Japan and the German-speaking countries and is lower in countries of Nordic and Chinese culture.

A Long-Term Orientation (LTO) becomes particularly apparent in East-Asian countries, especially in China, Taiwan, Japan and South Korea.

Anyone wanting to apply Hofstede's model, can find more information at

http://www.geert-hofstede.com/

Professor Dr. Geert Hofstede is honoured for his life's work

The highest prize as appreciation of his life's work in the field of further education and training is awarded to the pioneer in modern intercultural research, Professor Dr. Geert Hofstede. With his research, the social psychologist has revolutionised the comprehension of cultural diversity at the workplace. Up until now, his innovative studies among more than 10,000 IBM employees in over 50 countries have been considered some of the most comprehensive surveys in an enterprise. Based on their results, a concept of cultural dimensions was devised, with the help of which national cultures became measurable for the first time and, as a result, describable. With this model, he offered a manifold instrument which has been employed in the field of intercultural training until nowadays. For these attainments, Geert Hofstede is honoured with the Life Achievement Award in the further education domain.

Within solemn proceedings, Hofstede is awarded the honour by praiser Lothar Seiwert. The Past President of the German Speakers' Association e. V. is honouring the attainments of the social psychologist by a short speech. "For the field of further education, his work has the significance of paving the way" is the reason given for this honour. "For decades, the model devised by Geert Hofstede has served as an essential foundation for trainers, both female and male, who have been working successfully with senior managers and teams of employees on international projects and globalised markets," adds Renate Richter, vice president of the umbrella association of further education organisations (DVWO).

In: managerSeminare.de, Petersberger Trainingstage 2012; Life Achievement Award, March 2012 (Own translation)

Tab. 2.8:   Country-specific scores of the 5-D-Model
Source: Weidmann, 1995, p. 52 (compiled according to Hofstede, 1991)

Country	Power Distance PDI		Individualism IDV		Masculinity MAS		Uncertainty Avoidance UAI		Long-Term Orientation	
	Index	*Rank*	Index	*Rank*	Index	*Rank*	Index	*Rank*	Index	*Rank*
Argentina	49	*35–36*	46	*22–23*	56	*20–21*	86	*10–15*		
Australia	36	*41*	90	*2*	61	*2*	51	*37*	31	*14–15*
Austria	11	*53*	55	*18*	79	*2*	70	*24–25*		
Belgium	65	*20*	75	*8*	54	*8*	94	*5-6*		
Brasil	69	*14*	38	*26–27*	49	*26–27*	76	*21–22*	65	*6*
Canada	39	*39*	80	*4-5*	52	*4–5*	48	*41–42*	23	*20*
Chile	63	*24–25*	23	*33*	28	*33*	86	*10–15*		
Columbia	67	*17*	13	*49*	64	*49*	80	*20*		*5*
Costa Rica	35	*42–44*	15	*46*	21	*46*	86	*10–15*		
Denmark	18	*51*	74	*9*	16	*9*	23	*51*		
Ecuador	78	*8-9*	8	*52*	63	*52*	67	*28*		
Finland	33	*46*	63	*17*	57	*17*	59	*31–32*		
France	68	*15–16*	71	*10-11*	43	*10–11*	86	*10–15*		
Germany	35	*42–44*	67	*15*	66	*15*	65	*29*	31	*14–15*
Greece	60	*27–28*	35	*30*	57	*30*	112	*1*		
Guatemala	95	*2–3*	6	*53*	37	*53*	101	*3*		
Hongkong	68	*15–16*	25	*37*	57	*37*	29	*49-50*	96	*2*
India	77	*10–11*	48	*21*	56	*21*	40	*45*	61	*7*
Indonesia	78	*8–9*	14	*47–48*	46	*47–48*	48	*41–42*		
Iran	58	*29–30*	41	*24*	43	*24*	59	*31–32*		
Ireland	28	*49*	70	*12*	68	*12*	35	*47–48*		
Israel	13	*52*	54	*19*	47	*19*	81	*19*		
Italia	50	*34*	76	*7*	70	*7*	75	*23*		
Jamaica	45	*37*	39	*25*	68	*25*	13	*52*		
Japan	54	*33*	46	*22–23*	95	*22–23*	92	*7*	80	*4*
Malaysia	104	*1*	26	*36*	50	*25–26*	36	*46*		
Mexico	81	*5-6*	30	*32*	69	*6*	82	*18*		
Netherlands	38	*40*	80	*4-5*	14	*51*	53	*35*	44	*10*
New Zealand	22	*50*	79	*6*	58	*17*	49	*39–40*	30	*16*
Norway	31	*47–48*	69	*13*	8	*52*	50	*38*		
Pakistan	55	*32*	14	*47–48*	50	*25–26*	70	*24–25*	0	*24*
Panama	95	*2–3*	11	*51*	44	*34*	86	*10–15*		
Peru	64	*21–23*	16	*45*	42	*37–38*	87	*9*		
Philippines	94	*4*	32	*31*	64	*11–12*	44	*44*	19	*21*
Portugal	63	*24–25*	27	*33–35*	31	*45*	104	*2*		
Salvador	66	*18–19*	19	*42*	40	*40*	94	*5-6*		
Singapore	74	*13*	20	*39–41*	48	*28*	8	*53*	48	*9*
South Africa	49	*35–36*	65	*16*	63	*13–14*	49	*39–40*		
South Korea	60	*27–28*	18	*43*	39	*43*	85	*16–17*	75	
Spain	57	*31*	51	*20*	42	*37–38*	86	*10–15*		
Sweden	31	*47–48*	71	*10–11*	5	*52*	29	*49–50*	33	*12*
Switzerland	34	*45*	68	*14*	70	*4–5*	58	*33*		

Taiwan	58	29–30	17	44	45	32–33	69	26	87	3
Thailand	64	21–23	20	39–41	34	44	64	30	56	8
Turkey	66	18–19	37	28	45	31–33	85	16–17		
United Kingdom	35	42–44	89	3	66	3	35	47–48	25	18–19
United States of America	40	38	91	1	62	15	46	43	29	17
Uruguay	61	26	36	29	38	42	100	4		
Venezuela	81	5–6	12	50	73	3	76	21–22		
Yugoslavia	76	12	27	33–35	21	33–35	88	8		
Regions: Arab Countries	80	7	38	26–27	53	23	68	27		
East Africa	64	21–23	27	33–35	41	39	52	36	25	18–19
West Africa	77	10–11	20	39–41	46	30–31	54	34	16	22

Rank 1 = highest, 53 = lowest rank (regarding Long.Term Orientation, rank 23 is the lowest)

Point scores of 50 countries and three regions for the five dimensions of national culture)

Tab. 2.9:   Country-specific scores of the 5-D-Model – Supplement
Source: Weidmann, 1995, p. 53 (compiled according to Bond, 1986; Hofstede, 1991)

Country	PDI	IDV	MAS	UAI	LTO
Albania	90	20	80	70	
Baltic Republics	40	60	30	50	
Bulgaria	70	50	50	80	
Butane	94	52	32	28	
Caucasus	70	20	50	60	
China	80	20	66	30	118
Croatia	72	33	40	80	
Czechoslovakia	35	60	45	60	
Dominican Republic	65	30	65	45	
Egypt	70	25	45	80	
Ethiopia	70	20	65	55	
Fiji	78	14	46	48	
Ghana	80	15	40	65	
Hungary	19	55	79	83	
Kenya	70	25	60	50	
Lebanon	75	40	65	50	
Luxembourg	55	70	60	70	
Malawi	70	30	40	50	
Namibia	65	30	40	45	35
Nepal	75	30	42	40	40
Nigeria	80	30	60	55	
Poland	50	60	70	50	
Romania	90	20	40	95	
Russia & Ukraine	95	47	40	75	
Saudi Arabia	95	25	60	80	
Serbia	86	25	43	92	

Sierra Leone	70	20	40	50	
Slovenia	71	27	19	88	
Sri Lanka	60	40	10	55	45
Surinam	80	48	35	80	
Tanzania	70	25	40	50	30
Zambia	60	35	40	50	

(Point scores of 32 countries not included in Tab. 2.8: Country-specific scores of the 5-D-ModelTab. 2.8)

2.5.3   Trompenaars' 7-D-Model

Like Hofstede's research, Trompenaars' study is based on written interviews. He analyzed 30.000 questionnaires and presented the results in 1993. In contrast to Hofstede, the respondents did not come from one single company but from many different enterprises, among others Heineken, Philips, Volvo, Royal Dutch/Shell and Eastman Kodak. He received answers from 55 different countries. However, only 47 countries were included in the study, as the required minimum number of 50 returned questionnaires was reached here.

Universalism versus Particularism

The first dimension reflects the primacy of the "general" in opposition to the primacy of the "specific". While universalists particularly emphasize the compliance with rules, particularists pay more attention to the circumstances or personal backgrounds.

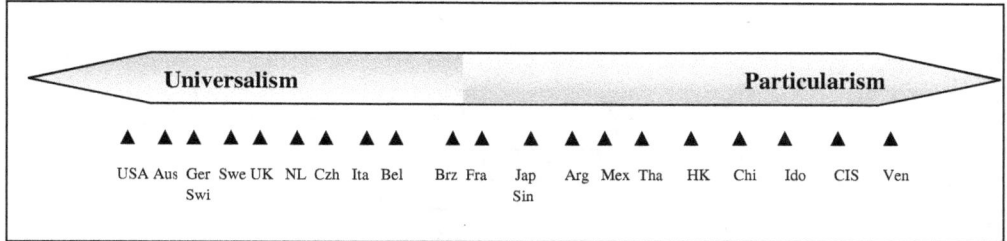

Fig. 2.6 :   Universalism versus Particularism – Country comparison
Source: Hodgetts/Luthans, 2003, p. 126

Tab. 2.10:   Universalism versus Particularism
Source: Hoecklin, 1998, p. 41

Universalism	**Particularism**
• Focus is more on rules than on relationships.	• Focus is more on relationship than on rules.
• Legally contracts are readily drawn up.	• Legal contracts are readily modified.
• A trustworthy is the one who "honors" their work or contract.	• A trustworthy is the one who "honors" changing circumstances.
• There is only one truth or reality that has been agreed to.	• There are several perspectives on reality relative to each participant.
• A deal is a deal.	• Relationship evolves.

Individualism versus Collectivism

As with Hofstede, the question of the relationship between people also arises with Trompenaars. For him, the central question is, whether individuals primarily see themselves as individuals, or whether they define themselves through the affiliation to a group.

Tab. 2.11:   Individualism versus Collectivism
Source: Hoecklin, 1998, p. 41

Individualism	Collectivism/Communitarianism
• More frequent use of "I" and "me".	• More frequent use of "we".
• In negotiations, decisions typically made on the spot by a representative.	• Decisions typically referred back by delegate to the organization.
• People ideally achieve alone and assume personal responsibility.	• People ideally achieve in groups which assume joint responsibility.
• Holidays taken in pairs or even alone.	• Holidays taken in organized groups, or with extended family.

Apart from the USA, e.g. Rumania, Russia, Nigeria and Israel are characterized as individualistic by Trompenaars, while e.g. Japan, India, Egypt and Mexico are classified as collectivistic.

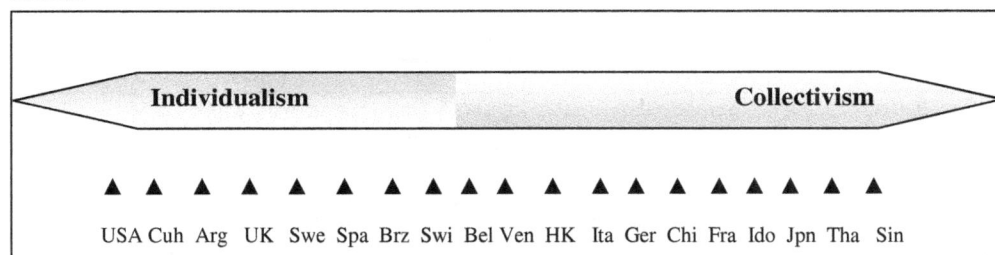

Fig. 2.7:   Individualism versus Collectivism – Country comparison
Source: Hodgetts/Luthans, 2003, p. 126

Neutral versus Affective

Trompenaars' third dimension deals with the importance of feelings and relationships. In affective cultures, feelings and emotions are not restrained, whereas instrumentality and rationality of actions are the main focus in neutral cultures. Simplified, one can say that one also differentiates between "impulsive behavior" and "disciplined behavior".

Tab. 2.12:   Neutral versus Emotional
Source: Hoecklin, 1998, p. 42

Neutral	Emotional/Affective
• Opaque emotional state.	• Show immediate reactions either verbally or non-verbally.
• Do not readily express what they think and feel.	
• Embarrassed and awkward at public displays of emotions.	• Expressive face and body signals.
• Discomfort with physical contact outside private cycle.	• At ease with physical contact.
• Subtle in verbal and non-verbal expressions.	• Raise voice readily.

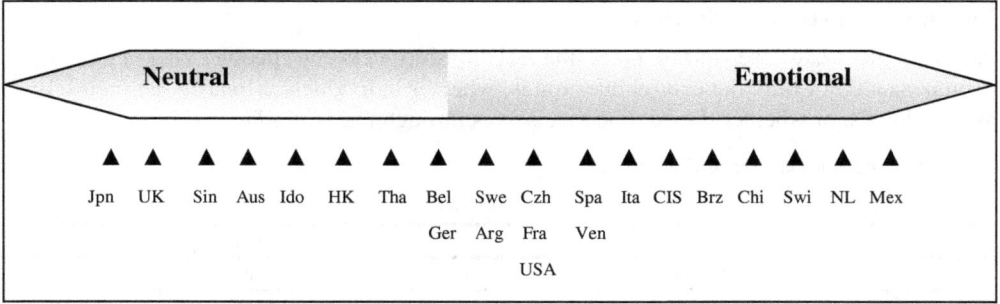

Fig. 2.8:   Neutral versus Emotional – Country comparison
Source: Hodgetts/Luthans, 2003, p. 126

Specific versus Diffuse

This dimension is in some cases also called "dimension of consternation/engagement" expressing an individual's degree of consternation in a certain situation or action. In "diffuse" cultures the different areas of life cannot be separated from each other. In "specific" cultures, however, the areas of life, e.g. work and family, are clearly differentiated.

Tab. 2.13:   Specific versus Diffuse
Source: Hoecklin, 1998, p. 45

Specific	Diffuse
• Rather "open" public space, rather "closed" private space.	• Rather "closed" public space, rather "open" private space.
• Direct, to the point, purposeful in relating to others.	• Indirect, circuitous, seemingly "aimless" forms of relating to others.
• Precise, blunt, definitive and transparent.	• Evasive, tactful, ambiguous, even opaque.
• Separates work and private life.	• Work and private life are closely linked.
• Principals and consistent moral stand independently of the person being addressed.	• Highly situational morality depending upon the person and context encountered.

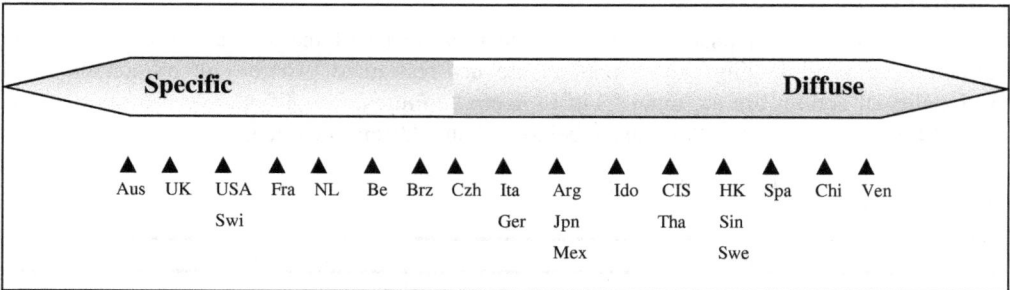

Fig. 2.9:   Specific versus Diffuse – Country comparison
Source: Hodgetts/Luthans, 2003, p. 126

Achievement versus Ascription

This dimension relates to the question whether an individual's status is determined by religion, origin or age or whether it is mainly reached by own achievements. According to

Trompenaars, the United States of America are strongly focused on achievement, whereas some Central European countries, such as Italy, Germany and Russia, obviously tend to ascription.

Tab. 2.14:   Achievement versus Ascription
Source: Hoecklin, 1998, p. 121

Achievement-oriented	Ascription-oriented
• Use of titles only when relevant to the competences you bring to the task.	• Extensive use of titles, especially when these clarify your position in the organization.
• Respect for superior in hierarchy is based on how effectively his or her job is done and how adequate their knowledge.	• Respect for superior in hierarchy is seen as a measure of your commitment to the organization and its mission.
• Most senior managers are of varying age and gender and have shown proficiency in specific jobs.	• Most senior managers are male, middle-aged and qualified by their background.

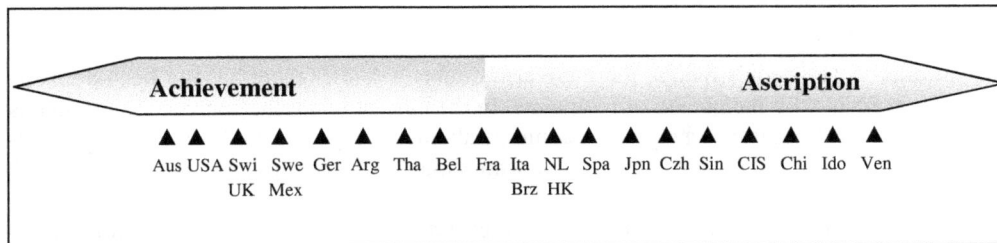

Fig. 2.10:   Achievement versus Ascription – Country comparison
Source: Hodgetts/Luthans, 2003, p. 126

Human-Time-Relationship

Similar to Hall, Trompenaars also included temporal considerations into his model. In some cultures, time management is seen as rather sequential, in others it is seen as rather circular or synchronic (see chapter about Hall and the described concept of time).

Tab. 2.15:   Sequential versus Synchrone
Source: Trompenaars 1998, p. 143

Sequential/Monochrome	Synchronic
• Do only one activity at a time.	• Do more than one activity at a time.
• Time is sizable and measurable.	• Appointments are approximate and subjects to "giving time" to significant others.
• Keep appointments strictly; schedule in advance and do not run late.	• Schedules are generally subordinate to relationships.

Human-Nature-Relationship

Trompenaars also examined the ways in which people deal with their environment. Specific attention should be given to whether they believe in controlling outcomes (inner-directed) or letting things take their own course (outer-directed). One of the things he asked manager to do was to choose between the following statements:

1.   What happens to me is my own doing.

2. Sometimes I feel that I do not have enough control over the directions my life is taking.

Managers who believe in controlling their own environment would opt for the first choice; those who believe that they are controlled by their environment and cannot do much about it would opt for the second choice (Hodgetts/Luthans, 2003, p. 130).

Tab. 2.16:   Internal versus External control
Source: Trompenaars, 1998, p. 159

Internal control	External control
• Often dominant attitude bordering on aggressiveness towards the environment.	• Often flexible attitude, willing to compromise and keep the peace.
• Conflict and resistance means that you have convictions.	• Harmony and responsiveness, that is, sensibility.
• Focus is on oneself, one's own group and organization.	• Focus is on "others", that is customer, partner and colleagues.

Critical review of Trompenaars' study

*   Similar to Hofstede's model, there are also doubts, whether there has not been a distortion of results by the choice of recipients. In the case at hand, the survey of participants of a management training course, it could be about employees who already had a comparably high intercultural awareness and who should only be further sensitized with the help of intercultural issues.
*   It remains uncertain how Trompenaars exactly derived the seven identified dimensions and whether he did not "mix" elements of other cultural models to an own model.
*   It stands out positively that Trompenaars' results of the study have been met with great interest by managers, trainers and students, since he shows, in opposite to authors in management research who assume a cultural independence of management, that the behavior in and of companies is - or at least can be - characterized by culture.
*   Trompenaars also provides results for countries which have not been considered by Hofstede, especially many countries in Central and Eastern Europe.

For further information on Trompenaars/Hampden-Turner, please see
http://www.7d-culture.nl/.

---

30 TIPS ON HOW TO LEARN ACROSS CULTURES (5–6)
(Andre Laurent)

5. If you are convinced that your ways of managing, motivating, making decisions, running meetings etc. are the best, avoid working across cultures. It would be a painful experience for everybody involved, including yourself.

6. Respect local customs, adapt your behaviour to local norms and expectations, but don't try to imitate. Clowning is not expected. It would be seen as phony and would not be respected.

In: SIETAR (Hrsg.), Keynote-Speech, Kongress 2000, Ludwigshafen

2.5.4   Schwartz' Cultural Model

Shalom H. Schwartz is one of the leading social psychologists in Israel and professor at the Hebrew University of Jerusalem. In 2007, the Israel Prize in Psychology was awarded to him (The Hebrew University of Jerusalem, Press Release, 28/02/2007). Not least had he deserved this tribute for his research on cultural values and the development of his three dimensions, which have gained considerable importance in the international environment. When creating his cultural model, Schwartz used an approach which is similar to the procedure of Trompenaars or the researchers of the GLOBE project and slightly different from Hofstede's approach. While Hofstede conducted an empirical study and as a result formulated his dimensions, Schwartz theorized a model for comparison of cultures in a first step. He considered three basic issues that confront all societies (Munro/Schumaker/Carr, 1997, pp. 77–78):

1. Relationship between the person and the group
2. Assuring socially responsible behaviour
3. The role of humankind in the natural and social world

The various ways in which cultures handle these problems are assembled along bipolar cultural dimensions: Embeddedness vs. Intellectual and Affective Autonomy, Egalitarianism vs. Hierarchy, and Harmony vs. Mastery.

After a comprehensive literature research, Schwartz established a list of fifty-six single values such as social justice, humility, creativity, social order or pleasure and ambition. He asked respondents to evaluate each item on a scale ranging from 7 to -1 according to their importance *"as a guiding principle in my life"* (Schwartz, 2004, pp. 43–73) with 7 meaning the value is of supreme importance, 0 that it is of no importance, and -1 that it is opposed to my values (Schwartz, 1994, p. 99). In advance, Schwartz assigned each value to one of the seven cultural orientations in a way that he expected them to relate to each other.

Between 1988 and 2000, he collected data of 67 countries and 3 sub-national ethnical groups. In heterogeneous societies, samples were drawn from the dominating cultural group representing the majority of the population. However, due to the considerable cultural diversity in some countries, Schwartz decided to include separate samples from French and English Canadians, from Black and White South Africans as well as from Israeli, Arabs and Jews. All respondents completed a questionnaire which was phrased in their respective native language. Schwartz distributed the questionnaires among his network of university professors and students (Schwartz, 2004, pp. 43–73).

Schwartz' Cultural Dimensions

Embeddedness versus Autonomy

Schwartz' first dimension addresses the relationship between the individual and a group. While in cultures with a tendency towards the embeddedness pole of the scale, individuals are integrated in established group relationships, in autonomous cultures, the individual is rather self-determined (Schwartz, 2004, pp. 43–73).

Schwartz differentiates between two types of autonomy: Intellectual and affective autonomy. Intellectual autonomy implies that individuals are encouraged to pursue their own ideas and intellectual directions independently. Consequently, important values are broad-mindedness, curiosity and creativity. Affective autonomy, in contrast, emphasizes pleasure as well as an exciting and a varied life. Therefore, individuals are encouraged to pursue positive experiences for themselves (Schwartz, 1994, pp. 102–103).

In cultures where embeddedness is prevailing, *"people are viewed as entities which are embedded in the collectivity"* (Schwartz, 2004, pp. 43–73) and they receive their meaning in life through social relationships and the identification with the group. A shared way of life is as important as striving towards joint goals. Maintaining the status quo is a superior aim in embedded societies and activities that are expected to disrupt solidarity or traditional order are impeded. People value social order, security, obedience and wisdom (Schwartz, 1994, p. 102).

Egalitarianism versus Hierarchy

The second dimension shows the extent to which responsible behavior, which preserves the social structure, is assured and the unequal distribution of power, ascendancy and resources is legitimized (Schwartz, 1994, p. 102). Egalitarianism stresses values such as equality, social justice or honesty and consequently, people are encouraged to neglect self-serving interest in favor of societal needs. In cultures with a strong tendency towards hierarchy, important values are authority, humility and health. Frequently, high egalitarianism and intellectual autonomy appear together, as it is the case in Western Europe (Schwartz, 2004, pp. 43–73).

Harmony versus Mastery

Harmony versus Mastery describes the relationships of individuals to the natural and social world. In this context, harmony refers to a person's harmonious fitting into the world under the present circumstances, while mastery describes striving for the active and ambitious accomplishment of challenges and aims. In harmonious cultures people try to understand and appreciate rather than to change, direct or exploit. World at peace, unity with nature, and protecting the environment are values that play an important role in people's lives. Mastery, as the opposite, emphasizes ambition, success, and daring as well as competence and self-assertion (Schwartz, 1994, pp. 102–103).

---

30 TIPS ON HOW TO LEARN ACROSS CULTURES (7–8)
(Andre Laurent)

7.   Watch for the illusion of similarity. "We are from the same industry." "We are all engineers." "We share the same language." "We are from the same company united by a strong corporate culture." We are all human beings too. Such statements often hide a desire to avoid confronting the reality of cultural differences.

8.   Beware of excessive politeness. It is another strategy contributing to the denial of differences. It often leads to superficiality, low risk-taking, avoidance and productive confrontation and achievement of the smallest common denominator.

In: SIETAR (Hrsg.), Keynote-Speech, Kongress 2000, Ludwigshafen

---

Critical review of Schwartz' study

Today, Schwartz is considered to be *"one of the most prominent and valued researchers in the world"* (The Hebrew University of Jerusalem, 28/02/2007). His study is consistently gaining in importance and has been cited in both Hofstede's "Cultural Consequences" and the GLOBE study for comparison and validation purposes. Schwartz managed to make use of the criticism raised against Hofstede's methodology and improved several of these aspects in his own research. One example is the check on the equivalence of meaning of the chosen values across all cultures in order to avoid a Western bias as in Hofstede's concept.

Nevertheless, Schwartz' model has not nearly reached the popularity of Hofstede, Trompenaars or Hall in intercultural matters. Despite valuable improvements compared to previous research, the approach Schwartz has chosen is somewhat problematic. As a basis for the validation of his dimensions, Schwartz used data on the importance of values in people's lives. However, it is questionable to what extent respondents were able to objectively measure the relevance of certain principles. Since this is something people generally do not consciously experience, they consequently are not able to rationally assess the meaning that certain values have in their lives. Additionally, the differentiation on a scale from 1 to 7 appears to be difficult in this context. People can presumably estimate whether certain values play an important role in their lives or not or whether they are even opposed to their personal attitude. However, a clear distinction between values being more or less important on a 7-point scale seems to be rather impossible especially considering that Schwartz presented a list of fifty-six items. This appears to be quite lengthy, since the evaluation of the relevance of values is a complex matter and is complicated to grasp and therefore, it could easily lead to untruthful answers.

Additionally, the choice of the sample leads to a limited representativeness of the whole study. Schwartz interviewed a relatively homogeneous group consisting of teachers and college students. Naturally, these respondents have received a considerable amount of education and for various reasons they are more similar across countries than the rest of the population.

Schwartz created a cultural model which has proven to be closely related to Hofstede's concept. The similarities are not only based on analogical theoretical considerations but also on empirical research which confirmed the interdependency. Schwartz himself considers his study to be a *"check on the replicability"* (Schwartz, 1994, p. 87) of Hofstede's five dimensions. Therefore, the validation of the findings of popular intercultural studies can be considered as an important gain through Schwartz's research.

---

30 TIPS ON HOW TO LEARN ACROSS CULTURES (9)
(Andre Laurent)

9.   The most negative outcomes in cross-cultural collaboration typically occur when the partners hold radically different assumptions about the situation (objectives, task, resources...etc.) and are fully unaware that this is the case.

In: SIETAR (Hrsg.), Keynote-Speech, Kongress 2000, Ludwigshafen

---

2.5.5   GLOBE-Study

The Global Leadership and Organizational Behavior Effectiveness Research Program, referred to as GLOBE-Study, is the most extensive cultural investigation in terms of scope, depth, duration and sophistication that has been conducted in recent times. The research project was initiated by the US-American university professor Robert J. House in 1991 and engaged 170 investigators in exploring cultural peculiarities of 62 societies (http://www.grovewell.com).

The GLOBE-Study aimed at establishing a theory about how culture influences leadership styles and organizational culture by gathering data from more than 17,000 managers from 951 different organizations in the industries of financial services, food processing, and telecommunications, as these sectors are expected to exist irrespective of the economic situation. In the questionnaires a 7-point scale was given on which respondents could indicate their level of agreement ranging from 1, low agreement, to 7, strong agreement (House/Hanges/Javidan/Dorfman/Gupt, 2004, p. 9).

The   criteria   decisive   for   the   sample   selection   were   the   following (http://www.grovewell.com):

1.   Several respondents had to be selected from one organization;
2.   In each country, two or more organizations had to be obtained from at least two of the three possible types of industries;
3.   In each country, at least two industries had to be represented;
4.   All respondents had to be middle managers.

The nine dimensions of the GLOBE-Study

The collected data led to the identification of the following nine cultural dimensions which are described in the following figure:

Tab. 2.17:   The GLOBE Study's Cultural Dimensions
Source: House/Hanges/Javidan/Dorfman/Gupt, 2004, pp. 12–13

1.	**Uncertainty Avoidance**	*"... is the extent to which members of an organization or society strive to avoid uncertainty by relying on established social norms, rituals, and bureaucratic practices."*
2.	**Power Distance**	*"... is the degree to which members of an organization or society expect and agree that power should be stratified and concentrated at higher levels of an organization or government."*
3.	**Institutional Collectivism**	*"... is the degree to which organizational and societal institutional practices encourage and reward collective distribution of resources and collective action."*
4.	**In-Group Collectivism**	*"... is the degree to which individuals express pride, loyalty, and cohesiveness in their organizations or families."*
5.	**Gender Egalitarianism**	*"... is the degree to which an organization or society minimizes gender role differences while promoting gender equality."*

6.	Assertiveness	*"... is the degree to which individuals in organizations or societies are assertive, confrontational, and aggressive in social relationships."*
7.	Future Orientation	*"... is the degree to which individuals in organizations or societies engage in future-oriented behaviours such as planning, investing in the future, and delaying individual or collective gratification."*
8.	Humane Orientation	*"... is the degree to which individuals in organizations or societies encourage and reward individuals for being fair, altruistic, friendly, generous, caring and kind to others."*
9.	Performance Orientation	*"... is the degree to which an organization or society encourages and rewards group members for performance improvement and excellence."*

The results of the GLOBE Study, i.e. which of the countries are at the highest, medium or lowest ranks in each of the dimensions, are shown in the figure below.

Tab. 2.18:   Results of the GLOBE Study
Source: Hodgetts/ Luthans, 2006, p. 119

Variable	Highest Ranking	Medium Ranking	Lowest Ranking
Assertiveness	Spain, U.S.	Egypt, Ireland	Sweden, New Zealand
Future Orientation	Denmark, Canada	Slovenia, Egypt	Russia, Argentina
Gender Differentiation	South Korea, Egypt	Italy, Brazil	Sweden, Denmark
Uncertainty Avoidance	Austria, Denmark	Israel, U.S.	Russia, Hungary
Power distance	Russia, Spain	England, France	Denmark, Netherlands
Collectivism/Societal	Denmark, Singapore	Hong Kong, U.S.	Greece, Hungary
In-group collectivism	Egypt, China	England, France	Denmark, Netherlands
Performance orientation	U.S., Taiwan	Sweden, Israel	Russia, Argentina
Humane orientation	Indonesia, Egypt	Hong Kong, Sweden	Germany, Spain

Critical review of the GLOBE-study

The GLOBE Study is the most extensive study that has ever been carried out in the field of cultural anthropology. It includes 59 countries and 62 cultures. The study differentiates between Eastern and Western Germany, German- and French-speaking Switzerland and the black and the white population of South Africa. By bearing in mind that significant differences between cultural groups within one country exist, the GLOBE-study turns out to be more sophisticated than the research of Hall, Trompenaars or Hofstede, who were criticised for neglecting the diverseness of cultures existing within one country. However, in other heterogeneous countries such as the United States, India or China, subcultures were not examined (House/Hanges/Javidan/Dorfman/Gupt, 2004, p. 97).

Yet, most critical is the choice of the sample. The GLOBE-project was restricted to interviewing middle managers. Managers have often received a broad education and have considerable experiences also on an international level. Therefore, they can be expected to be more sensitive towards cultural differences. Consequently, it is questionable whether cultural peculiarities can be observed adequately among managers.

2.6   Comparison of the cultural models

In the following overview, the analysis of differences in response patterns with regard to culture is focused on the area of quantitative market research. For this reason, Hall's model turns out to be less helpful especially considering that he used a primarily qualitative and less scientific approach for the development of his dimensions. Consequently, his model meets the requirements of subsequent statistical analyses only to a limited extent.

The following table allows a short comparison of the remaining four models, with Hofstede's 5-D model as the oldest and Schwartz's model as well as the GLOBE study as the most recent ones. Basically, they are all very similar in the way they are composed, however, at the same time they bear several considerable differences.

Tab. 2.19:   Hofstede, Trompenaars, Schwartz and GLOBE study in comparison
Source: Kutschker/Schmid, 2008, p. 763

	Hofstede	**Trompenaars**	**Schwartz**	**GLOBE Study**
1st Publication	1980	1993	1994	2004
Sample Size	116,000 IBM employees Chinese Value Survey: 2,300 Students	30,000	> 75,000	17,000
Time	1966–1973 Chinese Value Survey: Early 80s	1983–1992	1988–1992 1992–2000	1994–1997
Questionnaire	60 questions Chinese Value Survey: 40 questions	57 questions	Classification of 56 values according to their importance in life	292 questions
No. of Countries	53 countries Chinese Value Survey: 23 Countries	55 countries	67 countries	59 countries
No. Of Dimensions	5 (incl. Chinese Value Survey)	7	3	9
Genesis of Dimensions	Correlation and factor analyses	Conceptual categories based on literature review, followed by empirical validation	Conceptual categories based on literature review, followed by empirical validation	Conceptual categories based on literature review, tested in pilot studies; empirical validation

Furthermore, the next table provides an overview on how the four culture models can be compared to each other in terms of the cultural dimensions:

Tab. 2.20:   Comparison of the four cultural models
Source: Own illustration

Hofstede	GLOBE-Study	Trompenaars	Schwartz
Collectivism vs. Individualism	Societal Collectivism / In-Group Collectivism	Collectivism vs. Individualism	Embeddedness vs. Autonomy
		Achievement vs. Ascription	
Power distance	Power distance	Equality vs. Hierarchy	Egalitarianism vs. Hierarchy
		Internal vs. External orientation	
		Universalism vs. Particularism	
		Neutral vs. Affective	
Time orientation	Future orientation	Sequential vs. Synchronic time	
Uncertainty Avoidance	Uncertainty avoidance		
Masculinity vs. Femininity	Gender Egalitarianism / Assertiveness		Harmony vs. Mastery
	Performance orientation		
	Humane orientation		

It is obvious, that the GLOBE-Study is similar to Hofstede's approach. The first six dimensions of GLOBE have their roots in Hofstede's dimensions. The first three levels reflect the same construction as Hofstede's dimensions "Uncertainty Avoidance", "Power Distance" and "Individualism". Instead of adopting Hofstede's dimension "Masculinity", GLOBE changed it to "Gender Egalitarianism" and "Assertiveness".

Furthermore, Schwartz' analysis is closely related to Hofstede's 5-D-Model, yet their dimensions are still distinct. Although there is a considerable interdependency in many cases, still a high amount of cross-national variance is not shared by Schwartz' and Hofstede's dimensions. It is important to bear in mind that even the most similar dimensions differ conceptually and empirically in significant ways.

2.7   The application of cultural models in the training practice

With regard to the cultural models, the question to what extent they are used in practice arises. As part of a project in my lectures in 2008, a questionnaire was sent to 35 intercultural training institutes – including the following question:

Which cultural theories are the basis of your intercultural *trainings?*

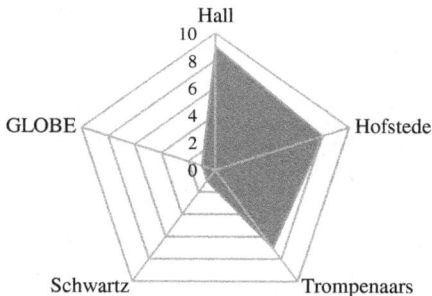

Fig. 2.11:   Application of the Cultural Models in Intercultural Seminars
Source: Hanisch/Warnke, Written Assignment, 2008 (unpublished)

Sixteen of the participating training institutes answered that they preferably use the models of Hofstede and Trompenaars for their seminars. Hall's cultural theory was also often mentioned, whereas the GLOBE-Study and Schwartz' cultural model have not yet become part of the seminars.

2.8   Levels and core elements of the cultural environment and its influence on international assignments

As the cultural models have shown, intercultural understanding does not only depend on the understanding of one's own culture but also extends the scope of action by getting to know other cultures. Or, to say it in the words of Huntington (1996, p. 74):

> *"Every civilization sees itself as the centre of the world and writes its history as the central drama of human history. This has been perhaps even more true of the West and of other cultures. Such mono-civilizational viewpoints, however, have decreasing relevance and usefulness in a multicivilizational world."*

2.8.1   Questioning one's own cultural point of view

"So many countries, so many customs" ("Andere Länder, andere Sitten") is the common phrase to say that different cultures also tend to act differently. Culture influences how individual people see themselves, which attitudes they have and which values and goals are pursued with that. That implies that also the assessment of others – be it in within the own or an unknown culture – depends on the own cultural point of view.

It is particularly difficult to assert oneself as a manager with divergent goals and values in another culture. Traditions always involve also adherence and hence also the fear and uncertainty of alterations. That proves that despite a very positive evaluation of the term "culture" the consequences can be negative nevertheless.

Therefore, not only questions on the individual level have to be raised and answered by respective expatriates. They also have to allow questions on a societal and international level about their attitude towards other cultures and which procedures and methods they want to use to realize their ideas. How such a list of questions could look like, show the following considerations (Friedrich, 1997, p. 87):

- On the individual level: Which culture does the person represent? Does he/she consciously use his/her strengths and weaknesses against others? What is his/her educational background?
- On the societal level: Which form of society does he/she represent? How tolerant against others is the person?
- On the international level: Are there particularities in the management in different cultures which can be explained only by cultural differences? Are they taken into account or does he/she try to spread the own culture as the "right" one?

2.8.2   Core elements of the cultural environment

In order to cope with the questions raised, certain elements of the cultural environments have to be factored into the manager's behavior. The cultural determining factors, which can be observed during business situations abroad and which have to be integrated into the respective behavior, mainly depend on the type of business and the venture's degree of internationalization. There are some elements that do influence the behavior in a different intercultural setting. Those, which have proved to be substantial determining factors and about whose importance for a successful intercultural behavior there is a broad agreement, shall be chosen here. (El Kahal, 1994, p. 33). However, without having reflected on culture as a system consisting of different elements on different levels, the exclusive focusing on the core elements of the cultural environment involves the danger of remaining too much on the surface without really understanding the underlying cultural standards.

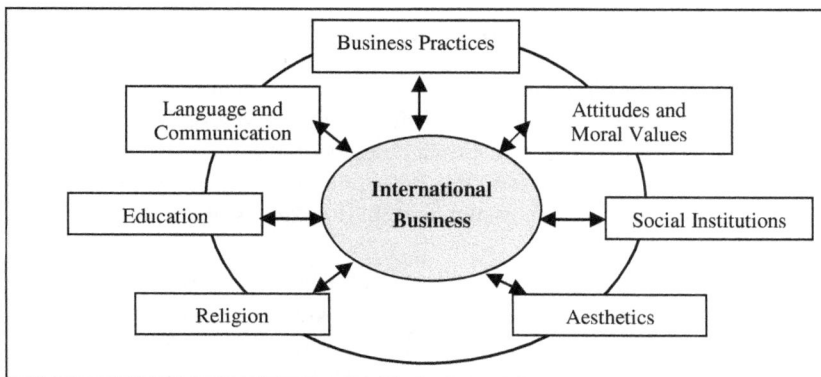

Fig. 2.12:   Elements of the cultural environment of international business
Source: El Kahal, 1994 p. 33

The cultural environment is represented by the following seven core elements: Language and Communication, Education, Religion, Aesthetics, Social Institutions, Attitudes and Moral Values and Business Practices. Thereby, an interdependency becomes obvious. It does not only affect the relationship between the respective core element and the way of doing business internationally but, moreover, shows that all core elements are also interrelated (see Fig. 2.12).

How not to embarrass yourself in Germany
(Matt Owens)

Alcohol	Drinking alcohol is common, but it's always acceptable to refuse a drink.
Birthdays	When it's your birthday, it's your responsibility to provide food and drinks.
Dress	Wear conservative business attire. Khakis make people think you're sloppy.
Garbage	Always recycle. Proper garbage disposal is extremely important to the Germans.
Hierarchy	Make your status known. Hierarchy is considered important.
Jaywalking	Never jaywalk, even if there's no traffic anywhere to be seen.
Meetings	Expect business meetings to be longer than in other countries.
Punctuality	Always be on time. Be direct and detail-oriented.
Sitting	Wait to sit down until you are invited to do so or until others sit.
Talking	Avoid exaggerations and high-pressure talk.
Tipping	Tip 10% to 15% on big meals. For coffee or small meals, round up to the next euro or half euro.
Titles	Always use titles, like Doctor, Frau, or Herr. Don't use first names unless invited.
Toasting	Make eye contact when toasting. Not doing so is said to bring bad luck.
Visits	When invited to someone's home, always arrive on time and bring a small gift.
Water	Expect to pay for bottled water at restaurants. Ordering tapwater is impolite.

In: Bloomberg Businessweek, October 4–10, 2010, p. 82 (excerpt)

2.8.3   Regarding the interrelation of the core elements

The mentioned interdependency of all elements influencing international business activities shall be clarified with an example. In order not to fail right in the beginning, everybody preparing him- or herself for a business with international partners has to orientate his actions to the respective cultural context. Considerations in this regard not only have to be made before a business trip abroad or a long-term foreign assignment. In the same way, preparations have to be made when international guests come to Germany for negotiations.

If we assume both options for a meeting with an Arabian business partner, and if we also consider the fasting month Ramadan, then the German businessman (respectively businesswoman) should know that the Muslim business partner fasts from dawn till sunset (religion/education). Respecting his counterpart's behavior, he should not eat or drink during the negotiations either. Concerning business practices, he has scheduled the major part of the meetings at 8 pm or later. Even though he cannot speak the Arabian language, he uses the simple greeting "Karim Mubarak", which means "Happy Ramadan" (language/communication).

Moreover, his English is business fluent, since he knows that his counterpart has mainly studied in English-speaking countries and therefore has a good command of the English language (education/communication). Regarding his present for the guest, he has wrapped it in green paper; a color which is highly esteemed by Muslims (aesthetics/religion). Beyond that, this is also seen as an act of politeness (attitude and moral values) (Rothlauf, 1997, pp. 28ff)

As to religion as a core element – an overview of various calendars: Happy New Year!
(Dieter Duneka)

Our calendar is based on the birth of a founder of religion 2011 years ago: in other cultures totally different chronologies prevail, and not in every case does the year comprise 365 days.

2011 – The Gregorian Calendar
This calendar used worldwide is a modification of the Julian Calendar stemming from Caesar and it was decreed by pope Gregory XIII in 1582. The old calendar, with its intercalary day interpolated every four years, had become put off its stroke, because the astronomical year does not exactly extend over 365.25 days, but is somewhat shorter. Nowadays, the leap year is omitted every 400 years, except when the number of the year is divisible by 400.
Beginning of the Year: January 1; lunisolar calendar; Duration: 365/6 days

1433 – The Muslim Calendar
In some countries, the Muslim Calendar is in use besides the Gregorian Calendar. It is purely a lunar calendar, with the year consisting of 12 "genuine" months. The chronology commences with July 16, 622. In this year, Mohammed emigrated from Mecca to Medina. Numerically, Muslims age faster: 32 solar years of the Gregorian Calendar correspond to 33 lunar years.
Beginning of the Year: November 26; lunar calendar; Duration: 354 days

5772 – The Jewish Calendar
The Jewish Calendar is a lunisolar one: the usual year spanning 354 days consists of 12 lunar cycles. In order for it to be synchronised with the solar year, there are 7 leap years with an additional month each within 19 years. "Zero" is the creation of the world. This was fixed on the basis of the Old Testament – on the year 3761 B. C.
Beginning of the the Year: September 29; lunisolar calendar; Duration: 354 days

4708 – The Chinese Calendar

The Chinese calendar is oriented both towards the sun and the moon. There is no rigid duration of the months. Continually, single days are intercalated to the lunar months, oriented to astronomical events; sometimes there are even complete leap months. In 1912, the Gregorian Calendar was introduced in China; nowadays, on the basis of the old one, particularly the dates of holidays are calculated.

Beginning of the Year: February 3; lunisolar calendar; Duration: 360 days

2554 – The Buddhist Calendar

Above all in the countries of "southern" Buddhism (Sri Lanka, Myanmar, Thailand), the chronology beginning with the death of Siddhartha Gautama (543 B.C.) is applied. As the "New Year" is not exactly determined, the year may commence on January 1, at the first new moon in spring (Tet-Festival, the Chinese New Year), but it may also start at the fourth full moon of the lunar year (some time in April).

Beginning of the Year: variable; lunar calendar; Duration: 360 days

1418 – The Bengalese Calendar

This calendar is employed particularly in East India, West Bengal, Assam and Bangladesh. The count commences in 593 A. D. Moreover, it is related to the Hedschra of Mohammed in 622, with the discrepancy resulting from the mathematical intermixture of solar and lunar years. Only in 1584 did Akbar Shah introduce the solar year in order to achieve common taxation dates.

Beginning of the Year: April 15; solar year; Duration: 365 days

In: DIE ZEIT, 30/ 12/ 2010, p. 39 (excerpt)

The consideration and adequate inclusion of these core elements are an important basis for successful actions in a different environment. However, a number of other conditions also have to be fulfilled to lead a long-term partnership to success. Thereby, the individual actions have to become part of a subordinate corporate strategy, which internally and externally conveys the company's international cultural guiding principle.

Which Culture Shock do Impatriates experience in Germany?
(Sylvia Schroll-Machl)

Whereas life in Germany is the normal thing for us Germans, impatriates, i.e. emissaries of international companies, in Germany face comparable difficulties as we do in their countries.

Their situation: a lot is new to them in every-day life. The problems range from A, namely how to address them (Christian name?) and driving a car (speed, TÜV) to food, child restraints (Do Germans shackle their children?), the climate (heating and airing?), the police (Do not tip!), security, the language (dialects), table manners up to environmental care (separation of rubbish?) and apartments (periods of rest?).

In line with these "Questions of Survival", our German mentality seems to be strange to impatriates. Some typical questions are: why are Germans so formal? Why is it difficult to form any friendship with them? Can Germans be flexible? Why do Germans frequently speak so aggressively and why are they so undiplomatic? Without any schedule nothing seems to work, not even in their private lives. Why?

In: FAZ, 22/07/2006, p. 53

2.9 The expert's view: Interview with Prof. Dr. Geert Hofstede

In the framework of an intercultural project, Lise Colombo, Valentine Engel, Leslie Knopf and Gianni Torregrossa, four students of the master degree course "Management Interculturel et Affaires International" at the Université de Haute-Alsace in Mulhouse, had the opportunity to conduct an interview with Prof. Dr. Geert Hofstede in Velp, the Netherlands, in November 2011. An excerpt of this interview can be found here:

Students: Do you think that languages are essential for multicultural experiences?

Hofstede: Languages are important but not sufficient. You can speak another language without understanding the culture, and you can also understand another culture without speaking the language – if you are aware of it. However, I think it is essential for someone who works internationally to speak at least two languages. If people have never learnt more than one language in their life, it is very difficult for them to understand other cultures. You know what happens when you speak another language: there is a little "switch" in your mind. You have to have this flexibility to say something in a very different way. As I was saying, language is important but not sufficient. It is not the case that if you are a better linguist, you are also a better culturologist. […]

Students: Could you give us your own definition of leadership?

Hofstede: First of all, leadership is a very cultural subject. What is leadership in one place is not necessarily the same in another place. You could say that leadership is an American subject, as the Americans always write about leadership and make lists about things you should do to be a good leader – but the world is not like this. If you have, for example, a collectivistic society, where relationships of people are very much determined by family and personal relations, leadership is less important, since the leader has already been determined by the situation.

If you want to understand leadership, you should also understand "followership" or "subordinateship", because a leader is not a person but a relationship between someone and an organization or a group. If you have a different group, you will need a different leader. This was especially interesting, when Japan became more important as an industrial power and people started to talk about Japanese leadership, and forgot to talk about Japanese "subordinateship", because the secret of Japan was not so much about the bosses, but about the subordinates and their way of working, and how they come to consensuses. You cannot separate these things.

It also becomes very interesting, when you talk about international situations, because then you need people who are able to relate to people from other cultures – and some people are better at that than others. In France, Carlos Ghosn is often given as an example of a very good cross-cultural manager. He was the CEO of Renault-Nissan in Japan and before he was there, people would say: 'In order to manage a Japanese company, you need a Japanese manager.' But then he, as a Brazilian-Lebanese-French manager, went there and became an extremely popular manager in Japan and actually, he has had a big influence on Japanese management. Therefore, never believe that something would not work – because it did work! [...] You need really special people for these international situations and it also depends on the situation. I do not think you can give general rules.

Students: *Is it the leader, who should adapt to the group or should the group adapt to the leader?*

Hofstede: In my opinion, it is the leader who should adapt himself to the group, but it is not always possible. First of all, you need the right kind of leader for the right kind of group because there is only a certain level of adaptation possible. Basically, I think the leader should be able to adapt to the group, but he should also be able to lead the group somewhere. However, you can only lead people if you first go over to where they are, and then you have to go with them. A group will never be able to fully adapt and during the process they will at least lose part of their creativity. They might be able to do what the leader wants them to do, but if you are a good leader, you try to get the best out of the group. Therefore, you have to be able to listen to the group. Groups have capabilities and a good group is one where its creativity is really coming out.

Students: *What is the best way to apply international leadership?*

Hofstede: I do not know what the best way is, but experience plays a very important role. Someone, who wants to be an international leader, should have international experience and should have discovered the pitfalls of working in a different environment. Another important point is interest. Good international leaders show an interest in the various parts of the world they are working in. A good property of an international leader is curiosity.

Students: *Which cultural dimension is the most influential one on leadership?*

Hofstede: The most obvious one is Power Distance. But there are other things, e.g. Masculinity and Femininity, because masculine values are more ego-focused: in a masculine culture, the "Ego" of the leader is more important. In a feminine culture, a too strong ego is counterproductive. A typical masculine leader is Berlusconi. He is almost a symbol of masculinity. Feminine values are modesty and low-key behaviour. People like Ghosn and [Jean-Cyril] Spinetta [CEO of Air France- KLM], for example, are more a feminine type of leaders and are much more sensitive to the situation and do not want to stand out that much.

Students: *What is the most challenging part of working in a multicultural team? What are the advantages?*

Hofstede: First of all, you must want it. Not everybody would want to work in a multicultural team, and so you must belong to the kind of people feeling challenged by that, and you must have the interest. In that case, it is very interesting because you can learn a lot of things you could not have learned otherwise. But there are people who are afraid of working in a situation they do not know and maybe these people should not work in an international environment. They should look for a safe situation in a culture they know.

Students: Could you tell us something about the importance of intercultural skills?

Hofstede: An important factor is personality. People must be able to listen to people from a different background and must not be afraid of situations that are different from their own. They must not judge too quickly only from their first impression.

Students: Do you think that a crisis tends to change cultural reactions, e.g. so that an individualistic society could evolve into a collectivistic one?

Hofstede: I would rather think that the opposite would happen. It could be that a crisis speeds up the adaptation of collectivistic societies into individualistic ones. Greece and parts of Italy, for example, are collectivistic societies. There is the term of "clientelismo": It is a collectivist concept, which means that you take care of the people within your group and you try to belong to the group of people who have the power. That has partly led to the crisis and also leads to corruption and the misuse of money. It is clear that there is a very high pressure to cut through that. This means there is a chance that these societies will be forced to support a more individualistic development, because they cannot function otherwise. It is a very interesting situation which will turn out one way or the other. I would say it could force collectivistic societies to become more individualistic because these individualistic forces are supported by international pressure.

Students: Concerning the onion model, you claim that only rituals, symbols and heroes but not values could change. Don't you think that this could evolve in our fast globalized world where differences between generations are getting bigger and bigger?

Hofstede: I am not sure that the differences between generations are getting bigger. The differences between generations are as old as the world. There are inscriptions in Egypt from 3000 BC where old people complained that the young people would not follow the virtues of the society any longer. [...]

My colleague Marieke de Mooij (www.mariekedemooij.com) is specialized in culture and consumer behavior. One way of people expressing themselves is how they spend their money, and there are strong national patterns, which continue to exist. Even with the internet: We all have it, but the way the internet is used differs a lot from one culture to another. These differences will not disappear as they are based on what people have learnt from their parents and their parents have learnt from their parents.

What I mean with the changes in the onion model is that the outside - the symbols, heroes and rituals - will change rather easily, but the values underneath will not change that easily. This is also a problem with the Euro-crisis. The Euro is at the level of the symbols and rituals but if the underlying values are too different, it causes a problem.

Students: *You have just mentioned the Euro-crisis. Has the supposed fail of the European Union been a consequence of too many different cultures in the union?*

Hofstede: It is easy to say "yes", but what is the point? I think that the European Union could cope with different cultures but having one currency is a step further, and this is where the problem is at the moment. Having the same currency without having at certain points the same values is not easy. All those different cultural dimensions play a role in there, e.g. Power Distance, because politicians are no longer free to decide what happens with the money, so they lose part of their power. It would be a lot easier without cultural differences, but they do exist.

Students: *In your books you say that in countries with a high power distance index you will find it in every institution. Does that mean that in countries where politicians have a strong political influence, this is also reflected by a high PDI of the managers?*

Hofstede: You find it in the family, in schools, in working and political organizations. These things tend to go together, but there is a certain flexibility. I could imagine that e.g. in areas of business and industry, the change is faster because there are more foreign influences. Now, I think the political level in Europe has pretty strong foreign influences and they may be forced to change.

It is interesting that the countries in Europe which have suffered most from the Second World War have changed fastest after the war. Germany, for example, has changed a lot. I have personal experience there because we were occupied by the Germans. I was 12 years when they came and 16/17 when they left, and I would have never imagined that I would have liked to go to Germany, but so much has changed and one of my sons works there and I will go there on Friday. And of course relationships across the border like you have in Mulhouse have changed so much since those years. These countries have changed the most because they were forced to, so maybe the present situation will lead to a similar effect. You see, I am an optimist.

Students: *Why do you think is your 5-dimension model still the most commonly used one by universities and training institutes?*

Hofstede: Actually, in the latest edition of the book, there are six dimensions and you also have to realize that dimensions do not "exist". They are ideas which develop and change. I came up with this model because this was the result of the material I had available and it turned out that – because I have been working a lot with people from practice – they recognize these things. So most of the issues I or other people write about dimensions are simply taken from the experience of those who have worked with it and who find it a useful way of understanding the differences. It is not the only way and it probably also depends on the things you want to explain. My experiences mainly come from businesses and partly also from universities.

However, we may need other dimensions if we try to explain differences in consumer behavior or in art. Music for example: Why do different societies have such a different taste in music? There is not one model that fits for everything and ideas will probably continue to develop over time. There are other people attempting to construct new models. The question always is: What is the extra value of that model and what can it contribute towards other ideas? I am not defending my own model so much, but we are now in a position, because a number of alternative models have been developed, that we can compare them and look at some practical things, e.g. consumer behavior. [...] Different models explain different aspects of consumer behavior and you can see that some do much better than others, or even one dimension of one model and another dimension of another one.

Students: In the latest edition of the book "Cultures and Organizations: Software of the mind" (Hofstede/Hofstede/Minkov, 2010) a sixth dimension was added. Based on data of the World Values Survey for 93 countries "Indulgence versus Restraint" shows to what extent people in these countries are able to gratify their needs and drives to enjoy life rather freely or whether they rather have to face restrictions. Why did you add this sixth dimension?

Hofstede: The sixth dimension is based on an analysis of World Values Survey data by my colleague and co-author Michael Minkov [...] These data cover a broad number of subjects, not only work but also family and religion, and show their evolution over the past decades. [...] In the American tradition, people are generally better in collecting data than in analyzing them – in Europe it tends to be the other way round. [...] I believe the World Values Survey, coordinated from the U.S.A., has been a place where we risk having lots of data without sufficient analysis. My friend Michael Minkov is a master in interpreting these data. Being Bulgarian he also inherited a different, East-European tradition which contributes insights missing in our society. There are many new ideas if you collate it. [...] The sixth dimension "Indulgence vs. Restraint" is related to optimism vs. pessimism and the feeling of happiness. [...] This element was not yet represented in the dimensions we had so far. It explains new aspects of consumer behavior, like the extent to which people engage in sports. In indulgent societies more people actively engage in sports. We suspect it explains some of the differences in music I just mentioned: Compare the indulgent Latin American music, which also contains African elements, to restrained Chinese music. [...]

Students: Prof. Dr. Hofstede, thank you very much for taking the time and giving us the unique opportunity of such an interview! We did really appreciate that!

In 2009, Susanne Kluth, Jonas Linke and Hendrik Walter, students of Baltic Management Studies at the University of Applied Sciences Stralsund, interviewed Dr. Liane Steiert, an international coach for intercultural management and also asked her about the cultural models she uses.

Students:	*Do the cultural models of Hofstede and Trompenaar play an elementary role in the preparation of your training?*
Dr. Steiert:	Absolutely! They are two specialists that in theory describe what is going on in cultures. I prefer using the theories of Hofstede, Lewis and Thomas and Cultural Standards. Every method I use is a toll to create discussion; so again, I am more interested in the practical adaptation.

In: Written Assignment, Stralsund, 2009 (unpublished), p. 76

2.10   Intercultural exercise: Bridge construction experts among the "Ulemans"

In the following exercise, your seminar group has to be divided into two groups: a group of German engineers and a group of Ulemans. The group of German engineers supposed to teach bridge construction to the Uleman people.

For the instructions for the Ulemans, please see page 299!

Assignment for the team of German bridge construction experts

Your expert team receives the order to build a bridge in the developing country of Ulema spanning the country's widest river. Thus, the local people of Ulema shall be saved from long detours in the future and the trade exchange with the neighbors on the other riverside shall be facilitated. Since there are further rivers in Ulemania, which the Ulemans will have to bridge themselves, it is not sufficient to take the work out of their hands and bridge the river. *The aim is rather to teach the Ulemans the principles of bridge construction. This requires a close cooperation with the delegation of Ulemans* chosen by the tribal elders to learn the techniques of bridge construction from you and your team.

The Ulemans are a people with a still native culture and archaic rituals. *The success of your deal will strongly depend on your degree of empathy with which you consider the people's cultural identity during the cooperation.*

Procedure of the exercise:

You have *10 minutes* to read the instructions and to develop *some basic ideas for your course of action.* During that time you will also have the chance to clarify technical problems concerning bridge construction.

Afterwards the Ulemans will enter the room and the *30-minute-long construction phase* starts, in which you will have to teach them the basics of bridge construction and building the bridge together.

After the Ulemans have gone back, you will have another *10 minutes* to discuss their cultural peculiarities with your colleagues. In order to facilitate future development aid projects, please develop a *list of rules of conduct* to be observed when cooperating with Ulemans.

Criteria of success:

The project has only been finished successfully when the bridge has been built within half an hour and you have been able to teach the Ulemans the techniques of bridge construction so they will not be dependent on your help in the future. Another important task is to find a correct evaluation of the Ulemans' cultural peculiarities together with your colleagues so that future aid workers can draw on your experiences with the foreign culture.

Material and construction regulations:

For the construction, you are only allowed to use materials, which will also be available to the Ulemans for future construction projects and which are not in contradiction to their religious beliefs. The following construction materials can be used:

- Paper
- Scissors
- Glue sticks
- Pencils
- Rulers

The materials have already been transported to Ulema some time ago and therefore do not have to be provided by you. *Please keep in mind, that, though the Ulemans have the appropriate materials at their disposal, they do not know how to use them for the construction of bridges.*

The bridge has to have a span of at least 40 cm and has to be as stable as possible. As a proof of stability, the bridge will have to carry the weight of a ruler in the end. The bridge may only be made of paper stripes with a maximum length of 14 cm and breadth of up to 6 cm. These paper stripes can be cut, bent, glued and jointed together in any way. However, every paper stripe has to be sketched out with a pencil and a ruler and cut out afterwards. *Remember that the construction time must not exceed 30 minutes* and your performance will be measured against the other group's performance.

In: Jürgen Rothlauf, Seminarunterlagen, 2011

---

30 TIPS ON HOW TO LEARN ACROSS CULTURES (10–13)
(Andre Laurent)

10. Whenever possible, check your assumptions and expectations with your partners.

11. Everybody holds some stereotypes about other cultural groups. Acknowledge your own stereotypes about other cultures. But try to use them only as prototypes ready to be updated and changed on the basis of your own experience.

12. Don't confuse the individual and his/her culture. Confusing these two units of analysis leads to sterile stereotyping. Both the individual and his/her culture are real but different entities. Culture is obviously not an individual property. It is a group attribute. Individuals carry culture. They don't own it.

13. Every individual is unique. Every culture is unique. Understanding individual differences and understanding cultural differences are equally important. It is not one or the other, it is both.

In: SIETAR (Hrsg.), Keynote-Speech, Kongress 2000, Ludwigshafen

2.11   Case Study: Getting people to play ball

An international company appointed two high potentials – Peter Mason from America and Takeo Tanaka from Japan – to run a project together. They seemed to get on well and, after much discussion, worked out a modus operandi and detailed schedule that they and their teams could agree to. Tanaka went back to Japan and submitted a written report, outlining what they had agreed, to his boss. A few days later, Peter had a brilliant idea. There was a much more efficient way of handling the project. Peter discussed that with his American team and, before long, everyone concluded that it would work perfectly. A delighted Peter submitted a revised schedule to the American steering committee. Then he called Tanaka:

Mason:	I've got some good news. We have managed to streamline the schedule. I'll mail you the details in a minute. But, basically, it means we'll be able to complete the project a couple of months earlier than we thought.
Tanaka:	*You've changed the schedule?*
Mason:	Yes. I suddenly realized that if we split the teams into eight work groups rather than six, we could overlap phases two and three, and run phases five and six concurrently.
Tanaka:	*You've changed the work groups?*
Mason:	Yes. It's so simple. I don't know why we didn't think of it before.
Tanaka:	*I see... But I told my boss that the schedule had been finalized. I've already submitted my report.*
Mason:	Well, just tell him we've had a better idea.
Tanaka:	*It will be very difficult for me to explain the changes to him.*
Mason:	I don't see why. I mean, changing the schedule is going to save a lot of time and money. I'm sure he'll be very pleased.

The project went ahead, but the relationship between the Japanese and the American team deteriorated fast. Tanaka and his colleagues were not openly obstructive, but Peter got the impression that they were somehow "working to rule". Before long, the project had fallen seriously behind schedule.

Rothlauf, J., in: Seminarunterlagen, 2005, p. 20

Review and Discussion Questions:

1.   What went wrong in the relationship between Mason and Tanaka?

2.   What was the decisive mistake Peter made?

3.   Structure the episode in a way that Tanaka can save his face!

3 Corporate Culture and Internationalization

3.0 Statement of the problem

Nepotism in Vietnam

A German company had established very clear global purchasing guidelines: no more than 30 percent of any particular item could be supplied by one vendor, and quotes had to be obtained from at least three different suppliers; and contracts were to be awarded purely on the basis of price, delivery terms, reliability and quality.

Meier, the German regional manager for South-East Asia, was disturbed to note that, despite several reminders, the subsidiary in Vietnam did not appear to be following the guidelines. In fact, the range of suppliers they used seemed to be very limited, and most of them were Vietnamese.

The subsidiary's Vietnamese manager seemed very unconcerned when Meier raised this problem with him. "Well, of course most of our suppliers are Vietnamese", he said. "I only use vendors I am related to." Meier was shocked and remained silent for a moment. Then he calmly explained that this practice was against company guidelines. "But why?" asked the Vietnamese manager. "Because it is unethical and anti-competitive. We are not allowed to do it in Germany, and we cannot allow our subsidiaries to behave in this way." It was the Vietnamese manager's turn to be shocked: "But I cannot see what the problem is", he said. "My family is much more loyal and reliable than people I do not know. I can call them any time of day or night. They cannot escape me. And, of course, they give me much better discounts. Surely, you do not want me to use suppliers I do not trust." Meier raised and lowered his eyebrows, and remained silent.

Rothlauf, J., in: Seminarunterlagen, 2005, p. 14

As the world is becoming increasingly interconnected, one could argue that intercultural competence is also gaining critical importance in numerous ways – whether it is in global workforce development, in resolving conflicts, in facilitating intercultural coexistence on a local level or in working together to address the world's most pressing issues – including the ethical, social, ecological and cultural challenges of globalization. Yet, the term "intercultural competence" has been notoriously difficult to define and assess.

There are a lot of different definitions as far as the term intercultural competence is concerned. Deardorff (2006, p. 5) says that intercultural competence *"is the ability to interact effectively and appropriately in intercultural situations, based on specific attitudes, intercultural knowledge, skills and reflection."*

Bennett (2011, p. 4) describes it as *"a set of cognitive, affective, and behavioural skills and characteristics that supports effective and appropriate interaction in a variety of cultural contexts"*

3.1   Corporate cultures in global interaction

Long neglected, the corporate culture has by now become one of the major competitive factors in the globalization process. Opening up new markets, either through mergers, acquisitions or start-ups, presents the management not only with economic challenges. Business success and economic continuity depend on the connection, design as well as the transparency and acceptance of the corporate culture's core values across the international corporate locations. Though intercultural problems are often recognized in the course of the daily working and communication processes, they are not yet sufficiently taken into account for important decisions, because reputedly "hard" economic arguments prevail. However, studies have shown that around 70 % of the business combinations do not achieve their goals. (Mohn, 2005, p. 4)

Toyota's corporate culture – guiding principles
(Sonja A. Sackmann)

1. Honour the language and spirit of the law of every nation and undertake open and fair corporate activities to be a good corporate citizen of the world.
2. Respect the culture and customs of every nation and contribute to economic and social development through corporate activities in the communities.
3. Dedicate ourselves to providing clean and safe products and to enhancing the quality of life everywhere through all our activities.
4. Create and develop advanced technologies and provide outstanding products and services that fulfill the needs of the customers worldwide.
5. Foster a corporate culture that enhances individual creativity and teamwork value, while honouring mutual trust and respect between labour and management.
6. Pursue growth in harmony with the global community through innovative management.
7. Work with business partners in research und creation to achieve stable and long-term growth and mutual benefits, while keeping ourselves open to new partnerships.

In: Bertelsmann Stiftung (Hrsg.), Toyota Motor Corporation: Eine Fallstudie aus unternehmenskultureller Perspektive, 2007, p. 16.

3.1.1   A research project on global cultural development

Between October 2003 and September 2004, 200 international managers from the focus regions Germany/Switzerland (88 interviews), Japan (39) and the USA (73) were asked in semi-structured in-depth interviews about their assessment of the possibilities and limits of a transnational corporate culture. The study explicitly concentrated on the pool of international executives (first to third management level). The participating companies were selected on the basis of accessibility and their willingness to cooperate.

Companies such as BASF, Henkel, Deutsche Post World Net, Volkswagen, Bertelsmann, Lufthansa, Pfizer, Toyota and Nestlé agreed to participate. In cooperation with the executives, a framework of action for an improved and more effective process of cultural development in multinational companies was developed. The aim was to promote intercultural collaboration within the company and to enhance the economic and social productivity and efficiency in the global corporate sector. (Spilker/Lippisch, 2005, p. 7).

3.1.2   Cultural integration drivers

Seven instruments for achieving cultural integration, which are described as cultural integration drivers by Blazejewski & Dorow (2005), have been identified as action-guiding in the course of the study. In the form of checklists, the respective activities, which allow putting the project's findings into practice all around the world, will be presented in the following (Blazejewski/Dorow, 2005, pp. 38ff):

Fig. 3.1:   Seven instruments for achieving cultural integration
Source: Blazejewski/Dorow, 2005, p. 11

"Check list: Cultural Vision
- *Written definition of core corporate values: This makes it easier to communicate values to new employees, after mergers or acquisitions, for example, and provides a binding, common framework for everyone.*
- *Clear, creative communication of core values: Values are often overlooked if they are sent out by e-mail or posted on the intranet. They should be brought to the attention of employees in their immediate work environments. It is important to encourage thinking about cultural issues as part of the everyday routine, for example by scheduling this regularly.*
- *Five to seven core values are sufficient: People cannot really absorb or comprehend more than that, let alone apply them in day-to-day decision making.*
- *Translation into local languages: When a list of values has been drawn up only in English, the result is frequent misunderstandings and uncertainty about how to interpret and*

apply them in practice. In addition, discussion about how these values should be translated and interpreted offers an excellent opportunity for dialogue within the subsidiaries on the company's culture.

- **Operationalize the core values:** *These often quite abstract values must be put into concrete terms, through examples or descriptions of appropriate behaviour. The concept of "integrity" can only be understood by giving examples, for instance by pointing out that employees are not allowed to exchange gifts with customers or suppliers.*

Check list: Local Dialogue

- **Systematically take the local perspective into account:** *It is not enough to only involve the top management echelon, which tends to focus on headquarters. It is important from the very beginning to include employees of the subsidiaries in developing global core values. This is crucial to ensure that the core values are accepted early on and reinforced throughout the company.*
- **Local application:** *Subsidiaries should be encouraged to give serious thought to interpreting core values from a local perspective at dedicated forums and workshops. Regional interpretations of company values and local codes of conduct should be put in writing so that erroneous or confusing interpretations can be identified early on and discussed.*
- **Solve conflicts through cooperation:** *Facilitate dialogue between the parent company and subsidiaries to resolve differences between the global core values and local interpretations or traditional business practices. If subsidiaries are left to resolve these conflicts on their own, local employees may react with cynicism or even reject the global value initiative altogether.*

Check list: Visible Action

- **Living one's values:** *Among leadership personnel in particular, consistency between words and deeds needs to be apparent and communicated at all times. The concept of a global corporate culture loses all credibility if those at the highest levels fail to take the company's values seriously.*
- **Emotional commitment to core values:** *It is not enough for the global values to be expressed as one more formal regulation within the organization. If values are to be credible, leadership personnel, serving as cultural role models, must demonstrate personal, emotional commitment and be able to enthusiastically communicate global values. Superficial, noncommittal lip service by superiors as an afterthought at management meetings, under the heading of "miscellaneous", results in cynicism and rejection on the part of employees.*

Check list: Communicator

- **Institutionalize platforms for dialogue:** *Make sure there is adequate room for cultural dialogue at both the regional and global level. This includes specific, formal opportunities for communication such as culture-focused workshops and discussion groups, as well as support for an informal cultural exchange. Set aside time for the latter during training sessions or at international project meetings. Personal communication between employees of different cultural backgrounds was consistently identified as the most important means of achieving cultural integration.*

- ***Promote fluency:*** *Even today many employees, including executives, lack the necessary language skills to participate meaningfully in a cultural dialogue. Inadequate language skills prevent them from contributing their own interpretations of core values to the discussion and from establishing intercultural communication networks. In addition to language problems, in some regions there are also cultural barriers to communication that prevent participation in open dialogue. When this is the case, executives must make a special effort to elicit opinions from employees in cultures where people are more reticent, thus enhancing the employees' ability and willingness to take part in dialogue over the long term.*

- ***Internationalize means of communication in a consistent way:*** *Inhouse intranet pages are still often available only in the language of the headquarters; no more than excerpts are provided in English, if that. This means that foreign employees are often simply unaware of information made available through that medium.*

- ***Globally appropriate artifacts:*** *Symbols, slogans, logos and other artifacts (architecture, room furnishings, work clothing) that are intended to enhance the integration of the company need to be internationally acceptable and associated with positive connotations. Poorly worded English slogans meant to encourage group cohesion end up being ridiculous and imperil the success of the entire initiative.*

Check list: Cultural Ambassador

- ***Ongoing rotation programs:*** *To save money, many companies have recently cut back on their expatriate programs. This can slow down or even prevent cultural integration within the larger company. Even though e-mail and telephone calls are options as well, personal contact with colleagues from other cultural regions is the main method of integration. It is important not only to assign employees from headquarters to other locations, but to increase the number of rotations from or among the regions.*

- ***Allow for flexibility:*** *Because of the different working and living conditions in many countries, rotation programs should be kept flexible in terms of such factors as length of stay, host country, responsibilities and career stage. Rotating younger employees at the beginnings of their careers can give them a global perspective, increase their intercultural competence and lay the groundwork for an international network of contacts. This puts in place important factors needed for intercultural understanding and cultural integration within the company.*

- ***Guarantee a return to the home office:*** *In many regions, foreign assignments fail to materialize for the simple reason that employees would rather forgo the international experience than risk that their return will be poorly organized. Guaranteeing that an attractive option for returning will be available would open up new possibilities for gaining foreign experience, also for American executives, who are often reluctant to be sent abroad.*

- ***Ensure on-site involvement:*** *In spite of the lip service paid to the idea of globalization, employees still frequently feel abandoned before, during and after a foreign assignment. Systematic intercultural mentoring programs in the respective home and host countries can help to facilitate cultural integration and enhance the benefit of cultural experiences for the entire company.*

Check list: Open Sky

- *Internationalize leadership positions:* Every career path in the company, including the highly symbolic management board, must also be open to foreign employees in the subsidiaries.
- *Put global hiring procedures into effect:* Many of the companies already have global procedures for choosing international executives, but foreign employees still have the impression that only those from the home country are actually hired into leadership positions. A lack of transparency quickly leads to the suspicion that headquarters is only paying lip service to the core values of internationality, interculturality and diversity.
- *Remedy image problems abroad:* A lack of international top executives is often defended by contending that the executives in the subsidiaries are "second-rate". It is still uncommon to see systematic efforts to deal with the problems of recruiting first-class employees in foreign countries, particularly those who share the company's basic values (through local sponsoring efforts, links with outstanding local universities).

Check list: Compliance

- *Binding core values:* When seeking to achieve global integration by developing core values jointly, it is helpful for a company to ensure that employees and executives worldwide share a binding commitment to those values, in order to reflect the importance of the corporate culture in central corporate policy.
- *Review compatibility with corporate core values:* In many companies the hiring, evaluation and incentive systems are not consistently geared to global corporate values. This can lead to contradictions and a loss of credibility of cultural integration initiatives.
- *Control and sanctions:* Cultural development needs to be monitored and ensured on a continual basis, through ongoing review processes (employee surveys, regular cultural diagnosis, opportunities to provide feedback, for example through anonymous hotlines). When individuals grossly violate company values, there must be a consistent response and visible consequences; only then will it be possible to ensure the credibility of the cultural initiative."

3.2   Mergers & acquisitions

The number of mergers and acquisitions (M&A) is on the rise, not only in Europe but all around the world. Reasons for this development include the efforts of companies to cut costs, save time for more improvements and innovations, and improve the quality of the products respectively the services, or simply to become bigger in many ways. The following table provides a short insight into those business transactions. The eastward expansion of the European Union as well as the new emerging markets in Asia have removed barriers and opened up new markets resulting in a quest for "fertile hunting grounds for takeover targets".

> *"Coming together is a beginning.*
> *Keeping together is progress.*
> *Working together is success."*
> (Henry Ford)

Mergers & Acquisitions – selected major deals in 2013

- 2nd September: Vodafone Group sold *Verizon Wireless Inc* to *Verizon Communications Inc* for US$bn 124.1.
- 14th February: *H.J. Heinz Company* was acquired by *Berkshire Hathaway Inc* and *3G Capital* for US$bn 27.4.
- 6th February: *Liberty Global Plc* acquired *Virgin Media Inc* for US$bn 25.0.
- 24th June: *Kabel Deutschland Holding AG* was bought by *Vodafone Group Plc* for US$bn 11.3
- 24th September: *Applied Materials* acquired *Tokyo Electron Limited* for US$bn 8.7.

Source: Mergermarket M&A Trend Report: 2013, January 2014

3.2.1 The terms "merger" & "acquisition"

To distinguish an acquisition from a merger, it is essential to understand that the term "merger" is usually referred to as a fusion of two approximately equal-sized companies, while the term "acquisition" describes the process of one larger corporation purchasing a smaller company which will then vanish (Pride/Hughes/Kappor, 2002, p. 146).

The basis for a merger are two or more economically and legally independent entities. A merger takes place when these entities give up their economic and legal independence and build a new entity. Three different types of mergers generally exist: horizontal, vertical or conglomerate. (Schmusch, 1998, p. 11).

Those three different types of mergers can be characterized as follows (Tremblay/Tremblay, 2012, pp. 522f):

- A **horizontal merger** describes a merger with one or more direct competitor in order to expand the company's operations in the same industry. Horizontal mergers are designed to produce substantial economies of scale and result in a decreasing number of competitors in the industry
- In a **vertical merger**, two companies which are operating in the same industry but at different stages of the value chain merge. On the one hand, this can e.g. be a company's take-over of its supplier of raw material (backward integration of activities) but also, on the other hand, a take-over of its retailer (forward intergration of activities).
- A **conglomerate merger** involves companies engaged in unrelated types of business activities, i.e. their businesses are neither horizontally nor vertically related. Conglomerate mergers are the unification of different kinds of businesses under one flagship company. Those mergers aim at the utilization of financial resources, an enlarged debt capacity and also the synergy of managerial functions. In the case of impure conglomerates mergers, however, the two businesses are to a certain degree related, either because they sell similiar products but in different geographic markets or because their products are related to a certain extent, e.g. both companies produce different kinds of groceries.

An acquisition is "essentially the same as merger", but the term is usually used in reference to a large corporation's purchase of other corporations. It can be performed by a direct purchase or a merger agreement that involves the exchange of assets. In many cases, an acquisition is carried out in agreement with both sides, but there are also hostile takeovers, which mean that the firm targeted for acquisition disapproves of the merger.

3.2.2   Cross-border M&A

Cross-border mergers and acquisitions have long been an important strategy to expand business abroad. Due to technological developments and globalization, M&A activity sharply increased over the last two decades. They skyrocketed in the 1990's reaching a peak in 2000 with the booming stock markets and the larger degree of financial liberalization worldwide, sharply declined in 2001 and 2002 and rebounded again with new developments in the world economy after 2003. Traditionally, developed countries, and in particular the developed countries of the European Union and the United States, have been the largest acquirer and target countries for M&A. During the 2003–2005 period, developed countries accounted for 85 % of the total USD 465 billion cross-border M&A, 47 % and repectively 23 % of which pertain to EU and US firms either as acquirer or as target companies. (Althaus et al., 2004, pp. 1ff)

Cross-border transactions pose bigger challenges for the executives and consultants involved than national mergers and acquisitions. Successful international M&A therefore require an extra portion of knowledge and assistance to all parties. On the one side, cross-border transactions conduce to achieving the strategic goals of the purchaser. On the other side, the seller can obtain a higher price as with a national transaction. (ibid.)

However, the following requirements are essential for successful cross-border M&A:

1.   **M&A Know-How**

In contrast to large firms, an M&A transaction usually is an event that is not part of the everyday business for mid tier companies and often means a unique event in the history of the company. Therefore, the knowledge about the whole M&A process is either rudimentary or not at all existing in a company. Big companies, however, have their own M&A units, which can correspondingly elaborate transaction concepts and have the necessary knowledge about countries and different cultures. (ibid.)

---

30 TIPS ON HOW TO LEARN ACROSS CULTURES (14)
(Andre Laurent)

14. Across cultures, attribution errors occur in both directions: genuinely individual characteristics are wrongly labelled as cultural, and conversely cultural patterns are wrongly attributed to an individual's personality.

In: SIETAR (Hrsg.), Keynote-Speech, Kongress 2000, Ludwigshafen

---

2.   **Understanding of other cultures**

The entrance into a new region is accompanied by the overcoming of cultural obstacles. This requires a solid knowledge about the respective national culture and their specific characteristics. Assuming that the market conditions, competitive advantages on their own and major political, economic and legal conditions have already been considered attractive, it is also a vital part of a cross-border transaction to specifically comply with the following aspects:

Fluent command of the transaction language (usually English), preferably basic knowledge of the language of the decision makers involved, familiarity with foreign cultures and the fundamental differences and different legal systems and tax systems, a sound knowledge of internationally significant accounting and valuation rules as well as know-how to efficiently integrate a foreign company. (van Gerven, 2010, pp. 44ff)

3. **Involvement of middle management and key persons**
Occasionally, the middle management and key employees of a company are informed about the pending takeover too late. Such an approach does not encourage the active commitment and the formation of new management teams. Especially in cross-border transactions, the start and the early involvement of the right people is vital. So-called kick-off-meetings and workshops have proved to be successful tools for the communication of basic information about the planned transaction. The work teams have to be merged in a way to enable the transition to start smoothhly in the acquisition phase and to be completed in the subsequent, comprehensive integration phase. In particular, the cultural and organizational integration often requires additional management resources. (Althaus et al., 2004, pp.1ff)

4. **Inclusion of a cross-border M&A advisor**
The management or a group, which is occasionally consulted, cannot simply handle the entire cross-border transaction. To be successful, it is advisable to involve a team composed of managers from different departments and an experienced M&A consultant. The consultant should accompany the process from the beginning to the end and have the following competences (ibid.):

- *Access to global resources:* International transactions are usually conducted under significant time pressure and expectation. Therefore, the rapid access to reliable and competent partners in all economically important markets and countries is a prerequisite. The customer will not accept if the M&A advisor must first establish own contacts in the relevant country. It is also expected that the members of an international M&A consulting firm know each other in person, have regular contact with each other and have already worked together on international projects. Their common understanding will have a positive impact on the course of the transaction. (ibid.)
- *Identification of numerous contacts*: For corporate sales, foreign buyers regularly pay a higher price than national prospects. It is therefore particularly important that many international contacts to prospective targets exist and can consequently ensure the optimization of value (the sale). An efficient global network of M&A professionals would perfectly cover the customer needs, which are identifying and contacting potential interested parties, information about transactions carried out country-specific developments in the industry, consulting on-site customer support and the involvement of local consultants. (ibid.)
- *Collaboration with local consultants:* For international transactions, it is imperative that – especially in the acquisition phase – local experts (lawyers, tax experts, accountants, banks) are consulted for special work (including Due Diligence, negotiation support, financing). Extensive contacts on a global scale facilitate the break-down of barriers in unknown cultures. (ibid.)
- *Comprehensive M&A surveillance:* For smaller domestic transactions it may be understandable that small and medium-sized companies consult with their lawyer, accountant or auditor only for specific services. The effort for the implementation of an international transaction, however, is often underestimated. An experienced M&A consultant

will relieve the company's internal project team and greatly optimize the entire transaction process, so that the managers can focus on other factors of success (commercial analysis, concept integration, communication, etc.). (ibid.)

Conclusion

The acquisition of an already existing company over a long period abroad is far more complex than a business expansion through the establishment of branch offices or subsidiary companies. Therefore, existing cross-border competences of the management are extremely helpful to the success of cross-border transactions (ibid.).

---

30 TIPS ON HOW TO LEARN ACROSS CULTURES (15)
(Andre Laurent)

15. To avoid wrong attributions, a paradoxical strategy is needed. When dealing with people from other cultures, as a starting point, make every effort to forget everything about culture and cultural differences. Try to meet the individual and its uniqueness first. Avoid categorizing. Concentrate on the individual. The cultural dimension will come next and soon anyhow.

In: SIETAR (Hrsg.), Keynote-Speech, Kongress 2000, Ludwigshafen

---

3.2.3   Reasons for M&A

There are several reasons why corporations are looking for external growth by merging with or acquiring other companies. Among a lot of factors, M&A are seen as supportive for cost savings through economies of scale and the realizations of synergies in order to increase the company value. Some of the most important reasons why companies consider M&A as a good deal are to be found in the following table (Hermann, 2008, pp. 6ff).

Tab. 3.1:   Benefits of M&A
Source: Hermann, 2008, p. 6ff

Horizontal	Vertical	Conglomerate
Increased market power	More control over quality and delivery of inputs	Gaining market power
Network externalities	Greater control over coordinating production flows through vertical chains	Efficient internal capital market
Leveraging marketing resources and capabilities	Monitoring supplier performance easier	Efficient diversification
Reduction of excess capacity	Contract disputes minimized	Bankruptcy risk reduction
Economies of scale and scope		
Creating new capabilities and resources		

In the course of globalization, M&A have become a useful tool for corporations to expand their business activities to foreign countries. With the help of cross-border M&A, companies can utilize the advantages of internationalization. One benefit of going international by merging with or acquiring foreign enterprises could be to overcome barriers to trade and thus serving foreign markets within certain trade blocs. In those blocs, firms can distribute their products without paying tariffs. Another advantage of cross-border and cross-cultural M&A are cultural synergies. To develop cultural synergies in newly-merged companies, global business leaders must be well trained and skilled at understanding and resolving cross-cultural conflicts. At the same time, they have to enforce a cooperative, cross-culture organizational behavior in a multicultural environment. (ibid.)

Another reason is the realization of economies of scale through cheap labor in low-wage countries as well as lower energy costs or overhead savings. A diversification with the help of a conglomerate M&A can be seen as a useful strategy to spread risks. By acquiring foreign assets, the diversification potential cannot only be seen in the diversification of the product range but also in expanding into different geographical markets. Thus, in times of an economic down-swing in the home market, companies can still benefit from their foreign activities, as different countries and regions do not have the same business cycle and the same stage of development. Therefore, the risk potential of weak national markets becomes less. The prevalence of M&A and the importance of various factors that give rise to M&A activity vary over time. (Finch, in web)

3.2.4   Drawbacks

Although there are many reasons for M&A, the major drawbacks can certainly be seen in the high rate of failures after deals have been closed. Most transactions fail to deliver the expected positive results and significant costs related to the failure are a major concern to companies' stakeholders. Most literature consults the so-called cultural clash to be the primary casual factor for the failure of cross-border M&A. As there are different values, beliefs, practices and attitudes between the different cultures, the new management must find a way to integrate culture into the corporate strategy. Thus, the top management has to set goals and lead employees in line with cultural beliefs and attitudes. (Hermann, 2008, pp. 8ff)

Other risks of cross-border M&A can be seen ingeneral risks of foreign business activities. One example could be political risks, like civil strife, revolutions and wars disrupting the activities in foreign countries. Another example could be fluctuations in the exchange rates between different currencies. (Hackmann, 2011, pp. 9ff)

3.2.5   The process of forming M&A

Pre-merger phase

Before the process of forming a new company is going to happen, a lot of issues have to be carefully considered. What are the benefits of such a project, what are the pros and cons, which risks have to be undertaken and which price has to be paid for such an undertaking are only a few questions that have to be addressed properly before a final decision can be made. In the pre-merger phase, the time frame for the integration and the planned development of synergies must be clearly marked out and it has to be discussed whether support from outside the company should or should not be asked for.

Post-merger integration

When the final decision has been made, the post-merger integration begins. Every integration process needs to be adapted to different situations. In order to understand the integration process properly it is useful to consider the four relevant phases. The following figure will give you an overview in connection with a general time frame.

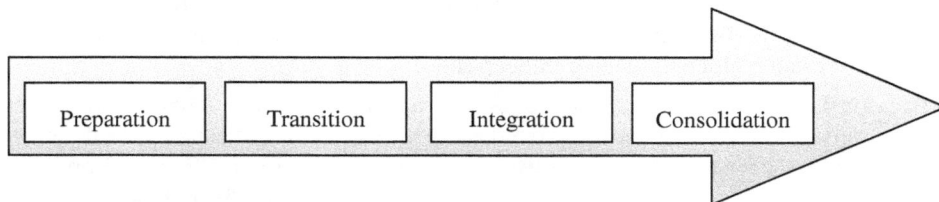

Fig. 3.2:   The integration process
Source: Gancel/Rodgers/Raynaud, 2002, p. 125

Preparation phase

In business, planning is one of the major objectives in everyday operations. For M&A, planning is the key to success in the preparation phase. Meetings will be held, the top management is involved, interviews and surveys are carried out. As far as the pre-deal planning is concerned, a practical example will demonstrate which activities are necessary and which departments are involved.

Transition phase

During this phase the partners begin to work together. Plans are put into actions and integration teams are formed in order to develop detailed plans for the merging process. It is the time when troubles begin. The cultural dimension comes into play; cultural differences will now start to become obvious. Each party is convinced that their behavior is the right one. Gancel/Rodgers/Raynaud (2002, p. 127) wrote in this context: *"The initial euphoria is replaced by a culture shock: a collision of values and beliefs that baffles and frustrates the individuals concerned."* The quality of communication and information will be negatively influenced. It is up to the integration team to work out a new and more detailed plan in order to safeguard the project. The newly merged companies are now confronted with cultural discrepancies. This is a dangerous situation when the project can actually fail.

Integration phase

At this stage, detailed strategies and plans are implemented as people start working together more comfortably and first synergies become apparent. Due to people's natural suspicion and reluctance towards change, building true commitments to the new way of doing things takes more time. The old cultural profiles of the partners begin to play a less critical role, as people begin to agree on common values and build up a history that they will share. This is not only a result of some employees leaving the company because they could not or did not want to adapt to changes, while new employees joined the team. Nevertheless, it is of great importance to be aware that, at any time, operational integration is usually further developed than cultural integration. Technical aspects may follow a set up plan, and quickly start to work in functional ways. However, people's attitude towards change is most likely to widen the time span of cultural integration (Gancel/Rodgers/Raynaud, 2002, p. 129).

Consolidation phase

During this phase, stability comes into the new organization. The overall goal has been reached, when all tools have been appropriately used and all plans have been successfully implemented. All operations involved in running the new organization will eventually be backed up with strength and stability. As a result, stakeholders begin to see clear evidence of the emerging synergies. Finally, the new corporate culture becomes deeper and deeper enrooted in the increasingly solid ground of the company (Gancel/Rodgers/Raynaud, 2002, p. 131).

Friendship and instinct
(Jeremy Williams)

Many Arabs have (or believe they have) special intuition or a "sixth sense" that guides them towards the correct decision in any matter. This can lead to sudden judgements and instructions that are difficult to dislodge, even in the face of new facts relating to the topic. Many Arabs will often trust their instinct rather than plough through a mass of boring detail. This special Arab sense may or may not exist (and there are many examples when Western "experts" were, in long term, proved quite wrong in their advice to their Arab principals). What is certain, in terms of judging people, is that almost all Arabs can quickly notice, and see through, false or shallow "friendship" sought or maintained simply to advance commercial or other activity. Be "genuine" in your friendship or relationship: don't "pretend" with Arabs.

In: Don't they know it's Friday?, 2004, p. 66

3.2.6   Cultural Due Diligence

Definition of Due Diligence

The term Due Diligence is used for various concepts involving either an investigation of a business or person prior to signing a contract. It can be a legal obligation, but the Due Diligence will more commonly apply to voluntary investigations. A common example of Due Diligence in several industries is the procedure through which a potential acquirer evaluates a target company or its assets for acquisition. (Hoskisson/Hitt/Ireland, 2004, p. 251) The Due Diligence is the careful analysis, review and assessment of an object of purchase, especially before an asset deal. The investigation of the strength and weaknesses of the target company, as well as the determination of the risks, are the goals of a Due Diligence. The implementation extends to the review of the business documents and a survey among the management, among other things. There are many implementation phases, according to the specific purchase intention of the buyer. The purchasing price will depend on the outcome of this inspection. The Due Diligence is intended to be an objective, independent examination of the acquisition target. In particular, it focuses on financials, tax matters, asset valuation, operations, the valuation of a business, and providing assurances to the lenders and advisors in the transaction as well as the acquirer's management team. (Angwin, 2001, pp. 35ff)

Importance of the Cultural Due Diligence

Next to the Financial and Tax Due Diligence, the Cultural Due Diligence should be of special relevance. Before and during every M&A-transaction, the cultural compatibility of all involved parties should be examined. Different business models, basic approaches, compensation systems, values, norms etc. could evoke serious problems in the case of international corporate mergers if their observation is neglected. The involvement of cultural investigations in mergers and acquisitions becomes increasingly important. Studies have shown that cultural coflicts were initiated when two business cultures had to merge and are one reason for the failure of business combinations. The Cultural Due Diligence methodically analyzes all business cultures involved. A business cultural analysis reveals cultural differences and their relevance and importance for the M&A parties. (Schneck/Zimmer, 2006, p. 593)

The Cultural Due Diligence should not play a secondary role, because it could also lead to a termination of the M&A negotiations. To a greater degree, there are more costly investigations avoidable if one assesses the barriers and differences in advance. Some consulting companies concentrate on culture management and cultural integration during corporate mergers, and have hence identified a market niche and new means of income in the traditional M&A business. The neglect of business cultures in the M&A process and the potential occurring problems of a following "culture clash" could endanger corporate mergers. Therefore, it would be beneficial if consulting companies generally extended their service package and made the Cultural Due Diligence an inherent part of the M&A process. (Schneck/Zimmer, 2006, p. 587)

For the last years, a Cultural Due Diligence for mergers and acquisitions has been suggested, so that more and more careful inspection of the integrative business cultures have taken place. Behind that is the concept of analyzing the financial data as well as the business cultural compatibility beforehand. A Cultural Due Diligence is useful for analyzing the different beliefs as well as the different leadership philosophies. It is important to distill the real risk factors for the cultural integration and to entirely concentrate on them during the integration process.

The main idea of a Cultural Due Diligence is simple. You just have to find out how similar or different the merging cultures are. During a merger and acquisition the sense and purpose of the contrast intensification is to delimit the own culture of origin and to preserve it, so that the own corporate culture will not be destroyed. Whether the cultural integration would be easy or difficult can only be answered by the comparison of the two cultures and their apparent similarity or dissimilarity. It is not necessary to have vast objective differences to cause a redoubtable "clash of the cultures". When you are faced with a possible threat from the outside like a merger or acquisition, people tend to band together with others of their ilk. During mergers or acquisitions, the concerns and distinction mechanisms on both sides are actually similar but can still separate them.

During takeovers, the staff and especially the executives of the transferred business try to explore the conditions of the "winner". They want to find out if they have a chance in this new constellation. For the executives of the acquisitive company it seems reasonable to act dismissively and authoritatively towards the competitors. They want to show right from the beginning that the others have to quit the field or be satisfied with a subordinate place in the operating pecking order. The result would be that even without vast cultural differences the dynamic of the system would generate two polarized factions and would promote the "clash of the cultures". The cultural integration stands and falls with the feeling of belonging. It is about having a place in the new organization where everyone feels accepted and contributes one's share to achieve a common goal. Only if people feel accepted by the community, they can concentrate on their tasks and generate a full load output. As long as the people are unsure about their place and acceptance and fear to be a discriminated minority, they are under stress and are primarily concerned with their own interests and their situation, which will create difficulties. As a result, they will work badly together. (Berner, 2008, p. 85)

The central factor for the success or failure of the cultural integration is whether it is successful at conveying trust among the staff and executives, so that the people have a place in the new company, feel accepted and can show full commitment. (ibid., p. 91) The risk factors consisting of difficult compatible values, convictions and habits could be early recognized during a Cultural Due Diligence. (Steinle/Eichenberg/Weber-Rymkovska, 2010, p. 254)

The two biggest risk factors of the cultural integration are, on the one hand, the belonging and, on the other hand, the perceived meaningfulness of the future occupation. (Berner, 2008, p. 85) The merger syndrome describes all the feelings and behaviors, including suspicion, coordination problems, disorientation, loss of control and misunderstandings, which occur, when two cultures collide because of the different cultural perceptions. The company is strongly influenced by those problems, so that the daily business suffers and competitors profit from it. (Balz/Arlinghaus, 2003, p. 179)

To sum it up, cultural differences could definitely lead to a failure or collapse of a merger or acquisition und should therefore be analyzed in a Cultural Due Diligence.

Conduction of a Cultural Due Diligence

Diverse data collection procedures for the investigation of a corporate culture exit. For that, instruments mainly from the empirical social research are used, which are very helpful for investigating people's opinions and attitudes. With the assistance of these instruments, it is possible to research the social phenomena and their cultural backgrounds. It is important to use the same tests, instruments and procedures in both companies to guarantee a high validity of the data. To ensure the comparability of the determined data, the analytical instruments should have fixed manuals and guidelines. Statements of the employees, internal documents as well as interviews of customers, shareholders and other persons related to the company should be included. A complete picture of the business cultures should be the result. The data collection is very important for the implementation of a Cultural Due Diligence, but it could lead to large difficulties. Sometimes, the top-management of the company does not give the permission to interview the staff or look into internal documents before the closure of the transaction. Fear to interrupt the peace in the company exists, because mergers involve concerns and a feeling of uncertainty among the staff. In this case, not all relevant information can be explored in the pre-merger phase. Consequently, certain analytical instruments can only be used or permitted during specific phases of the M&A transaction. (Schneck/Zimmer, 2006, p. 604) The following instruments could be used (Schneck/Zimmer, 2006, pp. 604ff):

- Document and Content Analyses
- Critical Event Analyses
- Observations
- Interviews

- Simulations
- Questionnaires

3.2.7 An evaluation of mergers & acquisitions

How good are companies at mergers and acquisitions? A survey conducted by KPMG (The initials stand for the founding fathers Klynveld, Peat, Marwick and Goerdele) shocked the business world in 1999. The findings say that only 17 percent of the examined mergers had led to an increase in the equity value of the companies after one year. Some 30 percent of the mergers created no value and 53 percent actually destroyed value (Kelly, 1999, p. 2–5).

According to Jahns (2003, p. 20) 60–70 % of all merger and acquisition transactions fail and do not achieve their long term growth objectives due to profitability losses of over 10 % during the merger process. Two years after a transaction the following developments were reported: 57 % of all "new" organisations suffered from enormous losses in their profitability, 14 % lingered with their original standard and only 29 % achieved an increment in their profitability.

Dielmann (2000, p. 478) has pointed to the fact that *"one major reason for the failure of many mergers and acquisitions is the insufficient consideration of the human factor"*. In 1999 top managers were asked and the findings show that the lack of internal communication (70 %) and the handling of cultural differences (46 %) had caused these problems (see Fig. 3.3).

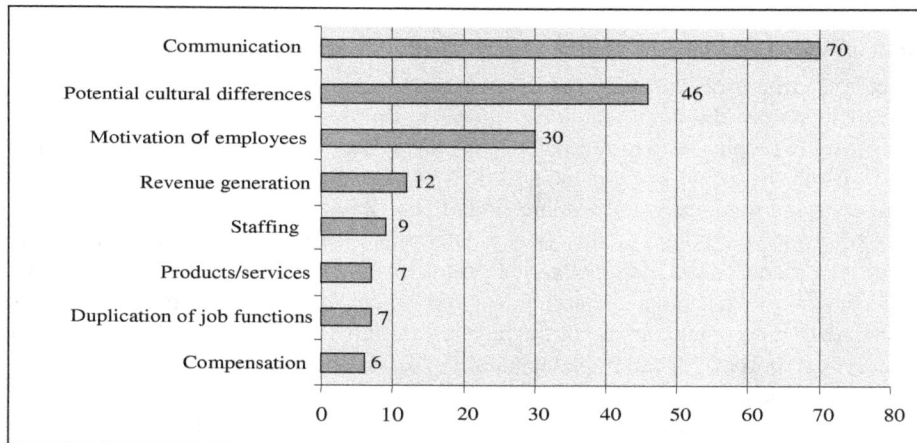

Fig. 3.3: Problems during the merger process
Source: Böning/Fritschle, 2001, p. 151

Another study showed that 85 % of he managers regarded cultural differences in the leadership styles as the main reasons for the failure (Bertels/de Vries, 2004, p. 2). For Dielmann (2000, p. 478) the conclusion is quite clear:

> *"The most important thing is that the new organization has to give highest priority to the creation of a new corporate culture. The heads of the organization and the board of management do not only need to control the process of integration and lead the*

new organisation into a new continuity, but they also unconditionally have to live the new culture themselves."

However, why is culture the leading factor for failures? One reason is a lack of awareness or blissful ignorance. Managers are simply unaware that the cultural dimension exists at all. Another possible answer is that, although they may be aware of the culture, leaders simply do not understand it well enough and therefore cannot assess the impact it could have.

Time-keeping – the biggest frustration?
(Jeremy Williams)

Probably all Westerners in the Gulf will quickly agree that the frequent inability of their Gulf colleagues to keep to time is the most significant of all cross-cultural aspects affecting their work in the Gulf. But many Gulf Arabs will comment that they are always available at any time and that access to them is simple. They may claim that it is only the unavoidable and unforeseen accident of other duties – such as those involving the family or friends – or unexpected duties placed necessarily on them by members of ruling families that draw them away from agreed meetings with Westerners. Westerners normally have no concept of the absolute duty that Gulf Arabs have towards family situations which are, in general, far greater than those undertaken, or expected, in Western society. "My brother telephoned and asked to see me, so I had to go to him; I am sorry I had to miss our meeting" is typical of a remark a Gulf Arab might make to a Westerner after a failed meeting i.e. genuinely believing that the explanation – because it involved a family member – would be understood, and failing to comprehend that for the Westerner such a reason would not be good enough. The Westerner would have been far less bothered if a phone call rearranging the meeting had been received, but the experience of almost all Westerners is that most Gulf Arabs do not reschedule meetings beforehand – they simply fail to appear when expected. "Time" is therefore a major area of culture clash.

In: Don't they know it's Friday?, 2004, p. 39

"A company's culture is often buried so deeply
inside rituals, assumptions, attitudes, and values
that it becomes transparent to an organization's members only when,
for some reason, it changes."

(Rob Goffee)

3.2.8   The influence of culture on M&A – selected results of two studies

In 2011 a study concerning the influence of culture on M&A transactions was conducted by Carolin Boden, Elisabeth Guth, Nelly Heinze and Sarah Lang, students of Baltic Management Studies at the University of Applied Sciences Stralsund. The questionnaire was filled in by 22 consulting companies and M&A-experts from 14 different countries, which are specialized on various aspects of international M&A. Some results of the study can be found here.

1) Do cultural differences often prove to be an obstacle?

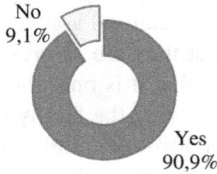

No 9,1%

Yes 90,9%

2)Would you consider the intercultural training as sufficient in most cases?

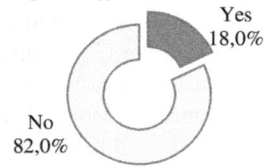

Yes 18,0%

No 82,0%

3) When would you recommend starting with the training?

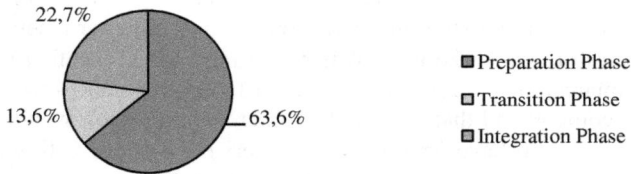

22,7%

13,6%

63,6%

- Preparation Phase
- Transition Phase
- Integration Phase

4) What is the most common reason for the failure of M&A?

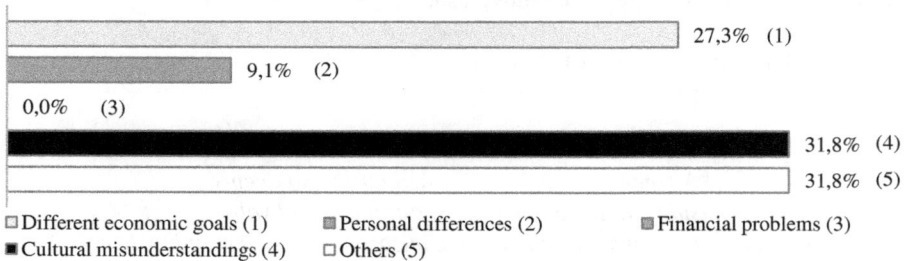

27,3% (1)
9,1% (2)
0,0% (3)
31,8% (4)
31,8% (5)

☐ Different economic goals (1)   ▨ Personal differences (2)   ▨ Financial problems (3)
■ Cultural misunderstandings (4)   ☐ Others (5)

5) How would you rate the influence of cultural misunderstandings on the failure of M&A?

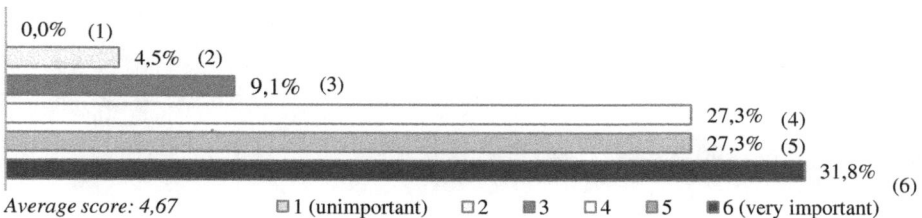

0,0% (1)
4,5% (2)
9,1% (3)
27,3% (4)
27,3% (5)
31,8% (6)

Average score: 4,67   ☐ 1 (unimportant)   ☐ 2   ■ 3   ☐ 4   ▨ 5   ■ 6 (very important)

Source: Boden/Guth/Heinze/Lang, 2011, pp. 75ff

Another study on culture and M&A was conducted by Amène El Mansouri, Laura Prestel, Nejma Samouh and Yang Wang, students of "Management Interculturel et Affaires Internationales" at the Université de Haute-Alsace, Mulhouse-Colmar. In this case, a questionnaire was sent to companies which had already conducted a merger or an acquisition. The following companies participated in the study: Abbey National-Banco Santander, Arcelor-Mittal, Gecina-Metrovecesa, Orange-France Télécom, Rhodia Chalampé-Slovay, Saint-Gobain/BPB and Wind-Weather Investment.

1) What cultural obstacles did you face during the M&A process?

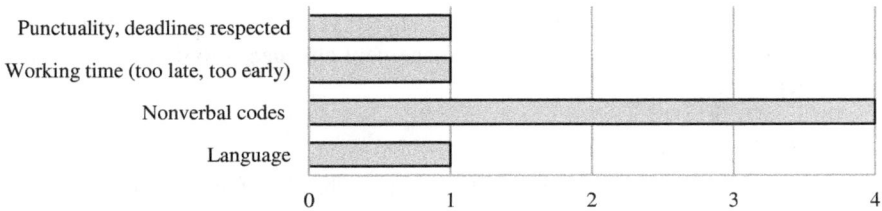

2) Did you get any intercultural training during the M&A process?

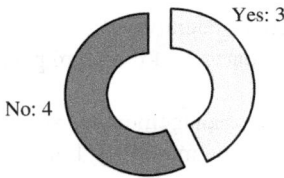

3) Do you think that intercultural management is important for an M&A company?

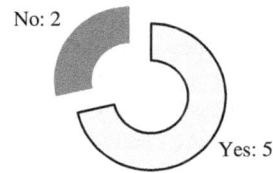

4) What are the most common reasons for a failure of M&A?

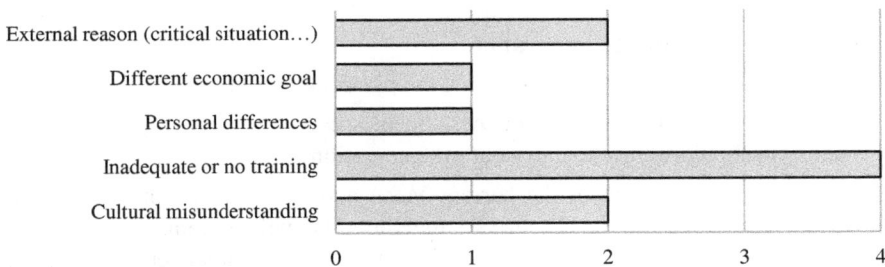

Source: El Mansouri/Prestel/Samouh/Wang, 2011, pp. 51

Both studies show that cultural aspects can have a significant influence on M&A transactions. However, the majority of participating companies did not offer any intercultural training. The lack of this kind of training was also among the most listed reasons for the failure of M&A. As far as the opinions of the consultants and experts are concerned, the result is even more impressive: cultural misunderstandings are on the top of the scale.

3.2.9   A practical example: a pre-deal planning by KPMG

Successful acquirers take the long term view and recognize that the cost of their investment in pre-dealing planning is minimal compared to the potential impact of failing to generate the desired level of return from the transaction. KPMG has developed a guide to pre-deal planning (Kelly, 2003, p. 5–8):

a)   Be clear about strategic intent

An M&A is a tool to meet strategic objectives, not an end in itself. Even if the integration process runs smoothly, a flawed strategy will inevitably lead to serious problems. Be sure that the strategic rationale is translated into a shared vision (ideally with measurable targets) and communicated to all stakeholders. Management also needs to determine what is valued in the target.

b)   Assess the top management team

Identify and involve the team who will be responsible for managing the new business. It will be important to:

- consider the role of the target company top team in the future plans of the business;
- consider whether between the two businesses there exists a management team capable of running the new, enlarged business. Often the management team needs external strengthening;
- determine how key executives need to be secured or incentivised;
- define succession and contingency plans as the departure of top team personnel from the target is common;
- define and communicate a process for selecting the management team;
- define any redundancy matters relating to the top team swiftly but be aware that the investigation process by its nature asks many questions and often results in a breakdown of trust, so it is ill-advised to make snap judgements about management during the pre-planning phase.

c)   Determine approach to integration

Two key questions must be addressed during the planning period:

- To what extent should we integrate these businesses?
- What style should we use to carry out the integration?

The motivation behind much of the current M&A activity is based on the opportunity to achieve synergies from bringing businesses together. Typically, organizations underestimate the extent of integration they should be undertaking early on. However, failing to integrate the target sufficiently is responsible for much of the disappointment around the extent of benefits derived from a transaction. By the time they realize this is the case, the 100 day period is over or inappropriate messages may have been communicated to stakeholders.

In terms of style of integration, it is clearly valuable to learn lessons from past experience; however, a successful approach adopted in one case may not work as well when applied to another. At one extreme is a directive approach, based on a "just do it" mentality entailing minimal involvement from the workforce. This may be appropriate in low tech industries. At the other extreme, facilitative approach puts emphasis on managers to find solutions. It assumes a highly skilled workforce working to a high level agenda and assures implementation through involvement and "buy-in". This can be appropriated in high growth markets. The decision on which approach to adopt may vary for different parts of the business (e.g. divisions, countries, functions) and is based on:

- quality of people;
- availability of resource;
- degree of risk;
- distance from customers;
- complexity of issues;
- access to best practice.

The approach requires careful consideration and evaluation during the pre-deal period to ensure the integration programme is tailored appropriately to the particular circumstances of your deal.

d)   Involve the "right team"

Given the range of internal management and external adviser involvement, it is vital to appoint an Integration Director responsible for the transaction process as a whole. One of the teams within the programme will be that of the integration planners. It is important for that team to:

- include a mix of M&A experience and operational management capability. The role of the operational team is key. Initially the acquiring team, but later the operational staff of both businesses, can impact on the ability to deliver value.

Their knowledge of the business can:

- have an impact on the value/price;
- help you to plan for the 100 days; ensuring integration programmes are achievable;
- ensure buy-in to the integration plan;
- have continuity through the deal completion into the initial post-completion phase so that immediate benefits can be realized;
- be full time to enable them to give the implementation process their undivided attention.

e)   Create the integration programme based on where benefits will be derived

Traditionally many of the original synergies will not materialize during integration due to:

- failure to test synergy assumptions,
- failure to recognize the role of the operational team.

It is therefore important to build a plan to identify benefits beyond those originally envisaged. Often these benefits are limited by prudence or city code rules. However, experience shows that 20% of integration activities will deliver 80% of the benefits, so it is advisable to focus on the projects which will create the biggest impact. Once benefit pools have been identified, it is important to build a plan to deliver them and to establish momentum in the first 100 days. At the planning stage, it is necessary to:

- ensure the process is underpinned and consistent with a common business vision/strategy;
- develop first action plans setting out what should be done to take control of the business;
- identify workstreams for the key benefit areas and identify work teams to deliver them;

- allocate tasks, timings, responsibilities, milestones and deliverables for the projects that have been identified;
- revisit plans on an on-going basis as information becomes available;
- plan to handle the overlap and interfaces between workstreams to avoid losing value.

f)   Address cultural issues

Assess cultural differences between the acquirer and the target. Too often these differences are underestimated and yet they can undermine the 100 day programme as well as the longer term implementation. Ability to identify cultural issues will depend on the extent of access to the target pre-deal, but should cover:

- leadership style, management profile, organisation structure;
- working practices and terms & conditions;
- perceptions from the marketplace.

g)   Develop a communications plan

Communication is a critical factor in the successful handling of M&As. Companies which are caught unprepared on deal completion find it difficult to reassure employees and other stakeholders. It is therefore important to produce a communications plan early on, before completion:

- the messages for the different stakeholder groups and the timing of their release;
- the process of cascading information through the organization is important, e.g. decisions on the mix of one to one, group meetings and written communication and the content of each will need to be addressed;
- the Day One communication programme is probably most critical of all; you only get one chance to make a first impression;
- how the press will be managed, the content of release and information packages and the points of contact;
- any immediate matters that will affect day to day business, such as the name to be used by the new organisation and how switchboard staff will answer the telephone.

"We regard the interplay among diverse cultures
as a strength and an opportunity
to boost creativity and productivity."
(ThyssenKrupp Stahl AG)

3.3 Interview with Peter Agnefjäll, CEO of IKEA

Natalia Brzezinski spoke with Peter Agnefjäll, CEO and President of the IKEA Group since September 2013, about successfully doing business across cultures.

Brzezinski: IKEA is a global company, is it challenging exporting your values-based leadership model to stores and managers in other nations that may have different cultural values?

Agnefjäll: We need to work actively with our values and culture to keep them alive. Today, this is integrated in the way we recruit and work with people development. We actively seek people who share our values and recruit on values first and second on competence. For our leaders there is constant follow up regarding culture and values and we measure how well they communicate the values. Culture and values are also an integrated part of our development and performance talks for all managers and co-workers.

Brzezinski: In your experiences, what are the policies and practices that really work in promoting and retaining top female talent? What truly sparks change?

Agnefjäll: We are working with a set of tools that we feel work very well. One is the leadership commitment. We also strive to create an environment that encourages all competent co-workers who come from different backgrounds, for example can flexible work arrangements accommodate for individual life situations. Practices vary between countries for example in Japan we have a day care centre next to one of our stores and we have introduced paternity leave; both enabling more women to have a career. Several countries are trying out job sharing where two people share a manager position to facilitate for combining manager position with for example parenting during a period.

Brzezinski: [...] How would you describe your leadership style and what works for you in empowering your employees, both male and female?

Agnefjäll: I am a believer in people and IKEA is a truly people and team oriented company. Our leaders appreciate working close together in a team with clear framework and clear goals, but we also leave room for freedom. I am enthusiastic so sometimes it is hard to let go but I try not to poke my nose into other people's areas of responsibility. Delegating and relying on others by giving them responsibilities is part of the IKEA culture. At IKEA we give straightforward, down to earth people a chance to grow, both as individuals and in their professional roles. It is essential for our growth to develop our business through our people.

Brzezinski: What workplace trends or market changes are you seeing on a global scale, perhaps from the United States to China or India? Are your stores and corporate culture in the U.S. very different than the ones in Sweden or elsewhere?

Agnefjäll: We have been on the U.S. market since 1986 and in China from 2000. We do often find that our values are universal and that there are more similarities than differences between the different markets. When we enter a market, experienced IKEA co-workers work together with locally recruited co-workers there to support and ensure that the values and concept are clear. Now, when we will enter the Indian market we will follow the same approach.

In: Huffington Post Business Online, extract, 20/12/2013

3.4 Case Study: From foundering consumer goods factory to cookware leader: A recipe for growth

When I. Smirnova arrived at the Demidovsky plant in Russia's Sverdlovsk region fresh with a management degree in 1999, her boss challenged her to use her newly acquired skills to come up with a last-ditch plan to save the business from closure.

The factory had made scarce consumer goods during the Soviet period since 1947, and even produced a non-stick Teflon range of saucepans from 1982. But the work of its 650 staff – almost entirely low-paid women – was an after-thought to the aluminium plant next door to which it belonged, and it made losses year after year. "I brought all the employees together, and felt as though I had the whole weight of Russia on my shoulders," she recalls. They were afraid that they would lose their social benefits, such as holiday camps for their children. I told them that to survive under capitalism, we need to be interesting for our shareholders and to the market." With support from the owner, which since 2000 has been Sual, she has increased wages 2.5 times for a slightly smaller number of staff, and turned the factory into a profitable venture, which now sells cookware throughout the country.

The secret was to give her autonomy. "When 99 per cent of management time was focused on the aluminium factory, we may have had a good product but we were losing more than $ 100.000 a month," she says. We started to calculate our production costs." Most savings came through more efficient techniques, sharply lessening waste. She is no longer required to use supplies form the aluminium plant next door, and has bought from Sual's competitors at home and abroad.

She has also instituted tough quality control. With staff paid by results, she docks up to 20 per cent for rejected saucepans. Late last year, she won the right to use Teflon's platinum coatings, allowing her to launch a new luxury range of pans.

Ms. Smirnova has retained some Soviet-era practices, including quarterly employee awards, mixed with profit-sharing and management training for a dozen senior executives in her team. She has recently opened a chain of shops to market the products.

One challenge has been overcoming Russian suspicion of domestically produced goods. So she launched the English-language brand, Scovo. She has adapted to local habits, including a preference for the colors red and yellow; detachable handles because Russians like to use saucepans in the oven; and the importance of longevity.

Jack, A., in: Financial Times, 11/02/04, p. 8

Review and Discussion Questions:

1. Which were the challenges Ms. Smirnova had to master in the beginning and during her work?
2. What is her philosophy concerning the salary policy of the company?
3. How did she succeed in combining old traditional structures with highly new management principles?
4. Which key qualifications are necessary to do such a good job and what do you think about her academic background?

4 Values under the Influence of Culture and Technology

4.0 Statement of the problem

Great Wall? Firm eyes great bridge
(S. Pounds)

Boca Raton's Genesis Technology Group is in the businesses of helping other small U.S. businesses establish roots in China

Call the offices of Genesis Technology Group and you are pleasantly prompted by a voice mail menu in two languages: English and Chinese. Not many companies do enough business with the world's most populous nation to need an office telephone voice mail in Chinese. But Genesis is trying to change that by helping smaller American firms establish roots in China. After all, with 1.3 billion consumers and low-cost workers, China is emerging as a major economic power. Philip Guo, born and reared in China and now an attorney with Becker & Poliakoff in Fort Lauderdale, sees only an upside to planting the seeds of U.S. commerce on the business side of the Great Wall. "China has been a hot topic. It has had such economic growth," Guo said. "Labour there is unbelievably cheap. That's why toymakers, furniture makers, shoemakers are moving their facilities there", he said. The global business world has embraced China and doesn't appear to be letting go.

Still, with Beijing in the middle of modifying its laws to comply with WTO rules and to attract international business partners, it is difficult for a foreign company to set up there. Its language is hard to learn and its business practices are based as much on personal relationships as they are contractual arrangements. "In China, they want to be friends and then do business", Genesis Technology Chairman James Wang said recently. "With Americans, it is 'Can we sign a contract tomorrow?' For Americans friendship is a nice side benefit. In China, it is a prerequisite."

Genesis, looking to this burgeoning sector of the consulting business to reverse a string of losses, drums up business by holding roundtable discussions with small and medium-sized firms interested into the Chinese market. From those roundtables, companies eventually come forward with business proposals for China. It can take a while, though. Take Custom Biologicals, a Boca Raton firm that makes biological agents for environmental cleanup. Company officials went to China 18 months ago and had meetings that Genesis arranged with Chinese businessmen. Custom Biologicals is still waiting for a deal to materialize, but Chief Executive Clarence Baugh is not giving up. "Chinese business is quite different. It is slower paced," he said. Viragen, a Plantation-based biotechnology firm, began working with Genesis in January 2003 to find Chinese distributors for a disease-fighting drug called Multiferon. After a year of meetings with Genesis and prospective Chinese partners and a slight interruption form the SARS outbreak, Viragen is close to forging distribution agreements, said Viragen Executive Vice President Mel Rothberg. "They go through a certain protocol of consensus. They will retest their thinking to validate it," Rothberg said. "If you can identify the best person to champion your program, you'll get the fastest track. You have to be patient." In China, business mannerisms make a difference. A premium is placed on politeness and process, even down to the presentation of a business card. "If you don't have a business card in Chinese, you are immediately recognized as unknowledgable," Rothberg said.

In: The Herald, Miami, 1 March 2004, p. 9

4.1   Values and responsibilities

As technology continues to transform national and international working environments, involving more people from different cultural background, the values, beliefs and ideologies of individual employees, consumers and other "constituents" have gained assumed added importance for the management. In order to understand cultural groups, the centrality of cultural values is vital. The word "value" has different meanings in English, depending on the context in which it is used (McEwan, 2001, p. 45). It may describe a thing's worth, desirability, usefulness, or qualities which influence these judgements.

Four different types of values can be distinguished (Rokeach, 1973, p. 17):

- Moral values – concern interpersonal behavior, e.g. being honest is desirable.
- Competence values – concern one's own valuation of one's own behavior, e.g. behaving imaginatively is desirable.
- Personal values – concern the goals or terminal states that are desirable for oneself, e.g. peace of mind.
- Social values – concern the goals that one would desire for the whole society, e.g. world peace is desirable.

The first two types in this list concern instrumental values that are about how a person should live and behave. The latter two are terminal values that concern the goals or purposes that we should be striving for.

In economics, value refers to the purchasing power of goods or services to acquire something else. In general, values are described as ideas how people should live and the goals they should seek. They are shared by a majority of people within a community or society. They are simply expressed generalities, often no more than single words such as peace and honesty. As they are very broad, they do not give guidance on how particular things should be evaluated (Fisher/Lovell, 2003, p. 111). In other words: values are the most deeply felt beliefs shared by a cultural group; they reflect a shared perception of what ought to be, and not what is. Equality, for example, is a value shared by many people in the United States. It refers to the belief that all humans are created equal, even though we must acknowledge that, in reality, there are many disparities, such as in talent, intelligence, or access to material goods.

Intercultural conflicts are often caused by differences in value orientations. For example, some people feel strongly that it is important to consider how things were done in the past. For them, history and tradition help provide guidance. Values often cause conflicts among participants in international projects, e.g. when future-oriented individuals show a lack of respect for traditional ways of doing things. Moreover, those conflicts may be exacerbated by power differentials, with some values privileged over others.

Different cultural patterns in the United States
(Erbert/Perez/Gareis)

A graduate student from India noted the U.S. patterns of greeting. In her native culture, people say hello to those they know. Initially, she was surprised by the frequency with which Americans greet each other; she later became disillusioned:
I thought, they are really interested in how I am. Then ... "I'm fine and how about you?" Then I realized that people are really not interested in the answer. It is just a way of acknowledging you.
A British student commented on how openly Americans share their religious affiliation: *At first, I felt like a bit separated because I didn't quite fit into any ... They didn't know quite how to respond to me. I thought, Oh, am I supposed to be religious? Am I going to fit in here?*
A graduate student from Iran noted how Americans are taught to "sell themselves": *The job search is another thing in this country that is culturally quite different... In my society, mostly, there is not, you know, no selling yourself. And for the first couple of months I wasn't very successful because I didn't have the experience in selling myself.*

In: Western Journal of Communication, 2003, p. 67, pp. 113-117

Reflections on human values, values-based leadership and organizational ethics belong to the issues that should be addressed when doing business. Corporations – personified by their leaders – have a great responsibility for establishing a values-based foundation for our work-life, and thus indirectly as well as for our whole life. The notion of values as standards is stimulated by an increasing concern amongst leaders about being able to measure how well the organization lives up to the values it proclaims to promote. In addition, demands from constituencies that are increasingly aware of their power to influence corporate behavior are bringing pressure to bear on enterprises to articulate their values and to describe their activities and results with respect to these values. Therefore, values can be considered to be a social-psychological concept with broad implication for any company and its leaders. The concept has a cognitive and emotive foundation that provides a basis for formulating long-term goals, for reflecting on individual and organizational identity and responsibility, and for measuring and communicating corporate success using an increased repertoire of measures and indicators. In other words, values provide a frame of reference for new perspectives on leadership, identity, responsibility and success (Pruzan, 2009, p. 134).

Value of collectivism in Korea: Kibun
(Shim/Kim/Martin)

For Koreans kibun is when *"an inner, peaceful environment is maintained."* For Koreans
to develop and maintain harmonious relationships, they must be able to accurately "read"
the kibun of others. Preserving the kibun of one or more parties in an interpersonal communicative exchange or relationship takes precedence in the termination of the communication interaction or even the relationship itself.

Due to the Confucian emphasis on harmony and hierarchal order in relationships, an individual should always express respect and concern for another's kibun, as well as express a
concern for the kibun of the entire group/situation... This sense is extremely important in a
business context. Within the business world it is socially important not to let your true feelings show through in your facial expressions. This may unconsciously show disrespect to
your clients or traders, and can essentially make or break your business relationship or
deal. To truly understand someone you must know how to maintain that person's kibun,
their mood, feelings, or state of mind.

In: Changing Korea: Understanding Culture and Communication, 2008, pp. 77–78

4.2   De Bono's Six Value Medals

Edward de Bono differenciates values in six medals: gold, silver, steel, glass, wood and
brass. This is supposed to make it easier to notice, look, see and act upon them (De Bono,
2005, p. 39). For all medals, negative values also exist, which one should try to avoid.

The Gold Medal Values

> *"This medal deals with human values, the values that affect people. Gold is a supe-
> rior material and human values are the most important values of all in the
> end."(ibid., p. 36)*

The gold medal deals with questions like "What matters to our employees?" and "How do
decisions affect the employees?"

> *"With human values there is exploitation, slavery and tyranny. The whole purpose of
> civilisation is a combined effort to attend human values." (ibid., p. 41)*

There is a range of human values, such as the basic needs of food, shelter, health and respect.
In addition to this, you will also find many "negative values" in the gold medal. Freedom
from those kinds of values becomes a value itself.

> *"Freedom from tyranny, oppression and bullying is a very high value. The life of a
> child at school or a worker in a factory may be made intolerable by bullying."(ibid.,
> pp. 43f)*

Psychological needs like recognition, appreciation and thanks, prestige and importance, simplicity, trust, reassurance, encouragement, achievement, human warmth and dignity, help and
hope also need attention (ibid., pp. 44ff).

Values
(Barack Obama)

Our individualism has always been bound by a set of communal values, the glue upon which every healthy society depends. We value the imperatives of family and the cross-generational obligations that family implies. We value community, the neighborliness that expresses itself through raising the barn or coaching the soccer team. We value patriotism and the obligations of citizenship, a sense of duty and sacrifice on behalf of our nation. We value a faith in something bigger than ourselves, whether that something expresses itself in formal religion or ethical precepts. And we value the constellation of behaviors that express our mutual regard for one another: honesty, fairness, humility, kindness, courtesy, and compassion.

In: The Audacity of Hope, New York, 2006, p. 55

The Silver Medal Values

"This medal focuses directly on organizational values. That means values related to the purpose of the organization (in business this would be profitability). Silver is associated with money. There are also the values involved in the actual running of the organization, such as cost control. The organization may also be a family, group of friends or social club." (De Bono, 2005, pp. 36f)

Some values of the gold and silver medals overlap in the sense that the employees affect the profitability of a company. If employees are not happy and do not work well, their unhappiness and discontent can also become an organizational value. (ibid., p. 49)

You can define two main types of silver medal values:

- How successful the organization is in achieving its intended purpose.
- How well the organization is running.

Using a car analogy, the first values relate to whether the car is on course for the chosen destination. The second values relate to how well the car is actually running. (ibid., p. 50)

The Steel Medal Values

"These are the quality values. Steel should be strong. The values are in the intended direction. What are the values of the product, service or function in terms of what it is trying to do? If it is tea, is it good quality tea?"(ibid., p. 37)

Steel medal values include customer values, quality of service and function quality.

The Glass Medal Values

"Glass medal values are concerned with creativity, innovation and simplicity. These values apply in all areas. Anything we do and anything we think about can possibly be improved through creative thinking." (ibid., p. 69)

Innovation, simplicity, creativity, fragility and potential are part of the Glass Medal Values.

> **The Strength of the Internet**
> (Li Yahong)
>
> In the 15 years since China joined the Internet in 1994 the number of Chinese net users has soared to 300 million, laying the ground for an information era in a nation that has barely accomplished industrialization. The Internet has stimulated technical progress and productive forces, changed the way in which information is spread, and consequently had a far-reaching impact on Chinese society and people's. Now the Internet is a popular channel for the public to voice their opinions and display their strength, giving rank and file citizens some access to top officials.
>
> In: China Today, Nr.4, 2009, p. 11

The Wood Medal Values

"In the broadest sense, the wood medal values assess the impact of a decision, project, activity or change on 'third parties'. These third parties are not directly involved in the operation but are affected by it." (ibid., p. 79)

Wood highlights environmental values in the customary sense: nature, community, ambience political climate, etc.

The Brass Medal Values

Perception is much more important than people assume, because people react to what they see, even if it is not real.

"The brass medal is all about 'perceptual values'. How does this look like? How else might it be seen?" (ibid., p. 89)

If an action is taken, in whose interest will it be done? If a famous actor is filmed visiting a children's hospice, will this happen for the children's benefit or selfish publicity reasons? If a big company donates USD 1 million to an environmental organization, is it because they want to save endangered species or because they need to whitewash their image? Often it is difficult to tell what the true intention is. Most times it is a mixture of self-interest and charity. What matters is how people perceive things. (ibid., pp. 91f)

Visualization of the Six Value Medals: The Value Triangle

Sometimes it is helpful to see things at one glance. The following triangle is made out of six equal circles, each representing one medal (ibid., pp. 144ff):

*   The silver medal is the top of the triangle, but not necessarily the most important value. It is on top, because the "value scan" is often made from an organization's point of view and the initiator of the scan is usually always most interested in those.
*   The steel medal is situated on the left side of the second row, because "quality values" are very important if you want to lead a successful business.
*   The gold medal is situated right next to the steel medal. It represents the human values which need to be taken into account, but are often not the "objective values".
*   The glass medal is in the lower right corner of the triangle. Although creativity and innovation are important, their emphasis is not superior.

- The cental circle at the bottom row represents the wood medal, because our choices and actions affect our environment. At this spot, the wood medal has the most surroundings.
- The brass medal is situated at the left bottom. This is the first spot you come across, if you scan a page, just like perceptions are the first things you notice in a situation.

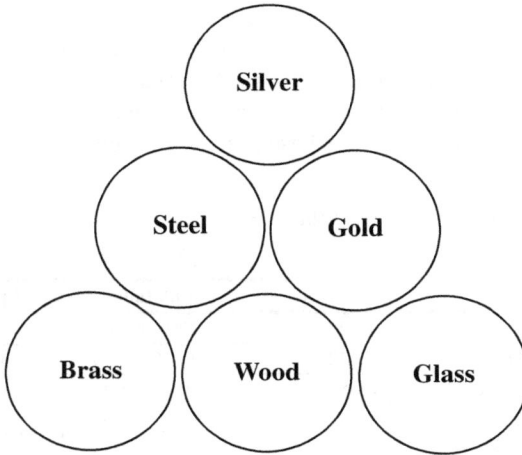

Fig. 4.1:   De Bono's Value Triangle
Source: Own illustration, according to de Bono, 2005, pp. 144ff

---

My Traditional Christian Faith
(Jimmy Carter)

One of my most interesting and perhaps most productive conversations was with the Chinese leader Deng Xiaoping, with whom I negotiated normal diplomatic relations between the United States and the People's Republic of China. During his state visit to Washington, Deng and I had a number of wide-ranging talks about many aspects of Chinese and American life, in order to establish as firm a friendship as possible between our two peoples. At a state banquet one evening, he asked what inspired my first interest in his country. I replied that I was raised as a Baptist and that our preeminent heroes were the women Christian leaders who went to China as missionaries to spread the gospel about Jesus Christ.

Deng was amused by my response, and pointed out that religious activities of that kind had been terminated when the People's Republic of China was established in 1949. The official policy was atheism, and worship services and the distribution of the Bibles and other holy books were prohibited. I asked if it might be possible to change these policies. Before returning home, Deng told me that the basic law of China would be changed to provide for religious freedom and that Bibles would be authorised. Within three years, he had kept both promises, with a proviso that any new church congregations would register with the government.

In: Our Endangered Values, p. 25–26

4.3   The World Values Survey

4.3.1   An overview on the project

The World Values Survey (WVS) is a global research project on values and beliefs of people in 97 different countries on all continents covering approximately 88 percent of the world's population. The World Values Survey Association, a non-profit organization, coordinates the worldwide network of social scientists. Those scientists are recruited from the respective culture/society studied. The first wave of WVS was based on the European Values Survey in 1981. The latest sixth wave was started in 2010.

Tab. 4.1:   Numbers of countries and people covered by the WVS
Source: World Value Survey, 2008, p. 5

Wave	Years	Countries	Population	Respondents
1	1981–1984	20	4,700,000,000	25,000
2	1989–1993	42	5,300,000,000	61,000
3	1994–1998	52	5,700,000,000	75,000
4	1999–2004	67	6,100,000,000	96,000
5	2005–2008	53	6,700,000,000	77,000
Four-wave aggregate data file		80		257,000

The questions are asked in the course of a face-to-face interview and address among others religious, political and social issues. The findings help to identify the most important values of each country and how they might change over time. The obtained values can be mainly divided into traditional/secular-rational and survival/self-expression values. The former show the differences between countries strongly influenced by religion and those which are not. Nowadays, secular-rational values dominate in the vast majority of industrialized countries. A similar situation also applies for the latter dimension of values, since the emphasis in developed countries is more on subjective aspects than on economic and physical security, like in developing countries. (The World Values Survey, 2008, pp. 3ff)

The findings of the WVS also show a correlation between certain values and the nation's political development, e.g. concerning the mass self-expression and democratic institutions. The results have also been the basis of Hofstede's new sixth dimension, Indulgence vs. Restraint. (ibid.)

> *"Keep your language.*
> *Love its sound, its modulation, its rhythm.*
> *But try to march together with men of different languages,*
> *remote from your own,*
> *who wish like you for a more just and human world."*
>
> (Hèlder Câmara, Spiral of Violence)

4.3.2   Sample questions from the World Values Survey

In order to give an insight into the nature of the questions of the World Values Survey (WVS), some sample questions taken from different questionnaires can be found here.

For each of the following, indicate how important it is in your life. Would you say it is:

	Very important	Rather important	Not very important	Not at all important
Family	1	2	3	4
Friends	1	2	3	4
Leisure time	1	2	3	4
Politics	1	2	3	4
Work	1	2	3	4
Religion	1	2	3	4

Taking all things together, would you say you are:

1 – Very happy   2 – Rather happy   3 – Not very happy   4 – Not at all happy

---

For each activity, would you say you do them every week or nearly every week; once or twice a month; only a few times a year; or not at all?

	(Nearly) Weekly	Once or twice a month	Only a few times a year	Not at all
Spend time with parents or other relatives	1	2	3	4
Spend time with friends	1	2	3	4
Spend time socially with colleagues from work or your profession	1	2	3	4
Spend time with people at your church, mosque or synagogue	1	2	3	4
Spend time socially with people at sports clubs or voluntary or service organization	1	2	3	4

Some people feel they have completely free choice and control over their lives, while other people feel that what they do has no real effect on what happens to them. Please use this scale [...] to indicate how much freedom of choice and control you feel you have over the way your life turns out.

No choice at all   A great deal of choice

  1   2   3   4   5   6   7   8   9   10

Which point on this scale most clearly describes how much weight you place on work (including housework and schoolwork), as compared with leisure or recreation?
1.   It's leisure that makes life worth living, not work
2.
3.
4.
5.   Work is what makes life worth living, not leisure

Now, I would like to ask you something about the things which would seem to you, personally, most important if you were looking for a job.
1   A good income so that you do not have any worries about money
2   A safe job with no risk of closing down or unemployment
3   Working with people you like
4   Doing an important job that gives you a feeling of accomplishment

Here are two statements which people sometimes make when discussing good and evil. Which one comes closest to your own point of view?

A.   There are absolutely clear guidelines about what is good and evil. These always apply to everyone, whatever the circumstances.

B.   There can never be absolutely clear guidelines about what is good and evil.

Do you think most people would try to take advantage of you if they got a chance, or would they try to be fair?

People would try to take   People would try to be fair
advantage of you

  1   2   3   4   5   6   7   8   9   10

In: The World Values Survey Association, The World Values Survey: Questionnaires of 2005, 2000 and 1995 (sometimes slightly summarized), 2012.

4.4 Valuing diversity and managing diversity

4.4.1 Definition of diversity

According to the Collins English Dictionary, diversity can be described as the state or quality of being different or varied. It is a point of difference and its synonyms are change, difference, variation and dissimilarities (Collins English Dictionary, 2009). The word "diversity" has its origin in the Latin word "diversitas" and means as much as contradiction, plurality and variety (Rüdiger, 2003, p. 92).

Diversity refers to the heterogeneity of the employees of a company as well as of its customers (Rühl, 2001, p. 56). The beginning of using the term "diversity" in matters of organizations and management is to be found in the U.S. and was established during the 1960s (Lindecke, 1995, p. 51).

When mentioning the term "diversity", only the obvious sign of diversity, like race and gender, come to people's minds. Whereas it used to be a code word for Black, it e.g. also includes people from different racial and cultural background, different genders, people with disabilities, with different religious backgrounds, sexual orientations or from different age groups.

One of the most influential UK scholars in the field of equality and discrimination, Bradley, defines diversity as the

> *"differences based on race, ethnicity, gender, sexuality, disability or age which are historically and socially constructed, and they draw the lines of inequality and discrimination in society. In turn, overcoming discrimination and inequality requires engagement with the effects of past discrimination and careful questioning of the common sense assumption that govern organization and society." (Tatli, 2010, p. 4)*

4.4.2 Diversity management

The aim of managing diversity is to learn to understand cultural and other differences among workers and creating an environment in which they will be productive (Anthony, 2002, p. 85).

To achieve this target, diversity management applies to individual differences and similarities as well as to group identity of the workforce.

Managing diversity is a holistic approach of how to use the potential of the employees for the good and profitability of a corporation. It does not offer a set of solutions and contrary to popular belief, it is not a program for addressing discrimination. (Rooseverlt, 1992, p. 167)

Diversity encompasses more than being "politically correct" or promoting an equal opportunities policy. The proper management of diversity actually brings benefits for an organisation. Its goal is more than

> *"simply minimising the effect of discrimination and encouraging equal treatment it takes positive advantage of the differences between individuals and works against prejudice." (The Scout Association, 2005, p. 1)*

A broader definition of diversity refers to all defined individual differences of people in social contexts (Gardenswartz/Rowe, 1998, p. 77) and will be discussed in the abstract about the Dimensions of Diversity.

Diversity in our workforce
(Jacklyn Koh)

Diversity means variety. In the workplace, the term is used to denote the variety among employees - those differences of age, gender, ethnicity, religion and nationality that make each one of us a unique and distinctive individual. In a global company like Siemens, we experience diversity during our everyday work. Diversified teams are commonplace. We regard the diversity of our workforce as an invaluable source of creativity and experience that makes us more competitive.

In: Siemens AG – Corporate Values, 2006

4.4.3   Diversity management within intercultural management

Diversity and multiculturalism

The first step towards an effective diversity management is embracing multiculturalism. The term may imply "culture", but it encompasses religion, language, ethnicity, nationality and race. (Song, 2010) Even though diversity and multiculturalism are interconnected, they are not interchangeable. In order to understand the differences between diversity and multiculturalism, the following two statements focus on their most important aspects:

> *"Diversity is who we are. It is quantitative. It is defined by 'otherness'." (National Association of Independent Schools, in web)*

> *"Multiculturalism is an evolving process. It is qualitative. It is the shift that occurs when we stop defining everyone by one cultural norm and move to an understanding of multiple norms." (ibid.)*

4.4.4   Theoretical approaches towards diversity management

Paradigms of diversity management

For the last few decades, managers believed that diversity automatically stands for discrimination. This assertion is wrong, both legally and morally. Today's managers are claiming a second notion, which stands for

> *"a more diverse workforce that will increase organizational effectiveness and bring greater access to new segments of the marketplace, and enhance productivity." (Thomas/Ely, 1996, p. 79)*

In short, they claim, diversity will be good for business.

Two perspectives have guided most diversity initiatives to date: The discrimination- and fairness paradigm and the access- and legitimacy paradigm. Thomas and Ely have identified a new, emerging approach to this management issue:

"The learning- and effectiveness-paradigm incorporates aspects of the two para-
digms but goes beyond them by concretely connecting diversity to approaches to
work". (ibid. p. 80)

Paradigm 1 – The discrimination-and-fairness paradigm

The perhaps most dominant way of understanding diversity is by the help of the discrimination-and-fairness paradigm. Leaders of organizations looking at diversity through this lens
usually focus on "equal opportunity, fair treatment, recruitment, and compliance with federal
Equal Employment Opportunity requirements. The paradigm's underlying logic can be expressed as follows:

"Prejudice has kept members of certain demographic groups out of organizations
such as ours. As a matter of fairness and to comply with federal mandates, we need to
work toward restructuring the makeup of our organization to let it more closely reflect
that of society. We manage processes that ensure that all our employees are treated
equally and with respect and that some are not given unfair advantage of others."
(ibid. p. 81)

Companies that operate with this philosophical orientation often institute mentoring and
career-development programs specifically for the women and people of color in their ranks
and train other employees to respect cultural differences.

With this paradigm, nevertheless, progress in diversity is measured by how well the company
achieves its recruitment goals, rather than by the degree to which conditions the company
allows employees to draw on their personal assets and perspectives to do their work more
effectively. You could say that the staff, gets diversified, but the work does not.

Organizations valuing this process of equal treatment of all employees are often companies
bureaucratic in structure, with control process in place for monitoring, measuring, and rewarding individual performance. Perhaps, the most extreme example is the United States
Army.

Paradigm 2 – The access-and-legitimacy paradigm

In the 1980s and 1990s, the new access-and-legitimacy paradigm was predicted on the acceptance and celebration of differences. The underlying motivation of this new paradigm can
be expressed this way:

"We are living in an increasingly multicultural country. And new ethnic groups are
quickly gaining consumer power. Our company needs a demographical more diverse
workforce to help us gain access to these differentiated segments. We need employees
with multilingual skills in order to understand and serve our customers better and to
gain legitimacy with them. Diversity isn't just fair; it makes business sense." (Thom-
as/Ely, 1996, p. 83)

Organizations using this paradigm, almost always operate in a business environment in
which there is increased diversity among costumers, clients or the labour pool.

"The access-and-legitimacy paradigm has its strengths. Its market-based motivation
and the potential for competitive advantage that it suggests are often qualities an en-
tire company can understand and therefore support." (ibid.)

The paradigm has therefore led to new professional and managerial opportunities for women and people of colour.

Paradigm 3 – The emerging paradigm: Connecting diversity to work perspectives

Organizations begin to recognize that employees make decisions and choices at work that draw upon their cultural background – choices made because of their identity-group affiliations.

Like the fairness paradigm, the emerging paradigm promotes equal opportunity for all individuals. Additionally, it also acknowledges cultural differences among people and recognizes the value in those differences.

Yet, this model for managing diversity lets the organization internalize differences among employees so that it learns and grows on the basis of them.

Discrimination is everyone's business
(Volvo Car Corporation)

The challenges of racism, discrimination and intolerance are obvious in our societies. This does not only mean suffering from individual perspective but also a missed opportunity for society to develop. From a business point of view diversity and non-discrimination are essential […]. Our commitment is based on the conviction that diversity is good and good for business. We believe that those customers who choose our products and services do so because they can identify with our values and purpose. In order to be able to expand our business and cater to the broad spectrum of customers our company must reflect diverse demands.

In: Volvo Car Corporation (Publishers), 2000, p. 2

The Four Layers of Diversity

Diversity can be distinguished in different characteristics: immutable characteristics (biological sex, age and race), variable or acquired characteristics (social status, education, religion and local membership) and organizational characteristics (hierarchy, region, experience).

The so-called "Four Layers of Diversity" – Model was described by Gardenswartz and Rowe and illustrates human diversity, which gets more and more important for organizations in every part of the world

> *"Managing Diversity means acknowledging and valuing the differences of race and gender in particular and moving toward integration." (Cross, 2000, p. 74)*

In this systematization of individual diversity, it is important to distinguish between the so-called personal immanent and the behaviour immanent diversity. This will help not to categorize the behavior of an individual based on personal immanent characteristics. Otherwise, such stigmatizations will reduce a person to a single attribute. (Koall, 2004, p. 4)

The model is divided into four layers. Beginning with the core of the modell, the "level of personality", "internal dimensions", "external dimensions" and, at the outer layer, the "organisational dimensions" can be seen.

The following figure illustrates a possibility of how to structure the different factors of diversity:

The dimension "personality" can be found in the middle of the model and includes all aspects of a person, which can be described as the "personal style". It is the most hidden dimension. The individual is not directly able to control the development of its personality; it is rather a subconscious process and as a result, truly unique.

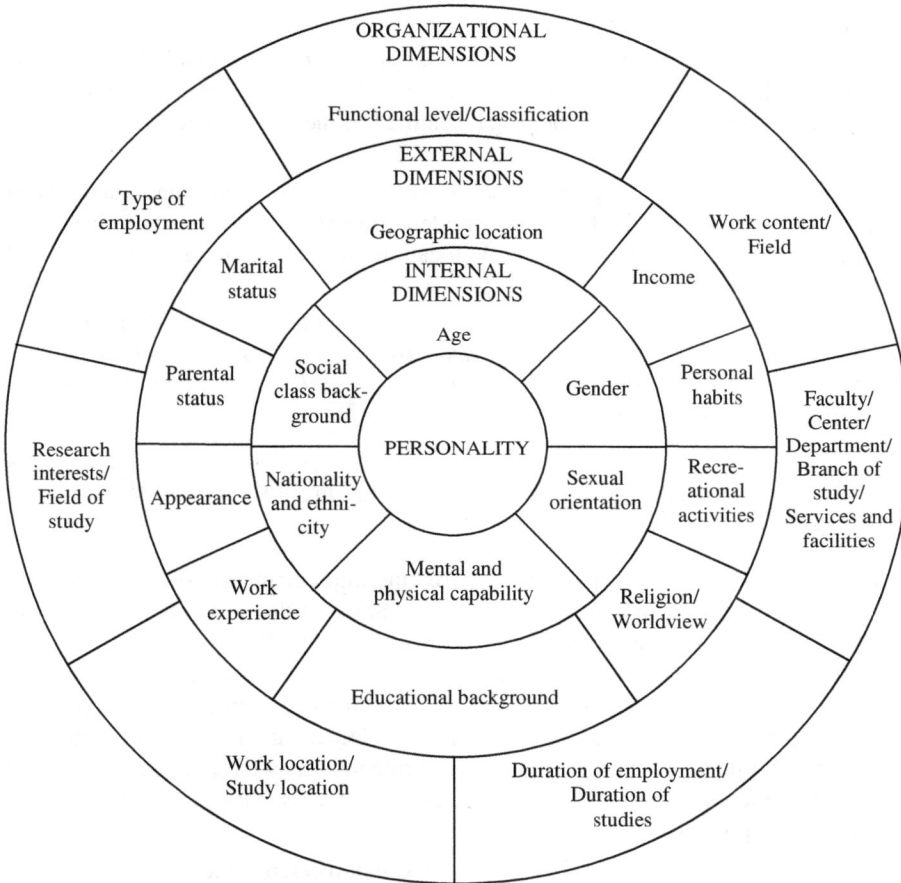

Fig. 4.2: The Four Dimensions of Diversity
Source: Based on Universität Wien, Diversity – 4 Dimensions of Diversity, in web

The following dimensions are relatively immutable for the individual person: age, gender, sexual orientation, mental and physical capability, nationality and ethnicity, and social background. These dimensions generate the core of the model, also known as the "internal dimensions". All of the previously named dimensions have a significant influence on our life. Such criteria are fixed from an individual's birth and represent the most obvious differences and similarities of people and result in the split-up into several small groups.

The third circle contains all "external dimensions", such as geographic location, income, personal habits, recreational habits, religion/worldview, educational background, work experience, appearance, parental status, and marital status. All these dimensions have one thing in common: their variableness, except for "religion" and "worldview".

They could also be counted to the "inner circle" because of two reasons:

> *"On the one hand 'Religion and Worldview' are not always free to choose, on the other hand there exists a juridical restraint on discrimination." (Universität Wien, in web)*

Thus, all these dimensions are directly linked to work-related decisions and behavior of the individual related to the factors marital status, residence or habit. Their influence on creating diversity is higher than the one of the organizational dimensions, but not incisively. (Workpapers Mitte Consult, 2004)

The outer circle contains the "organizational dimensions", such as functional level/classification, work content/field, faculty/centre/department/field of studyservices and facilities, duration of employment/study, work location, research interests, and type of employment.

> *"These dimensions are defined by the kind of affiliation inside of an organizations. It appears independent form the individual and, consequently, the impact on the diversity factor is not really far-reaching in comparison with the three inner layers, examind in the above." (Universität Wien, in web)*

4.4.5   The benefits, dangers and limitations of an active diversity management

Many managers share the opinion that efforts towards the implementation of diversity management can only be made in economically stable times. Some of them consider the growing interest in diversity and the discussions arising from it as a hype that has no decisive importance for their enterprise. (Furkel, 2008, p. 50) They often argue that diversity-activities are a luxury which their current situation does not allow them to indulge in. On the other hand, it is beyond question that equality of opportunities is legally and morally necessary and there is also a growing demand from customers, governmental as well as nongovernmental organization to bring the topic to a new level. Managers find themselves faced with a serious dilemma. (Krell, 1998, pp. 14f)

Having gained a deeper insight into the background and the different fields of diversity, it is time to ask: What makes it worthwhile from a manager's point-of-view to deal with the topic and which concrete arguments could drive an enterprise to actively start managing its workforce diversity?

Since a number of business scientists and other experts have already discussed this critical question in the course of the past two decades, those opinions on benefits and arguments in favour of implementing diversity-management-measures as well as weak points and limitations of the concept shall be briefly presented.

Assumed business-benefits of diversity management

It is beyond question that avoiding and working against discrimination corresponds to legal, moral and ethical standards. While this is the starting point of diversity management, it also has to be pointed out that diversity management is more than an anti-discrimination-measure. Already in 1996, Ely & Thomas pointed out that there was a second notion to the concept, which had lately also been recognized by managers. A diverse workforce, they believe, will increase organizational effectiveness. (Thomas/Ely, 1996, p. 79) As this is a rather spacious term, we shall have a closer look at which impacts of diversity are actually accountable for its beneficial effect.

In 1994, Kandola & Fullerton examined the interrelation between diversity management and organizational efficiency including the evidences for these relations. (Kandola/Fullerton, 1994, pp. 35ff) Their work was discussed and revised by Jung in 2003, who designed a scheme of proven, debatable and indirect benefits, which gives a profound overview of the majority of possible benefits analyzed within the scientific discussion. (Jung, 2003, p. 100)

Irrespectively of the degree of their evidence, the benefits of a successful diversity management will be categorized by using the following three arguments speaking in favor of the implementation of diversity management: (1) The Human-Resource-Argument, (2) The Marketing-Argument and (3) The Cost-Argument.

Tab. 4.2:   Benefits of diversity management
Source: Own translation according to Jung, 2003, p. 102

	Impact on efficiency	**Evidence**
Proven benefits	• increased choice of human resources • better personnel binding • cost-savings in the fields of recruiting, education and advanced training • reduction of fluctuation- and absent-time • organizational flexibility	• factual-analytical proof • empirical support by organizations' statements • empirical support debatable
Debatable benefits	• promotion of team-creativity and innovation • advancement of problem-solving and decision-finding • better understanding of customers' requirements • increase of selling-numbers to members of cultural minorities • enhancement of quality	• creativity, innovation and partly problem-solving-qualities are empirically supported; for other efficiency-variables, results are also converse • factual-analytical proof; no definite empirical data • factual-analytical proof; no sufficient empirical data
Indirect benefits	• satisfying work-environment • advancement of working morals and satisfaction • advancement of relationships between different groups of workers • increase in productivity • competitive advantage • advancement of public image	• partly analytically proved; empirical proof due to multi-factorial influence difficult, if not impossible

The Human-Resource-Argument

Human resources are the most important strategic factor for the success of a company. This holds true for the past and the present but especially for the near future. The percentage of the working population is increasing while the demographic change leads to a lack of new potential skilled employees in Western countries. (Aretz, 2006, p. 65; Mor Barak, 2005, pp. 57ff) Even in consideration of these two single facts, it would be more than unreasonable to focus on the "average" white, male employee, on which many monolithic companies still concentrate (Süß/Kleiner, 2007, p. 1935) and treat women, elderly people, ethnically different or disabled people as a marginal group. The recognition of the value of diversity plays an advantageous role in the fields of recruiting, employee-binding and employee-satisfaction. (Aretz, 2006, p. 65)

Regarding the diversity of a company's workforce, experts point out that diverse perspectives increase the probability of innovation – which is a decisive competitive factor in the modern, rapidly changing world. To say it in simple words: The more diverse views there are regarding a problem – this problem may concern organizational functions, procedures, products, strategies, operations or any other field - the greater the pool of proposed solutions to choose from. In addition, a diversity of perspectives among decision-makers can improve the quality of predictions made on future trends, environmental changes and company performance. Long-term strategies and visions of a company will hence be based on more solid ground. (Page, 2007, pp. 6–20; Thomas/Ely, 1996, pp. 7f, 12f; Ely/Thomas, 2001, p. 80)

As a conclusion, it can be said that a sensible diversity management program can contribute to an even better output by the company's workforce.

The Marketing-Argument

Following the access- and legitimacy paradigm, which values diversity management as a market-oriented strategic instrument of an enterprise, it can be said that diversity management allows access to a greater number of markets and customers. By recruiting a diverse workforce and managing its potentials effectively, a company will gain deeper insights into the needs and ways of thinking of their customers and will also have a greater ability to respond accordingly. This will increase the customer-closeness. (Seidel, 2006, pp. 244ff) Thinking of phenomena like Ethno-Marketing and Relationship Marketing – approaches towards marketing concentrating on the company's relationship and appearance towards the customer – it becomes obvious that the positioning of employees with specific identities in the corresponding positions will give access to niche markets. (Ely/Thomas, 2001, p. 80) An example for the German market are Turkish customer consultants operating for Volkswagen or Deutsche Bank. (Furkel, 2008, p. 30)

The more diverse the perspectives, ways of thinking and ideas are within a company, the better it will comprehend its groups of customers within a diverse market and can adapt their product and marketing instruments. (Shen et al., 2009, p. 236)

The advantages of diversity management are also reflected in product- and personnel-marketing. A successful diversity management ensures flexibility and adaptability considering the company's surroundings as well as an increased creativity and problem-solving-capability during the formulation of a marketing strategy. (Seidel, 2006, pp. 244ff)

Another important point is that to a certain extent, purchase decisions rely on the company's image, which is also constituted by its diversity-management-policy. Companies are often evaluated in accordance to their efforts for equality of opportunities for diversity groups. In markets with a clientele stressing ethical values and equality, a successful diversity policy and the related company-image present a competitive advantage. (Krell, 1998, pp. 14f; Kandola, 1995; Aretz, 2006, p. 65)

The Cost-Argument

Many laws include non-discrimination rules. The costs that occur because of a violation against these legal norms are not as high in Germany as in the USA, but can be the beginning of a long row of court trials. Costs due to discrimination can also be caused by the loss of motivation of affected employees as well as damages on the organization's image.

Due to the changing basic conditions, like globalization and the demographic change, diversity policies are gaining importance as a factor of competition. To achieve the expected positive effects, it is necessary for organizations to make certain activities and success visible. (Krell, 1998, pp. 14f) An effective diversity management will lower costs and increase returns in the long run. (Shen, 2009, p. 236)

An indicator for the financial effects of diversity management is the study carried out by the American magazine "DiversityInc." which proved that multicultural companies are more successful on the stock market than other companies without a diversity management program. (Furkel, 2008, p. 30)

Dangers, limitations and criticism

Aretz (2006) claims that until now, there has been no sufficient scientific proof for the efficiency-improving effects of diversity management. Furthermore, he points out that the degree up to which diversity-management-measures can have beneficial effects on the company performance greatly depends on the society, culture and the corresponding values within which the company is operating. Hence, diversity management is sensible to its context and the question should not be whether diversity management is beneficial for a company or not, but which conditions in its environment have to be fulfilled to make it successful (Aretz, 2006, p. 65)

A similar limitation is pointed out by Page, who refers to Ely & Thomas (2001, pp. 229ff) when claiming that if people do not believe in the value of diversity, diversity management is not likely to have a good outcome. Hence, it is a second challenge for those companies striving for the benefits of diversity management to make their employees believe in it. (Scott, 2007, pp. 6ff, Thomas/Ely, 1996, p. 7)

Concerning Scott's theories on organizational problem-solving, predictions and decision-finding, another restriction has to be made: The value diversity can display cannot easily be identified. The fact that an Asian woman who counts herself as a Hindu sits in the management of a company does not guarantee that she delivers the desired perspectives and heuristics to unleash the beneficial effects of diversity within the decision-finding-processes. (Page, 2007, pp. 6ff; Thomas/Ely, 1996, pp. 16f)

Thomas and Ely came to a similar result: To simply equate diversity with identity-group representation inhibits effectiveness. They point out that diversity has to go beyond increasing the number of different identity-groups on the payroll. (2001, p. 80)

The active recognition of diversity within a company's workforce may also have direct negative effects, which Seidel points out as the following: Cultural and linguistic differences may constrain communication among employees and difficulties in understanding the co-workers' points-of view may obstruct decision-finding processes and cause conflicts in the daily routine (Seidel, 2006, pp. 246ff). The biggest challenge of diversity management is hence communication, either as perceptual, cultural or language barrier:

> *"Ineffective communication of key objectives results in confusion, lack of teamwork, and low morale."*

In some cases, however, diversity management can be avoided on purpose by employees or employers who have a strong resistance to change. (Greenberg, 2004, in web)

What is more, a diverse workplace could be hard to establish without diversity-related policies which we will deal with in an upcoming chapter. Nevertheless, some employees in position of authority may be unwilling to adopt such policies and to implement them by delegating responsibility to a person or a department.

A potential threat, which was pointed out by Kirton, who interviewed managers about diversity management, is that

> *"being an advocate for diversity could be potentially damaging for mainstream management careers".*

Managers claimed that an active diversity management would damage their reputation and career. (Kirton, 2009, p. 172)

With regard to the direct effect of diversity on the company turnover, Leonard and Levine simply highlight the fact which has not changed in the past years and is unlikely to change in the near future:

> *"(...) diversity does not consistently predict high turnover."* (Leonard/Levine, 2006, p. 568)

India: Family amd Societal Values
(Zubko/Sahay)

Indian society is family oriented and collectivistic where emphasis is on harmony and conformity with established cultural norms, social values, and family traditions. Elders command deep respect and family is a priority. Traditionally, individuals who are self-oriented were viewed with distrust, although with the changing socioeconomic conditions and growing disposable income, young professional Indians have started to indulge in a culture of consumption. A long-term relationship is the centerpiece of core Indian values and is the coveted goal of everyone from newspaper vendors to business tycoons and industrial houses.

In: Inside the Indian Business Mind, 2011, p. 5

4.4.6   The drivers for implementing diversity management

After this insight into why it is beneficial for organizations to pay respect to diversity as a management topic, and knowing that good reasons are not enough to make people step into action, it will be interesting to analyze what drives organisations to integrate diversity management into their operational business reality.

It was primarily Pitts, Hicklin et al. who examined this question with the help of examples from public organisations in the USA in 2010. In addition, Süß & Kleiner examined the dissemination, design and drivers for diversity management in Germany in 2007.

"Any governance regime, from the local to the international, is embedded in a wider social, fiscal, and cultural context." (Lynn et al., 2001)

This quote from Lynn implies that organizations adapt to their surroundings, especially values of external society. A consistent relationship between management activities directed on the company's environment and organizational performance could be shown by various researches. (Goerdel, 2006, pp. 351ff, Meier/O'Toole, 2001, pp. 271ff)

Acting on the assumption that organisations develop diversity management programs as a response to opportunities and challenges in the internal and external environments, three main drivers of diversity management implementation can be defined: (1) environmental uncertainty, (2) environmental favourability and (3) institutional isomorphism. All of these forces have an influence on diversity management in different ways and in varying degrees. Companies or their managers might be motivated by more than one factor and the factors may change over time. (Pitts, 2010, pp. 867ff)

The practical implementation of diversity management

Corporations are quickly realizing their lack of diversity management is now negatively impacting their bottom line and they can no longer ignore it. The main challenge of managing diversity at any business is to

"create conditions that minimize its potential to be a performance barrier while maximizing its potential to enhance organizational performance". (Taylor, 2001, p. 4)

How diversity policies can be implemented within a company and what is included in an active diversity management shall be looked at in the following.

Implementing diversity management

In many cases, organizations which consider diversity management in their corporate strategy have introduced a special function in the company's organization which directly reports to the CEO. This shows the high importance of diversity for the company. Especially at the beginning of the implementation of diversity management measures, the special attention of the top management is of critical importance – later, diversity management may be included in other departments. In some companies, the implementation of diversity management starts with a diversity council, which is convened by the top management and acts parallely to the daily business. In later phases of the development, the council's agenda will then be integrated into the operative business.

Regarding the organization of the implementation of diversity – for which there are many possible ways – a recent model will be displayed in the following, which uses the top-down-approach and will additionally demonstrate concrete measures which account for an active diversity management.

Rosken's Top-Down-Approach

In her article from 2011, Rosken claims that it should be an aim of diversity management to assert the acceptance of diversity management even though the single employee might not feel any personal benefit from it in the beginning. This indicates an attainment of corporate goals beyond all social borders. Necessary pre-conditions for diversity management are a clear commitment and an undoubting initiative for diversity among the management and the employees. In addition, a positioning of diversity management within the management's agreement of objectives and within all operative, normative and strategic levels which affect the employees is also of great importance in this context.

Diversity can only work if all employees take responsibility and are willing to live the defined values in a vital diverse corporate culture. Diversity cannot be an order – it prospers on the participation of all members of the organisation.

PHASE	GOALS	MEASURES
Strategy Definiton Strategic level	• Development of an organizational-strategic diversity approach to use resources for solving complex problems • Creating a diversity-just culture inside the organization • Foundation of diversity rudiments in a set of values	• Convincement of the leadership level • Crossover from normative diversity rudiments to a strategic level and embedding these into the overall goals of an organization • Foundation of diversity inside the system of values to describe the self-perception of an organization • Decision and commitment for a wide transition of the organization
Diversity Concept Middle level	• Operative realization of strategic diversity rudiments • Establishment of the set of values in the position of employees	• Crossover of strategic diversity reflection on the operative level • Development of an integrated concept for the cultural change in the long run • Integration of diversity goals into plans and target agreements of every individual involved; measurement of those goals
Reali-zation Operational level	• Creating role models • To train diversity maturity	• Identification and training og diversity champions • Training of available employees • Identification and implementation of core competences • Recruitment of new, qualified staff • Adjustment of recruiting methods • Development of incentive systems
Continuous improvement		**Monitoring of strategic and normative shifts**

Fig. 4.3:   The phases, goals and measures of implementing diversity management
Source: Own translation of Rosken, 2009, p. 265

An implementation on different levels in order to slowly prepare the system for changes is of decisive importance. Rosken suggests a top-down-approach for the implementation of diversity management, as its success relies on persons with the necessary power to make basic decisions and to actively change procedures and communication. Nevertheless, there should also be measures including the entire workforce, for example with the help of a diversity-co-management.

The top-management has the special responsibility for securing the realization of diversity management on all levels. The executive management has the task to set pre-conditions on the operative levels – e.g. creating a diversity-friendly work-climate. On the employees' level, there are two perspectives which need to be considered: recruiting and selecting – here, diversity competence can be a decisive factor – and personnel development, e.g. diversity trainings could be offered. (Rosken, 2011, p. 33ff)

Measures of managing diversity

In 2005, a survey dealing with the dissemination and design of diversity management in Germany was carried out by Süß & Kleiner, two German economists. In order to develop a profound scientific questionnaire, they asked 17 experts from research practice, economic journalism and diversity associations to determine diversity management measures that could be applied by organizations. 13 central measures representing core activities for managing workforce diversity could be identified (Süß/Kleiner, 2007, p. 1941):

- Flexible working time agreements
- Mixed teams
- Determining the requirements for diversity management
- Mentoring programmes
- Integrating DM into corporate culture
- Consulting service for diversity groups
- Works council agreement
- Communicating diversity
- Diversity trainings
- Institutionalizing diversity management
- Diversity-oriented facilities
- Diversity-oriented design of the human resource management
- Evaluating diversity

The Diversity Manager

Having implemented diversity management as a fixed position in the company's organization, the question arises: What exactly do those people responsible for diversity management actually do? In the following, the core tasks of a diversity manager according to Jablonski (2006, pp. 197ff) will be outlined:

Definition of diversity criteria

Defining the criteria essential for a company's diversity actions is a central task of the diversity manager. Those could be gender, disability, age, ethnical origin or any other aspect discussed previously. It is the diversity manager's task to consult, inform and to create sensitivity for the diversity criteria among employees and management.

Support and control of diversity groupings

The diversity manager primarilyis a supporting task, as the overall power of decision still lies with the top management. He or she prepares diversity council meetings, moderates them and gives content-related advice.

The forming of such a council follows a top-down-approach. If on the other hand a bottom-up-approach is used, a group of employees gets together in a so-called resource group in order to discuss issues. Later, their findings and ideas will be presented to the management and can be introduced at different levels of the organization. Here, the diversity manager supports the resource-group's work and creates an environment, in which it is possible for those ideas to take root.

Diversity training

A central aspect of introducing diversity management is diversity training – as it is necessary to make employees aware of the usefulness, aspects and the value of diversity. The diversity manager has to arrange trainings and decide on the contents of those sessions, which should ideally have clear parallels to the operative work of the employees and correspond to their knowledge and interests. In addition, the diversity manager has to make sure that the training results will be evaluated.

Parameters and success measurement

For all managerial systems, the collection and interpretation of data as well as parameters for control and evaluation play an important role. The success and the future demand of diversity programmes can be assessed by comparing empiric data with benchmarks. Hence, the diversity manager has to develop a system which makes the collection and comparison of data possible.

Outer appearance

As diversity management is an instrument that influences the public opinion of the company, it is the diversity manager's task to promote and communicate diversity activities and achievements also to the public – including customers, the media, other companies, trade unions and other external parties. Constructs like corporate social responsibility and corporate citizenship have to be communicated in a way so that they account for diversity.

4.4.7   The future development of diversity management

Diversity management has originally developed from the traditional human resource management and now incorporates topics such as corporate strategy, corporate social responsibility, organizational design and effectiveness, corporate marketing and even sales. Thus, in order to be an effective Chief Diversity Officer (CDO), there is need of a more holistic management approach. This would be a prerequisite so that diversity is embedded within common threads that touch all functional areas (on an internal level) and the supply chain (on an external level). (Llopis, 2011, in web)

In order to foresee the future of diversity management and its role as a potential business growth factor, a comparison between the functions of a CIO (Chief Information Officer) and a CDO could be made. Information technology used to be perceived just as a cost factor and not as a business driver; however, this view has completely changed. The same might be said about diversity management in the future, because its main driver, demographic change, is gaining pace. It is expected that the responsibilities of CDOs will expand and probably shift in terms of their functional role – like it has already happened with CIOs.

> *"We believe that the participation and cultural diversity*
> *of our employees are the keys to our future success."*
>
> (IKEA)

4.5 The expert's view: Interview with Ryohei Arai

Ryohei Arai is the managing director of SAN consulting and marketing GmbH. He left Japan to come to Germany at the age of 27. In 1989 he co-founded the SAN GmbH in Germany. He shared his experiences about different values in Germany and Japan with the students Sophie Buliczak, Lisa Gottschalk Karol Kontny and Cornelia Strehlke.

Students: *Which experiences have you made in Germany?*

Arai: I like Germany a lot. You can live here your own life. In Japan it is more difficult because you must work between 12 to 14 hours. There is no time for something else. Japanese companies demand from their employees strong loyalty and the Japanese employees demand strong loyalty from the companies. Today it changed a little. In Japan I must spend all my time in the company.

Students: *You always hear, that Japanese are not telling her opinion not as directly as we are used to – on the business as wells as on the private level. Is it true?*

Arai: The young generation tells its opinion also directly. In my generation and older people it is different. I have in Germany the problem that I (a shy person) show my opinion not so obviously and that is why I get less help from others. In Germany you must show strong signals to get help from friends and business partners.

Students: *When Japanese business managers are together, what do they talk about?*

Arai: Europeans make businesses and just talk in the business time about this. If you get an invitation for dinner, the discussion is about interests and some private activities. In comparison Japanese managers behave differently. Their main focus in such a discussion is on issues that are related to the company, private things do not matter.

Students: *What would you say to a German who wants to make a deal with Japanese?*

Arai: First of all, you need a lot of patience doing business in Japan. In Germany, the final decisions are made by the top management. The decision making process in Japan differs in many ways. The initial idea created by the top management will be communicated over all levels and in all departments. Sometimes they try to consult people from outside the company getting their opinion. When I worked with German managers, the decision making process can become very short if there is a certain necessity. The Japanese process, they call it "Ringi Seido", requires extremely more time and the partners form all around the world are not very familiar with such a situation.

In. Buliczak/Gottschalk/Kontny/Strehlke, Written Assignment, 2012 (unpublished)

4.6   Case Study: A vision of a modern Arab world

In his old life in Cairo, Rami Galal knew his place and his fate: to become a maintenance man in a hotel, just like his father. But here, in glittering, manic Dubai, he is confronting the unsettling freedom to make his own choices. Here Galal, 24, drinks beer almost every night and considers a young Russian prostitute his girlfriend. But he also makes it to work every morning, not something he could say when he lived back in Egypt. Everything is up to him. Everything he eats, whether he goes to the mosque or a bar, where his friends are.

"I was more religious in Egypt," Galal said, taking a drag from yet another of his ever-burning Malboros. "It is moving too fast here. In Egypt there is more time. They have more control over you. It is hard here. I hope to stop drinking beer – I know it is wrong. In Egypt, people keep you in check. Here, no one keeps you in check." In Egypt, and across much of the Arab world, an Islamic revival is being driven by young people for whom faith and ritual are increasingly the cornerstone of identity. But that is not true in the ethnic mix that is Dubai, where 80 percent of the people are expatriates, with 200 nationalities.

This economically vital, socially freewheeling yet unmistakably Muslim state has had a transforming effect on young men. Religion has become more of a personal choice and Islam less of a common bond than national identity. Dubai is, in some ways, a vision of what the rest of the Arab world could become – if it offered comparable economic opportunity, insistence on following the law and tolerance for cultural diversity. In this environment, religion is not something young men turn to because it fills a void or because they are bowing to a collective demand.

That, in turn, creates an atmosphere that is open not only to those inclined to a less observant way of life, but also to those who are more religious. In Egypt, Jordan, Syria and Algeria, a man with a long beard is often treated as an Islamist – and sometimes denied work. "Here, I can practice my religion in a natural and free way because it is a Muslim country and I can also achieve my ambition at work," said Ahmed Kassab, 30, an electrical engineer from Zagazig in Egypt who wears a long dark beard and has a prayer mark on his forehead. "People here judge the person based on productivity more than what he looks like. It is different in Egypt, of course." No one can say for sure why Dubai has been spared the kind of religion-fueled extremism that has plagued other countries in the region. There are not even metal detectors at hotel and mall entrances, standard fare from Morocco to Saudi Arabia. Some speculate that Dubai is like Vienna in the Cold War – a playground for all sides. There is a robust state security system. But there is also a feeling that diversity, tolerance and opportunity help breed moderation. Dubai dazzles, but also confuses. It appears to offer a straight deal – work hard and make money. It is filled with inequities and exploitation. It is a land of rules: No smoking, no littering, no speeding, no drinking and driving.

"They should give you an introduction when you arrive", said Hamza Abu Zanad, 28, who moved to Dubai from Jordan about 18 months ago and works in real estate. "It is very distorting. I felt lost. There are fancy cars, but don't speed. You can have prostitutes, but don't get caught with a woman." Dubai offers a chance to lead a modern life in an Arab Islamic country. Abu Zanad raises his beer high, almost in a toast, and said he liked being able to walk through a mall and still hear the call to prayer.

Back in Cairo, Galal is reconnected with his family. He fasted for Ramadan, including giving up cigarettes during daylight hours. And he went out looking for his friends on the bustling streets of his neighborhood, which is the antithesis of Dubai. It is filled with people – men, women, children – all night long, shopping, chatting, smoking, enjoying the cold night, the warmth of the neighborhood and a common culture.

"My friends are all stuck at a certain limit. That's as far as they can go," Galal said after three weeks at home. "Nothing is new here. Nothing is happening. My friends feel like I changed. They say money changed me." Galal and a cousin went out for a night of fun the day before he was scheduled to return to Dubai. "I want to go back," he said."I was living better there. It is the simple things – sitting at the coffee shop, talking to people. Their mentality is different." He said he had broken off his engagement. Marriage in Egypt is usually a practical matter, a necessary step to adulthood, to independence. It is often arranged. A year in Dubai changed his view of marriage. "You are looking for someone to spend you whole future with," Galal said. "I want to go back and have fun. My future is there, in Dubai."

Slackman, M., A vision of a modern Arab world, in: International Herald Tribune, 23/09/2008, p. 1

Review and Discussion Questions:

1. Describe in your own words Galal's mixed feelings related to the place he comes from and the way he is living in Dubai!

2. Could you imagine that Dubai's policy of religious openness will become a role model for other Islamic countries? Explain your opinion!

3. What are the reasons for Galal to stay in Dubai?

5 Intercultural Competence

5.0 Statement of the problem

Negotiations in Japan

Thomas Schneider, a distinguished and successful employee in the export department of a medium-sized German pharmaceutical company, has just returned from a business trip to Japan. He is asked by his colleague Bernd Neumann, how the sales negotiations with the Japanese partners have gone.

Neumann: How did the negotiations in Kyoto proceed? Could you apply the Japanese skills from your last language course?

Schneider: *Things worked out well with the Japanese, but the negotiations didn't go as smoothly as I'd imagined. We had to make significant price concessions.*

Neumann: Did the Japanese drive such a hard bargain? That wasn't normally to be expected.

Schneider: *The case is this: After the usual introductory words, I informed Mr. Yoshida about our offered price and he reacted with a strange silence.*

Neumann: He didn't answer?

Schneider: *No, he sat there with a very serious facial expression. After a few seconds of silence, I thought that the offered price would not meet his expectations. Therefore, I started reducing the price. When he still didn't answer but just looked rather startled, I marked down the price even further, well, actually down to my absolute limit.*

Neumann: And what happened then?

Schneider: *After another short silence, Mr. Yoshida finally accepted our offer.*

Neumann: Well, at least we've got the contract. You should be pleased.

In: Rothlauf, J., Seminarunterlagen, 2011

Globalization caused an increase of ethnic, religious, and cultural heterogeneity in our societies as well as a rise in contacts between people of different cultural and social values accordingly. Hence, in the coming years, intercultural competence will be a necessity. Boecker and Jäger (2006) argue that

> *"(…) the ability to deal constructively on an interpersonal level with cultural diversity and the multitude of attitudes and values will not only become a key qualification required of business executives working in international settings, it will also be required generally of each individual as a key factor for ensuring that cultural diversity can be experienced positively and productively."*

5.1   Definition

Intercultural competence has been a term difficult to define and assess. Over the past thirty years, scientists have tried to define this concept, but there was no general agreement. The policy paper on intercultural competence by Deardorff (2006) addressed this issue and collected the personal definitions of intercultural competence and appropriate assessment methods from 23 top intercultural experts, especially from the USA.

The top-rated definition was one in which intercultural competence was defined as *"the ability to communicate effectively and appropriately in intercultural situations based on one's intercultural knowledge, skills and attitudes"*.

Following this definition Boecker and Jäger (2006, p. 5) expressed it like this: *"Intercultural competence is the ability to interact effectively and appropriately in intercultural situations, based on specific attitudes, intercultural knowledge, skills and reflection."*

Intercultural Competence
(Janet M. Bennett)

Cognitive
- Cultural self-awareness
- Culture-general knowledge
- Culture-specific knowledge
- Interaction analysis

Affective
- Curiosity
- Cognitive flexibility
- Motivation
- Openmindedness

Behavorial Skills
- Relationship building skills
- Behavorial skills: listening, problem solving
- Empathy
- Information gathering skills

In: Developing Intercultural Competence, AIEA Conference, 22/02/2011, p. 3

With respect to specific components of intercultural competence, the intercultural experts came to the conclusion that one component alone is not enough to ensure competence, for instance knowledge or the language by itself. 80 percent or more of the intercultural experts and administrators participating in this study were able to reach consensus on 22 essential elements of intercultural competence. These elements are a very important finding of this study, since there has previously been no agreement among intercultural experts as to what constitutes intercultural competence (Boecker/Jäger, 2006, pp. 13f):

- *"Understanding others' world views*
- *Cultural self-awareness*
- *Adaptability / adjustment to new cultural environment*
- *Skills to listen and observe*
- *General openness to intercultural learning and to people from other cultures*
- *Ability to adapt to varying intercultural communication and learning styles*
- *Flexibility*
- *Skills to analyze, interpret & relate*
- *Tolerating and engaging ambiguity*
- *Deep knowledge and understanding of culture (one's own and others')*
- *Respect for other cultures*
- *Cross-cultural empathy*
- *Understanding the value of cultural diversity*
- *Understanding of role and impact of culture and the impact of situational, social, and historical contexts involved*
- *Cognitive flexibility – ability to switch frames*
- *Sociolinguistic competence (awareness of relation between language and meaning in societal context)*
- *Mindfulness*
- *Withholding judgment*
- *Curiosity and discovery*
- *Learning through interaction*
- *Ethno-relative view*
- *Culture-specific knowledge/understanding host"*

Only the element *"the understanding of others' world views"* received a 100-percent agreement. This is in line with other literature which regards the respect for other world views as essential to crucial for intercultural competence. In this context, "world views" are defined as *"basic perceptions and understandings of the world"* (ibid., p. 15). Looking at the findings of the study, three clusters present themselves as particularly compelling. (ibid., pp. 15ff)

---

30 TIPS ON HOW TO LEARN ACROSS CULTURES (16–18)
(Andre Laurent)

16. Listen, observe and try to understand before judging and evaluating.

17. Accept the fact that your conception of time may not be shared. You can only win through understanding and negotiating.

18. Be patient. Accept the fact that it may take a much longer time to get results.

In: SIETAR (Hrsg.), Keynote-Speech, Kongress 2000, Ludwigshafen

---

"Culture is like gravity,
you only experience it, when you jump two meters in the air."

(Fons Tromenaars)

5.1.1   Cluster 1: Attitude

Attitude is a highly important basis and specifically openness, respect (valuing all cultures), curiosity and discovery (tolerating ambiguity) are viewed as fundamental to intercultural competence. As "*after all the books have been read and the skills learned and practiced, the cross-cultural effectiveness of each of us will vary. And it will vary more by what we bring to the learning than by what we have learned.*" (Lynch/Hanson, 1998, p. 510).

A question of attitude
(Westcombe, J./Boye, S.)

If you really want to develop your intercultural skills, you need to start by looking at yourself and especially at your own attitudes.

Tick the following statements that you think apply to you.
□ I love finding out about other cultures, and I have friends from different countries.
□ I enjoy learning other languages.
□ I'm a good listener.
□ I observe what is going on around me and try to understand it in a neutral way.
□ I don't panic when I don't understand what's going on.
□ I'm not afraid to ask for help.
□ I can look at my own actions and reactions and reflect on how I behave.

These statements show some important intercultural skills – the qualities of curiosity, openness and the ability to deal with difference and uncertainty. If you can answer most of them with "yes", then you are on your way to being interculturally competent – although you might still want to get some feedback about how others see you. And remember: even if you develop your intercultural skills in theory, it is still difficult to overcome your own cultural comfort zone and need to try skills out that you feel this push and pull most strongly.

In: Spotlight, 5/2012, p. 32

5.1.2   Cluster 2: Knowledge and skills

The required knowledge includes cultural self-awareness as a prerequisite for beginning to understand other cultures – as well as a deep understanding and knowledge of other cultures; in particular of others' world views.

The "skills" are not only cross-cultural skills but rather general skills necessary to acquire and process knowledge about one's own and other cultures, e.g. listening and observing and cognitive skills like analyzing and evaluating. Thus, the development of intercultural competence goes along with intellectual competencies (Yershova/DeJeagbere/Mestenhauser, 2000).

The following Fig. 5.1 shows a list of competencies which are important when working for international organizations.

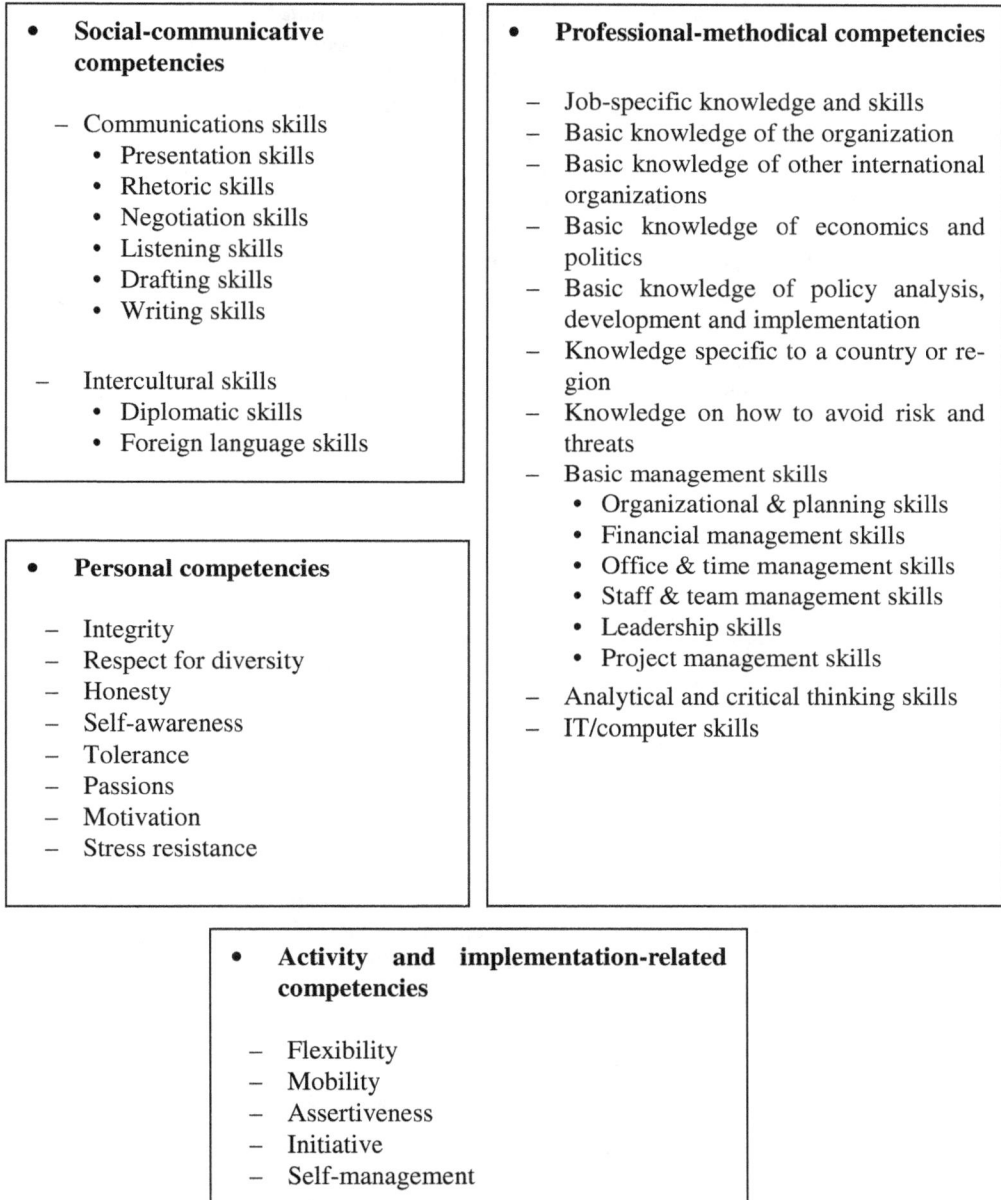

- **Social-communicative competencies**

  - Communications skills
    - Presentation skills
    - Rhetoric skills
    - Negotiation skills
    - Listening skills
    - Drafting skills
    - Writing skills

  - Intercultural skills
    - Diplomatic skills
    - Foreign language skills

- **Personal competencies**

  - Integrity
  - Respect for diversity
  - Honesty
  - Self-awareness
  - Tolerance
  - Passions
  - Motivation
  - Stress resistance

- **Professional-methodical competencies**

  - Job-specific knowledge and skills
  - Basic knowledge of the organization
  - Basic knowledge of other international organizations
  - Basic knowledge of economics and politics
  - Basic knowledge of policy analysis, development and implementation
  - Knowledge specific to a country or region
  - Knowledge on how to avoid risk and threats
  - Basic management skills
    - Organizational & planning skills
    - Financial management skills
    - Office & time management skills
    - Staff & team management skills
    - Leadership skills
    - Project management skills
  - Analytical and critical thinking skills
  - IT/computer skills

- **Activity and implementation-related competencies**

  - Flexibility
  - Mobility
  - Assertiveness
  - Initiative
  - Self-management

Fig. 5.1:   Important competencies for international organizations
Source: PROFIO-Forschungsteam

5.1.3   Cluster 3: Internal and external outcomes

Finally, the remaining elements were classified as desired internal and external outcomes of intercultural competence. The former include *"the elements of adaptability, flexibility, empathy and in ultimately adopting an ethno-relative view"* (Boecker/Jäger, 2006, p. 16). This view refers to being comfortable with many sets of standards and customs and to having an ability to adapt behavior and judgments to a variety of interpersonal settings (Bennet, 1998, p. 26). One's own cultural, religious or ethnocentric world view is not seen as absolute, but is reflected upon and an ethno-relative view is adopted (Boecker/Jäger, 2006, p. 9). The ethno-relative view is the ultimate stage of Bennet's "Developmental Model of Intercultural Sensitivity" (ibid.) describing the development of the increasing ability to interpret and evaluate behavior from different intercultural perspectives. New elements can then be accepted emotionally and rejection or fear of the unknown reduced and this is the prerequisite for developing empathy.

Those internal outcomes result an internal shift in the personal frame of reference, which, can boost the external and consequently the observable outcomes of intercultural competence.

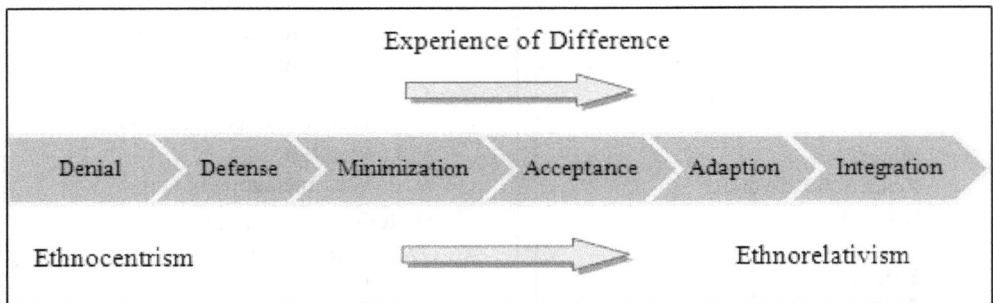

Fig. 5.2:   Development of intercultural sensitivity
Source: Own graph based on Bennet, 1998, p.26

The external outcomes can be described as *"behaving and communicating appropriately and effectively in intercultural situations"*, whereby "appropriateness" is defined as the avoidance of violating valued key "cultural" rules and "effectiveness" as the achievement of objectives (Spitzberg, 1989, p. 242).

---

30 TIPS ON HOW TO LEARN ACROSS CULTURES (19)
(Andre Laurent)

19. If you like to make jokes, watch out for those that do not fly so well across cultures. Although, humor can sometimes be an effective lever in cross-cultural situations, it is also one of the most culturally sensitive aspects of social life.

In: SIETAR (Hrsg.), Keynote-Speech, Kongress 2000, Ludwigshafen

Deardorff (2006, p. 17) elaborated two graphic representations depicting these clusters: the pyramid model and the process model.

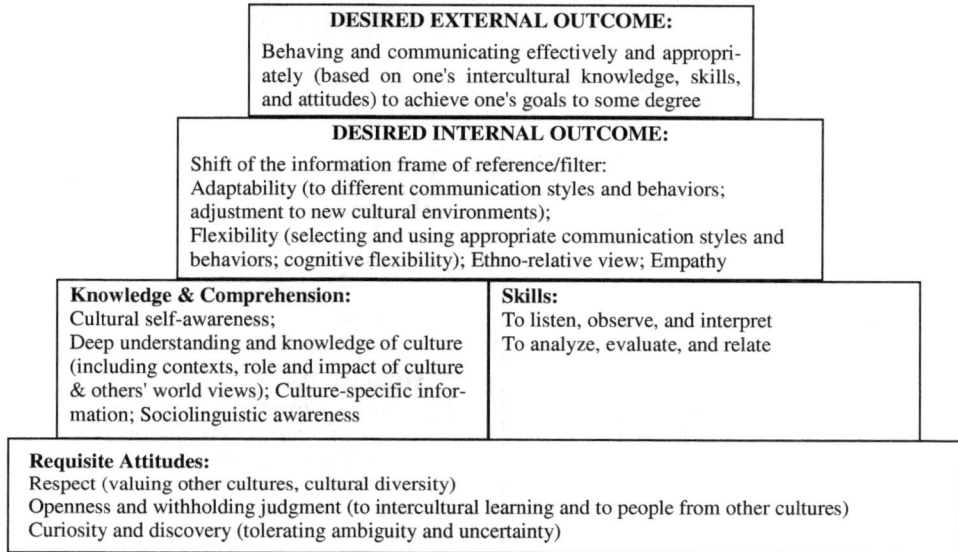

DESIRED EXTERNAL OUTCOME:
Behaving and communicating effectively and appropriately (based on one's intercultural knowledge, skills, and attitudes) to achieve one's goals to some degree

DESIRED INTERNAL OUTCOME:
Shift of the information frame of reference/filter: Adaptability (to different communication styles and behaviors; adjustment to new cultural environments); Flexibility (selecting and using appropriate communication styles and behaviors; cognitive flexibility); Ethno-relative view; Empathy

Knowledge & Comprehension:	**Skills:**
Cultural self-awareness; Deep understanding and knowledge of culture (including contexts, role and impact of culture & others' world views); Culture-specific information; Sociolinguistic awareness	To listen, observe, and interpret To analyze, evaluate, and relate

Requisite Attitudes:
Respect (valuing other cultures, cultural diversity) Openness and withholding judgment (to intercultural learning and to people from other cultures) Curiosity and discovery (tolerating ambiguity and uncertainty)

Fig. 5.3:   Pyramid model of intercultural competence
Source: Deardorff, 2006, p. 17

Given attitudes of openness, curiosity, and respect, one can then gain the requisite knowledge and skills that will lead to the desired internal and external outcomes. Boecker and Jäger (2006, p. 16) opine that this model reflects a more linear way of thinking and may be construed as somewhat simplistic, thus not illustrating the complexity of the construct. Thus, they promote the process model, since ongoing process orientation is essential, this means being aware of the learning that takes place at each point and the necessary process skills that are needed for acquisition of intercultural competence.

---

30 TIPS ON HOW TO LEARN ACROSS CULTURES (20)
(Andre Laurent)

20. One of the problems across cultures is that we naturally tend to interpret and evaluate behavior on the basis of our own culture. We apply our standards where they may not apply. This leads to misunderstanding. Behavior does not talk for itself. Trusting behavior per se can be highly confusing. What matters is the actual meaning of behavior which is embedded in different values across different cultures.

In: SIETAR (Hrsg.), Keynote-Speech, Kongress 2000, Ludwigshafen

---

This process model of intercultural competence also depicts the movement and process orientation that occurs between the different elements. For instance, this process model displays possible movement from the personal level to the interpersonal level (intercultural interaction). It shows that it is possible for one to go from attitudes or skills (knowledge) directly to the external outcome, but the appropriateness and effectiveness of the outcome may not be nearly as strong as when the entire cycle is completed and begins again. To them, this process model demonstrates the ongoing complexity of intercultural competence development.

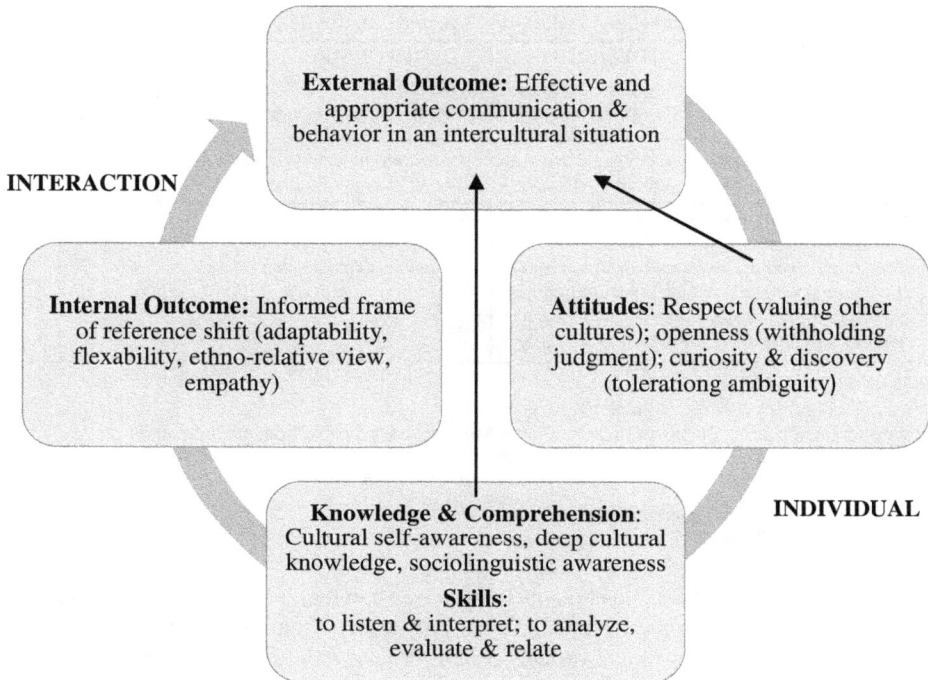

Fig. 5.4:   Process model of intercultural competence
Source: Own graph based on Deardorff, 2006, p. 18

Boecker and Jäger (2006, p. 6) opine that intercultural competence is neither a static state nor the direct result of one discrete learning experience. Language ability and explicit learnable knowledge of cultural characteristics alone do not suffice for intercultural competence, nor by visiting a foreign country (Gibson/Tang, 2004, p. 238). "[I]*ndividuals must learn and master the ability to deal with ongoing processes*", since they understand also "*culture as a dynamic flow and ongoing process of negotiation between norms, values and lifestyles*" (ibid.). The acquisition of intercultural competence is a continual, dynamic process. Boecker and Jäger (ibid.) describe this process like a movement through "*diverse dimensions while developing and enriching itself in an upward spiral*".

Boecker and Jäger (2006, p. 10) argue that

> "*[w]ith its focus on communication-related skills and a process-oriented definition of culture, the intercultural competence learning spiral presented here reflects a Western perspective*",

due to the fact that in overall research on the topic of intercultural competence seems to reflect theories of Anglo-Saxon orientation. Therefore they assume that the inclusion of non-

Western perspectives, in particular Asian perspectives, would lead to new definitions of intercultural competence, because indirect forms of communication and group-related background attitudes influence the analysis of inter- and intra-social interactions in Asia much more extensively than in the West.

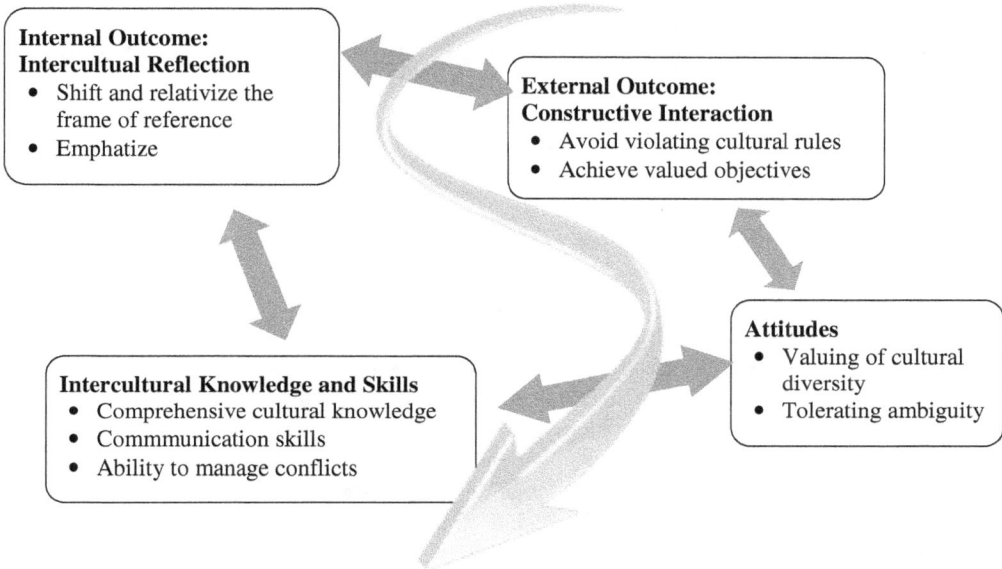

Internal Outcome:
Intercultual Reflection
- Shift and relativize the frame of reference
- Emphatize

External Outcome:
Constructive Interaction
- Avoid violating cultural rules
- Achieve valued objectives

Intercultural Knowledge and Skills
- Comprehensive cultural knowledge
- Commmunication skills
- Ability to manage conflicts

Attitudes
- Valuing of cultural diversity
- Tolerating ambiguity

Fig. 5.5:   The Intercultural Competence Spiral
Source: Based on Boecker/Jäger, 2006, p. 7

5.2   Relevance of intercultural competence

Intercultural competence concerning business life is important for a variety of employments (Gibson/Tang, 2004, pp. 1–2):

- Employees working in the parental company, but collaborating with colleagues from different countries
- Managers in the parental company trying to integrate foreign employees
- Expatriates who take over manager responsibilities abroad
- Technical specialists travelling abroad for their assignments
- Project managers leading international projects
- Multicultural team work
- Purchasing agents who buy globally
- Marketing and sales manager elaborating and implementing international marketing and sales concepts
- Managers who establish global business strategies

Exercise concerning the topic of "intercultural competence"

Born in Germany: Taking a close look at the German culture
Please answer the following questions by writing down keywords:

- Three German heroes/heroines
- Three important basic rules/principles Germans have to observe to be accepted by the society
- Three popular conversational topics of Germans
- Three to five characteristics of German women
- Three to five characteristics of German men
- What do Germans want to reach in life?
- What do Germans expect from their government?
- What do Germans expect from their employer?
- What do Germans expect from their children?
- What do Germans expect from their neighbors?
- What do Germans expect from foreigners and other minority groups?
- Which are the most important leisure-time activities in Germany?
- What does "friendship" mean to Germans?
- How does a German react when someone is successful?
- How does a German react when someone makes a mistake?
- Name a German way of behaving which is considered as a repulsive act.
- This exercise can be applied to other cultures as well!

5.3   Intercultural competence in the framework of the 7-S-Model

Peters/Waterman (1982) called it "productivity through people", when they were asked about the fundamental criteria for successful companies. In the framework of culture-comparative management research and in cooperation with Pascale/Athos (1981), they have developed the so-called "7-S-Model", which creates a framework for systematization and which can also be linked to the development of intercultural competence.

The 7-S-Model distinguishes between "hard" and "soft" elements. While the formal organizational "structure", the "systems" (in the sense of "business systems") and the corporate "strategy" represent the "hard" variables, the terms (managerial) "staff", "skills", "style" and subordinate goals ("shared values") are referred to as "soft" elements (Heinen, 1997, p. 12). How they fit into the intercultural framework shall be briefly described on the following pages.

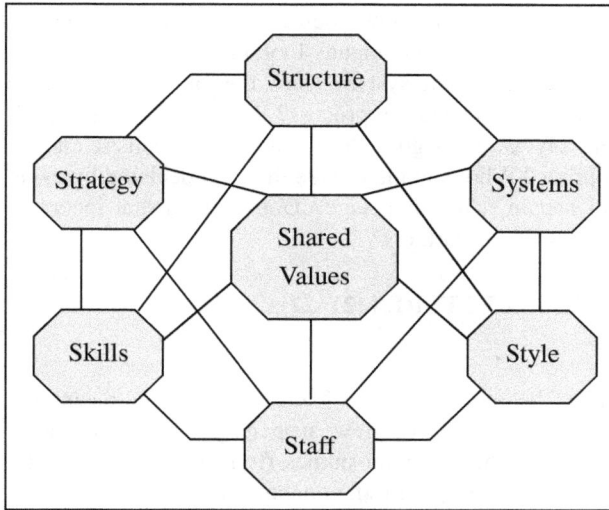

Fig. 5.6:   The 7-S-Model
Source: Peters/ Waterman, 1982, p. 10

The importance of intercultural knowledge for the future
(Annette Ulrich)

Everything we do across national and cultural borders, or within diverse societies, needs to take cultural differences into account. Intercultural specialists are beginning to move into strategic decision making and marketing in large companies: the perception of companies, products, and marketing approaches can differ tremendously across cultures. A wide variety of management strategies, such as recruiting procedures, need to be adapted when operating in a different country. The possibilities of applying intercultural knowledge in business are vast, and go far beyond the traditional area of expatriate support. While international business has played a key role in bringing intercultural concepts into use, other fields have been slower to put them into practice. Yet public administration in diverse societies and international relations too, will increasingly need to use intercultural knowledge.

In: BSN, Nr. 16, 2004, p. 3

5.3.1   The "hard" elements of the 7-S-Model

- **"Strategy"** is understood as the plan or course of action in order to reach certain goals with the given means. Questions which have to be raised in this intercultural context are: In which foreign markets, respectively at which locations do we want to or have to be present? Do we have a quantitative and qualitative potential analysis of all employees worldwide? Do we have support plans for all those activities?
- **"Structures"** ask for the relevant structures for the internationalization process. Do we want a centralized or a decentralized structure of our organization? Should organization-

al forms take local requirements into account and how does an organizational structure and process organization of a worldwide operating company look like?

- **"Systems"** deal with controlling and the reporting system. Here, the following questions arise: Do our systems support the internationalization process? Which information policy is currently applied in our company? Are our guidelines everywhere realistic and effective? Are they culturally appropriate? Who is going to take the final decision by using which managerial leadership tool and in which language? Does our current incentive program reflect the intercultural needs of our partners?

---

30 TIPS ON HOW TO LEARN ACROSS CULTURES (21–22)
(Andre Laurent)

21. When you encounter some "strange" behavior that looks bizarre, ineffective, meaningless, crazy or even stupid from your own point of view, suspend your judgment and make every effort to understand where this behavior comes from, what it means. If you work hard enough at this, you may end up with the conclusion that this behavior makes a great deal of sense. You may even discover that you can learn something from it.

22. Learning across cultures can only occur when differences are not only understood but truly appreciated. Appreciation feeds the motivation to learn. Lots of people are aware of cultural differences. Some people understand. Few people really appreciate. Positive appreciation of cultural differences is a requirement for effective collaboration.

In: SIETAR (Hrsg.), Keynote-Speech, Kongress 2000, Ludwigshafen

---

5.3.2   The "soft" elements of the 7-S-Model

Especially the success of Japanese companies in the 1980s with a special focus on the so-called "soft" elements – in opposition to an overemphasis on the "hard" factors in the Western world – has led to a paradigm change among companies.

- In the intercultural context, this means that there are questions connected e.g. with the element of **"style"** referring to the leadership style and all associated tasks a manager has to fulfill. How does the communication behavior look like, how is the climate in a post-merger situation or how are German staff members treated, trained, supported or promoted for an international assignment. Which role do our international managers play in this context? Is our management philosophy also unrestrictedly effective abroad and how does a manager see him-/ herself in this context?
- The element **"staff"** especially deals with the company's employees. Which employees are involved in the internationalization process, which nationalities do they represent, where do they work and which qualifications do they have? What do we know about the potential of our employees? Do we have all the necessary information related to their knowledge, skills, international experiences and so on? Do we have a policy that enables them to promote their career even as far as top positions in our company are concerned, regardless where they come from?

- In an international setting, the element "skills" with a specific focus on intercultural competences is the decisive prerequisite for success and is in the heart of any internationalization strategy. Questions like the following ones determine if we are internationally competitive or not: Do our employees have these skills in order to act efficiently and effectively on an international level? Which are these intercultural skills and how can we adequately adapt them, before we send our employees abroad? Are the same skills needed everywhere and who is able to identify them at an early stage?

- **"Shared values"** reflect the guiding values of any company and are expressed in the corporate culture. Questions concerning technology and quality, reliability, corporate ethics, environmental sustainability as well as the company's visions are connected to that. With regard to the internationalization strategy, questions like the role and importance of the internationalization strategy should be a vital part in the mission statement. Moreover, a holistic approach to the values includes principles that underline how we act as a company. What are our internal and external structures? How does our social commitment look like? How is the public perception of all our activities and is the image we have created in line with our values? Even the role model of the behavior of our managers must not be neglected in this context.

Chinese and Germans see time and quality in very different ways
(Robert Gibson interviewed Veronika Rolle, an intercultural development specialist)

Gibson: *What are the main problems the Germans have when working with the Chinese?*

Rolle: It depends on the kind of project. Project managers are confronted with different attitudes to project management. Chinese and Germans see quality and time in very different ways. German companies tend to be driven by quality, seeing it as an essential part of success. The Chinese are educated to believe that flexibility and meeting the needs of the consumer are paramount. They find it hard to understand why Germans spend so much time and money on producing 100 per cent quality. Why make a car with a perfect finish that will get scratched soon after it's on the road? The irony is that Chinese are attracted to German products precisely because of their reputation for high quality.

In: Business Spotlight, Nr. 4/2001, p. 35

"Culture makes people understand each other better.
And if they understand each other better in their soul,
it is easier to overcome the economic and political barriers.
But first they have to understand that their neighbour is,
in the end, just like them, with the same problems, the same questions."

(Paulo Coelho)

5.4   WWW – a selection of intercultural sites

If you want to concentrate even more on intercultural issues, you should take a look at the following websites:

- **Journal of Intercultural Studies, Monash University, Australia**
  www.tandf.co.uk/journals/carfax/07256868.html
- **(Journal of) Intercultural Education, Netherlands**
  www.tandf.co.uk/journals/carfax/14675986.html
- **Centre for Intercultural Studies, Austria**
  www.cis.or.at
- **Nordic Network for Intercultural Communication**
  http://sskkii.gu.se/nic/
- **Centre for Intercultural Communication**
  www.sik.no
- **Centre for Intercultural Studies, Dept of Anthropology, University of New Mexico (Alfonso Ortiz Center for Intercultural Studies)**
  www.unm.edu/~ortizctr/programs.html
- **School of Applied Language Intercultural Studies, Dublin City University**
  www.dcu.ie/SALIS
- **Intercultural Studies: Scholarly Review of the International Association of Intercultural Studies (IAIS)**
  www.intercultural-studies.org
- **Intercultural Communication Institute, Portland, Oregon, USA**
  www.intercultural.org
- **UK Unesco**
  www.unesco.org.uk
- **Cultnet**
  www.cultnet.english.arts.tu.ac.th
- **Culture Source**
  www.culture-source.de
- **Guardian quizzes on popular culture**
  www.guardian.co.uk/quizzes/
- **University of Minnesota, Center for Advanced Research on Language Acquisition (CARLA)**
  www.carla.umn.edu
- **Society for Intercultural Education, Training and Research (SIETAR) sites:**
  - **Sietar Austria**
    www.sietar.at
  - **Sietar Europe**
    www.sietareu.org
  - **Sietar France**
    www.sietar-france.org
  - **Sietar Germany**
    www.sietar-deutschland.de
  - **Global Network**
    www.sietar.org

- **Sietar UK**
  www.sietar.org.uk
- **Sietar USA**
  www.sietarusa.org
- **Young Sietar**
  www.youngsietar.org

- **Official website of the European Union**
  www.europa.eu
- **Eurodesk**
  www.eurodesk.org
- **Innovation across cultures, Cordis (archived)**
  www.cordis.lu/tvp/src/culture3.htm
- **Delta Intercultural Academy, Konstanz**
  www.dialogin.com
- **European Youth Training**
  www.europeanyouthtraining.com

5.5   The experts' view

5.5.1   Interview with Abdulaziz Al-Mikhlafi

Extract from an interview conducted by the TÜV SÜD Journal with Abdulaziz Al-Mikhlafi, General Secretary of the Ghorfa – Arab-German Chamber of Industry & Commerce since 2000.

TÜV SÜD: *To what extent are German-Arab business relationships characterized by the different cultures?*

Al-Mikhlafi: German-Arab business relationships are fundamentally very good. Of course, there are cultural aspects that must be taken into consideration when you develop new business. But you can learn about such practices in such places as seminars on intercultural communication.

TÜV SÜD: *Can you describe the most important difference?*

Al-Mikhlafi: One special feature is that you do not just sit down with Arab business people and talk about business. That is almost doomed to fail. The Arab culture is based on personal relationships. This means that a personal relationship has to be established first. Business only comes afterward.

TÜV SÜD: *Is etiquette more important than hard facts?*

Al-Mikhlafi: Of course not. But business is also done at dinner or through recommendations. But this does not mean that business is not conducted in a professional manner. In the end, it is just like everywhere else in the world: personal contacts and local presence are the critical factors behind success. In the Arab world, maybe even a little more.

TÜV SÜD: *What is the biggest mistake a foreign investor can make?*

Al-Mikhlafi: That would be to give up too quickly. At Ghorfa, our advice is: If you have selected this region as a target market, you should have patience. Invest in personal contacts. A mid-sized German company generally wants to see results after the second or third on-site meeting. But patience and long-range thinking pay off in the Arab world: For instance, a business partner from Saudi Arabia views his company not simply as an import-export operation. He views his business partner as a friend with whom he also does business

TÜV SÜD: *How important is Germany as a business partner for the Arab world?*

Al-Mikhlafi: Germany always assumes one of the leading positions in all Arab countries. "Made in Germany" is in real demand, particularly in flourishing economies seeking good quality and good services.

In: TÜV SÜD Journal, 2nd quarter 2011, p. 29

5.5.2   Interview with Peter Wollmann

Peter Wollmann, the executive vice president, is responsible for planning and controlling corporate strategy within Deutscher Herold, the insurance arm of Deutsche Bank. His job requires him to chair and participate in international meetings. Bob Dignen spoke to him.

Dignen: *What kind of chairman are you?*

Wollmann: I try to be very open and friendly and to develop an approach that suits the situation. The main thing is to get the participants committed to the objective and the procedure. But I'm also very German in that I am very strict with the timing and the agenda of the meeting. I don't allow digression. In fact, I'm famous for finishing meetings ahead of schedule.

Dignen: *What are the main challenges for you when speaking English at meetings?*

Wollmann: First and foremost, it's speaking fluently. I often find I don't have the vocabulary to say what I would say in German. I get round this by writing down key points or statements. I also find it difficult to be as precise and concise as I would be in German and have to go round and round a subject until I've explained it, rather than finding the right word straight away. Understanding native speakers who speak quickly, or certain non-native accents, is also a challenge. To deal with this, I always ensure that there is someone producing a written note of the meeting on a white board so that everyone, including myself, understands the decisions, I also ask a lot of clarification questions to make sure that I understand.

Dignen: *Is there a specific way of conducting meetings in German business culture?*

Wollmann: This depends a lot on what you mean by "culture". My first response would be to say that departmental culture has an enormous impact on a meeting and how I have to handle people. Working with IT or technical experts is very different from working with more "creative" marketing people.

But in terms of national culture, one interesting difference between the British and the Germans is that German chairpersons are far more technically oriented and will spend much more time discussing technical details. In Britain, such details are left to engineers. Also, as I said earlier, Germans are very strict with time and agenda meeting and tend to be less socially oriented, especially at the beginnings of meetings. I notice that southern Europeans will invest a lot of time in developing rapport and in relationship-building before getting down to business. It can cause real friction when we Germans arrive and want to jump straight into the agenda. Another important difference is that Germans are more direct. Negative comments or disagreement are often communicated hammer-style. People from other nations, Austrians in particular, are far more charming in their disagreement. Finally, on a more positive note, I find that Germans are less hierarchical than other cultures, with staff members free to contribute their expertise within meetings.

In: Dignen, B., Business Spotlight, Nr. 4/2001, p. 77

5.6   Case Study: Why did Walmart leave Germany?

Walmart can boast that it has more than 8,500 stores in 15 countries, under 55 different names, that it's the largest private employer in the United States, the largest in Mexico (as Walmex), and the third largest in Canada. In fact, it's the biggest private employer in the whole world. It has 108 stores in China alone, and operates another 100 Chinese outlets under the name of Trust-Mart.

Still, for all of Walmart's conspicuous success, the retailing giant, after having set up shop in Germany in 1997, was forced to withdraw from the country in 2006, abandoning Germany's lucrative $370 billion retail market. Even though this happened five years ago, the German debacle still reverberates. It's still being discussed. After all, as anyone who's been paying attention can tell you, Walmart rarely fails in these endeavors.

Because America and Europe share similar cultural and political antecedents, one might naturally assume that an American enterprise would have a better chance of succeeding in Europe than in Asia. But the German smackdown proved that's not always the case. Indeed, while the nominal Communist regime of the People's Republic of China embraced Walmart's corporate philosophy, the Germans rejected it.

Though no one can say precisely why the venture failed, there's been no shortage of explanations. One is that Germany was too "green" for a slash-and-burn outfit like Walmart, with its plastic bags and plastic junk. Another is that Walmart couldn't hack the pro-labor union culture of Germany. Another is that Germany is anti-American when it comes to name-brand retailers (even though Dunkin' Donuts and Starbucks are popular there). Another is that German consumers prefer small neighborhood stores rather than impersonal chain (even though Aldi, a discount supermarket chain, is successful).

While there is probably some validity to all of these explanations, three additional cross-cultural idiosyncrasies have been identified as determining factors.

One issue was the chanting. Walmart employees are required to start their shifts by engaging in group chants and stretching exercises, a practice intended to build morale and instill loyalty. Fiendish as it sounds, Walmart employees are required to stand in formation and chant, "WALMART! WALMART! WALMART!" while performing synchronized group calisthenics.

Unfortunately, this form of corporate boosterism didn't go over particularly well with the Germans. Maybe they found it embarrassing or silly; maybe they found it too regimented. Or maybe they found this oddly aggressive, mindless and exuberant exercise in group-think too reminiscent of other rallies...like one that occurred in Nuremberg several decades earlier.

Another issue was the smiling. Walmart requires its checkout people to flash smiles at customers after bagging their purchases. Plastic bags, plastic junk, plastic smiles. But because the German people don't usually smile at total strangers, the spectacle of Walmart employees grinning like jackasses not only didn't impress consumers, it unnerved them.

The third was the "ethics problem". Back in 1997, Walmart not only required employees to spy on fellow workers (and report any misconduct), but prohibited sexual intimacy among its employees. Apparently, while the folks running the Bentonville, Arkansas-based company had no problem with screwing the environment, they couldn't abide employees doing it to each other (alas, a German court struck down Walmart's "ethics code" in 2005).

Whatever the specific reasons, the German market is now verboten to Walmart. Clearly, the failed experiment was a severe blow to the company's pocketbook and pride. And while no one can predict where a company as aggressive and acquisitive as Walmart will turn up next, presumably, they will pick up the slack by opening a store in Libya.

Source: Macaray, D., in: Huffington Post Business Online, 29/08/2011

Review and Discussion Questions

1. Describe those of Walmart's mistakes which are related to intercultural issues!

2. In order to avoid intercultural mistakes in the future, which kind of suggestions would you offer Walmart in general and particularly if they considered a second attempt of coming to Germany?

3. If Germans and Americans have to work together – either as a team or at the top management level – certain intercultural differences will become apparent. Name three of them!

6 Intercultural Communication

6.0 Statement of the problem

How to work with heavy accents
(Sasivimol Suchinparm)

May Choi's China Chef restaurant was located in an area where many of the customers were Mexican. Most of the restaurant employees were Chinese and could not understand or speak Spanish. One day a Mexican customer came in to order dinner. During the order, the Mexican asked for *arroz* – rice in Spanish. May Choi, who was taking the order, thought the customer was asking for "a rose" and directed him to a florist located in the same mall. After this incident, May Choi hired a number of Mexican employees who spoke both English and Spanish to help communicate with her Mexican customers.

In: Global Smarts: The art of communicating and deal making anywhere in the world, New York, 2000, p. 153

6.1 The importance of intercultural communication

Global communication is a major part of every international business. The success of every international business activity depends on the effectiveness of the communication with other cultures. Apart from the language differences, they need to focus on the social attributes, religion, attitudes and other facts from different cultures. All these communication terminologies are known as "Intercultural Communication". Intercultural communication is not only about language but also about managing a different language. There are different understandings about culture and language in other countries. People travelling and living abroad should make an attempt to become familiar with the local culture and show respect, which will leave a positive impression and improve the relationship with the host. Moreover, using native-language slang and style in foreign countries is not recommended, because it will confuse listeners. Hence, it is always better for more effective communication to explain things in simple words. People should not judge the behavior of others on the basis of their own culture. People from different cultures e.g. have different ways of greetings and should understand diverse behaviors around the world for effective intercultural communication. Sheida Hodge responds to the question about the impediments of good communication:

> *"Problems with meaning are especially important in cross-cultural communication. What you mean when you say something is not necessarily what the other side hears. Messages derive a large part of their meaning from their cultural context. In a cross-*

cultural communication, messages are composed or 'coded' in one context, sent, and then received or 'decoded' in another cultural context." (Hodge, 2000, p. 145)

The communication process and the influences of different cultures will be explained in more detail with the help of a communication model in the following.

6.2   The communication model

Communication can be defined as the process of transmitting meanings (Blom and Meier, 2002, p. 73). Gibson (2002, p. 9) also states that communication is the exchange of meaning, involving the sending and receiving of information between a sender and a receiver. This happens not only through words, but also non-verbal factors are involved. The problem is that the message received can be very different from the message that was sent. Adler (1991, p. 64) even states that *"(...) the sent message is never identical to the received message"*.

A common model for communication is as follows:

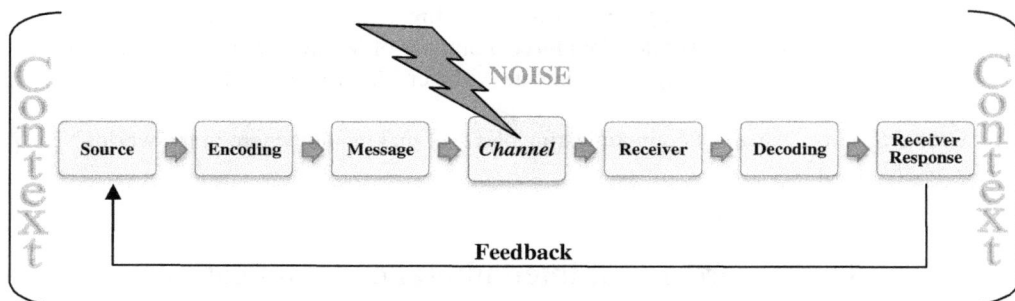

Fig. 6.1:   Communication model
Source: Own graph based on Jandt, 1995, as cited in Gibson, 2002

The idea or feeling is sent by the source by putting it into symbols. Several conditions influ-ence the communication capacity, for example his/her communicative capabilities and his/her socio-cultural system, which disposes of implicit norms and values that influence the message (Blom and Meier, 2002, p. 75). The message is transmitted through a channel. A channel is a medium used for communication, for instance emails, letters, telephone calls or face-to-face conversations (ibid.). Then, the message is interpreted (decoded) by the receiver, who responds. To see if the message has been understood, one has to measure the reaction and the feedback of the receiver (ibid.). The context is seen as the general environment, also called extra-verbal communication level (Hasenstab, 1999, p.154), in which the communica-tion takes place. Noise means anything that distorts the message. To see if the communica-tion has been effective one has measure

"(...) the degree to which a message is received and understood, and if the receiver's reaction to the message correspond to the sender's purpose in sending it."(Tosi et al. 1990, pp. 450f)

Intercultural communication takes place when the sender and the receiver are from differing cultures, meaning

> *"(...) the process of communication between individuals from different cultures" (Jacob, 2003, p. 72).*

Communication can be very difficult if there is a big difference between the two cultures. Hence, if there is too much "cultural noise", communication can fail (Gibson, 2002, p. 9).

Intercultural communication generally involves face-to-face communication between people from different national cultures. The main personal traits that affect intercultural communication are:

1. *self-concept* (refers to the way in which a person views his- or herself);
2. *self-disclosure* (refers to the willingness of individuals to openly and appropriately reveal information about themselves to their counterparts);
3. *self-monitoring* (refers to the use of social comparison information to control and modify one's self-presentation and expressive behavior);
4. *social relaxation* (the ability to reveal only little anxiety in communication).

Effective communicators must know themselves well and, with the help of their self-awareness, initiate positive attitudes. Individuals must express a friendly personality to be competent in intercultural communication. (Jandt, 2013, pp. 35f)

Nowadays, the telecommunication revolution permits rapid correspondence with business partners around the world. Communication via fax, telex, e-mail, cell phone and video conferencing enables us to constantly stay in touch with our international counterparts.

Nevertheless, these technological marvels have not eliminated the need for face-to-face contact with our relationship-focused customers and partners. Relationship-focused people are less comfortable to discuss important issues in writing or by phone. They expect to see their suppliers and partners in person more often than is considered necessary in "deal-focused" markets. (Gesteland, 2002, p. 29)

6.3   Negotiating across cultures

Namaste is a common greeting used on the Indian subcontinent. Literally translated it means "I bow to you" and is used to express deep respect by Hindus, Jains and Buddhists in India and Nepal. In these cultures, the word is spoken at the beginning of a conversation, accompanied by a slight bow made with hands pressed together, palms touching and fingers pointed upwards, in front of the chest. As such, Namaste is a form of both verbal and non-verbal communication. It may be only one word, but it carries significant symbolism.

Within one culture or language group, communication can often be problematic – generally across age groups, geographic regions and gender. However, these problems pale in comparison to the challenges of communicating across cultures. (Nardon/Sanchez-Runde/Steers, 2010, p. 200) However, most researchers, employees, and business owners agree that the most important element in effective intercultural communication is language.

> *"Language issues are becoming a considerable source of conflict and inefficiency in the increasingly diverse work force throughout the world [...]. No corporation can be competitive if co-workers avoid, don't listen to, perceive as incompetent, or are intol-*

erant of employees who have problems with the language. In addition, these attitudes could be carried over into their interactions with their customers who speak English as a second language, resulting disastrous effects on customer relations and, thus, the corporate bottom line." (Fernandez in: Hillstrom, in web)

Some Notes on Business Meetings
(Scott D. Seligman)

- Chinese organizations typically request background information before they agree to formal discussion. Provide as much information as possible about the individuals who will present, the organization you are representing, and the topic you wish to discuss, and give the Chinese time to study the request.
- In China, meetings are generally held in conference rooms rather than offices. Seating is not rigid, but there typically are designated places for the principals.
- Punctuality is considered a virtue, so it is important to arrive at a meeting on time – not late and not early. Guests are greeted upon arrival by a representative and escorted to the meeting room.
- Chinese generally expect foreign delegation leaders to enter a room first, and this prevents confusion. Important guests are escorted to the seats, which the principal guest placed in a seat of honour.
- Chinese meetings begin with small talk.
- Chinese meetings are structured dialogues between principals on both sides; others participate in the conversation only upon explicit invitation. The Chinese prefer to react to others' idea, and not to bear the onus of setting the scope of the discussion themselves.
- Chinese often signal the speaker with nods or interjections that they understand what he or she is saying. Such ejaculations do not necessarily signal agreement.
- Don't interrupt a speaker.
- A good interpreter can help you immeasurably in China. When talking through an interpreter, pause frequently and avoid slang and colloquialisms. Always talk to the host, never directly to the translator.
- Restate what was accomplished at the close of a meeting to guard against misunderstanding. Ask for a contact person for future dealings.

In: Chinese Business Etiquette, 1999, p. 107

Often, intercultural communication exists concerning the practice of listening. Numerous tips about establishing culturally sensitive verbal and written communication practices within an organization exist. While the prevailing norms of communication in American business may call for the listener to be silent and offer body language intended to convince the speaker that his or her words are being taken into account. Many cultures have different standards that may strike the uninitiated as rude or disorienting.

"A person who communicates by leaning forward and getting close may be very threatening to someone who values personal space. And that person could be per-

ceived as hostile and unfriendly, simply because of poor eye contact." (Monson in: Hillstrom, in web)

In any cross-cultural exchange between managers from different regions, the principal purpose of communication is to seek common ground – to exchange ideas, information, gain customers, and sometimes even establish partnerships between the parties. Business in general and management in particular rely on people's willingness and ability to convey the meaning between managers, employees, partners, suppliers, investors and customers. There are numerous comprehensive models that attempt to capture the various elements of the communication process.

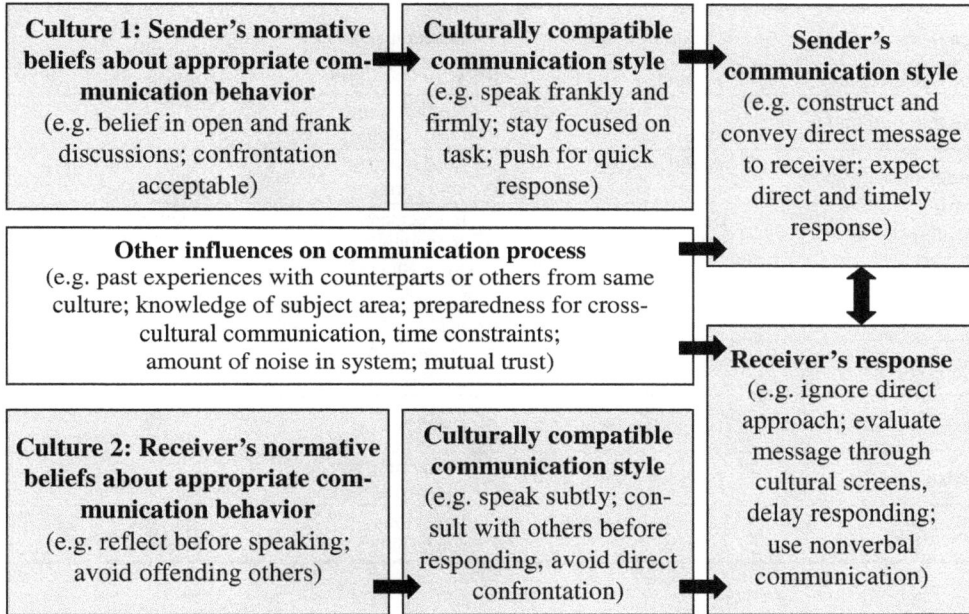

Culture 1: Sender's normative beliefs about appropriate communication behavior (e.g. belief in open and frank discussions; confrontation acceptable)	Culturally compatible communication style (e.g. speak frankly and firmly; stay focused on task; push for quick response)	Sender's communication style (e.g. construct and convey direct message to receiver; expect direct and timely response)
Other influences on communication process (e.g. past experiences with counterparts or others from same culture; knowledge of subject area; preparedness for cross-cultural communication, time constraints; amount of noise in system; mutual trust)		**Receiver's response** (e.g. ignore direct approach; evaluate message through cultural screens, delay responding; use nonverbal communication)
Culture 2: Receiver's normative beliefs about appropriate communication behavior (e.g. reflect before speaking; avoid offending others)	**Culturally compatible communication style** (e.g. speak subtly; consult with others before responding, avoid direct confrontation)	

Fig. 6.2:   Cultural influences on the communication process – a model
Source: Adapted from Nardon/Sanchez-Runde/Steers, 2010, p. 202

According to this model (Fig. 6.2), characteristics inherent in the cultural environments of each participant help to determine various beliefs underlying the communication process. In a cross-cultural environment, these cultural drivers often influence the extent to which communication would be open and frank.

As a result of these normative beliefs, certain culturally compatible communication strategies emerge, including people's expectations and objectives in initiating or responding to a message or comment, choice of language and transmission strategies. Three principal communication behaviors can be identified as verbal, non-verbal and virtual. These strategies are aimed at achieving a number of intended message outcomes.

Limitations on both message content and the choice of message transmission can be found across cultures. This is mostly a challenge for the senders as well as the recipients of the message. Senders must decide how to formulate a message, so it is consistent with the sender's culture but also consistent with the recipient's culture. However, what is acceptable in one culture might not necessarily be acceptable in another. Communication patterns include message content, message context, communication protocols, single-language communication, technology-mediated communication, and information-sharing patterns. These all patterns illustrate many of the challenges faced by global managers when communicating across cultures. (Nardon/Sanchez-Runde/Steers, 2010, p. 203)

Tab. 6.1:   Selected elements of the negotiation process in comparison between US-Americans, Japanese and
            Arabs
Source: Based on Chaney/Martin, 1995, p. 183

Element	United States	Japanese	Arabians
Group composition	Marketing oriented	Function oriented	Committee of specialists
Number involved	2–3	4–7	4–6
Space orientation	Confrontational competitive	Display harmonious relationship	Status
Establishing rapport	short period; direct to task	Longer period; until harmony	Long period; until trusted
Use of language	Open, direct, sense of urgency	Indirect, appreciative, cooperative	Flattery, emotional, religious
First offer	Fair ±5 to 10%	±10 to 20%	±20 to 50%
Second offer	Add to package; sweeten the deal	–5%	–10%
Final offer package	Total package	Makes no further Concessions	–25%
Decision-making process	Top management team	Collective	Team makes recommendation
Decision maker	Top management team	Middle line with team consensus	Senior manager
Risk taking	Calculated personal responsibility	Low group responsibility	Religion-based

6.4   Levels of communication

According to Watzlawick et al. (1969) every message has a content aspect and a relationship aspect. Therefore, in our way of communicating with another person we also show our opinion about this person and in which relationship we are in. Hence, the aspect of content transmits information, facts, results etc. and the relationship aspect makes statements about the contact, climate, emotional aspects and the interpersonal relationship.

Relationship aspects are especially transmitted by non-verbal communication. With laughs, intonation, mimic and gestures the speaker expresses for instance what he thinks about the receiver of the message and how important conversation is for him/her. This makes it clear that non-verbal language is often the source of misunderstandings during intercultural meetings (Blom/Meier, 2002, pp.79–80). The interpretation of non-verbal behavior according to own cultural norms, although the conversational partner has his/her own encoding, leads to misunderstandings (ibid.). To understand intercultural communication requires an accurate perception of what is conveyed in the verbal as well as the para- and non-verbal mode. Regarding to that, Jacob (2003, p. 72) states that *"beliefs and attitudes about a person from another culture can often be communicated through behavior, even when nothing has been verbalized."*

In the following figure, the modes of communication – verbal-, para-verbal-, and non-verbal – are illustrated.

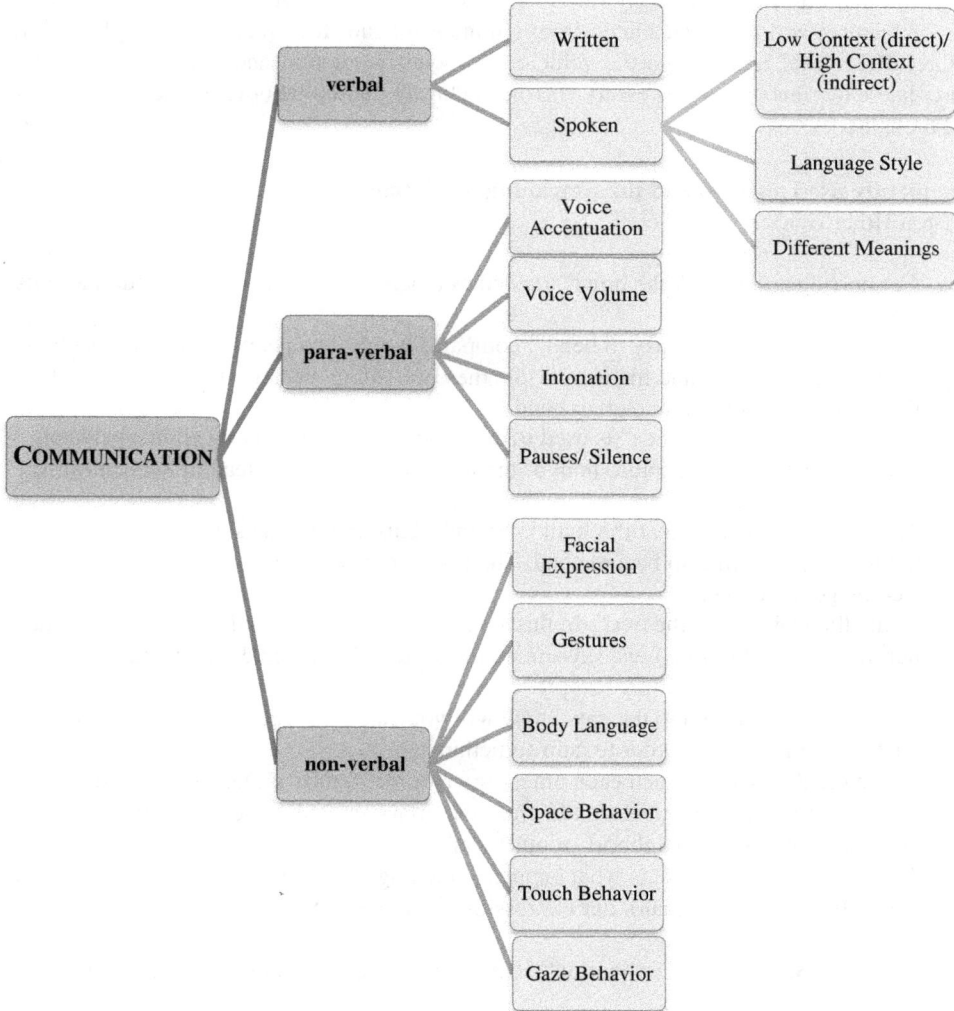

```
COMMUNICATION
├── verbal
│   ├── Written
│   └── Spoken
│       ├── Low Context (direct)/ High Context (indirect)
│       ├── Language Style
│       └── Different Meanings
├── para-verbal
│   ├── Voice Accentuation
│   ├── Voice Volume
│   ├── Intonation
│   └── Pauses/ Silence
└── non-verbal
    ├── Facial Expression
    ├── Gestures
    ├── Body Language
    ├── Space Behavior
    ├── Touch Behavior
    └── Gaze Behavior
```

Fig. 6.3:   Modes of communication
Source: Own graph based on Blom/Meier, 2002

*"A journey of a thousand miles
must begin with a single step."*

(Lao Tzu)

6.5   Verbal communication

6.5.1   Language

Language and culture are strongly interrelated. Language is a symbolic system which consists of features and rules detectable in any human tongue. It is shared by people within a culture. The verbal language is the vehicle for social interaction and empowers to express and create experience. It is necessary for the social mutual collaboration and enables to reveal thoughts.

Frequently used phrases and their meaning in Vietnam
(Elston/Hong Hoa)

- "Eat porridge, then kick the bowl", describes a person who receives a favour and fails to express gratitude.
- "The young bamboo is easy to bend", compares bamboo to people. We must teach our children good morals and manners while they are young, because when they get older, like bamboo, become too thick to bend.
- "Catch fish with both hands" is used to describe a person who has a choice between two things and tries to capture both of them in a frantic way instead of concentrating on just one thing at the time.
- "Near the ink is black, near the light is bright". This one instructs us that if we make bad friends, we will also become bad. The flip side: if we keep good friends, we also become good people.
- "Same the fruit, know the tree". In this sentence, the fruit is a child, the tree is the father. In English (German), we say something similar, "The apple doesn't fall far from the tree".
- "If you don't venture into the cave, how will you catch the tiger?" tells us that we must risk something in order to gain something.
- "Close the doors, then teach each other" refers to the family circle. When there is a dispute inside the family, we should close the doors and solve the problems privately without involving our neighbors or outsiders".
- "Far faces, distant hearts" is what happens in a long-distance relationship between two lovers. In English (German), our expression might be "Out of sight, out of mind".

In: Vietnamese Sayings, in: Destination Vietnam, July/August, San Francisico 1997

6.5.2   Distinctive language features

Language indicates and graduates phenomena like experiences, feeling, ideas, objects, groups, people and many other. There are a lot of differences, but also many similarities in the world-wide language varieties. All of them have the four distinctive features of: arbitrariness, abstractness, meaning-centeredness and creativity.

Arbitrariness

"Language is viewed as an arbitrary symbolic system" (Chung/Ting-Toomey, 2012, p. 112).

The words are formed with letters, which depend on the graphic representation, and the sound of the word is formed with sound units, which depend on the phonemic. Consequently, words and sounds of each culture have no inherent meaning to the phenomena the word is trying to describe.

In general the meaning of words emerges

"from the specific conventions and expectations shared by members of a given speech community, conventions and expectations that can and do change dramatically from time to time and place to place" (Allen/Jensen, 1995, p. 35).

Abstractness

Language can be used abstractly or for hypothetical thinking. The language abstraction is the process of moving away from concrete and external phenomena. Because of different ethical and moral beliefs, the expression of abstract thoughts, feelings or ideas can differ between cultures, which can cause discomfort and uncertainty. In order to avoid this, it is better to use less abstract and more concrete words, when talking to people from another culture. (Chung/Ting-Toomey, 2012, p. 113)

How to start a conversation iu China
(Scott D. Seligman)

Initial encounters with the Chinese often follow strikingly similar patterns. The following "top ten" questions can help you to build up a conversation:
- Where are you from?
- How long have you been in China?
- Have you visited China before?
- Do you speak Chinese?
- What do you think of China?
- What kind of work do you do?
- Which places in China have you visited?
- Are you accustomed to Chinese food?
- Are you married?
- Do you have children?

In: Chinese Business Etiquette, 1999, p. 26

Meaning-centeredness

Although it is possible to label phenomena like situations or feelings with language, the use of second meanings like metaphors are very helpful, because they can express our thinking. George Lakoff, a cognitive scientist and linguist, proposes, that metaphors are *"a major and indispensable part of our ordinary conventional way of conceptualizing the world, and that our everyday behavior reflects our metaphorical understanding of experience" (Martin/Nakayama, 2010, p. 226).*

Meaning-centeredness describes the two different, the denotative and connotative, meanings.

"The denotative meaning of a word emphasizes its objective, dictionary definition shared and recognized by the majority members of a linguistic community.

The connotative meaning, on the other hand, stresses the subjective, interpretive meanings of a word constructed by individual members based on their cultural and personalized language experience." (Chung/Ting-Toomey, 2012, p. 112)

An example for the two different meanings is the word "hook up". The denotative meaning is *"an arrangement of mechanical parts"* and the connotative meaning can be interpreted as a casual sexual encounter or dealing drugs.

Within intercultural communication it is necessary to get familiar with metaphors and other connotative meanings to avoid confusion and anxiety.

Creativity

Creativity as a distinctive feature of language consists of three parts: productivity, displacement and meta-communication.

The productivity is the creative capacity to understand the complex structure of a language and vocalize and understand sentences never heard before. The displacement element is the capacity to talk about different time and space, because of the possibility to pass memories end experiences over generations. The meta-communication is the opportunity to use language for cooperative work and communal life. (Chung/Ting-Toomey, 2012, p. 114)

The "fourth" floor

When a group of British people attends a meeting on the "fourth" floor of a London business tower, they know it actually refers to the fifth floor of the building, since Brits distinguish between the ground floor and the first floor. On the other hand, communicating across cultures can be challenging, since the link between words and their meaning is not always clear. When a group of Americans attends a meeting on the "fourth" floor of a New York high-rise, they do, in fact, go to the fourth floor. However, when foreign travelers attend a meeting on the "fourth" floor of a Seoul high-rise, even the more experienced travelers can become puzzled. While the number four ("sa" in Korean) is not unlucky itself, it is pronounced like the Korean word for death. As a result, many Korean buildings either use the English letter "F" for this unnamed floor or simply do not have such floors.

Based on: Nardon/Sanchez-Runde/Steers, 2010

6.5.3   Translation problems

Even within one language and/or culture, translation problems can occur, e.g. when a metaphor is unknown or someone is sarcastic or misunderstood as being sarcastic.

Five problems that can lead to intercultural communication barriers are described here:

Tab. 6.2:   Five possible translation problems

Vocabulary equivalence	*"Languages that are different often lack words that are directly translatable."* *(Jandt, 2013, pp. 141f)*
Idiomatic equivalence	*"In translating idioms, the translator meets various difficulties that are not so easy to overcome. The main problem is the lack of equivalence on the idiom level. It would be perfect if a translator could find an idiom in the target language which was the same in its form and meaning as that of the source language. However, even though each language has its idioms, it is still hard to find the exact equivalent." (Straksiené, 2013, p. 1)*
Grammatical-syntactical equivalence	*"That simply means that languages don't necessarily have the same grammar."* *(Jandt, 2013, p. 143)*
Experiential equivalence	*"If an object or experience does not exist in your culture, it's difficult to translate words referring to that object or experience into that language when no words may exist for them." (ibid.)*
Conceptual equivalence	*"The problem of conceptual equivalence refers to abstract ideas that may not exist in the same fashion in different languages." (ibid., pp. 143f)*
Vocabulary equivalence	*"Languages that are different often lack words that are directly translatable." (ibid., pp. 141f)*

6.5.4   English as a lingua franca

In the whole world, the use of English has become more common and essential. In order to be able to communicate in the wide range of international business, English is set as the common communication language. While in the 19th century, English was the language of commerce, French of diplomacy and German of science, today English is the universal language of all three of them, although it is not the world-wide most widely spoken language, as you can see in the following figure. (Jandt, 2013, pp. 147f)

Through colonialism and emigrations the English language spread over to other continents and counted by 1990 an estimated number of 750 million people using English as their second language. Today English dominates areas like science, technology, commerce, tourism, diplomacy and music. It is the native language in 12 countries and 33 others use it as official or semiofficial language. The study of English is mandatory or admired in at least 56 countries. Through global communication English has become necessary for companies, scientists and politicians. (Jandt, 2013, pp. 148f.; Rothlauf, 2012, pp. 202f)

Tab. 6.3:   The five most widely spoken languages worldwide
Source: Ethnologue.com, 2014

Language	Approximate number of speakers
1. Chinese (Mandarin)	1,197,000,000 (848,000,000)
2. Spanish	414,000,000
3. English	335,000,000
4. Hindi	260,000,000
5. Arabic	237,000,000

6.5.5   Direct and indirect styles of verbal communication

The shape of a message can differ even when the purpose is the same. The differences are often the tone of voice and the immediacy of the content. The direct styles distinctly unveil the speakers' intentions with a notable tone of voice, while the indirect styles camouflage the speakers' aim with a calm voice. Of course these styles are mixed up in many different forms, however the direct is commonly used in individualistic, and the indirect style is frequently used in collectivistic cultures. (Chung/Ting-Toomey, 2012, p. 125)

The difference of these styles is most obvious in a request situation. A direct style user just asks for a request giving the information about what he needs. An indirect style user would not ask that straightforwardly, but would give background information expecting that the listener or interpreter can infer what he or she needs. While the direct style user wants to get a clear "yes" or "no", the indirect style user would never get him-/herself caught in a situation where the listener has to say "no", because this would mean that both of them lose their face. (ibid, pp. 125f)

When a direct and an indirect style user meet in a business environment, a misunderstanding or even a conflict situation is inevitable and no result will be reached. Therefore it is necessary for intercultural businessmen to analyze the cultural background of their negotiation partner to prevent misunderstandings and to achieve a goal.

"Warming-up" phase in China

"It's important, not to come in swinging, but to establish the foundation of a relationship and build slowly. There is no need to rush into a discussion of business; the topic will come up naturally in time. Most Chinese gatherings begin with small talk, especially when the host and guests do not know one another well."
(Seligman, 1999, p. 95)

"Business meetings typically start with pleasantries such as tea and general conversation about the guests' trip to the country, local accommodations, and family. In most cases, the host already has been briefed on the background of the visitor."
(Harris/Moran, 1991, p. 410)

6.5.6   Written communication

The written word can have a huge impact. It is even more influential than the spoken word, because it can be read over and over again. William Howard Taft, the 27th president of the USA, once said:

> *"Don't write so that you can be understood, write so that you can't be misunderstood."*

Written communication in general

Written communication means that the writer is usually distant from the reader. Therefore, the written word is mostly very different from the spoken word. In order to understand the message it is necessary to leave out any ambiguity in writing. In the written communication, there are no additional linguistic features, such as eye-contact or other nonverbal behavior. When writing a message, the context has to be clear and understandable for the receiver. (Indrová, 2011, pp. 7f)

Written communication in business

It's not possible to imagine business without written communication, because it has so many usable features. Because of its durable nature, important facts can be recorded to re-read or to analyze at any time. It can show some information in a more detailed, logical or effective way, e.g. through graphs or tables, messages can be distributed faster to a bigger group of people. (ibid.)

To effectuate written communication in business some rules should be followed:

- Make sure your spelling and use of grammar is correct.
- Keep your message short to make sure it will soon be read and easily understood.
- Pay attention to the "subject" and the first sentence of your message. The attention of the receiver must be raised and he/she should also be able to quickly grasp your intention.
- Try to avoid negative verbalizations but rather formulate your message positively.
- Keep in contact with business partners, e.g. by sending – congratulatory notes or thank-you-emails etc.
- Always double-check your message before sending it off.

Forms of Address: Chinese Names
(Scott D. Seligman)

The first thing you need to remember about Chinese names is that the surname comes first, not last. More than 95 percent of all Chinese surnames are one syllable – that is to say, one character – in length; some of the most common examples are Wang, Chen, Zhang, Li, Zhao, and Lin.

For business purposes it is traditionally acceptable to call a Chinese person by the surname, together with a title such as Mister or Miss or even Minister or Managing Director. Thus Mr. Wang, Managing Director Liu, or Ms. Zhao would all be acceptable forms of address, and there is no problem with mixing an English title and a Chinese surname in just that order.

In: Chinese Business Etiquette, New York, 1999, p. 32

6.5.7   Listening skills

Winston Churchill once said:

> *"Courage is what it takes to stand up and speak. Courage is also what it takes to sit down and listen."*

Every effective speaker should have an effective listener. Being a good listener means he or she (Arent, 2009, p. 8):

- *"stays focused on the speaker's main point (more global than discrete)*
- *tunes out all potential distractions (or ask for time to remove them)*
- *offers the fullest possible attention (manages any emotional reaction, especially if a particular word or phrase is used.)*
- *gives signals that he or she is listening as objectively as possible (use eye contact or other nonverbal cues, or fillers, such as yeah, uh huh, ok, I know what you mean, or equivalent expressions in another language)*
- *is flexible and open-minded when new topics or ideas are raised (these concepts are cultural specific in practice, but the general point remains that these traits have a positive impact on overall listening effectiveness)*
- *asks for clarification if anything is unclear (how that is done will depend on the language and culture involved; all languages have a way to ask questions and make clarification requests)*
- *validates the speaker's main points (conveying that they are received, considered and under review, such validation may be verbal, non-verbal or both)."*

The factors mentioned are depending on the culture of the country.

6.6   Paraverbal communication

One of the most important elements in intercultural communication is paraverbal communication. It encompasses the instrument of the voice and consists of the loudness of our voice, the speech melody, the speaking tempo, the pitch of our voice and the emphasis of different words in a sentence. (Mruk-Badiane, 2007, p. 4)

Those things are different from culture to culture, which makes it more complicated to understand the message of people from other counties and cultures correctly. It is important to know how to use the voice efficiently to reach certain goals, either in private conversations or in business negotiation. Around about 38 % of our messages are made up by paraverbal communication (see Fig. 6.4).

A paraverbal message and its interpretation
(Jürgen Rothlauf)

A sentence can have entirely different meanings depending on intonation and emphasis. Six different conclusions are possible as far as the following statement is concerned:

"I didn't say you were impolite."
"I DIDN'T say you were impolite."
"I didn't SAY you were impolite."
"I didn't say YOU were impolite."
"I didn't say you WERE impolite."
"I didn't say you were IMPOLITE."

In: Seminarunterlagen, 2013, p. 14

6.6.1   Communicating to display emotion

Showing emotion in nonverbal and verbal communication varies between high-context and low-context cultures. In China, Japan, Korea, Thailand, Vietnam, and other collectivist Asian countries, culture socializes people from an early age not to show emotion publicly. No doubt, this is because a display of emotion could have potential consequences of disrupting the harmony that is so important to collectivist cultures. In Iraq, Dubai, Jordan, Kuwait, and other collectivist Middle Eastern countries, culture teaches people from an early age to show emotion and how to do it (Varner/Beamer, 2011, p. 159).

Obviously, the level of emotion shown can have consequences in work environments, where people from emotion-expressive cultures interact with people from emotion-repressive cultures. When someone from an emotion-expressive culture – say Polish – "performs" a communication transaction about a perceived mistake with someone from an emotion-repressive culture – say Thai – both could be sending messages the other has trouble decoding correctly because of the different communication styles. The Pole may be perceived to be immature, out of control, and egocentric. The Thai might be perceived to be remote, unsympathetic, and uptight. These perceptions then form the context for the worded message, which is subject to distortion and misinterpretation, or in other words, faulty decoding.

Egyptians display socially acceptable emotion. The emotion of anger is not socially acceptable, but not to show emotion in the face of another person's grief, jubilation, or disappointment is regarded as self-centered and egoistic. To be impassive can result in a denied group membership.

6.6.2   Effect of speaking

Silence
(Hayashi Shujl)

A Japanese company and a German firm were considering a tie-up. Preliminary discussions were promising, and negotiating teams from each corporation met to hammer out a basic agreement. Throughout the meeting the senior Japanese Representative sat straight in his seat, said nothing and often closed his eyes. Angered by his apparent aloof indifference, the German team finally broke off the talks." […] If they had understood local customs better, the negotiations would not have collapsed.

In: Culture and Management in Japan, Tokyo, 1991, p. 113

The speaking tempo includes the sound and syllable lengths of the words, and pauses. The lengths of the pauses differ in every country and culture and can be interpreted in a wrong way if people have no information about them.

In general, there are two different types of pauses, "filled pauses" and "unfilled pauses". "Filled pauses" consist of words, are stuffed with words like "then" and "well" and are used for thinking about how to go on in a sentence without saying anything. "Unfilled pauses" are pauses in which nobody says something, there is absolute silence. The amount of seconds with absolute silence differentiates from culture to culture. (Gebhard, 2012, pp. 39ff) In negotiation and business meetings, pauses can be used to reach a certain effect or to support the meaning of a sentence and let the other team member or partner think about the words. In the culture of China it is usual to use pauses in speaking to show the guest who of them is the leader of this conversation. Especially Chinese team leaders use longer pauses for making clear which team member is the leader with the highest position. (Berkemeier/Scholz, 2006, p. 6)

Sharing
(Wilson/Donaldson)

Four Russian friends meet. One has a chocolate bar. He pulls out his pocket knife and carefully cuts the chocolate into four minuscule but equal pieces and divides it among the four. In other countries, four friends would not typically think of equally distributing such a small portion. "If I want one, I will buy my own" would perhaps be the attitude. In Russia, the sharing of food or consumables is of primary importance.

In: Russian Etiquette & Ethics in Business, Chicago, 1996, p. 71

For Japan, Kaminura describes this kind of communication as follows (1995, p. 670):

> *"The person who is self-confident but very humble in attitudes is rather respected in Japan. We do not use direct expressions, but a listener should read and understand between the lines to get a message. As a result, I think that Japanese are passive in their general attitude whereas Westerners are aggressive based on individual mind."*

6.7   Nonverbal communication

Nonverbal messages can be broken down into subcategories. Although this makes the discussion easier, one has to be careful not to assume that speakers use nonverbal signals in isolation. In most cases, speakers use many different signals at the same time. We may move our hands, nod with our heads, smile, and keep close eye contact, all at the same time. The nonverbal messages that give listeners the most trouble are those with accompany words. It's the tone of voice, the look on someone's face, or the lack of eye contact that makes you wonder if you are understood.

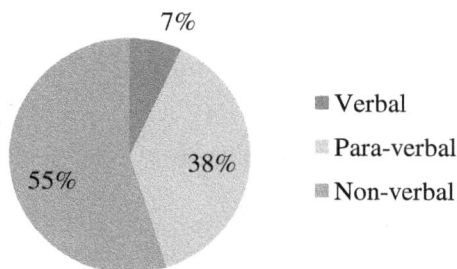

7%

55%   38%

■ Verbal
■ Para-verbal
■ Non-verbal

Fig. 6.4:   Elements of communication
Source: Based on Mehrabrian, 1976

Most people still believe that the main part of communication is the verbal part, which includes the written part. However, it is not. The verbal part accounts for only 7 % of the communication. The other 38 % include the tone of voice, in other words the paraverbal part and the biggest part is the nonverbal part, which covers 55 % of the overall communication.

6.7.1 Six categories of nonverbal communication

Nonverbal or nonworded communication includes all communication beyond the spoken or written word. Gesteland (2002, p. 73–78) has defined six categories that can help to get a better understanding of the complexity of nonverbal communication.

Proxemics – the study of space

"Proxemics is the branch of knowledge that deals with the amount of space that people feel it necessary to set between themselves and others." (Oxford Dictionaries)

In the early 1960s, the term "proxemics" – originating from "proximity" or nearness – was introduced by the American anthropologist Edward Hall (Pease/Pease, 2004, p. 192). Many people never think about how much space should be between us. We do it intuitively. During our childhood, we develop a feeling for our own "space bubble" (Gesteland, 2002, p. 72.), because we recognize it from our parents, friends and other members of our culture. Indeed it is not inborn, but we learn it by observation. (Beamer/Varner, 2011, p. 234)

The closet zone is the intimate space. Only those people who are familiar to us such as family, close friends or animals are allowed to be in this zone. The personal space is used for interactions between colleagues, acquaintances or people we meet at social parties. The next zone is the social space which we use for interaction with strangers, such as a new employee at work or a craftsman repairing things at your own house. The public space is the zone which we use when we meet people in a large group. (Pease/Pease, 2004, p. 192)

People from one culture can easily interact with each other without disturbing their personal space. Nevertheless in business it is important nowadays to interact within different cultures. The use of space differs a lot from culture to culture which means people from the Mediterranean Region can stand very close to each other. However, if a person from the Mediterranean Region stands next to a person from the United States, such as they would do it intuitively, the person from the United States (distant culture) would step back because it is too close and it is not anymore in the personal zone. In other words, the person does not feel comfortable anymore. Close and distant cultures are displayed in the following table.

Tab. 6.4: Distance behavior: The use of space
Source: Gesteland, 2002, p. 73

CLOSE: 20–35 cm (8–14 inches)	DISTANT: 40–60 cm (16–24 inches)
The Arab World	Most Asians
The Mediterranean Region	Northern, Central and Eastern Europeans
Latin Europe	North Americans

Haptics – the study of touch

"Haptic is related to the sense of touch." (Oxford Dictionaries)

Holding or shaking hands, kissing cheeks and also brushing arms belong to this kind of non-verbal communication.

In every culture, there is a different association towards touching. People from a high contact culture, such as the Mediterranean Region, feel comfortable with touching one another, e.g. kissing the cheek or hugging when one has just met. In other cultures, such as North America, it is uncommon to touch people one has just met. People would say "Hello" to one another and maybe wave their hands as a greeting sign. When people of this culture know each other better, they like to hug one another as greeting. The third kind of classification is the low contact. Those cultures, for example in the United Kingdom, do not like to touch in public at all, neither good friends nor family members. (Gesteland, 2002, p. 74) This association of the cultures towards touching is comparable to the distant zones of the cultures. The bigger the distant zone of one culture, the less people from this culture like to touch and vice versa.

In Asian countries, people do not shake hands. They usually bow as a greeting sign in Japan. The bow starts from the hip with a straight back and the neck also remains straight. Men hold their hands at the side, but the women put their hands on their legs. In other countries, such as Argentina, it is common for men and women to touch the women's right cheek. In Lebanon, men give three cheek kisses to other men, first on the right side, then on the left side and again on the right side. (Beamer/Varner, 2011, pp. 231f) In India, it is also possible that a man takes the other hand of a man when walking side by side. It is only a sign of friendship and is not connected to homosexuality. (Gesteland, 2002, p. 75)

Nevertheless, in many cultures, the handshake has become the most common form of greeting in formal business situations, which was first used when closing a commercial transaction in the nineteenth century. It is *"a sign of trust and welcome"* to the other person. (Pease/Pease, 2004, p. 41) This greeting ritual differs from region to region. While some cultures shake hands softly and long, other cultures do it distinctly and quickly.

The biggest problem is the way of exchanging handshakes. People from other cultures may wonder why the handshake feels too soft or too strong, or in some cases the other person might not have been allowed to reach for the counterpart's hand first. The result might be an uncomfortable situation. Germans and French people like to pump very briefly, only one to two times. In the United Kingdom, they give a pump of three to five times and the Americans like to pump even five to seven times. It might happen that the short-shaker can seem as restrained for the long-shaker. (Pease/Pease, 2004, p. 114)

In some circumstances it can happen that a woman has to wait until she gets the other men's hand reached for handshaking, such as in Czech Republic. (Gesteland, 2002, p. 323) Another example, in Mexico it is also possible that a woman has to extend her hand first after the man gave a slight bow, or in some other countries while the people shake hands they put their free hands on the forearm of the other person, such as in the Arab World. (Gesteland, 2002, p. 222; Beamer/Varner, 2011, p. 231) Moreover, good eye contact while shaking hands is important in other countries, such as Germany, Spain and Canada. (Gesteland, 2002, pp. 261, 313, 335)

Kinesics – the study of movement

Kinesics is *"the study of the way in which certain body movements and gestures re-garded as a form of non-verbal communication" (Oxford Dictionary)*.

Facial expressions

Every human likes to smile and to laugh. However, there can be differences in meaning: smiling and laughing can stand for happiness, joy and also for embarrassment. For example people from the United States like to smile and laugh as often as they can. They do not try to hide any feelings. Indeed, Japanese people also smile, but they usually do not try to show it in public. The German culture also seems to be cautious with smiling. The difference to the East Asian culture is that the German do not try to hide any feelings. They just do not want to smile or to laugh because most of them are very serious. The opposite are the Arab and Latin countries. They like to smile and laugh, and they also use their hands and arms to show their emotions. (Beamer/Varner, 2011, p. 224)

Frowning is another important form of facial expressions. In their own culture can the mean-ing of that frowning easily be identified, but in a different cultures can it be differently inter-preted. For example in North America mean raised eyebrows interest and surprise. British are skeptic and Chinese people disagree when they raise their eyebrows. Filipinos like to say "Hello!" with this gesture and for Arabs is it a sign for "No!". For doing business in a differ-ent culture, it is important to be careful with one's own facial expressions, because they might even mean the opposite. (Gesteland, 2002, p. 79)

Head gestures

Everybody around the world nods. Nodding can be a form of agreement, disagreement and listening. In most cultures, moving the head up and down means that you agree with some-one. And shaking your head from side to side means that you disagree. One exception is Bulgaria. Bulgarians agree with shaking their heads from one side to the other and disagree with moving the head up and down. Moreover, moving the head up and down might in some cultures only mean that the person listens and understands what has been said but does not necessarily mean that the person actually also agrees. (Beamer/Varner, 2011, p. 226)

Arm movements and gestures

In Latin cultures and also the Arab World, they like to internsively use their arms and hands to show their emotions and to underline what they are saying. It is possible that the other person is touched while a person from those cultures talks. This would disturbe e.g. a Japa-nese person. They usually do not use their hands and arms to underline their message, be-cause they do not want to get into another person's space zone, which is very large in Japan in contrast to Latin and Arab cultures. Those cultures have problems to interpret the other's gestures, because using the arms and hands means in the Arab World that you are interested in the conversation while in Japan it means that you destroy the harmony of the group. (Beamer/Varner, 2011, pp. 226f)

To hand over things, such as papers or business cards, it is important to know how hand them over correctly. For example in Muslim, Hindu and Buddhist countries, you should not use your left hand for giving papers or business cards to another person or even to shake left hands with somebody. The left hand is used for cleaning rituals. Therefore, always use your right hand there (Gesteland, 2002, p. 79). We will take a closer look at business cards later in this chapter.

Gestures in China
(Morrison/Conaway/Borden)

- Avoid making exaggerated gestures or using dramatic facial expressions. The Chinese do not use their hands when speaking, and become distracted by a speaker who does.
- The Chinese do not like to be touched by people they do not know. This is especially important to remember when dealing with older people or people in important positions.
- Use an open hand rather than one finger to point.
- To beckon, turn the palm down and wave the fingers toward the body.

In: Kiss, Bow, or Shake Hands: how to do business in sixty countries, Massachusetts, 1994, p. 61

Posture

According to Oxford Dictionaries, posture can be defined in two ways:

1. It can be "*a particular position of the body*", "*in which someone holds their body when standing or sitting.*"
2. It can be "*a particular approach or attitude*", which is "*a way of behaving that is intended to convey a false impression (a pose)*".

In international business is it important to know how to do it correctly. To stand upright with shoulder back and a high held head is a good way to show self-confidence. Everybody can read this posture around the world. However, there are differences as far as the right sitting position is concerned. Some companies in Japan are not westernized and the people are supposed to sit cross-legged on the floor. In other cultures where women are really new in business, they should not cross their legs at the knee. It is better when they put their legs together and do not occupy too much space. (Beamer/Varner, 2011, p. 228)

Oculesics – the study of eye behavior

Oculesics is another form of the nonverbal language.

> "*Several oculesics behaviors, including eye contact, gaze and pupil dilation, can convey immediacy in interpersonal communication.*" *(Manusov, 2009, p. 12)*

The eye gaze is a not only a sign of respect for the own culture. It is also a very important part in cross-cultural business. When Arabian and Japanese people meet, uncomfortable situations can often be expected. Both sides misunderstand the repective gaze by interpreting with the help of their own cultural understanding. For the Arabs, it is usually a significant matter to look at somebody's eyes. They consciously read the feelings and also the truthfulness of the counterpart's statement. If they cannot see the other person's eyes clearly, they move closer. Japanese people do not even try to make eye contact. It is disrespectful for them. They like to keep their distance and their privacy, too. In this particular case, when an Arab meets a Japanese person, the Arab would like to come closer and to look in the Japanese person's eyes, whereas the Japanese would try to look away and probably try to escape this situation. The Japanese person could also try to avoid this situation by wearing sunglasses. Consequently, the Arab will not be able to read the Japanese person's eyes and will perhaps not try to come closer. Not only when you meet a person in business situations but also in public, you should try to avoid eye contact in Asian countries. When you pass people just look at the ground or look past them. Otherwise, it would be considered as impolite. In other countries, such as the Mediterranean Region and Latin America, do not try to look away. It is often a sign that a person has something to hide or even does not like the other person. For "Westernized" women, it could also be interpreted as a sign of sexual harassment, but it is a cultural norm in those countries and should not be misinterpreted. (Beamer/Varner, 2011, pp. 221ff)

INTENSE EYE CONTACT

The Arab World and the Mediterranean Region

Latin Europeans and Latin Americans

FIRM

Northern Europe and North America

MODERATE

Korea and Thailand

Sub-Saharan Africans

INDIRECT EYE CONTACT

Most of Asia

Fig. 6.5:   The four types of eye contact in different cultures
Source: Gesteland, 2002, p. 76

Olfactics – the study of scent

"The study of communication via smell is called Olfactics. In all cultures, women can detect odors in lower concentrations, identify them more accurately and remember them longer than men." (Doty et al., 1984)

In business as well as in private life, a good first impression can make things easier. As far as the interpretation of body odor and perfume is concerned, every culture has a different approach. For example in the Western culture, the usage of deodorant and perfume is a must. People of this culture do not like any natural body smell, because it is a sign of untidiness. The culture of the Arab World regards the natural body odors as usual and does not mind if another person smells. For Asian cultures, the smell of body odor is a criticalpoint. They use at least deodorant and often perfume. A person from the Arab World should use deodorant and perfume but not too much, so the person of Asian cultures is not bothered of it. (Jandt, 2013, p. 123)

Chronemics – the study of time

"The study of the communicative function of time." ("Definitions", in web)

Traditional cultures regard the time as cyclical. The rhythms of nature and the cosmos dictate this view: Day yields to night, which in turn yields to day again; rain follows dry periods that come after rain; the time to plant leads to the time to nurture, then to the time to harvest and to the time plants die. Everything follows a pattern of birth, life, death and renewal – even daily activities, after which the weary body sleeps and awakes refreshed. Within the cyclical framework, events that occur take as long as they take; their duration is dictated by their essential nature. This view is common among agrarian cultures whose members are closely attuned to the rhythms of cultivation. The corn will be ripe when it has finished ripening, in its own time. It is also persistent in cultures that value human interaction and relationship (Varner/Beamer, 2011, p. 130–131).

What does it mean to be "on time"? The definition of punctuality varies from culture to culture. The cultural priority of time has close links to another priority: relationship versus results. When people are important and the nurturing of relationship matters, the time necessary for those activities is flexible.

You might have an appointment in Jeddah/Saudi Arabia at 10 a.m. and you might be the second appointment on the person's agenda, and you might still be waiting at 11 a.m. Everybody is so important that no meeting can be rushed for the sake of a schedule that is imposed arbitrarily. In Buenos Aires/Argentina, traffic snarls often delay people from arriving on time at meetings, and although an apology is expected, lateness is not considered an insult. Both Saudi Arabians and Argentinians have strong orientations towards building relationships in order to do business effectively.

In results-oriented cultures, adherence to schedules is much more important. In Israel, for example, promptness is a basic courtesy as well as an indication of seriousness about work. In Russia, time is not related to cost or profits, and punctuality – being "on time" – is an alien concept:

"Russians are notoriously not on time, and they think nothing of arriving long after the appointed hour, which is not considered as being late" (Richmond, 1992, p. 122).

As shown in chapter 2, Hall differentiated between monochronic (one-dimensional) time and polychronic (multidimensional) time. Monochronic time is linear and people are expected to arrive at work on time and work for a certain number of hours at certain activities. In polychronic cultures, time is an open-ended resource that is not to be constrained. Context sets the pace and rhythm, not the clock. Events take as long as they need to take; communication does not have to conclude according to the clock. Different activities have different clocks.

6.7.2   Dress code

Businesspeople must be particularly sensitive to dress in other cultures because of the negative image tourists have created. Westerners often assume that their leisure dress is appropriated everywhere. The standard business dress around the world is the suit, shirt, and tie for men, and some sort of suit or dress for women. That sounds easy, yet there are enough variations indicating authority that businesspeople must be aware of local customs and tradition. Some examples how to dress correctly are to be found in the following box.

Dress Code around the world – some examples
(Morrison/Conaway/Borden)

Argentina:
- Dress is very important for making a good impression. Your entire wardrobe will be scrutinized.
- While Argentines are more in touch with European clothing styles than many Latin Americans, they tend towards the modest and the subdued. The provocative clothing in Brazil, for example, is rarely seen in Argentina.
- Business dress is fairly conservative: dark suits and ties for men; white blouses and dark skirts for women.
- Both men and women wear pants as casual wear. If you are meeting business associates (outdoor barbecues, called asado, are popular), avoid jeans and wear a jacket or blazer. Women should not wear shorts, except when invited to a swimming pool.

China:
- For business, men should wear conservative suits, shirts, and ties. Loud colors are not appropriate. Women should also wear conservative suits, with high-necked blouses, and low heels – their colors should be as neutral as possible.
- At formal occasions, no high heels or evening gowns are necessary for women unless the event is a formal reception given by a foreign diplomat. Men may wear suits and ties.

France:
- The French are very aware of the dress. Be conservative and invest in well-made clothes and shoes.
- Men should wear dark suits and the women should also wear conservative suits.

India:
- For business dress, men should wear a suit and tie, although the jacket may be removed in the summer. Businesswomen should wear conservative dresses or pantsuits.
- For casual wear, short-sleeved shirts and long trousers are preferred for men. Women must keep their upper arms, chest, back, and legs covered at all times.
- Note that wearing leather (including belts, handbags, or purses) may be considered offensive, especially in temples. Hindus revere cows, and do not use leather products.

Saudi Arabia:
- Foreigners should wear Western clothes that approach the modesty of Saudi dress. Despite the heat of the desert, most of the body must remain covered.
- Men should wear long trousers and a shirt, preferably long-sleeved. A jacket and tie are usually required for business meetings. Keep shirts buttoned up to the collarbone. Saudi law prohibits the wearing of neck jewelry by men, and Westerners have been arrested for violating such rules.
- Women must wear modest clothing. The neckline should be high, and the sleeves should come to at least the elbows. Hemlines should be well below the knee, if not ankle-length. The overall effect should be one of baggy concealment; a full-length

> outfit that is tight and revealing is not acceptable. Therefore, pants or pantsuits are not recommended. While a hat or scarf is not always required, it is wise to keep a scarf at hand.
>
> In: Kiss, Bow, or Shake Hands, 1994, p. 24ff

The overall message is clear: you have to show respect and sincerity by the way you dress and by respecting certain rules of appearance of the host culture. That does not mean you have to adopt your clothes to the customs of the host culture. Keep in mind that you are a representative of your country and the way you are dressed is based upon your own point of view as a business man or a business woman.

6.7.3   Business cards

To communicate well and build successful relationships with people from around the world, the right handling of business cards is part of any intercultural competence. One of the first official acts in being involved in international business is the exchange of business cards. Business cards have an important function.

> **Forms of Address: Chinese Names**
> (Scott D. Seligman)
>
> The first thing you need to remember about Chinese names is that the surname comes first, not last. More than 95 percent of all Chinese surnames are one syllable – that is to say, one character – in length; some of the most common examples are Wang, Chen, Zhang, Li, Zhao, and Lin. For business purposes it is traditionally acceptable to call a Chinese person by the surname, together with a title such as Mister or Miss or even Minister or Managing Director. Thus Mr. Wang, Managing Director Liu, or Ms. Zhao would all be acceptable forms of address, and there is no problem with mixing an English title and a Chinese surname in just that order.
>
> In: Chinese Business Etiquette, New York, 1999, p. 32

This can be best demonstrated by the example of Japan. Like other countries of the world, Japan has its own business customs and culture. If someone fails to adhere to these traditions, the individual runs the risk of being perceived as ineffective or uncaring. The exchange of business cards is an integral part of Japanese business etiquette, and Japanese businesspeople exchange these cards when meeting someone for the first time. Additionally, those who are most likely to interface with non-Japanese are supplied with business cards printed in Japanese on one side and a foreign language, usually English, on the reverse side. This is aimed at enhancing recognition and pronunciation of Japanese names, which are often unfamiliar to foreign businesspeople. Conversely, it is advisable for foreign business people to carry and exchange with their Japanese counterparts a similar type of card printed in Japanese and in their native language. These cards can often be obtained through business centers in major hotels. Of course, this also applies to other countries and an example of a bilingual business card from Vietnam can be found in the following.

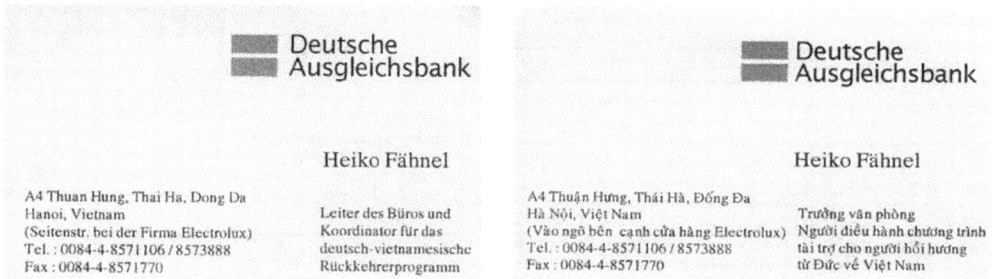

■■ Deutsche
■■ Ausgleichsbank

Heiko Fähnel

A4 Thuan Hung, Thai Ha, Dong Da
Hanoi, Vietnam
(Seitenstr. bei der Firma Electrolux)
Tel. : 0084-4-8571106 / 8573888
Fax : 0084-4-8571770

Leiter des Büros und
Koordinator für das
deutsch-vietnamesische
Rückkehrerprogramm

■■ Deutsche
■■ Ausgleichsbank

Heiko Fähnel

A4 Thuận Hưng, Thái Hà, Đống Đa
Hà Nội, Việt Nam
(Vào ngõ bên cạnh cửa hàng Electrolux)
Tel. : 0084-4-8571106 / 8573888
Fax : 0084-4-8571770

Trưởng văn phòng
Người điều hành chương trình
tài trợ cho người hồi hương
từ Đức về Việt Nam

Fig. 6.6:   A bilingual Vietnamese business card
Source: Rothlauf, 1998, p. 12

Vietnames names and forms of address

The full Vietnamese name is usually composed of two or three parts. In contrast to the European tradition, the surname comes first. As a middle name, "Thi" for a girl and "Van" for a boy are often used. For the actual first name, a careful selection takes place, since it is common belief that especially the first name will influence the person's life. Girls are often named after flowers or trees, e.g. Hong (rose) or Lien (lotus), while the boys' names are often connected to certain characteristics, such as smart (Minh) or virtuous (Duc). (HIWC, 1998, p. 9)

MINISTRY OF PLANNING AND INVESTMENT

EPCTC   Dr. PHAM VAN PHO
Director
The Economic - Planning Cadre Training Center
Executive Manager
The Central Club of Directors

Office : 68 Phan Dinh Phung   Res : Flat 502, House K18
Street, Hanoi   Bach Khoa, Hanoi
Tel : 8.431818 - 8.431812   Tel : 8690309

When exchanging business cards, one often asks for the other person's name. This is also done to be able to address the counterpart correctly. If you have seen that the contact's name is "Dr. Pham Van Pho" and he holds the title "Director", as you can see in this example, the correct form of address would be "Dr. Pho". In general, people are addressed with their title and their first name, or only with their title ("Thank you, Director").

As far as the formal description of the visitor's current position within a company is concerned, there are some particularities one should keep in mind. As an example, we suppose that you are a Marketing Director in your home country and you are allowed to sign contracts. The counterpart in Japan is on the same level and is called Kacho, but without any competence to give you all the necessary information for a final deal. Only for this purpose, one should get promoted, for example to an Executive Managing Director in order to meet somebody who has the relevant information and the support from the top management.

Tab. 6.5:   Titles and positions in Japanese companies
Source: JETRO, 1975, p. 9

Japanese titles	English translation
Kaicho	Chairman
Shacho	President
Fuku Shacho	Vice-President
Senmu Torishimariyaku	Senior Executive Managing Director
Jomu Torishimariyaku	Executive Managing Director
Torishimariyaku	Director
Bucho	General Manager
Bucho Dairi	Deputy General Manager
Kacho	Manager
Kacha Dairi	Assistant Manager
Kakaricho	Chief

When receiving a card, it is considered common courtesy to offer one in return. In fact, not returning a card might convey the impression that the manager is not committed to a meaningful business relationship in the future. Business cards should be presented and received with both hands. When presenting one's card, the presentor's name should be facing the person who is receiving the card so the receiver can easily read it. When receiving a business card, it should be handled with care and if the receiver is sitting at a conference or other type of table, the card should be placed in front of the individual for the duration of the meeting. It is considered rude to put a prospective business partner's card in one's pocket before sitting down to discuss business matters. In order to avoid a certain kind of embarrassment, you should have a sufficient number of business cards at hand, respectively in your hotel.

6.7.4   Gifts

Arab Business Culture
(Jehad Al-Omari)

As business is personal, exchanging favors is very common in the Arab world. There is no stigma or sense of shame attached to the giving and receiving of favors. So you should neither be embarrassed to ask for a favor, nor reluctant to grant one when asked. This is especially true for small favors: for example, arranging to visit your host's son who is studying in the West; sending medicine to his sick mother; arranging to meet a friend at the airport. These would be standard favors that would not cost much financially, nor interfere with general moral codes.

In: Simple Guide to the Arab Way: Practical tips on Arab culture, 2003, p. 22

In cultures where business is personal, gift-giving and exchanging favors is a universal way to please someone. However, a lot of misunderstandings can occur in this context if one is not fully aware about the right or wrong doing. The following example may underline what can happen if such a misinterpretation takes place (Martin/Nakayama, 2010, p. 279):

> *"One colleague of mine, Nishehs, once tried to impress our boss, Joe. Nishehs brought a well-wrapped gift to Joe and he was pleased as he received the gift, but his smile faded away quickly right after he opened the gift. Joe questioned Nishehs angrily, "Why is it green?" Shocked and speechless, Nishehs murmured, "What`s wrong with a green hat?"*

The misunderstanding resulted from the cultural differences between them. Nishehs is an Indian, whereas Joe is Chinese. For the Chinese, a green hat means one's wife is having an affair.

Gifts in China
(Scott D. Seligman)

Because gift-giving is an area in which common practice departs from the rules, it's hard to be categorical in giving advice on how best to proceed. The most conservative approach remains the traditional one: a single large gift for the whole group, presented to the leader either during a meeting or a banquet. On the more reckless end of the spectrum would be a very valuable gift presented in private to a powerful individual; the chances of this being construed as bribery if discovered are great.

In: Chinese Business Etiquette, New York, 1999, p. 169

There are a lot of questions that have to be answered:

- Which colors should be avoided and which colors are associated with positive feelings?
- When has the right time come to hand over gifts and to whom first?
- Who starts with the exchange of gifts?
- Which kind of gifts are prohibited?
- What is the role of women in this context?
- Is there a difference between a business and a private invitation?
- What is the right value of a gift?
- Does the body language play a role?
- What about imitation as a gift?
- Is bribery a topic in this context?

People of all cultures like to be surprised with a gift that fits into the given context. Here, your intercultural skills are required. The best intercultural recommendation one can give is to take a look at books that specifically deal with those questions.

The following box will help you to gain such an insight.

Gifts all around the world – some examples
(Morrison/Conaway/Bordon)

Finland:
- A bottle of wine is a good token of appreciation when you go to a Finnish home (along with the flowers for the hostess).
- Business gifts should not be too extravagant or too skimpy, and should not be given at a first meeting.
- A personalized gift, such as a book on a topic of interest to your client, is appreciated.
- Fiskars scissors (with the orange handles) are the most commonly imitated Finnish product. Avoid giving any type of gift that may compete with them.

Indonesia:
- Gift giving is a traditional part of Indonesian culture. Although gifts may be small, they are given often.
- You will give gifts to celebrate an occasion, when you return from a trip, when you are invited to an Indonesian home, when a visitor comes to your office or workplace, and in return for services rendered.
- It is not the custom to unwrap a gift in presence of the giver. To do so would suggest that the recipient is greedy and impatient.
- Since pork and alcohol are prohibited to observing Muslims, do not give them as gifts to Indonesians. Other foods make good gifts, although meat products must be halal (the Muslim equivalent of kosher).
- Muslim Indonesians consider dogs unclean. Do not give toy dogs or gifts with pictures of dogs.

Israel:
- Avoid giving a gift until you know something about the person you are giving it to. Especially with Orthodox Jews and Arabs, a gift must not violate one of the restrictions of their belief system.
- If you are invited to an Israeli home, bring a gift of flowers or candy. Be sure a gift of food is kosher if it is going to an Orthodox person.
- Make sure you give or receive gifts with the right hand, not with the left (although using both hands is acceptable).

Mexico:
- Giving gifts to executives in a business context is not required. However, small gifts, such as items with a company logo (for an initial visit) or a bottle of wine or scotch (on subsequent trips), are appreciated.
- When giving flowers, be aware that Mexican folklore maintains that yellow flowers represent death, red flowers cast spells, and white flowers lift spells.
- Secretaries do expect gifts. A government secretary who performs any service for you is given a token gift. For secretaries in the private sector, a more valuable (such as perfume or a scarf) should be given on a return visit. A businessman giving such a gift to a female secretary should say that the gift was sent by his wife.

- Avoid giving gifts made of silver; silver is associated with trinkets sold to tourists in Mexico.
- Gifts of knives should be avoided in Latin America, as they can symbolize the severing of friendship.

United States of America:
- Business gifts are discouraged by the law, which allows only a $25 tax deduction on gifts.
- When you visit a home, it is not necessary to take a gift; however, it is always appreciated. You may take flowers, a plant, or a bottle of wine.
- If you wish to give flowers, have them sent ahead so as not to burden your hostess with taking care of them when you arrive.
- If you stay in a U.S. home for a few days, a gift is appropriated. You may also write a letter of thanks.

In: Kiss, Bow, or Shake Hands, 1994, p. 33ff

6.8   The expert's view: Interview with Daniel Frisch

Living and working in South Korea as a German, Daniel Frisch, Head of Business Management APAC for Siemens Ultrasound/Vice President for Sales and Marketing of Ultrasound could provide valuable insights into intercultural communication in Korea.

Students: *How did the first conversations with the people in the new surroundings proceed?*

Frisch: The welcome was warm; the Korean partners were very interested in getting to know a lot of things and asked a lot of very personal and direct questions: age, married, children, how many, how old, studied, where, hobbies, parents etc.

This is for a German manager (very job- and fact-focused) very confusing in the beginning. The reason is they need this, to position you within their hierarchy matrix (Confucius)! Due to extreme English language issues (in almost all North East Asia countries, most worse in Korea, because of above mentioned culture reasons), it is more difficult to get involved. People talk mostly everyday Korean and and the German partners are not included in their daily conversations.

Another challenge is the extreme hierarchical order (mostly Confucius-driven/minded country: men/women, senior/junior, boss/employee) that makes things much more difficult.

Moreover, it is hard to understand how the communication can be interpreted. Korean people talk most of the time indirectly, which means that they never say "no, we cannot do this". At the same time they smile and the Germans are getting confused to find out the right message. On the other hand, if one says "no", they see it as an attack on them. The same is going to happen if one speaks too fast or tries to get directly down to business. On such a basis it will become hard in building up trust. Keep in mind that loyalty and respect are valued most going back to the philosophy of Confucius. So, it will take a while to get familiar with all those cultural barriers.

Students: *Which specific cultural differences are to be observed compared to the European culture?*

Frisch: Formal differences are that you give the right hand as a welcoming and take every time the left hand to your elbow of the right hand, to "hold" the arm. This is a very respectful gesture within Korea which is also used for exchange of biz cards and credit cards or money. For a good bye, you do not use hands mostly (using hands is very German - also hugs are a no-go) and just make a bow. Is the counterpart much higher in hierarchy or a customer, you have to make more bows (2–3 times) and also very deep ones (level of hips).

The exchange of business cards plays an important role in doing business in Korea. For example: a view on the card tells you the rank of your partner within his company and you can draw the right conclusion for the further collaboration.

Students: *How is communication in business?*

Frisch: Koreans need 2–3 meetings for the introduction of people and the project, before the real negotiation process can start. Then they expect also a lot of flexibility from the other party to respect their challenges and needs. So straight, fast and to the point negotiation, combined with strong rules and processes (like German companies and in particular Siemens is doing) are not so easy to be accepted. On the other side, German companies are respected for their quality, reliability, loyalty, brand of products and technology of hardware (not IT)! [...]

A special tA very peculiar thing in Korea is that there is a specific focus on entertainment for business meetings. Almost every deal is connected to a dinner, real music entertainment or the famous Golf play (major hobby within Korea)!

Students: *What are characteristics of the para-verbal communication in Korea?*

Frisch: The communication in Korea is focused on harmony and comfortable feelings for every party involved. As I said, it is very indirect and a direct "No" is very rude. Every time (even if not possible) people will give you a satisfying positive answer. This can come to that level, that even 3 times asking for a simple direct question, can bring an indirect answer ("we will try best", "we have to see the challenges", "it should be possible"), sometimes even answers to a very different topic. It can go even to the level of lying, but not in a bad way, just to keep everybody's "face".

In: Darmer/Geigle/Persidska/Sikinger, Written Assignement, 2013 (unpublished)

The 16th Annual IMI Conference on Incultural Relations

For more than 50 years, the Intercultural Management Institute (IMI) – formerly the Business Council for International Understanding Institute (BCIU) – has worked toward promoting cultural understanding through innovative and dynamic intercultural communication training. Never before have the effects of international communication been so far-reaching and immediate. The lesson is clear: in our global community, we tend to ignore the importance of intercultural relations at our own peril. Reciprocally, collectively we have made tremendous strides in the field of intercultural relations, and it is those successes and best practices that we continue to share at our annual conference. Join us for the ***IMI 15th Annual Conference on Intercultural Relations: A Forum for Business, Education and Training Professionals***, March 13–14, 2014, in the School of International Service building at American University in Washington, D.C

In: Annual IMI Conference-Website, 2014

6.9   Case Study: German manager meets Saudi Arabian chairman

Dr. Bauer, managing director of the construction machinery factory "Tiefhoch GmbH", and the chairman of the Saudi-Arabian construction company "Marsala", Mr. Muhammed Mubruk, have arranged to meet for a first exchange of information in Riad. The meeting has been preceded by some correspondence dealing with Tiefhoch's product range in general. Moreover, Marsala's wish to receive more information about specific building cranes for a major project in Saudi-Arabia has become obvious. Finally, both sides have agreed upon a visit of Dr. Bauer in Saudi Arabia from 3rd to 5th March.

Today is the first encounter of both managers in Mr. Mubruk's office. The first meeting has been scheduled at 10 o'clock. Dr. Bauer arrives shortly before the appointed time. The door to the office of Mr. Mubruk is open and Mr. Bauer has already spotted him as he is waiting for the meeting. After about 15 minutes he is now asked by the secretary to follow him to Mr. Mubruk's office.

Instructions for the Role Play

In brackets, you will find instructions for the adequate use of body language.

The following characters are to be casted (all men):

- Dr. Bauer
- Mr. Mubruk
- Two friends of Mr. Mubruk
- Mr. Mubruk's secretary

Initially, the role play is supposed to show Dr. Bauer's wrong behavior. After an intensive discussion, a second role play should take place, which shows how to behave interculturally correct.

Secretary:	*(Ushers Dr. Bauer into the conference room)*
Mubruk:	Welcome to Riad, Dr. Bauer. *(Offers him his right hand)*
Dr. Bauer:	As-salamu alaikum, Mr. Mubruk *(Dr. Bauer acknowledges the salutation with both hands.)*
Mubruk:	How was your journey, Dr. Bauer?
Dr. Bauer:	Basically, without any problems. Only the hot temperatures here in Saudi-Arabia are very discomforting for me.
Mubruk:	Fortunately, we have chosen March for our first meeting. In the following months, the temperatures rise up to 40°C. However, I think it should be bearable here in my office, thanks to the air conditioning.
Dr. Bauer:	May I give you my business card? *(printed on both sides in German respectively English, handing it over with his left hand)*
Mubruk:	*(Takes the business card with his right hand and turns it to read it first; afterwards he hands his own business card over to Dr. Bauer, who quickly accepts it and immediately puts it into his jacket pocket)*

	Shall we sit down? *(Subsequently, Mr. Mubruk asks Dr. Bauer to take a seat in an armchair opposite to his desk)*
Mubruk:	May I offer you a cup of coffee?
Dr. Bauer:	I would prefer a glass of mineral water.
Mubruk:	Most certainly.
Secretary:	*(Shortly afterwards, his secretary comes in with the requested refreshments for Dr. Bauer and pours a cup of coffee for Mr. Mubruk.)*
	(The telephone is ringing and the call takes quite a long time. After hanging up Mr. Mubruk continues his conversation with Dr. Bauer.)
Mubruk:	How do you like our capital Riad?
Dr. Bauer:	Unfortunately, I haven't seen much of it yet. Immediately after my arrival yesterday afternoon, I was tired, took a rest and then went to the hotel restaurant for dinner.
Secretary:	*(Mr. Mubruk's secretary enters and presents a signature folder to Mr. Mubruk. Both shortly converse in Arabian.)*
Mubruk:	Are you interested in horse racing?
Dr. Bauer:	No. My favorite sport is golf. By the way, how is your family?
Mubruk:	*(After some hesitation)* In Saudi-Arabia, we really appreciate family businesses, which we also run like a family.
	(Visitors appear in the outer office. Two friends of Mr. Mubruk enter the room. After a cordial greeting with kisses on the respective cheek, they start talking and drinking coffee which is brought in by the secretary. After approximately 10 minutes, the conversation comes to an end.)
Mubruk:	Dr. Bauer, may I now offer you a cup of Arabian coffee?
Dr. Bauer:	Well, let's try it.
Secretary:	*(The secretary enters and pours coffee from a typical Saudi-Arabian coffee pot into a small mocha-like cup.)*
Mubruk:	How do you like our Arabian coffee?
Dr. Bauer:	My imagination of your Arabian coffee was a little bit different. It has a slightly bitter taste. So, may I have some sugar, please? *(The telephone rings. A five-minute-long conversation follows.)*
Secretary:	*(The secretary comes in and asks Dr. Bauer:)* Would you like to have some more coffee, Dr. Bauer?
Dr. Bauer:	*(Refuses with an abrupt gesture.)*
Secretary:	Would you like to have some more coffee, Mr. Mubruk?
	(Mr. Mubruk twiddles his cup three times with his right hand.)
Mubruk:	In Saudi-Arabia, we're very keen on football and we really want to qualify for the World Cup again.
	Our big role model here is Germany and we'd be very proud to have a football player like Franz Beckenbauer!

Dr. Bauer:	Unfortunately, I'm not very interested in football, but maybe I could briefly present you our range of product.
Mubruk:	*(After glancing at his watch)* Maybe we should continue our conversation in the evening. I've chosen a special restaurant for that. My driver will pick you up at around 8 pm.
	Shortly, the muezzin will call to prayer. By the way, we pray five times a day in Saudi-Arabia.
	I assume that my driver may pick you up at the time mentioned. *(Mubruk rises; Dr. Bauer is still obviously consternated)*
	See you tonight! Good bye, Dr. Bauer!
Dr. Bauer:	Good bye, Mr. Mubruk! *(Dr. Bauer bids good bye to Mr. Mubruk with a handshake and a deeply bowed head.)*

Source: Rothlauf, J., in: Seminarunterlagen, 2005, S. 28

Review and Discussion Questions:

1. Which verbal und non-verbal mistakes of Dr. Bauer became obvious during his meeting with Mr. Mubruk? List them all and then describe how a solution should look like! You should find at least five mistakes.

2. How would you assess Dr. Bauer's intercultural preparation and what do you think is absolutely necessary to deal effectively and interculturally correctly with Arab partners?

3. Dr. Bauer arrived in Riad on Monday afternoon and has booked his return flight for Thursday. Do you think that his time schedule will meet the expected requirements of both sides? Give a profound answer!

4. During the time of Ramadan you are expecting a delegation of Kuwaiti managers, who will be arriving in Hamburg on Sunday. How should you develop the schedule for Monday with a specific focus on time tables and infrastructural needs (presents for the guests, drinks on the table, lunch, dinner, etc.)? How would you welcome your guests before the dinner starts?

7   Leadership Across Cultures

7.0   Statement of the problem

Bridging the culture gap
(Carté/Fox)

You are running an international project with very tight deadlines. Your colleague, Susan, knows that she needs to send you a detailed progress report at the end of every month. It's now 5 July and Susan's June report has only just arrived – nearly a week late. To make matters worse, some of the figures are inaccurate. You decide to call her.

How would you instinctively handle the conversation with Susan? Would you feel more comfortable taking approach A, or approach B?

Approach A
You: I'm calling about your June report. It was a week late and some of the figures were inaccurate.
Susan: Yes, I know. I'm very sorry about that. A couple of my people were off sick.
You: Yes but, Susan, you must respect the deadlines. If you don't, we'll fall behind schedule. And, in future, please make sure that you check all the figures very carefully.

Approach B
You: I'm calling about your June report.
Susan: I was just about to call you. I'm sorry it was late, but a couple of my people were off sick.
You: Oh dear… The thing is, I've just been through the figures and I'm afraid some of them don't seem to add up.
Susan: Don't they? Oh, I'm sorry. I had to put them together very quickly.
You: Right. But what about this month? Will you be able to spend a bit more time on them?
Susan: Yes, of course.
You: Great. Because, as you know, there's an important deadline coming up, and we'll be in real trouble if we miss it.

In: Bridging the culture gap, London 2004, p. 81

7.1   The foundation for leadership

Leadership is often credited for the success or failure of international operations. When one realizes that much of history, political science, and the behavioral sciences is either directly or indirectly related to leadership, the statement that more concern and research has been focused on leadership than on other topic becomes believable (Hodgetts/Luthans, 2003, p. 412). Numerous leadership theories variously focus on individual traits, leader behavior, interaction patterns, role relationships, follower perception, influence over followers, influence on task goals, and influence on organizational culture. But so far, there is no generally agreed-on definition. Effective leadership involves the ability to inspire and influence the thinking, attitudes, and behavior of people or in other words: leadership can be defined as a process by which a person influences others to accomplish an objective and directs the organization in a way that makes it more cohesive and coherent.

A leader is someone who stands not only for his cause but takes responsibility and motivates other individuals as well. There is a clear difference between being a boss and a leader. A leader motivates and inspires others to aim high and attain that aim. However, a boss only supervises over his subordinates. Power comes naturally to a leader, but power is not a tool of the leader.

Leadership is not a quality but it is an individual's behaviour. A leader showcases a positive attitude and high self-esteem. He assertively works towards the goal but never gets pushy for it. The task of helping employees to realize their highest potential in the workplace is the essence of leadership. Today's global managers are aware that increased competition requires them to be open to change and to rethink their old culturally conditioned modes of leadership. A continuous self study, training, evaluation and imbibing positive things in life develop the characteristics of a leader.

Ronald E. Riggio, Professor of Leadership and Organizational Psychology at Mc Kenna College, Claremont

Question: Are leaders born or made?
Dr. Riggio: This isn't something that requires my opinion, because this question has been well researched. The twin studies by Richard Arvey and his colleagues have estimated that leadership is about 2/3 "made" and 1/3 "born". This makes sense, though, if we see much of leadership as a set of learned skills and competencies: ability to communicate, strategize, problem solve, etc. This takes time to develop.

This question would have broad implications for leadership, for if it were all (or mostly) born, then our efforts should be directed toward identifying and selecting leaders, and we would be wasting our time on leader development programs. But, the research suggests that putting resources into leadership development makes sense, and recent meta-analyses of these programs suggest that, in general, they work and lead to positive gains.

Cutting-Edge Leadership, in: Psychology Today, October 7, 2012, p. 12

7.2   Leadership styles

The importance of the leadership role cannot be overemphasized because the leader's inter-actions strongly influence the motivation and behavior of employees, and ultimately, the entire climate of the organization. Modern leadership theory recognizes that no single leader-ship style works well in all situations. Leader behaviors can be translated into three common-ly recognized styles: (1) authoritarian; (2) paternalistic; and (3) participative. Moreover, there are four more types (4) laissez-faire; (5) transformational; (6) charismatic; and (7) transac-tional style that are presented here to get a better understanding how the process of influenc-ing people to direct their efforts toward the achievement of some particular goal(s) takes place.

7.2.1   Authoritarian leadership

Authoritarian leadership can be described as the use of work-centered behavior that is de-signed to ensure task accomplishment. (Hodgetts/Luthhans/Doh, 2006, p. 400)

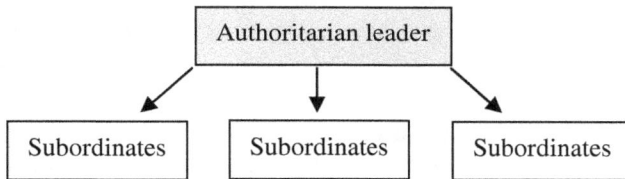

Fig. 7.1:   Authoritarian leadership
Source: Hodgetts, 2002, p. 264

This style is characterized by the use of one-way communication. The information goes only from the manager to the subordinate. Authoritarian leaders are keeping their focus on the work performance of the employees and reaching goals. The personnel needs of the employ-ees are less important. This leading style is used by managers who follow the Theory X or also to manage crisis in organisations. (Hodgetts/Luthhans/Doh, 2006, p. 400) One of the biggest advantages is that the manager is able make decisions very quickly. There is not a long working process because the leader has the sole responsibility. Furthermore, the au-thoritarian style can be a perfect working style for a leader who likes to have the total control and overview on the company activities. There is also a down side because the managers who follow the authoritarian style are under high pressure and that can have a negative im-pact on their health. This style can be difficult for certain subordinates as well. The commu-nication goes only from one direction so the leader tells his employees what to do. The em-ployees are not allowed to produce new ideas or improvement suggestions. Consequently there is a big risk that the employees get frustrated and unmotivated.

The graph makes also clear that in case of the authoritarian leadership style the communica-tion and exchange of information go downwards, only in one direction from the leader to the subordinates.

7.2.2   Paternalistic leadership

Paternalistic leadership is understood as a work-centred behavior coupled with a protective employee-centred concern. (Hodgetts/Luthhans/Doh, 2006, p. 400)

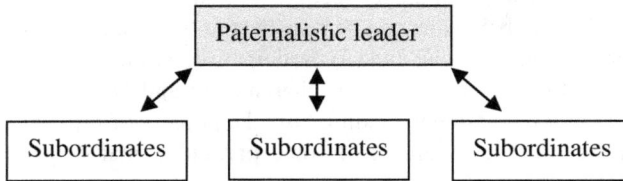

Fig. 7.2:   Paternalistic leadership
Source: Hodgetts, 2002, p. 264

The paternalisatic style is often characterized by "work hard and the company will take care of you" (ibid.). The major benefit is that the leader gives the subordinates support such as medical or retirement benefits. He is acting like a father and taking care of the social needs of his employees. They are highly motivated to deliver a good work performance. The relationship between these co-workers and the leader are extremely solid. The employees are expected to stay with the company for a longer period of time because of the loyalty and trust (Erben, 2008, p. 12).

The figure illustrates that in the case of paternalistic leadership style the information flow goes from the leader to the subordinates and back. It makes also clear that there is a continual communication between those two parties.

7.2.3   Participative leadership

The particpative leadership style leadership style is a combination of a work-centered and a people-centered approach and also known as a democratic leadership where the subordinates are involved in the decision making and controlling processes of the company.

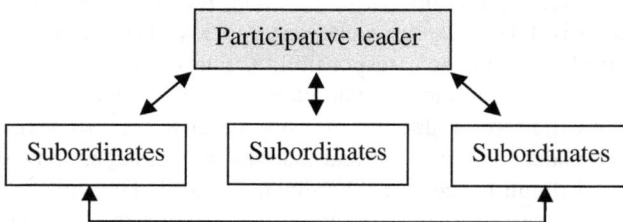

Fig. 7.3:   Participative leadership
Source: Hodgetts, 2002, p. 264

This style of leadership encompasses discussion, debate and sharing of ideas and encouragement of people to feel good about their involvement. The advantage is that the employees have the opportunity of being creative which enables the company to be innovative. Furthermore, the employees can improve their skills and knowledge which leads to a higher qualification and at the end to more money. One of the mayor disadvantages linked to this style is that the decision-making process requires a lot of time because more or less all employees should be actively involved.

The figure shows that in the case of a participative leadership, the flow of information is continuous and goes from the leader to the subordinates and back. Furthermore, this style supports the interaction and communication among the subordinates.

7.2.4   Laissez-faire leadership

Laissez-faire leadership is based upon the philosphy "let them do" and describes leaders who allow their people to work on their own. This type of leadership can also occur naturally when managers do not have enough control over their work and their people. Those leaders give their employees the possibility to take their own decisions. This kind of leadership will be supported by providing all necessary information and resources for the employees. This type of leadership is connected with a strong motivation, improved productivity and a high amount of satisfaction. However, this style is only successful when the employees are used to bear responsibility and experienced enough to carry out all main activities on their own. (Cherry, 2013)

7.2.5   Transformational leadership

The transformational leader treats each co-worker as a "whole" individual rather than as an employee and considers the individual's talents and levels of knowledge to decide what suits him or her best (Couldfield, 2013, p. 14).

They are able to inspire and motivate their team members. Consequently, the transformational style has a positive impact on the work performances of the team. Furthermore, this style keeps the major focus on interaction between the leader and the subordinates. Communication and a continuous flow of information among the leader and the employees are the major keys to fulfil company goals.

7.2.6   Charismatic leadership

The charismatic leader inspires and motivates employees through his or her charismatic traits and abilities. (Hodgetts/Luthhans, 2006, p. 415)

Charismatic leaders are essentially very skilled communicators – individuals who are both verbally eloquent, but also able to communicate to followers on a deep, emotional level. They are able to articulate a compelling or captivating vision, and are able to arouse strong emotions in followers (Riggio, 2012, p. 2). There is also a downside, because charismatic leaders trust only themselves, not their employees. This creates a high risk because the whole organization depends on the performance of the leader and when he or she fails the entire company might collapse. Furthermore, the employees are less motivated when their leader does not believe in the team.

"As long as you are going to be thinking anyway, THINK BIG."

(Donald Trump)

7.2.7   Transactional leadership

Transactional leadership is based upon the assumption that subordinates and systems work better under a clear chain of command. The implicit belief in the leader-follower relationship is that people are motivated by rewards and penalties (Marurano, 2008, p. 166). "Transaction" includes paying employees in return for high productivity and a good work performance. On the other hand, the transactional leader can "punish" the team members when he or she is not satisfied with their performance.

The transactional leadership style is the most effective style in international business and is characterized by the following factors, which are also known as the "I's" (Hodgetts/Luthhans, 2006, p. 416):

1.   *"**Idealized influence:** Transformational leaders are a source of charisma and enjoy the admiration of their followers. They enhance pride, loyalty, and confidence in their people, and they align these followers by providing a common purpose or vision that the latter willingly accept.*

2.   ***Inspirational motivation:** These leaders are extremely effective in articulating their visions, missions, and beliefs in clear-cut ways, thus providing an easy-to understand sense of purpose regarding what needs to be done.*

3.   ***Intellectual stimulation:** Transformation leaders are able to get their followers to question old paradigms and to accept new views of the world regarding how their things need to be done.*

4.   ***Individuals consideration:** These leaders are able to diagnose and elevate the needs of each of their followers through individualized consideration, thus furthering the development of these people."*

7.2.8   Leadership styles in the international context

Which leadership style an internationally operating manager applies depends on the country and the area a company is doing business. The cultural background has a strong influence, but also the size of the company, the organizational structure, the age and the experiences a leader has made play a big role. Much research has shown that the leadership style in Europe keeps focused on decision-making, controlling, risk-taking, planning and organizational structure (Hodgetts/Luthhans, 2006, pp. 404f).

> *"For example, British managers tend to use a highly participative leadership approach. This is true for two reasons: one because the political background of the country favours such an approach; and two because most top British managers are not highly involved in the day-to-day affairs of the business, they prefer to delegate authority and let much of the decision making be handled by middle- and lower-level managers. This preference contrasted sharply with that of the French and the Germans, who prefer a more work-centred, authoritarian approach. In fact, if labour unions did not have legally mandated seats on the board of directors, participative management in Germany likely would be even less pervasive than it is. This is a problem that currently confronts firms like Volkswagen that are trying to reduce sharply their overhead to meet increasing competition in Europe. Scandinavian countries however make wide use of participative leadership approaches, with workers representation on*

the board of directors and high management-worker interaction regarding workplace design and changes." (Hodgetts/Luthhans, 2006, p. 405)

Consequently, most of the European managers follow the more participative and democratic leadership style.

Leadership and decision making in Japan
(Richard Mead)

The following conversation between two Japanese women managers took place during a lunch break of an international conference:

Fukuyama:	*Some Japanese people don't like job rotation. But we have to do it. Normally we don't change companies. If you join a Japanese company, and then leave, that looks like disloyalty.*
Imai:	And nobody else wants to employ you. You might never find another job. It is very difficult, if you hope to move to a respected Japanese company
Fukuyama:	*A western company might employ you, if you have the skills they need.*
Imai:	Sometimes, yes.
Fukuyama:	*So most Japanese hope to stay with their company for all their working life.*
Imai:	Loyalty to the company is an issue when it comes to accepting job rotation, because you accept the company's plan to train you.
Fukuyama:	*Of course, many managers welcome the opportunity. Those who don't, well, they have to go along with it. The company expects its managers to learn all aspects of business. They have to learn all the functions of the company.*
Imai:	So they rotate their managers around the departments. Most Japanese managers are generalists, not specialists. And still very few go to business schools. We learn within the company, and only the skills that the company requires.

In: Cases and Projects in International Management – Cross-Cultural Dimensions, 2000, p. 71

7.3   Four types of leaders

In a study, Thomas has pointed out how leaders react in an intercultural setting. He distinguishes between four different types of reactions (Thomas, 2006, pp. 31ff):

Ignorant types ignore that operation in the intercultural context includes the consideration of differences across cultures. They do not notice the differences between different cultures. It is impossible to cooperate with the ignorant type in the international arena.

Universal types are the same around the world. Cultural differences across countries do not influence their style of leadership. The Universalist meets intercultural challenges by reacting in a friendly and tolerant way as well.

Action types do not focus on intercultural differences across countries. The most important features for the action-oriented type to be successful are setting well defined goals, persuasive power and being assertive as well.

The **Exponentiator** understands that every culture consists of its own knowledge, beliefs, arts, moral laws, customs, habits and other capabilities. Those managers keep focus on the differences across culture. Furthermore, those managers believe that different cultures can be synchronized and bound together with the aim to get a competitive advantage in international business.

The four types of reaction also differ regarding the following dimensions:

- Simplicity
- Complexity, activism
- Reflexivity and intercultural dominance
- Intercultural competence

CEO: Still crazy after all these years
(Steve Jobs)

For most things in life, the range between best and average is 30 % or so. The best airplane flight, the best meal, they may be 30 % better than your average one. What I saw with Woz was somebody who was fifty times better than the average engineer. He could have meetings in his head. The Mac team was an attempt to build a whole team like that, A players. People said they wouldn't get along, they'd hate working with each other. But I realized that A players like to work with A players, they just didn't like working with C players. At Pixar, it was a whole company of A players. When I got back to Apple, that's what I decided to try to do so. You need to have a collaborative hiring process. When we hire someone, even if they're going to be in marketing, I will have them talk to the design folks and the engineers. My role model was J. Robert Oppenheimer. I read about the type of people he sought for the atom bomb project. I wasn't nearly as good as he was, but that's what I aspired to do.

In: Isaacson, W.: Steve Jobs, 2011, p. 363

7.4   The Lewis Model

The Lewis model is a diagrammatic demonstration, which is based on the evaluation of thousands of cultural profiles of 68 nationalities. It shows the cultural distance between each nationality. Richard Lewis (2006, p. 42–46) established this model to classify several hundred national and regional cultures of the world into three groups: multi-active, linear-active and reactive.

Multi-actives are doing many things at once and are planning their priorities not according to a time schedule, but according to the relative thrill or importance that each appointment brings with it. People in this group are emotional in confronts and people-oriented. Feelings have a higher value than facts and the body language is unrestrained. Members of this group are e.g. Italians, Latin Americans and Arabs.

Linear-actives are planning, scheduling, organizing, and pursuing actions and doing one thing at a time. Characteristics are, being polite, direct and confront with logic. Moreover, they are highly job-oriented and sticking to the facts and have a restrained body language. Germans and Swiss are an example for this group.

Reactive cultures prioritize courtesy and respect. They listen quietly and calmly to their interlocutors and react carefully to the other side's proposals. Those cultures are focusing on general principles and never confront someone in business. They are very people-oriented and statements are promises. Due to the subtle body language the face-to-face contact is very important. Besides, they are polite, indirect and often ask for "repeats". Chinese, Japanese and Finns belong to this group.

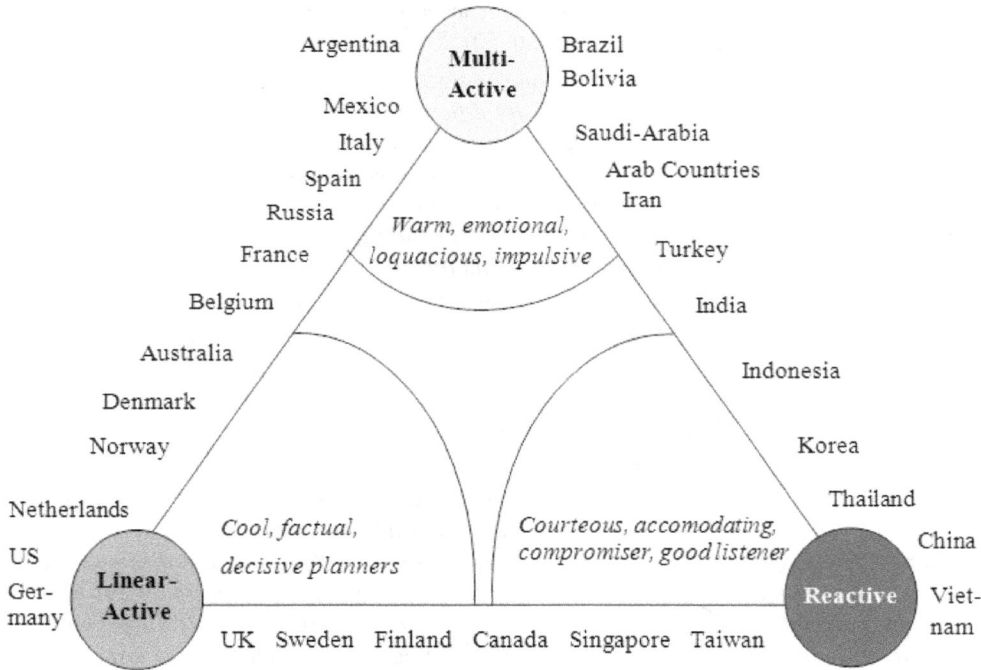

Fig. 7.4:   Cultural Types: The Lewis Model
Source: Lewis, 2006, p. 42

The Lewis model aims to promote *"harmony through understanding"*. This means that it shows how people from different cultures vary in their concepts of time and space, how they handle interpersonal distance, silence and eye contact. In addition it clarifies how their communication styles are reflected in the language patterns they use. It promotes harmony in intercultural relationships by allowing empathy and understanding to develop.

Lewis says that this categorization of national norms does not change significantly over time. The behavior of people from different cultures is not something indefinite. Clear trends, sequences and traditions exist. Reactions of Americans, Europeans, and Asians alike can be forecasted, usually justified and in the majority of cases managed. Even in countries where political and economic change is currently rapid or sweeping (Russia, China, Hungary, Poland, Korea, Malaysia, etc.), deeply rooted attitudes and beliefs will resist a sudden transformation of values when pressured by reformists, governments or multinational conglomerates.

All in all, the Lewis model guides a person to an understanding of various communication characteristics among cultures. A person is better able to get along personally as well as professionally with other cultures and is able to foresee how they are likely to react in various situations.

7.5   Leading across cultures: personality versus authenticity

The following text is part of a presentation that Michael Nagel, Manager at BearingPoint Frankfurt, held at the 14th International Baltic Sea Forum in Stralsund, entitled "A Global View on Intercultural Management" (2009, p. 50).

"Let's come to the famous take home message, what I would like to remember after this presentation. First of all, cultures are different. We can learn a lot from others. Why? Just consider none of the big emerging economies, so called BRIC countries (Brazil, Russia, India, China) is linear. So, why should the management style, let's say, the western management style better than the rest? Just look at the BRIC countries. We shouldn't think that we are the best or the superior. We are all at the same level. We have to learn from each other to find the best solution to work together.

The majority of senior managers blame cultural differences for the failure of mergers, so not the financials. It is not the product, it is not marketing. It is how the people communicate. A manager from Finland being now responsible for a Brazilian team, not being emotional, not winning the hearts, not following some simple rules, some simple advices, and all of a sudden all breaks down.

You could now say, well I want to be authentic. If I present, I want to present this Michael. I do not want to change, I do not want to act. I want to follow the rule of authenticity. You do not lose your personality or your values or your beliefs if you change. This is a stage and what do you want to do here? You want to sell something. You want to bring across a message. Here is the audience. So try to figure out what are the expectations. Do they expect a show? Or do they expect very detailed figures about analysis or whatever. So you are not changing your personality. It is just a simple practical step. Try it. The best place to try is being a student. In every single presentation you can try to be someone different. And anyway, I experienced lots of people and they told me 'I do not want to play roles'. The truth is you are playing roles all the time. I play the role of a husband when I am at home, I play the role of a presenter here, I play the role of a consultant in my company, and tonight I will play the role of a guest in a restaurant. So we are playing roles all the time. The difference makes it if you are playing a role successfully. And this does not mean changing the personality."

"Emotional leadership is the spark
that ignites a company's performance,
creating a bonfire of success or a landscape of ashes"

(Robert Gill)

7.6   Leadership affected by religion

In the majority of international organizations, homogenous teams belong to the past. More and more teams are made up of people with different nationalities and therefore you can find different religion, cultures, languages, ideas, behaviors and ways of doing things. When people of different religious backgrounds come together, it is not easy to find a common ground. This is because they bring with them their own cultural baggage in terms of how they do things and expect things to be done. As an example, religion in India is rated as extremely important, whereas, in Germany, the topic rather fades into the background

But nevertheless: The religious background is getting more and more important because the number of believers all around the world is steadily increasing. How Confucianism, Islam, and Hinduism influence international business in general and the leadership style in particular will be described in this chapter.

There are various types of religions, so it is impossible to generalize it or even look at all and examine their influence on leadership styles. The following short descriptions concerning the Confucianism, Islam and Hinduism, should try to give an idea of how leadership styles can be influenced and what consequences can appear for leaders going abroad if they try to ignore them.

Are there Shinto hierarchical structures?
(John Renard)

Like so many other religious traditions, Shinto community structures often reflect the belief that human life mirrors divine life. Just as there is at least an implicit hierarchy among divine beings, human society needs a certain degree of structure. Longstanding Japanese tradition much influenced and reinforced by Confucian teaching over the centuries, lay great emphasis on knowing one's place in society. Each individual stands in a relationship of higher-to-lower, or vice-versa, with his or her fellow human beings, and basic etiquette requires that one bewares of social subordination in every context. Everyday Japanese speech, with its various levels of polite address, reflects that awareness. Although contemporary Japan is a democratic society, with all the political institutions needed to support a democracy, hierarchy runs deep in the culture and so too in Shinto belief and practice.

In: The Handy Religion Answer Book, 2002, p. 510

7.6.1   Confucianism influencing leadership

It is interesting to note that many Asian countries have been influenced historically in one way or another by the Confucianism and its form and style of leadership.

China for instance is playing a very dominant role among the nations of the world. They did not adapt completely any Western leadership style so far; instead they remained to their tradition of Confucianism (Adair, 2013, pp. 3f).

Confucius was a thinker whose ideas have shaped the life of one third of the entire world and he is not at all representing many Western stereotypes. He developed a system in which men could learn to perfect themselves and the relations to one another. Furthermore, *"Confucius believed that it was the person who led an organization defined its success and failure"* (Cihak, 2007, p. 75). This means if the leader is good, any difficulty can be overcome.

Confucianism
(Scott D. Seligman)

China's bureaucracy probably owes as much to its Confucian heritage as it does to the Soviet Union, on whose government structure it was largely modeled. Far from the "classless" organization of communist mythology, it is in fact strictly hierarchical, with rank and its privileges defined extremely clearly. People relate to one another not purely as individuals, but rather according to their relative ranks. Personal loyalty is highly valued, and it is common for high-ranking cadres to install cronies in important positions under their control.

In: Chinese Business Etiquette, 1999, p. 51

People within an organization should be led by virtue and instructed by example not by telling. Relationship is a very important and powerful issue when doing business with China. Openness starts right at the top of an organization. So as a consequence for leadership you should neither require an attitude of helpfulness, nor should you issue any rules which you are not following personally. Otherwise your behavior will not only be counterproductive, it will also be seen as offensive. A leader in China is more a type of father figure who expects and receives loyalty and obedience from colleagues. In return, the leader is expected to take a holistic interest in the well-being of his colleagues. It is a mutually beneficial two-way relationship. Another key issue regarding leadership in China is listening. Take your time and listen to staff. If you as a leader do not listen carefully, you might not reach any good progress within your company. (Cihak, 2007, pp. 76ff)

Confucian Management at Hyundai
(Lee Chang-sup)

Confucian-oriented management was introduced by Chung Ju-yung at Hyundai. The Confucianism goal was defined by frugality, religious belief in achieving this goal, and diligence. His management strategies were defined as follows:
- As long as employees are diligent and dedicated to attaining a goal, life employment was guaranteed.
- All employees were treated the same way.
- At no times, strikes were accepted or tolerated.
- The management strategy was based upon group thinking and team work was seen as a key factor for success.

In: Korea Times, 28.03.2001, p. 12

In Confucian philosophy, all relationships are deemed to be unequal. Ethical behaviour demands that these inequalities are respected. Thus, the older person should automatically receive respect from the younger and so should the senior from the subordinate. *"This Confucian approach should be seen as the cornerstone of all management thinking and issues such as empowerment and open access to all information" (WorldBusinessCulture.com, in web).*

7.6.2 Islam influencing leadership

Islam is the world's second most followed religion, with about 1.6 billion believers. It began in its present form about 1,400 years ago, in the year 622 AD, which is in fact the year 0 in the Islamic calendar. That explains why Muslims consider the year 2014 to be in fact 1435.

The Qur'an is the principal source of every Muslim's faith and practice. The revelations in the Holy Book in form of 114 chapters (surahs) contain the fundamental beliefs and touch upon all aspects of human existence. The name Qur'an means recitation and it is believed to be the final message and word of Allah to mankind. It was written in Arabic and is only authoritative in that language as it is considered to be a divine book which has not and cannot be altered.

The following five basic principles are central to the Muslim faith and do influence any business in a Muslim country.

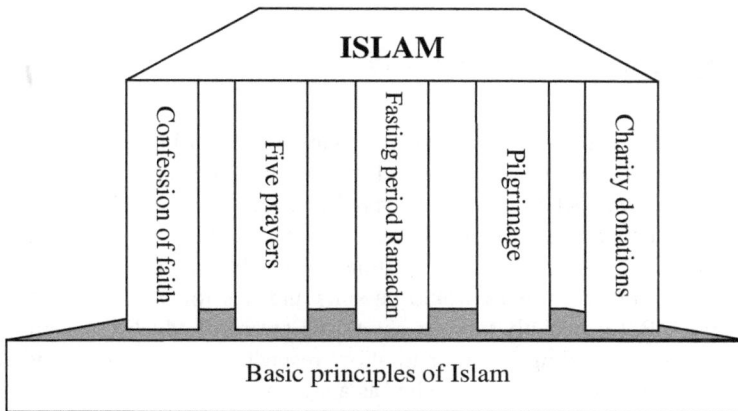

ISLAM

Confession of faith · Five prayers · Fasting period Ramadan · Pilgrimage · Charity donations

Basic principles of Islam

Fig. 7.5:   The five pillars of Islam
Source: Rothlauf, 2003, p. 5

1. Pronouncing the confession of faith (**Shahadah**): "There is no god worthy of worship but Allah, and the Prophet Mohammed (Peace Be Upon Him) is the last Messenger of Allah."
2. Praying (**Salah**): There are five obligatory daily prayers. They are exercised before sunrise (Fajr), at noon (Zuhr), in the mid afternoon (Asr), at dawn (Maghrib) and after darkness appears (Isha).

3. Fasting (**Saum**): Healthy Muslims fast during the ninth month of the lunar calendar called Ramadan. Fasting, which means abdication from eating, drinking, smoking and having sexual relations, is exerted from daybreak to sunset and is a demonstration of love and submission to Allah as well as a means to fortify one's willpower.
4. Pilgrimage (**Hajj**): It is an obligatory duty for Muslims to take the Hajj to Makkah (Mecca) once in their lifetime. There are certain rules, which have to be followed during the Hajj in order to make it valid. The rites e.g. include going around the Ka'bah seven times in a two-piece unstitched cloth (Ihram).
5. Charity donations (**Zakah**): Once a year, Muslims are required by religion to pay a minimum of 2.5 % of their yearly savings to the poor and needy. It is a means of purification of one's self and wealth.

Why is the Koran important for Muslims?
(John Renard)

Muslims believe the beautiful prose of the Koran to be the words of God Himself who spoke through Muhammad. Further, it is believed to be only a copy of an eternal book, which is kept by Allah. The Koran is also held up by Muslims as proof that Muhammad was indeed a prophet since no human is capable of composing such a text. Among the most widely read texts today, the Koran is also taught orally so that even Muslims who are not illiterate and do not speak Arabic might learn to recite the most important verses in Arabic.

In: The Handy Religion Answer Book, 2002, p. 192

In Western business culture, people e.g. make a strong separation between work and religious belief. Even a very devout Christian would not mention the will of God in a typical business encounter. However, when doing business in Saudi Arabia (and elsewhere in the Gulf) or in other Muslim countries, it is important to bear in mind the all-pervasive nature of the influence of Islam. When you are e.g. attending normal business meetings in Western countries, an appropriate business dress would be suits and ties for men and suits or skirts and blouse for women. But especially women should be aware of Muslim sensitivities and clothes should not be too revealing in order to show respect to their culture and religion. Muslim women are required to cover their bodies as a sign of modesty. Interpretations of the Qu'ran differ so you may see Muslim women wearing just a head covering whereas others may only show their eyes.

Life and business as an important aspect of life are governed by religion which forms the backdrop to society. In Islam religion nothing happens which has not been willed by God. If a deal comes off it is due to the will of God, if it fails it was not meant to be. Thus, a sense of fatalism and a resulting lack of urgency are often quoted by business people from non-Islamic cultures as being the over-riding impressions of a trip to for instance Saudi Arabia. The observance of religious ritual takes precedence over all other aspects of life and prayer punctuates the business day. Meeting discourses contain numerous references to God and His Prophet Mohammed and offices display numerous Koranic texts. Do not underestimate the deep conviction of your e.g. Saudi Arabian contacts and do not believe that reference to religion is in any way a ploy or insincere. (Abbas, 2005, pp. 50ff)

You should also know something about special religious festivities, like Ramadan or Hajj. Especially your right intercultural behavior is asked for if the holy month of Ramadan has come. Imagine you are expecting a delegation from Oman during this time. Make sure that no beverages – even no tea, coffee or water – are offered. It will also be seen as an insult if you drink, eat or smoke during this business session. As far as the time frame is concerned, keep in mind that only one meeting during the day is expected. You can continue your talks at dinner. Put it all together, and it does not matter if such an encounter will happen in Germany or in Kuwait, the time for doing business is very limited. Moreover, the last four days of Ramadan are reserved for the Eid al Fitr celebration, when definitely no business will take place. A certain greeting pays respect to your counterparts' religious feelings. Either you use the phrase "Happy Mubarak" or the more extended saying: "Kull am wa antum bichair" which means that you wish him all the best for Ramadan.

Why is Mecca a holy city for Muslims?
(John Renard)

Mecca (Western Saudi-Arabia) is the birthplace of the prophet Muhammad (c. 570) and was his home until year 622, when those who opposed him forced him to flee to Medina (about 200 miles north of Mecca). Muhammad later returned to Mecca and died there in 632. Mecca is the site of the Great Mosque in the heart of the city. The outside of the mosque is an arcade, made up of a series of arches enclosing a courtyard. In that courtyard is the most sacred shrine of Islam, the Ka'ba, a small stone building that contains the Black Stone, which Muslims believe was sent from heaven by Allah. When Muslims pray, they face the Ka'ba. It is also the destination of the hajj, or pilgrimage.

In: The Handy Religion Answer Book, 2002, p. 212

When doing business in very conservative Muslim countries like Saudi Arabia or Indonesia it is always good to be aware when the time of praying has come. Especially at noon (Zuhr) and in the mid afternoon (Asr) no business meeting will take place. If the praying time is at 11.45 am, the relevant time can be read in the morning newspaper, then the time between 11.30 till 12.30 is reserved for the religious duty. The same is going to happen if the time for Asr will come. Even the invitation for dinner should reflect the last praying time (Isha). If you think that 8.00 pm might fit into your schedule make sure that this is in line with Isha. If we presume that the last praying time is 7.45 pm, nobody will arrive earlier than 9.00 pm.

As far as the right leadership style is concerned, organizations are run along strongly hierarchical lines and managers tend to be very instructional in their approach. Subordinates view it as the boss' role to take decisions and to convey those decisions down the chain for implementation (Mawdudi, 1960, pp. 249ff). However, the leader will often include the group in a consensus-style discussion, while the final decision is taken by the leader.

The role of the manager is to accept the position of superiority and to use that position to further the aims of the organization or group. The manager is expected to make decisions and to convey them, in detail, to subordinates. The subordinate then expects to carry out those instructions, even if it is obvious that the instructions or decisions are flawed. A subordinate would not disagree with the boss – and especially not in public. (Beekun/Badawi, 1999, p. 21)

In return for accepting the role of manager and the loyalty that naturally accrues from that position, the manager is expected to look after group interests as well as the interests of the individuals within the group. Special attention should be paid to ensure that people are not placed in a position where they could possibly "lose face". Do not give people roles which will stretch their capabilities, hoping that they can learn from any mistakes they make - mistakes made can cause loss of face. Similarly, any praise or censure is best addressed to the whole group rather than any individual – being singled out can cause enormous embarrassment. It is of course important to remember that this deference is probably not only being shown to the organizational position of the boss but also to his family status, class connections and age.

7.6.3   Hinduism influencing leadership

There are several sections in Hinduism based on different philosophies of the religion, such as Advaita, Vishiciltadvalta, etc. It is in fact really difficult to precisely define Hinduism. It is more like *"a tree with several branches and yet the root of all these branches is common"* (Singh, 2003, p. 95). India had a long tradition of oral history. Indian folklore is full of kings and noblemen of all shades – good, brave, from wise to bad, cowardly, foolish. A constant refrain in folklore is the presence of sages, seers, and saints who renounced the material world, and practiced and propagated spiritualism. (ibid., pp. 92ff)

Basham claims that

> *"Indian history emerged from legend and dubious tradition in the 6th century BC, and what emerged was a society highly developed materially, intellectually, and spiritually. It was also characterized by a great sense of fairness in social and civil relations."*
> *(Basham, 1967, p. 345)*

The evolution of Indian society and culture has continued its course along with the march of time. Social progress since independence has served to heighten the awareness of cultural pluralism. Beneath the manifold diversity of physical and social type, language, custom and religion there is an Indian character, a general Indian personality which we cannot resolve into its component elements". (Singh, 1990, pp. 102ff) There has been a resurgence of some strong beliefs in Hinduism in India coinciding with the resurgence of strong religious beliefs elsewhere in the world (e.g. Islam, Christianity, etc.) (Basham, 1967, p. 347).

The power distance plays an important role in the Hindu system. However, authority is based on moral integrity. That is why a leader in a Hinduism culture should be kind, caring, inspirational and directional. The named characteristics all go along with transformational leadership style which is promoted. (Rampersad, 2009, p. 45).

In Nehru's words:

> *"Hinduism as a faith, is vague, amorphous, many sided, all things to all men. It is hardly possible to define it, or indeed to say definitely whether it is a religion or not, in the usual sense of the word. In its present form, and even in the past, it embraces many beliefs and practices, from the highest to the lowest, often opposed to or contra-*

dicting each other. Its essential spirit seems to be to live and let live." (Kumar, 2003, p. 33)

Leadership in India
(Chhokar/Kakar)

Indian leaders manage to balance, accommodate, and integrate contradictions between thoughts and actions; they do not necessarily lead to dissonance and confrontation. Face saving has great importance in Indian autocratic leadership. For instance, Indians can keep secrets much longer than their Western counterparts. Even lying can be acceptable if it serves a just purpose. If the team or the business can be protected by bending the truth, this is very much acceptable.

Relationship orientation is more important for effective leadership than performance or task orientation. When building a team, one would usually prefer team members whom one can trust and is comfortable to interact with over the team members with a perfect skill-fit but not on the same wave length. There is a comparatively high commitment by employees and also senior managers to the leadership of their companies. In fact, they almost adore and idealize their CEOs. Because of the socialization pattern in the family, Indians are more likely to be inclined to perceive the leader of a company as a wise, caring, dependable yet demanding figure – just like the elders in the family or social community. However, today this idealization of leaders is no longer completely blind to their deficiencies or the organizational needs to they might not fulfill.

In short, the most effective leadership style in India combines charisma, action orientation, autocracy, bureaucracy, collective relationship orientation, being a problem solver, self-starter, entrepreneur, and visionary. This appears a difficult task for one person to fulfill. But in Indian organizations, individualism coexists with vertical collectivism. This is seemingly contradictory, but it is the coexistence of values that in other cases would be mutually exclusive, which makes Indians effective leaders in their world.

In: J.S. Chokar, India: Diversity and Complexity in Action, New Jersey, 2007, p. 994; S. Kaher et al., Leadership in Indian Organizations from a Comparative Perspective, In: International Journal of Cross Cultural Management, Vol. 2, 2002, p. 239–242

7.7   The Intercultural Manager

With the march of globalization and internationalization growing louder and stronger, few successful businesses can now escape the need to work across cultures. With this move towards a cross-cultural business environment comes a need for people to be aware of how culture impacts the workplace. Unfortunately, as many quickly discover, the rest of the world does not do things "like we do". Cultural differences impact everything from inter-personnel communication to health and safety procedures to project management. In short, no corner of any business escapes.

In addition to the normal pressures of management, managers are now required to deal with challenges, friction and misunderstandings emanating from cross-cultural differences. Effective management in the modern environment necessitates cross-cultural competency in order to get the best out of a multicultural team.

Global Managers: What makes them different
(Maxine Dalton)

John Smith is sitting at his desk in New York City. The phone rings. It is the British plant manager in Beijing announcing that the plant is closed down because workers are demonstrating against the accidental bombing of their embassy. John turns to his e-mail. There is a message from the plant manager in Mexico. Inflation remains rampant and employees are once again complaining that they are not making enough to pay their ever-increasing rent. The phone rings again. The Saudi Arabian plant manager in the U.K. informs him that consumers are becoming increasingly resistant to the idea of genetically engineered foods. John leaves to go to a meeting, then turns back to his office to ask his secretary to arrange a conference call of all plant managers. This call will take place across 12 time zones. John knows this means that he will be up at 3 a.m. to participate in the call. The secretary reminds him that he will be flying to Mexico on Monday for a five-day stay and then going on to England for an additional week. She wants to know if John wants the call scheduled before he goes or while he is travelling....

And so it goes:
John Smith is a global manager. He lives in New York and his office is in New York but he manages across distance, country borders and cultural regions through the use of telephone, e-mail, fax and frequent airplane trips. Every time John picks up the phone, gets off the airplane, or logs onto his e-mail, he is faced with a management issue – as is any manager – but John must assess and respond to each issue through the ever-shifting lens of distance, country and culture.

In: Success for the New Global Manager: How To work Across Distances, Countries, and Cultures, New York 2002, p. 5

It is within this context that the idea of leadership is being challenged. Our conceptualization of who a leader is, what they do and how they do it is not shared by all. Today's leaders need to adapt to leading and managing people of different cultures; they need to listen to the voices of the people as well as understand what those voices may actually be telling them. In the essence is the crux of the challenge; when people perceive the world, communicate and view their leaders in different ways, the leader's ears may be ringing with misunderstood messages. The leader will come across cultural issues in many different guises. In the following, there are some guidelines how to behave correctly in this context.

The role of a manager is evolving from the needs of companies operating on the international stage. The complexities of globalization brought to the area of management are great and require the 21st century manager to adapt in order to offer modern solutions to modern problems. One area in particular of growing importance is intercultural management skills.

The majority of companies can no longer escape the necessity to buy from, sell to or work with people from different cultures. Multinationals have offices spanning the globe; manufacturers increasingly rely on foreign markets and distributors; services and products are no longer solely marketed to native audiences. In short, very few businesses escape the need for intercultural communication. As a result, companies are increasingly recognizing that, in order to grow, diversify and retaining a competitive advantage, intercultural management skills are crucial, especially for an intercultural manager.

Internally, he or she needs to be able to act as a medium between senior personnel and staff; communicate clearly and effectively with colleagues; build and nurture efficient intercultural and transnational teams and display strategic global thinking. Externally, an intercultural manager must demonstrate business acumen with a framework of intercultural awareness to supervise entrance into foreign markets, oversee the proper selection, mentoring and guidance of company.

The intercultural manager is therefore tasked with the responsibility of ensuring that communication is clear, coherent and free from intercultural misunderstandings on all levels. In order to achieve this, the intercultural manager must possess certain key attributes. These are namely intercultural awareness, flexibility, capitalizing on differences and patience.

The following 10 tips on intercultural management are meant to provide a starting point to managers dealing with culturally diverse teams. They might only touch the surface, but can be helpful especially right at the beginning of your intercultural career as a manager (Kwintessential, 2009):

1. **Respect and Courtesy:** The fundamental pillar of intercultural communication is respect and courtesy. Showing your appreciation of and consideration for others breeds a culture of openness. If colleagues request special treatment due to cultural or religious circumstances these are meant.
2. **Tolerance:** Tolerance is the key to intercultural leadership. It is not only needed in terms of respecting people's views and beliefs but also for different working practices and mistakes. If an atmosphere of non-tolerance is created, it is more likely that you will not be getting the best out of your employees.
3. **Identify Problems:** If cross cultural differences are proving an obstacle to communication within the workplace, try and analyse where things are going wrong. Take a step back and look at who is involved, the context, the situation, the means of communication (i.e. face to face, email, phone) and the outcome. Only by properly recognising the root of a problem you will be able to solve it.
4. **Cultural Taboos:** An understanding of all the cultural nuances is a tall task. An intercultural manager should therefore be aware of the major cultural taboos of his/her staff to ensure that offence or misunderstandings are not caused. Simple things such as providing a vegetarian alternative for Hindu colleagues or a food based upon the halal slaughtering method for Muslims makes a big difference for that employee.
5. **Know the Law:** If the country you work in has legislation covering diversity issues in the workplace, familiarize yourself with these to ensure you comply. Cultural diversity can and does lead to unnecessary employment tribunals.

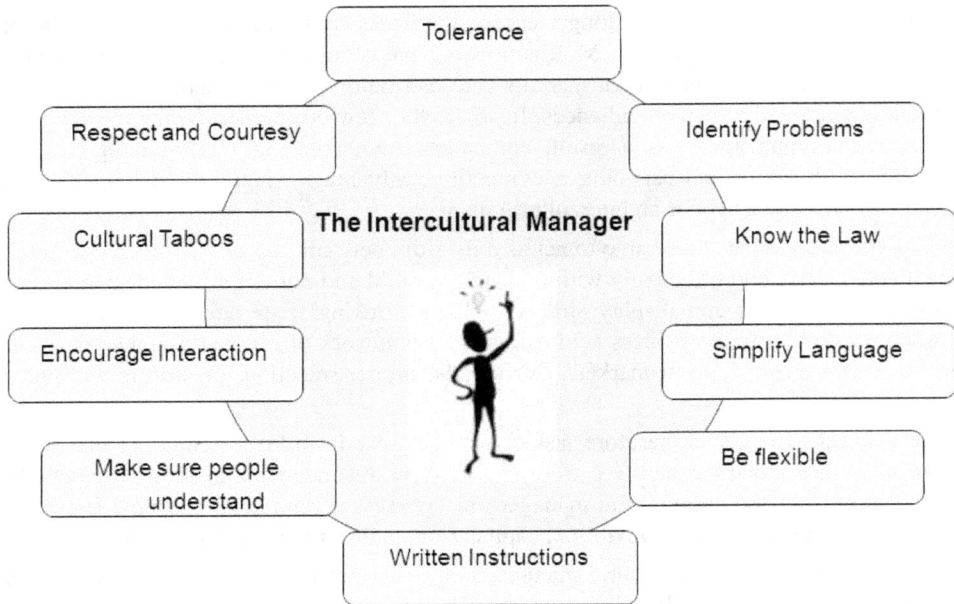

Fig. 7.6:   The Intercultural Manager
Source: Own illustration based on Kwintessential, 2009

6. **Encourage Interaction:** It is a good idea to encourage frequent and positive interaction within a culturally diverse workforce. This leads to stronger interpersonal relationships and a greater awareness of one another.
7. **Simplify language:** Although many of your staff or all will speak and use English, this does not mean they are fully competent. There is a strong desire from the team members to improve their English knowledge. For those that speak English as a second or third language it is best to avoid using slang or phrases.
8. **Make sure people understand:** Always make sure that a message has been processed and understood.
9. **Written instructions:** It is always a good idea to write instructions down to ensure that a message or request is fully understood.
10. **Be Flexible:** The good intercultural manager is a flexible manager. Understanding where potential obstacles lie in communication and adapting is good practice. For example, graphics are sometimes a more useful way of presenting information. So, rather than using text to explain health and safety issues, simply use illustrations that can be grasped across cultures.

> *"Leadership is a matter of having people look at you*
> *and gain confidence, seeing how you react.*
> *If you're in control, they're in control."*
>
> (Tom Landry)

7.8   The experts' view

Lisa-Marie Korth, Christina Schlabritz, Julia Segger and Gabi Wegner, students of Baltic Management Studies at the University of Applied Sciences Stralsund had the chance to question two internationally experienced managers about their experience with intercultural leadership.

7.8.1   Interview with Juergen Dlugi, CEO, Konecranes

Juergen Dlugi, the CEO of Konecranes has a wide range of Intercultural knowledge. He has worked in Finland, Spain, France, Egypt, Indonesia and many other countries.

Students: What is your understanding or personal definition of leadership?

Juergen Dlugi: I think a leader is a person who is guiding or let's say motivating other persons. He is someone who is giving them a direction, who is taking care of them and who is helping them to achieve their goals. Now leading by example you know I would like to refer to one of my favourite sayings. You need to be an example to your people to motivate them, to guide them. People need to look up to someone, they have to find something positive in the person, something they like, it may be because of his personality or his character but it can also be because of his professional career or education.

Students: So, you think characteristics and behaviour definitely matters for being a leader?

Dlugi: I would absolutely say that. There are two issues. Basically, the personal thing, you know, the charisma, the empathy. And the other one is the professional side. What have you achieved in your career before, how can you lead your people? I mean you lead your people because you have experience. Probably, you have been to similar things before and that's why you maybe can encourage them. So to sum it up: One is the personal thing and the other one is the professional thing.

Students: Would say that this assumption of charisma and education is common all over the world? Does it play the same role everywhere?

Dlugi: Of course, I would say the best thing is if you have a good mixture. Charisma as well as education is important but for me the personality is more important than the education. On the other hand you need also a high-qualified educational background to lead a team. You definitely cannot be a successful leader if you do not know anything about the business.

Students: How important is it to be prepared before you go abroad?

Dlugi: I would say it depends on the country where you are going. In general, it is important to be prepared. If you for example go for a short business trip to Turkey or Indonesia there are some "No-Goes" you have to know beforehand as touching Russia for business you should know that you will be offered some vodka during the business dinner. There is a big difference if you only go on a short business trip to a foreign country or if you plan to stay there longer. If you live in a foreign country you need to be much more systematic and well prepared. Furthermore, a good cultural understanding is needed and very important for success in business. For example in Germany or Finland it is more important to be technically well prepared than it is in Spain or Latin America where the people have more time and you can have an open discussion and will find the technical topics.

Students: Did you work in a country where religion influenced your daily business life strongly?

Dlugi: Yes, I have some experience where the religion influences the business as e.g. in Egypt and Indonesia. Of course you have to know for example that alcohol is forbidden, or that you don't give the hand to the wife. So, some behavior issues are always important to know when visiting another country.

Students: Do you think that people who go abroad should adapt their leadership style to the different countries and religions?

Dlugi: I don't think that adapt is the right word for that. You have to keep focus not only on religion but also on the local habits. Sometimes we mix up those two topics: religion and social habits. I always put habits before religion because that is how the culture and society developed in that country. I totally agree that respecting the other culture is a very important issue. I had the experience that very small things often matter the most as e.g. going to Barcelona and not being interested in soccer at all. That would be strange for the Spanish people living there. Due to my personal experience I would say that people in foreign countries accept that you have different attitudes and you do not need to do everything what they do. But you always need to be polite. In France they e.g. serve the brain of a sheep for lunchtime and I actually couldn't eat it. But it was not a problem because I dealt with it in a professional and respectful way and explained why I cannot eat it.

Students: What would you personally say, was the biggest challenge abroad?

Dlugi: This is of course something that is individual for everybody. Every person is different and everyone has his own challenge. For me, it was sometimes pretty hard when I worked for the Finish company. I needed to slow down and not rush into conclusions. So I needed to take a little bit the speed out. That's why it for me personally will even be more challenging to deal with countries like Japan where business is more slow and where people need a little bit more time thinking about business.

In: Korth/Schlabritz/Segger/Wegner, „Leading across different countries – with examples form Russia, China, Japan, Germany, USA, India and the UAE" (unpublished assignment), Stralsund, 2014, pp. 26ff

> *"The people who are crazy enough*
> *to think they can change the world*
> *are the ones who do."*

(Apple's "Think Different" commercial , 1997)

7.8.2   Interview with Steffen Keil, Siemens Saudi Arabia

Steffen Keil is the Saudi Arabia's country head of Sales Engineer and Advisory Expert Engineer in the Energy Sector at Siemens and has also gained international experience in Indonesia, South Africa, South Korea, Israel, Kuwait and the VAE among others.

Students: How did the leadership style within the different countries change?

Keil: Compared to Germany where everybody and everything sticks to a plan, working abroad is completely different. The democratic leadership style of Germany cannot be taken on because of the different religious and cultural influences of the different countries. Even the climate plays an important role during the everyday work. To develop a good working environment it is important to consider other persons and being respectful of their cultural values.

Students: How is the relationship to your employees and are there advantages/disadvantages an international team brings up?

Keil: My team consists of many different people from all over the world. From my point of view there are no recognizable advantages or disadvantages an international team offers. Teamwork is the most important key driver for successful international business. The working atmosphere at our company is always friendly and based on team spirit. In some countries, e.g. the Oman, one is forced to have a certain percentage of local people. Nevertheless, on average, there is no nation which is numerically superior but it differs from project and country. In Saudi Arabia, my team consists of many Chinese engineers.

Students: Which kind of leadership style does Siemens follow in Saudi Arabia?

Keil: First of all, it is important to know that Saudi Arabia is a monarchy. Following the authoritarian leadership style most of the time but since Siemens is a German company the democratic leadership style plays an important role too. Also the basis of comparison is the assumed level of bureaucratic formality within Saudi Arabia.

Students: What kind of influence does the religion has, especially the Islam, considering the leadership style and working conditions?

Keil: The Islam is a very important driver when it comes to leadership styles and working conditions, especially the hours of prayer influencing the work. During Ramadan the working hours for Muslims are reduced to 5 working hours because of the Lenten period. A decrease of the labour productivity is also visible. All other foreign employees, whether they are Muslims or not, also have to conform to the local rules and laws. It is not allowed to drink, eat or smoke in public. Breaking the local Ramadan rules will have drastic consequences such as flogging, prison or other penalties. It is also important to know that no body parts should be exposed or even outlined by tight clothing, no matter during work or during free time. When you are invited in a Saudi Arabian home, be sure to accept the invitation and bring a gift for your hosts.

Students: What are the most important features to become an international leader?

Keil: For me the 7 most important features are assertiveness, sensitivity to other cultures and religions, high sense of responsibility, fairness, kindness and honesty towards the team and a positive charisma.

In: Korth/Schlabritz/Segger/Wegner, "Leading across different countries – with examples form Russia, China, Japan, Germany, USA, India and the UAE" (unpublished assignment), Stralsund, 2014, pp. 79f

---

Extract from an interview with Rüdiger Baumann from Bavarian TV alpha (recorded 04/11/2008)

Baumann: Now I would like to ask you about the influence of religious questions in this intercultural context. How important is religion in general and which role does it play in international business? You just came back from India where Hindus and Muslims live together, but not always peacefully. What is your opinion?

Rothlauf: First of all, you have to be fully aware that religion is an issue that definitely can't be ignored. Which direct impact those religious questions can have in the everyday life of an international manager will be demonstrated by the following example: Does it make sense to arrange a meeting with Indian managers in Mumbai in mid-November or is it a good time to fix an appointment with Vietnamese or Chinese managers around the middle of February either in Germany or in the relevant Asian region? There is only one answer and it is a simple "no". Why? In India they celebrate at this time Diwali and the mentioned two Asian countries celebrate in February their New Year! Let me just pick up another example. If the holy month of Ramadan starts, the Muslim world celebrates this as an outstanding religious event. During this time they do not smoke, either they do not drink or eat. How can a business meeting during this time become a successful manifestation? Be aware of the feelings of your counterparts. Wish the Hindus in India or elsewhere a "Happy Diwali" or send your Vietnamese friends a "Chuc mung nam moi" or greet the Muslims with "Kull am wa antum bichair". This is the right intercultural behavior and this makes the difference between those who are interculturally sensitive and those who think they can neglect these religious questions.

"A leader…is like a shepherd.
He stays behind the flock, letting the most nimble go out ahead,
whereupon the others follow, not realizing
that all along they are being directed from behind."

(Nelson Mandela)

7.9   Case Study: International assignments

Imagine the following situation: You are working for the company "Roschmann" in the department of international assignments. Within this newly established department located at the German headquarters, you are responsible for India. Only recently Roschmann has bought a local Indian company which should now be integrated into the corporation. This Indian company has several locations and has not yet had any experiences with expatriates. In about three months' time, it is planned to send 25 German employees from different departments, hierarchy levels and corporate locations to India. On average, those international assignments are scheduled for three years.

Task:

A) Develop a concept for the future assignment process, which should consist of three modules referring to the phases of expatriation:
   1. Preparation in the home country
   2. Support during the international assignment
   3. Return to the home country – including a potential earlier termination of the assignment
   The individual preconditions of employees (length of service with Roschmann, private environment, foreign language skills etc.) have to be taken into account.
B) Develop a manual of "Do's and don'ts in India" (especially with regards to intercultural communication), which should be handed out to all expatriates posted to India.
C) Create a list of "Ten Commandments for international travelers" (culture-independent).
Present your results to your manager and your colleagues including a handout.

In: Rothlauf, J., Seminarunterlagen, 2006

8 Multicultural Teams

8.0 Statement of the problem

A failed teamwork project
(Hodgetts/Luthans)

In attempting to plan a new project, a three-person team composed of managers from Britain, France, and Switzerland failed to reach agreement. To the others, the British representative appeared unable to accept any systematic approach; he wanted to discuss all potential problems before making a decision. The French and Swiss representatives agreed to examine everything before making a decision, but then disagreed on the sequence and scheduling of operations. The Swiss, being more pessimistic in his planning, allocated more time for each suboperation than did the French. As a result, although everybody agreed on its validity, they never started the project.

In: International Management, 5th ed., 2003, p. 187

8.1 The necessity of multicultural teams

With the increasingly diverse workforce of this century, managers in today's multicultural organizations will need skills to realize the full potential of both domestic work teams and cross-border alliances. The ability to develop effective transnational teams is essential in light of the ongoing proliferation of foreign subsidiaries, joint ventures and other transnational alliances.

> *"Multinational groups of many types are evident: the management team of an international joint venture, a group developing a product for multiple-country markets, a group responsible for formulating an integrated European strategy, a task force charged with developing recommendations for rationalizing worldwide manufacturing, and, increasingly, even the top management team of the firm itself" (Hambrick/Davidson/Snell/Snow, 1998, p. 181).*

The term "multicultural teams" describes compositions of team members from several countries who must rely on group collaboration if each member is to experience the optimum of success and goal achievement. To achieve the individual and collective goals of the team members, international teams must provide the means to communicate the corporate culture, develop a global perspective, coordinate and integrate the global enterprise, and be responsive to the local market needs.

Group multiculturalism
(Hodgetts/Luthans)

1. **Homogenous groups,** which are characterized by members who share similar backgrounds and generally perceive, interpret, and evaluate events in similar ways. An example would be a group of male German bankers who are forecasting the economic outlook for a foreign investment.

2. **Token groups,** in which all members but one have the same background. An example would be a group of Japanese retailers and a British attorney who are looking into the benefits and shortcomings of setting up operations in Bermuda.

3. **Bicultural groups,** which have two or more members of a group, represent each of two distinct cultures. An example would be a group of four Mexicans and four Canadians who have formed a team to investigate the possibilities of investing in Russia.

4. **Multicultural groups,** in which there are individuals from three or more different ethnic backgrounds. An example is a group of three American, three German, three Uruguayan, and three Chinese managers who are looking into mining operations in Chile.

In: International Management, 5th ed., 2003, p. 185–186

8.2 Challenges for multicultural teams

The role and importance of international teams increases as the company progresses in its scope of international activity. Similarly, the manner in which multicultural interactions affect the firm's operations depends on its level of international involvement, its environment, and its strategy. For multinational enterprises, the role of multicultural teams again becomes integral to the company; since the teams consist of culturally diverse managers and technical experts located all around the world or at different subsidiaries.

> *"Situations in which a manager from one culture communicates with a native of another culture (one-on-one) or supervises a group from a different culture (token groups) can be quite difficult. What happens in work or project groups with members from two cultures (bicultural group) and in those with members representing three or more ethnic backgrounds (multicultural groups)?" (Kopper, 1992, p. 235)*

The team's ability to work together effectively is crucial to the success of the company. However, each group member has a different perception of his or her contribution towards effectiveness and efficiency. Smith/Berg (1997, p. 7) have described in which ways those perceptions can differ:

- *"acceptance of authority*
- *goal building process*
- *motivation*
- *corporate strategy*

- *time management*
- *decision making process*
- *conflict solution*
- *emotions"*

Moreover, in culturally diverse groups, the perceptions of team members can widely differ as far as the analysis, the process situation itself, the evaluation and the contribution each team member has to deliver are concerned (Schroll-Machl, 1995, p. 212). In such a situation, the team members are looking for orientation and help which is normally part of their own cultural background. The logical consequence out of this scenario is quite obvious: irritation and mistrust will arise, because the expectations are not in line with the relevant perceptions. The situation will become worse if companies do not interculturally prepare their staff for international assignments.

The "Zürich-Versicherungs-Gesellschaft" belongs to those companies which have recognized the importance of providing intercultural training. A seminar entitled "Working Together in a Multicultural Organization" underlines the readiness of the company to prepare their staff for working in multicultural teams. The reasons for those intercultural trainings can be found in an analysis the company had carried out (Saunders, 1995, p. 94):

- *"premature return of the expatriate*
- *missing contacts with the local society*
- *communication problems within multicultural teams*
- *private problems, mainly caused by the dissatisfaction of family members"*

8.3   The multicultural learning process

In a multicultural team, it is necessary to understand that the diversity of the team members is the starting point for any successful diverse team. The old approach that diversity is given and over the time problems will be solved in a certain way is outdated and counterproductive. If you want to have success for such a multicultural group, any team member has to show the willingness to be actively involved in learning situations.

Which are the stimulating factors that help to overcome learning problems? In a study, Smith/Berg (1997, p. 9–12) asked participants about their opinions. Some of the factors that could stimulate the learning process are described here:

- *"a positive as well as a negative feedback*
- *an environment that appreciates openness*
- *no lies*
- *the acceptance of mistakes*
- *sufficient time for the analysis of mistakes*
- *active listening even if a bad message has to be communicated*
- *open exchange of experiences*
- *an atmosphere that stimulates the learning process and honors a good performance"*

In order to find out which elements can obstruct the intercultural learning process, Smith/Berg (1997, p. 10–11) asked the participants to describe a situation in which they had the opportunity to learn something new but did not have the chance to realize it. Afterwards, they should name the reasons that did hamper this realization process. The following arguments were named:

- *"lack of information*
- *fear*
- *not sufficient time for mutual reflection*
- *the imagination one can escape from problems*
- *a negative climate that allows recrimination*
- *not sufficiently qualified teachers and mentors*
- *focus on egocentric needs"*

With the help of this exercise, Smith/Berg could identify factors that facilitate the start of a positive learning process, which is a decisive prerequisite for the cohesion of a multicultural team. Long before such a team actually starts with a project, every team member has to keep the basic principal of *"learn how to learn from each other"* in mind.

> *"It provides a way for potential group members to prepare for the learning that will be needed as they get started. It reveals a universality at the level of learning process that undergrids their experience even when the specifics of that experience vary widely. It encourages all to recognize that some environments are not hospitable to productive group life. This helps them to be more understanding and patient with each other when group crisis occur. It also inspires them to put energy into altering the context as a means of increasing group effectiveness, energy which serves as an antidote to the natural tendency to blame each other when, inevitably, the group encounters bumps in the road." (Smith/Berg, 1997, p. 9)*

8.4   Multiculturality and group formation

Culturally diverse groups have members from different nations and from different cultural backgrounds. One of the most challenging tasks is now how to bring all these differences positively together in order to come to a common group understanding.

> *"For a multi-cultural group to function effectively it is important for its members to know that the unique contributions each brings will be listened to, understood and embraced. This is not easy to achieve when such groups are left to navigate group formation on their own." (Smith/Berg, 1997, p. 9)*

Based upon the perception that all members of a multicultural team share a lack of information as far as the relevant cultural understanding of the other team members is concerned, an intercultural preparation for working in such a team is required.

> *"For example, individuals of two different nationalities tend to know, assume, and perceive different things about their respective countries." (Walsh, 1995, p. 285)*

In order to avoid prejudices and stereotypes right from the beginning, Smith/Berg suggest to start with the following exercise: The participants will be separated into groups of people from the same geographical area. Afterwards, the participants should describe events that happened in the selected region during a certain time period (1980s/1990s/2000s).The focus should be on social and economic issues and about 10–20 situations should be listed. The variety of potential topics, like the European Union, the breakdown of communism, the importance of the Asian region, in particular China, the population growth, the environment, and the aggravating unemployment situation, reflect the diverse thinking of the participants and shall help to create a completely new picture of opinions and trends.

With this in mind, everybody will understand that the world is far more different than they have been aware of until now. The logical conclusions for the participants should be:

1. There is a lot of information we have never heard about.
2. Each participant recognizes that one can personally contribute to a better understanding of this part of the world.
3. Such a brainstorming is helpful in order to get a different view about things that happen in a distant area.
4. There is a common understanding that things happening in one part of the world will also happen in another part of the world after a while.
5. The world becomes more and more interdependent.
6. The participants get the feeling that the description of different cultural standards is good for group cohesion.
7. This exercise underlines that everybody has only a rudimentary knowledge of the world and that there is much more to learn about it.

Drinking beer
(Carté/Fox)

Two firms in the brewing industry, one German and the other Japanese, were in the final stage of negotiating a contract. Neither side was prepared to concede on some minor details. It was Sunday afternoon in one of the Japanese company's breweries. The German team asked for a break, and, when offered drinks, requested some beers – they were in a brewery, after all. The Japanese left the room. Instead of the usual 10 minutes, the break lasted nearly an hour. On their return, the leader of the Japanese delegation bowed deeply and said they were now prepared to accept all the remaining demands the Germans had made. The delighted Germans and considerably less enthusiastic Japanese shook hands on the deal. Only later did the Germans discover that their request for alcohol had been interpreted by the Japanese as a subtle: "Accept our demands or the deal is off." Traditionally in Japan, alcohol only comes out to celebrate an agreement.

In: Bridging the culture gap, London 2004, p. 133

The learning process is not only determined by the exchange of general information. In the next step, the question should be discussed which experiences the participants have already made as far as their group experiences are concerned. For this purpose, Smith/Berg suggest the following exercise: Each team member, who will become part of a multicultural team, is asked to develop 8–10 rules that are accepted in his or her home country. Afterwards, the participants from different countries are divided into several groups in order to exchange their opinions towards their group experiences. After the discussion has been finished, each group has to present their discussion results. At the end, all participants should agree on ten common rules that are binding for all team members.

This exercise makes clear that there are different cultural views which can have a strong impact on the success of the teamwork. Therefore, it is necessary that such an exercise takes place before a multicultural team starts with the project. All the stereotypes that negatively influence the group formation process can be discussed very openly. Furthermore, the already broad discussion about cultural differences will enable everybody to develop a better understanding of the cultural background of those participants that will become member in a multicultural team.

The following polarizations have been found in multicultural teams (Smith/Berg, 1997, p. 12):

- confrontation versus harmony
- individualism versus collectivism
- task- versus process-orientation
- direct versus indirect criticism
- productivity versus creativity
- quality focus versus quantity focus
- authoritarian versus democratic decision making process

Success criteria for multicultural teams
(Indrei Ratiu)

1. Do the members work together with a common purpose? Is this purpose something that is spelled out and felt by all to be worth fighting for?
2. Has the team developed a common language or procedure? Does it have a common way of doing things, a process for holding meetings?
3. Does the team build on what works, learning to identify the positive actions before being overwhelmed by the negatives?
4. Does the team attempt to spell out things within the limits of the cultural differences involved, delimiting the mystery level by directness and openness regardless of the cultural origins of participants?
5. Do the members recognize the impact of their own cultural programming on individual and group behavior? Do they deal with, not avoid, their differences in order to create synergy?
6. Does the team have fun? (within successful multicultural groups, the cultural differences become a source of continuing surprise, discovery, and amusement rather than irritation or frustration.)

In: Managing Cultural Differences, 1991, p. 32

The problem now is how to bridge these different poles. This is a very challenging part in the teambuilding process, because the cultural understanding of the team members differs in many ways. With this exercise in mind, everybody is fully aware of the divergences and the logical conclusion for all is to find a compromise in which the different cultural aspects and views are settled.

"As members acknowledge the range of differences that exist within a multinational group, we observe several things happen. First, there is surprise that this exploration was easier than expected and that it felt collaborative and non-threatening. Second, there is an emerging excitement that membership in this group could be rewarding.

Third, there is anxiety over how they are going to manage these differences which are now out in the open and much more difficult to ignore. Fourth, there is fear that the group will be paralyzed by the tensions that will naturally arise as a result of the differences among the members. Finally, there is a wish that these differences can be regulated, controlled, and subordinated to the collective purpose of the group." (Smith/Berg, 1997, p. 11)

8.5 Multicultural team effectiveness

The potential benefits and difficulties posed by a cultural diverse workforce and a multicultural marketplace are crucial challenges for the future that companies must manage in a positive way. In achieving the greatest amount of effectiveness from diverse teams some parameters determine the success or failure of such a multicultural team.

8.5.1 Conflict as a chance

A former study from Smith/Berg (1987) has found out that team members are ready to bow their own goals to that of a team. Nevertheless different positions and views can lead to conflicts within a team and can hamper the effectiveness of the project. Therefore all efforts should be made to look for a positive solution.

"We argue that conflict in groups is a problem primarily because we think of it as a problem. If we saw conflict as a source of group vitality we would seek it out rather than avoid it in and effort to harness it in the service of the group's mission." (Smith/Berg, 1997, p. 11)

The conclusion drawn from this study is that conflicts should not be rejected but seen as an element that handled in the right way can be helpful for the further teambuilding process.

8.5.2 Team effectiveness and nationality

Culturally diverse groups have members from different nationalities with different cultural backgrounds. Problems potentially arising in this context can also have a negative impact on the group cohesion and effectiveness. The construct of "nationality" for example relates to the mother tongue, to group experiences made in the home country or the kind of task that had to be fulfilled at a home. All these elements have to be taken into account to guarantee the success of the project.

"When the patterns of differences were analyzed, variations in responses could be partly explained by characteristics such as age, education, job professional experience, hierarchical level, and company type. Less expected, however – particularly in an institution that places great emphasis on an international ethos – was the fact that the nationality of the respondents emerged as an explanation for far more variations in the data than any of the respondents' other characteristics." (Laurent, 1991, p. 201)

8.5.3   Team effectiveness and international work experience

Two companies – two different results

As the following extract from a conversation between two executives shows, there is often only a thin line between success and failure of multicultural teams:

"When we first launched our research programme on multinational groups, we discussed it with a group of senior executives from major multinational corporations. The comments of two executives, both from European-based companies, symbolize the complexity and subtlety of the issues involved. One executive said: 'I don't see why this is an important topic of study. Our company puts people of different nationalities together all the time. It's how we do business: there is nothing particularly special about such groups. What's the big issue?'"

The second executive responded:
"Wait a minute. In my company, we are having great difficulties with such groups. We've had strategic plans suffer and careers derail because complications arising from multinational groups. Just last month we killed a global product development project because the team had taken so long that the competition had already sewn up the market."
(Hambrick/Davison/Snell/Snow, 1998, p. 182)

In a study carried out by Hambrick/Davison/Snell/Snow (1998, p. 182), the scientist have combined the factor "nationality" with the construct of "international work experience" and came to the conclusion that those team members who possess international work experiences are better used to work in a multicultural teams in comparison to those lacking this experience. Moreover, if a company has an international corporate structure, the element "nationality" will be replaced by the identification with the new enterprise.

As far as the effectiveness of multicultural teams is concerned, Watson (1993, p. 590) has found out that time will play an important role for the success of any multicultural team. On the one hand, he pointed out that without a sufficient intercultural preparation for all team members – even though it is time-consuming – the success is not guaranteed. On the other hand, he underlined the importance of international work experiences of some team members, which can facilitate the teambuilding process mainly in the initial phase.

> *"[...] newly-formed multinational groups are likely to be the most vulnerable to the drawbacks of diversity, but over time, if they survive and meet nominal performance thresholds, they develop more trust and rapport."* *(Hambrick/Davison/Snell/Snow, 1998, p. 199)*

8.5.4   Team effectiveness and language

In the past, managers talked about the need for faster and more efficient communication, as if speed would guarantee effective communication. They paid lip service to the need for good intercultural communication, but staffing decisions were typically rather based on technical knowledge than on good language skills. In order to give instructions, a manager has to have a good command of the relevant business language. Even if the manager is fluent in English, the surface knowledge, the speed of speaking and a good accent might hide the fact that this person misses many of the fine points which can be important for doing business (Varner/Beamer, 2011, p. 432). There is a vast difference between being reasonably functional in a language and being bilingual and bicultural. A lot of problems derive from related misunderstandings, regardless whether a manager or team members are addressed.

> *"The influence of language proficiencies in a multinational group setting has been observed to be profound. For example, an individual's facility with the group's working language greatly affects one's amount and type of participation, as well as one's influence in the group." (Gudykunst, 1991, pp. 5f)*

In another study, Gehringer (1988, p. 214) found out that a good command of the language that is used in a multicultural team has a significant impact on the success of a multicultural team, respectively in a joint venture situation.

> *"The simple ability to communicate with one's counterpart in a partner firm often makes a significant difference in a JV's prospects for success; the absence of this ability has caused more than a few disasters." (Geringer, 1988, p. 214)*

Our studies carried out in France and Germany (2008–2012) have also come to the conclusion that without the suffiecient knowledge of the respective business language, misunderstandings will occur and the project is at risk to fail.

If one takes a look at the relation between language and the task itself, there are different correlations to be observed.

> *"[…]the harmful effects of limited shared language facility will be greatest for groups engaged in coordinative tasks, least for computational tasks, and in-between for creative tasks. Increases in shared language facility result in corresponding increases in group perfor-mance for each type of task" (Hambrick/Davison/Snow/Snell, 1998, p. 198)*

Compromise
(Helen Deresky)

In Persian, the word "compromise" does not have the English meaning of a midway solution which both sides can accept, but only the negative meaning of surrendering one's principles. Also, a "mediator" is a meddler, someone who is barging in uninvited. In 1980, United Nations Secretary-General Kurt Waldheim flew to Iran to deal with the hostage situation. National Iranian radio and television broadcast in Persian a comment he was to have made upon his arrival in Tehran: "I have come as a mediator to work out a compromise." Less than one hour later, his car was being stoned by angry Iranians.

In: Managing Across Borders and Cultures, 2000, p. 177

> *"When a team outgrows individual performance*
> *and learns team confidence,*
> *excellence becomes a reality."*
>
> (Joe Paterno)

8.5.5   Team effectiveness and international composition

The composition of a multicultural team plays an important role for the success of any project. Hambrick (1998, p. 192) and the OCCAR study carried out in 2008, which will also be presented in this chapter, underline the fact that the more nationalities are represented in a team composition, the more difficulties the team has to face. One the other hand, the belief that representatives with a similar cultural background would form a good team is questioned by the study of Hofstede. In his 5-D-study and particularly the individualism dimension, he has made clear that the differences, e.g. between Finland and the United States of America, might be significantly higher than one would normally expect.

Moreover, if one believes a team composition with members from neighboring countries can become a cornerstone for the success in a multicultural team, one has to realize that there are a lot of tensions among different countries tracing back to historical events. Representatives from Japan and Korea might face similiar problems like members in a team coming from Greece and Turkey or from Vietnam and Cambodia. Whether this kind of heterogeneity has a positive or negative impact depends on the tasks that have to be fulfilled.

8.5.6   Team effectiveness and the nature of the task

A lot of studies (Hoffmann/Maier, 1961, pp. 401–404, Rothlauf, 2012, pp.12–15) have come to the conclusion that normal tasks are better solved by a homogeneous group. However, if the task is not quite clearly defined and if there are no standard solutions at hand, the composition of a heterogeneous group proves to be more suitable. In terms of effectiveness and creativity, Hambrick/Davison/Snow/Snell (1998, p. 195) have found out that a multicultural team would be the best option. Different opinions and views from members with a diverse cultural background create new ideas which can be extremely helpful if the team has to develop products for regional or worldwide markets or has to identify market gaps for new services or products.

> *"When the group is engaged in a creative task, diversity of values can be expected to be beneficial for group effectiveness. The varied perspectives and enriched debate that comes from increased diversity will be helpful in generating and refining alternatives." (Hambrick/Davison/Snow/Snell, 1998, p. 195)*

If the task requires an analysis of a lot of facts and figures based upon objective criteria, the nationality as well as the cultural value system can be neglected for a successful collaboration within a multicultural team.

> *"When the group is engaged in a creative task, diversity of values can be expected to be beneficial for group effectiveness. The varied perspectives and enriched debate that comes from increased diversity will be helpful in generating and refining alternatives." (Hambrick/ Davison/Snow/Snell, 1998, p. 195)*

If team interaction is required as part of the task, the correlation is negative (Hambrick/Davison/Snow/Snell, 1998, pp. 197–198). Now the value diversity of the team members plays an important role and it takes time to find a consensus among them, especially if a critical situation has to be managed.

> *"However, when the task is coordinative, involving elaborate interaction among group members, diversity of values will tend to be negatively related to group effec-*

tiveness. In such a task situation, fluid and reliable coordination is required; debates or tensions over why or how the group is approaching the task - which will tend to occur when values vary - will be counter-productive. In addition, disparate values create interpersonal strains and mistrust which become damaging when the group is charged with a coordinative task." (Hambrick/Davison/Snow/Snell, 1998, p. 197)

Moreover, there are some studies (Bantel/Jackson, 1989, Eisenhardt/Schoonhoven, 1990, Hambrick, 1996) taking a look at the relationship between the multiculturalism of the top management and its effectiveness. They all came to the conclusion that there is a positive correlation between task orientation and the heterogeneity on this managerial level.

Managing multicultural teams
(Brett/Behfar/Kern)

The structure of a team is usually flat meaning that everybody has the same right and is treated equally. However, the flat structure of a team might be uncomfortable for a member who is coming from a culture where he or she is used to have a strict hierarchy and people are treated differently according to their status in the organization. The opposite situation can occur, when there is a strict hierarchical structure in the team that might be humiliating for teammates coming from egalitarian cultures.

The most serious violations of hierarchy occured when a junior-manager from a low-context culture was sent to contact or negotiate with a senior manager from a high-context culture, since this was seen as disrespectful from the point of view of high-context cultures. For example, in one US-Korean team of due diligence US team members were having difficulties with accessing information from their Korean team members. Therefore, Americans decided to complain directly to the Korean management, which offended higher-level Korean management, because Korea is a culture with a high power distance according to Hofstede. Koreans would have accepted complaints from at least same level manager, but not from the lower-level. Moreover, such an action of their American team members created tensions within the team. This conflict was only resolved when higher-level managers from US visited Korean higher-level managers with an apology and a gesture of respect."

In: Harvard Business Review, November 2006, p. 87

8.6 Tuckman's stages of group development

In the course of analyzing his study results on group development, Tuckman (1967, pp. 25ff) originally identified four stages, which he characterized in terms of group structure and task allocation:

8.6.1 Forming

In the first stage of group formation, members get to know the other group members and try to figure out what kinds of behaviors are expected. In multicultural groups, this stage is likely to be fraught with problems because people tend to distrust anyone but themselves – generally because of a lack of understanding. All kinds of verbal and nonverbal behavioral differences can lead to misinterpretation, which in turns leads to mistrust or dislike. Employees' expectations about the form of communication, respect for authorities, status and work division often produce variations in their perception of acceptable interpersonal behavior. In order to reduce this kind of possible tensions, some group activities can help to create a good climate for further collaboration. Playing football or basketball together and/or a multicultural dinner prepared by all group members are some good examples how mutual trust can be steadily developed and how the most important part of the team building process, namely cohesion, can be achieved in the long run.

8.6.2   Storming

The biggest challenge of this stage is how the group defines and responds to its task and what type of group structure emerges. Even in homogeneous groups, this is often a period of hostility and conflict, as group members have emotional responses to their commitment to the task and to emerging leadership patterns. In diverse groups, even greater conflict may arise because members may bring varying expectations with them about who is capable of doing what. The tendency of some people to stereotype others rather than to consider their skills and potential contributions to the group objectively can cause serious problems which have to be solved in order to successfully continue with the group project. An important part of creating a positive climate is to show that the skills of all group members are valued. Either in this phase or in the previous forming phase, the group has to develop team rules that are at the end of the discussion process binding for all group members.

8.6.3   Norming

The key issue at this stage is the ability of the group to further build up cohesion. Cohesion requires to accept everybody's role in the team. In this phase, group members establish a consensus on norms of behavior within the group with the aim of becoming united. The achievement of such consensus is not as easy, especially in a culturally diverse group with members from different cultural backgrounds and varying values. This stage is the most important one in the teambuilding process, because the danger of a failed teamwork project can become a reality. The success of the team therefore depends on whether the group was able to develop trust and respect in the initial stage.

8.6.4   Performing

Once the group has developed that kind of cohesion necessary for a successful collaboration, it can turn to the actual work stage and concentrate on the tasks for which it was created. A mature group – one that has worked through its problems and reached a consensus on allocating roles in the light of the group's needs for expertise and leadership – should be productive. At the end, the actual accomplishments of the group are realized at the performing stage: The relative level of effectiveness or productivity depends on how well the group's diversity has been managed.

8.6.5   Adjourning

Later Tuckman also added a fifth phase, which describes the completion of all tasks as well as the termination of the group work. The manager is required to keep this phase as short as possible and to assist the team members in finding new fields of activity and tasks.

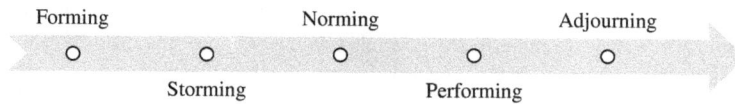

Forming	Norming	Adjourning
○ ○ ○ ○ ○		
Storming	Performing	

Fig. 8.1:   Tuckman's five stages of group development
Source: Own illustration based on Tuckman, pp. 25ff

8.7   Multicultural team building

As businesses success depends upon effective cooperation and communication within teams, intercultural business structures have been radically transformed over the past few decades. Changes in areas such as communication and information technology and shifts towards global interdependency have resulted in companies becoming increasingly international and therefore intercultural. In addition, the need to "go global" and to cut outgoings is demanding that companies protect international interests whilst keeping down staff numbers. The solution in most cases has been the forming of intercultural teams. However, the intercultural dimension of today's teams brings new challenges. Successful team building does not only involve the traditional needs to harmonise personalities but also languages, cultures, ways of thinking, behaviours and motivations.

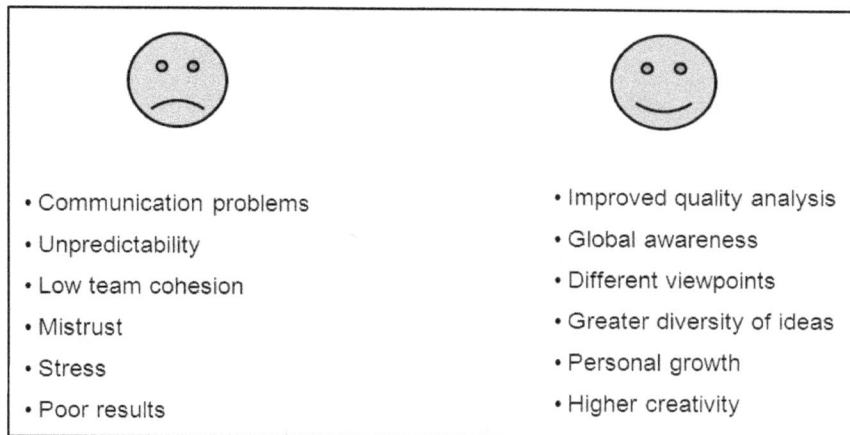

• Communication problems	• Improved quality analysis
• Unpredictability	• Global awareness
• Low team cohesion	• Different viewpoints
• Mistrust	• Greater diversity of ideas
• Stress	• Personal growth
• Poor results	• Higher creativity

Fig. 8.2:   Strengths and weaknesses of multicultural teams
Source: Own illustration

Over the last decade, a lot of research work has been done in the framework of Bachelor- and Master Theses regarding the collaboration within multicultural teams. Companies like German Lloyd, Rickmers GmbH & Cie.KG, or OCCAR were part of our studies. Interviews with Don A. Neuman, who is the manager and chief pilot of domestic and international flight inspection for the Federal Aviation Administration in Atlanta, with Tom Dinkelspiel, CEO at the Swedish Investment Bank Öhman, or with Dr. Boll, Head of Corporate Office of Internationalization, Bosch GmbH, only to name a few, made clear that there are some advantages as well as disadvantages that occur if members with a different cultural background have to work together. Because of the assurance to treat all information strictly confidential, only some general observations will be described in the following.

Intercultural teams have an inherent disadvantage. Cultural differences can lead to communication problems, unpredictability, low team cohesion, mistrust, stress and eventually poor results. However, intercultural teams can in fact be very positive entities. The combination of different perspectives, views and opinions can lead to an enhanced quality of analysis and decision making while team members develop new skills in global awareness and intercultural communication. Normally, one can expect a different viewpoint that broadens the horizon of each team member and leads to a greater diversity of ideas, which enables the members to be extremely creative. Moreover, each team member can personally benefit from the work within a multicultural team and can promote their career.

However, in reality, this best case scenario is rarely witnessed. More often, intercultural teams do not fulfill their potential. The root cause is the fact that, when intercultural teams are formed, people with different frameworks of understanding are brought together and expected to naturally work well together. However, without a common framework of understanding, e.g. in matters such as status, decision making, communication etiquette, this is very difficult, and thus requires help from outside to truly commit to the team.

Again, it becomes obvious that without a qualified intercultural training the overall goals of a company cannot be met. A good intercultural training is the decisive factor helping to bind a team together. Through an analysis of the cultures represented in the team, their particular approaches to communication and business and how the team interacts, intercultural team builders are able to find, suggest and use common grounds to assist team members in establishing harmonious relationships.

Multicultural Team Building
(Elashmawi/Harris)

As the result of team-building activities, which rested in a better understanding of cultural differences and working toward common goals, participants came up with the following motto:

$$T\text{ogether } E\text{verybody } A\text{chieves } M\text{ore (TEAM)}$$

In: Multicultural Management 2000, p. 260

Intercultural training sessions aim at helping team members to understand their differences and similarities in areas such as status, hierarchy, decision making, conflict resolution, showing emotion and relationship building. From this basis, teams are tutored how to recognise future communication difficulties and their cultural roots, empowering the team to become more self-reliant. The end result is a more cohesive and productive team.

Many exercises are offered for team trainings. The following are the major ones used for intercultural team development (Reinecke/Fussinger, 2001, p. 179):

- *"Contact exercises*
- *Sensitisation- and awareness exercises*
- *Role plays about the own culture and its values*
- *Exercises on flexibility*
- *Creativity- and communication exercises*
- *Team exercises*
- *Reflection exercises*
- *Closure exercises"*

Therefore, the concept of intercultural team training is divided into the following five steps:

Tab. 8.1:   Stages of the intercultural training,
Source: Reineke/Fussinger, 2001, p. 180

Analysis	<ul><li>What is the goal?</li><li>Where are we?</li><li>What are our hurdles of working together effectively?</li><li>What are our quirks?</li></ul>
Clarification	<ul><li>of the situation</li><li>of relationships</li><li>of problems</li><li>of goals</li><li>of resources</li></ul>
Feedback	<ul><li>Personalities: characteristics and preferences</li><li>Feedback exercises</li></ul>
Agreement	<ul><li>Goal orientation</li><li>Action plan</li><li>Rules and structures</li></ul>
Reflection	<ul><li>What happened?</li><li>How did we model our situation?</li><li>What and how do we want to use our experiences?</li></ul>

In conclusion, for intercultural teams to succeed, managers and HR personnel need to be attuned to the need for intercultural training in order to help cultivating harmonious relationships. Companies must be supportive, proactive and innovative if they wish to reap the potential benefits intercultural teams can offer. This goes beyond financing and creating technological links to bring intercultural teams together at a surface level but goes back to basics by fostering better interpersonal communication. If international businesses are to grow and prosper in this ever contracting world, intercultural synergy must be a priority.

Interview with Tom Dinkelspiel, CEO at the Investment Bank Öhman:

Students: *What are the risks for a project manager of a multicultural project?*
Dinkelspiel: There can be difficulties in assessing the skills and competencies of team players. Training and education standards and the relative value of qualifications can be very different in different parts of the world.

In: Projektunterlagen, Bachelor- und Masterarbeiten, Stralsund, 2000–2009

8.8   A study on multicultural teams: The OCCAR example

Abdelkarim El-Hidaoui, Monika Fehrenbacher, Michaël Koegler and Yvonne Kempf, students of the Université de Haute-Alsace, were part of a research project with a specific focus on staff members of the OCCAR in 2008. The Organisation Conjointe de Coopération en matière d'Armement (Organization for Joint Armament Cooperation) is an intergovernmental organization with the aim to provide more effective and efficient arrangements for the management of certain existing and future collaborative armament programs. Currently, the member states are Belgium, France, Germany, Italy, Spain and the United Kingdom. Some of the group's findings can be found below.

1)   What are the positive effects of culturally diverse teams?

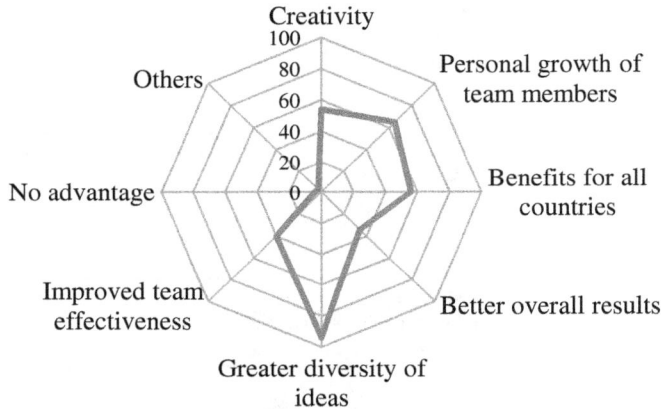

2)   What are the negative effects of culturally diverse teams?

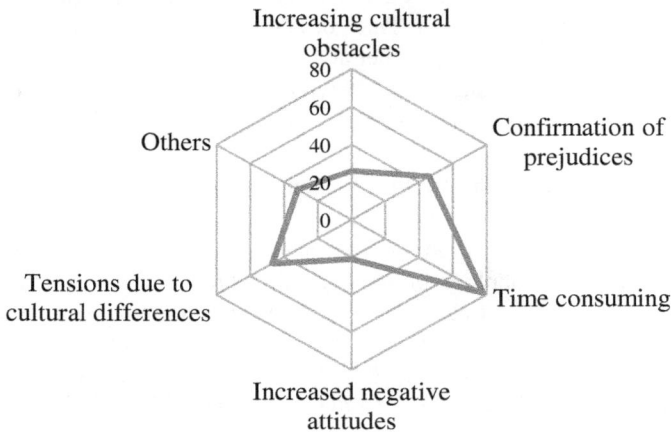

3) ***What do you expect from your colleagues?***

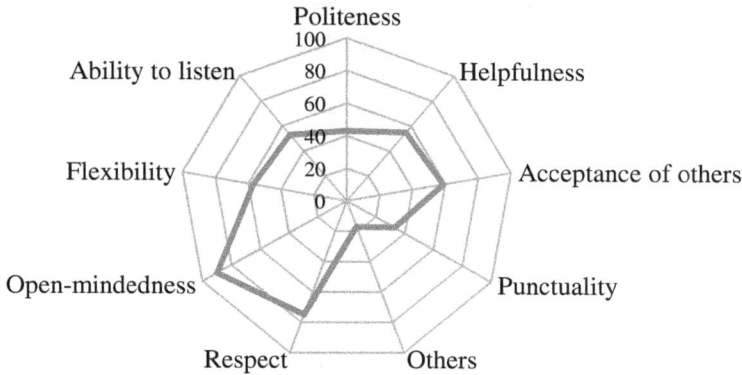

4) ***Have you ever been confronted with cultural conflicts arising from...***

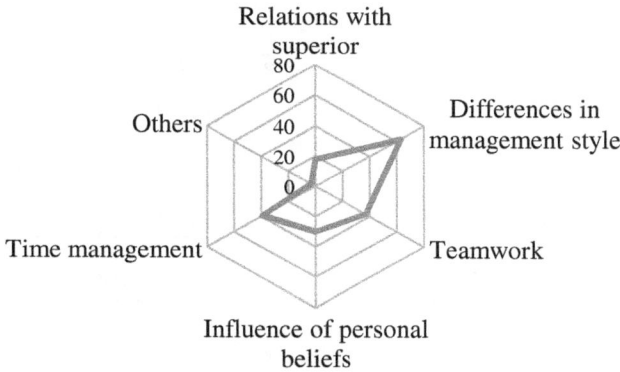

5) ***Which managerial skills are important for an efficient intercultural team?***

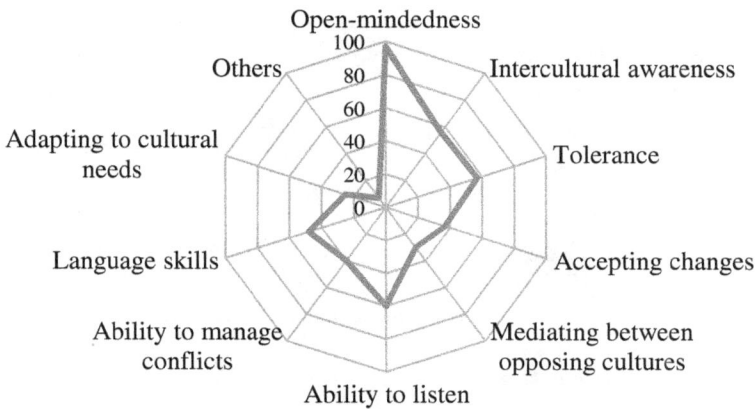

In: El-Hidaoui/ Fehrenbacher/ Kempf/ Koegler, International Teams – Practical application regarding to the teamwork of OCCAR, Mulhouse, 2008, unpublished

8.9   Questionnaire on cross-cultural teamwork (extract)

The following questions were taken from a questionnaire with 128 questions on cross-cultural teamwork. They can be provide a basis for assessing the work of one's own multicultural team and analyzing the cultural influences on the team's performance.

1.   Which language do you normally use when working in the team?

2.   How would you rate your knowledge of the team's business language?

☐ insufficient (5)   ☐ poor (4)   ☐ satisfactory (3)   ☐ good (2)   ☐ very good (1)

3.   If you have marked 2–5, what are the impacts on the team work?

☐   You sometimes back off in the discussion.
☐   Some things remain unclear and open.
☐   Misunderstandings occur.
☐   You sometimes have difficulties to understand what others say.
☐   You sometimes have difficulties to follow the team's discussions.
☐   Sometimes, you cannot fully apply your skills.

4.   Please mark the appropriate space.

	Strongly disagree						Strongly agree
I prefer to be direct and forthright when I talk to people.	☐	☐	☐	☐	☐	☐	☐
I would do what would please my family, even if I detested the activity.	☐	☐	☐	☐	☐	☐	☐
It is important for me that I do my job better than others.	☐	☐	☐	☐	☐	☐	☐
If a co-worker gets a prize I would feel proud.	☐	☐	☐	☐	☐	☐	☐
Without competition it is not possible to have a good society.	☐	☐	☐	☐	☐	☐	☐
I hate to disagree with others.	☐	☐	☐	☐	☐	☐	☐
Before taking a major trip, I consult with most members of my family and many friends.	☐	☐	☐	☐	☐	☐	☐
When we communicate with each other in the business language, this works very well.	☐	☐	☐	☐	☐	☐	☐
There are people who should really be more careful with their style of communication they use within our group.	☐	☐	☐	☐	☐	☐	☐
On the whole, I am very satisfied with the way our communication works.	☐	☐	☐	☐	☐	☐	☐
I feel free to express my opinion within the group.	☐	☐	☐	☐	☐	☐	☐
The experiences with this group are very helpful for the development of my personality.	☐	☐	☐	☐	☐	☐	☐
Perhaps I would work more efficiently if I had worked by myself.	☐	☐	☐	☐	☐	☐	☐

5. Prior to the actual teamwork, we got the chance to get to know each other.
   ☐ one   ☐ some   ☐ many   ☐ all   ☐ none

6. Which different nationalities are part of your team? How many team members belong to each nationality?

7. Please describe your tasks within the team.
   ☐ rather routine/simple   ☐ rather innovative/complex   ☐ both

8. Communication within the group takes place…

	several times a day	several times a week	several times a month	several times a year	not at all
face to face	☐	☐	☐	☐	☐
in meetings	☐	☐	☐	☐	☐
by telephone	☐	☐	☐	☐	☐
electronically (e-mail)	☐	☐	☐	☐	☐
in written form by letter/fax	☐	☐	☐	☐	☐
by video-conference	☐	☐	☐	☐	☐

9. How would you evaluate your team's performance regarding…?

	insufficient	Poor	satisfactory	good	very good
efficiency ("input-output-ratio")	☐	☐	☐	☐	☐
Quality	☐	☐	☐	☐	☐
(technical) innovations	☐	☐	☐	☐	☐
adherence to schedules	☐	☐	☐	☐	☐
adherence to budgets	☐	☐	☐	☐	☐
working excellence (achieving high performance and excellent results)	☐	☐	☐	☐	☐

10. Please state with how many of your team colleagues you would like to continue to work in the future:
    ☐ at least one   ☐ the majority of them   ☐ all   ☐ none of them

11. Please state how much you would like to work on further projects with the same group:
    ☐ not at all   ☐ rather not   ☐ maybe   ☐ readily   ☐ gladly

Source: Herrmann, D., in: Multikulturelle Teams – Ein Risikofaktor in der Projektarbeit, Passau 2009, Auszug aus einer Diplomarbeit, unpublished

8.10   Exercise: Cross-cultural team building scale

All human beings have values preferences that significantly impact work group cohesion. To see your values profile, mark an X along the continuum for each item and then connect the Xs. The benefit from this exercise to your team is that you will all see where the similarities and differences are. From there, the next step is to discuss how to turn your individual differences into a collective advantage.

	+2	+1	0	+1	+2	
Value change						Value tradition
Specificity in communicating						Vagueness in communicating
Analytical, linear problem solving						Intuitive, lateral problem solving
Emphasis on individual performance						Emphasis on group performance
Communication primarily verbal						Communication primarily non-verbal
Emphasis on task and product						Emphasis on relationship and process
Surface different views						Harmony
More horizontal organization						More vertical organization
Informal tone						Formal tone
Competition						Collaboration
Rigid adherence to time						Flexible adherence to time

Plett/Franz, in: mitte consult, Berlin, 2004, S. 16

"It is much more rewarding to get to the top of the mountain
and share your experience with others
than to show up by yourself, exausted."
(Shandel Slaten)

8.11   The experts' view

8.11.1   Interview with Jerry Holm, DB Schenker

The BMS students Anna Dünnebier and Matthias Hoffmann had an interview with Jerry Holm, Trade Lane Manager for South-East Europe within the DB Schenker Concern in Gotheburg on 22nd November 2011. Here are some of his answers:

Students: What is your general understanding of the term "international teams"?

Holm: Although all human beings are living in different countries with different mentalities, habits and thinking, they must all work in a network, because you should help each other to build up a network, which should be as perfect as possible.

Students: When you are planning an international team meeting, which planning steps, according the relevant time requirements and the introduction phase, are necessary?

Holm: DB Schenker used to organize development meetings at the head quarter in Essen, Germany. Such meetings are planned for all important members within the company from all around Europe. The schedule during such meetings provides group meetings for all participants and workshops to develop new ideas and solutions. In these workshops, consensus and strategies will be developed, which come into force in the regional departments. In a start-up phase the new ideas will be discussed and finally set into action.

Students: Which advantages/disadvantages do you see as far as international teams are concerned?

Holm: I suppose that you have many possibilities to move around. If you are young you can start at the company in the country you like and the level you like. The disadvantage in working for a big company is that you could feel sometimes as a number and your influence on the decision-making process is very modest.

Students: What do you think about modern communication tools? Which are used frequently?

Holm: With the modern telecommunication system that is offered nowadays the communication exchange has become much easier. We have many conference rooms which are equipped with a video-system; because it is a way to save time and money, but I think it will never take away the need of meeting a person face to face, especially if trust and confidence play a vital role. Very problematic is the usage of too many E-mails. I think people have to be trained to use this tool wisely, that means only if it is absolutely necessary.

In: Dünnebier/Hoffmann, Written Assignment, Stralsund 2012 (unpublished)

8.11.2   Interview with Heidrun Buss, AHK Guangzhou

Heidrun Buss is the Executive Chamber Manager at the Delegation of German Industry and Commerce (AHK) Guangzhou in China.. An extract from the interview conducted by the students Pia Boni, Anna Prötzig and Caroline Friemel in July 2012 provides insights into working in multicultural teams.

Students: How important is working in multicultural teams for you?

Buss: It is very important to me. Problems can never be solved alone and you always need a specialist. If a company has problems with taxes you need to talk to your legal department. Or you talk to another guy who has already had the same problem and knows how to solve it. Especially in a foreign country you need to get as much information as possible because you don't know how to solve problems. In China you need to collect much more information and consult more people.

Students: In which way do you have to adapt to your team members and their cultural specifics?

Buss: We have the Chinese New Year holiday where they have to have holidays. So we need to take this into account if you have any big projects. There are companies, not our company, where they consider the Chinese habit of sleeping after lunch. They always schedule meetings after 1.30 pm, because they know their Chinese colleagues have a break before that. In my part of China the people speak Cantonese, so on business meetings I always ensure to have someone with me who speaks that language. From the religious point of view we do not see any obstacles doing business in China.

Students: What are the strengths in working in a intercultural team?

Buss: It is definitely the different input and ways how to approach things. The other persons might know of other obstacles we didn't think of. In overall it is the enrichment for the whole project; to have different directions and opinions. It might be more difficult to come to an agreement later but at first it is broadening the whole view, so in the end you have better results.

Students: How important do you think is time management for working in a multicultural team?

Buss: Very important because time concepts are totally different in every nationality and you don't know that if you have never thought about that before because normally you might assume if you set a deadline on 5 pm you think you have it by then. What about the consequences? Especially the Chinese people don't see the whole picture. They don't know that if they miss their deadline by one day or even the next morning the whole process is screwed. It is very important to have a plan and to make sure they know what the problem is if they don't do their work.

In: Boni/Prötzig/Friemel, Written Assignment, Stralsund 2012 (unpublished)

8.12 Role play: Multicultural team work

The following role play was created by the students of Baltic Management Studies at the University of Applied Sciences Stralsund, Juliane Wormsbächer and Christoph Kolbin.
At the end, you are asked to find out, how the managers in the role play behaved based on their cultural background. Furthermore, write down the mistakes you have found as far as Dr. Wagner's behavior is concerned and let us know what your solution looks like.

(Part 1)
The American, the German and the Chinese company representatives of "Colors United", Mr. Peter Smith, Dr. Wagner and Mr. Byung Ningchu, meet in Berlin at 10 o'clock in the morning, since several decisions concerning the production of a new sports suit have to be made. After the greetings, they all take their assigned seats.

Wagner: *(He stands up, looks at the people in the room constantly gesticulating because he is full of enthusiasm.)* I would like to welcome you to our meeting today. I'm glad to have the representatives from China and also the US here in Germany to talk about the development of "Colors United's" new sports suit. I'm looking forward to this meeting and hope that we will be able to decide on the further development of our product. But before we get down to business, I would like to express my appreciation towards you and your teams for the fantastic work that has been done so far. We have had some great research and a feedback from the States, which was more than helpful. The results we got from China were outstanding. Mr. Ningchu, let me just ask: Who has come up with the new "skin" textiles?

Ningchu: *(He smiles, a little shyly.)* That was our innovation and development group.

Wagner: And who is the head of this group?

Ningchu: The head is Mr. Young.

Wagner: Would you please tell Mr. Young that we are very satisfied with his work and that we are glad to have someone with his competence as a partner!

Ningchu: *(He looks a little confused and answers with a short delay.)* Yes, I will tell him.

Wagner: Thank you very much! All right, then let us now talk about our new product.

(Part 2)
Wagner: As you all know, we have already selected the material and have developed a design for the jacket as well as for the pants. Today we will talk about the colors and the motifs or symbols and the name for our new sports suit.

Smith: *(He interrupts the German and looks at his notes while starting to speak.)* Let me comment on the design of the jacket and the pants. Our research and marketing team has just finished a couple of series in research concerning design and style trends for the upcoming year. We would suggest shortening the collar of the jacket and tightening it around the neck. This would make it look sportier; the same can be said for the pants. The trend seems to go in a direction where tight pants will be asked for. We suppose that our product would fail and would not be able to compete with other products on the market if the changes weren't made. We've already produced a few suits in the modified style and even carried out a survey with both suits. We asked people which of

| | them they were more likely to buy and the one with the changes was 40 % ahead. We'll soon be able to send our new plans to our partners in China so that they can adjust the production. |

Wagner: So, what you are trying to say is that we should change the design we have previously agreed on? Do I understand you correctly? We have spent most of the time on questions related to the design and we have all agreed that this design will be competitive on the market.
(He pauses for a moment) I would say we leave the design as it is.

Smith: Trust me! *(a bit angry)* We have spent a lot of time discussing these changes with the development group. Our efforts to change the design will be rewarded. I'm absolutely sure about that!

Wagner: I still don't agree with changing anything. We have planned our work and now have to implement our plan. There is no room for changes.

Smith: What is your opinion, Mr. Ningchu?

Ningchu: I have to agree with Dr. Wagner! We have spent a lot of time on the design and it seems to be good. But your team has done all those researches and if the trend goes towards what you've just said, it will be important to make the changes because we are going to launch a product with which we want to be successful and if the changes are necessary for that, we should consider them carefully.

Smith: *(impatiently asking)* So, do you say we should make those changes?

Ningchu: Well, we would have to discuss that within our group in China. I can't decide that on my own.

Smith: But we are running out of time, we need to finalize the changes and send them to China so you can implement them. Don't you think your colleagues would agree to these changes as much as you do?

Ningchu: I understand that we have a tight schedule, but I'm unable to decide this matter without having discussed anything within the group.

Wagner: Gentlemen, we are losing precious time. Let us get back to our actual topic. We can talk about possible changes if we still have time later on.

(Part 3)

Wagner: We should now focus on the colors. Mr. Smith, it's your turn. Would you please be so kind to share your results with us?

Smith: I'd love to. *(He rises from his chair and goes towards the flip chart)* The main idea of the whole project was to create a suit which is sportsmanlike, comfortable and of course stylish. *(He demonstrates it with his index finger.)*
The design makes it look sporty and the new material makes it comfortable. But the right combination of the colors together with the design will determine whether the suit has style or not. After our researches and long discussions we have decided for a combination of black and blue. *(He reveals his model on the flipchart and gives the group a moment to look at it)* We have tried out a variety of color combinations, but this one is just putting the main ideas of the project together. Sporty, comfortable and stylish! *(He looks at his audience and notices the nodding of the Chinese partner; smiles towards the Chinese)* I'm glad you agree with me. Dr. Wagner, what is your opinion?

Wagner: I'm impressed. It certainly is a sports suit with style.

Smith: Mr. Ningchu, what do you think?

Ningchu:	*(a long pause)*
Smith:	*(impatiently asking)* You have an opinion on that, don't you?
Ningchu:	*(little shy)* The design is wonderful and the main ideas are very well implemented. Even the colors look great. *(He pauses for a second.)* But might other colors be possible, too?
Smith:	We do have other color combinations, but the black and blue one is certainly the best one and will lead to success. But didn't you also agree to the blue and the black earlier? I remember you nodding to me when I presented the suit.
Wagner:	Mr. Ningchu's nodding meant that he understood what you were saying. But in China, I believe, nodding doesn't necessarily mean agreement. Is that right, Mr. Ningchu?
Ningchu:	*(with a calm voice)* Yes, that is true.
Smith:	*(He looks a bit confused)* Well, I didn't know that. Now, let us get back to the topic, I'm afraid we are running out of time. *(in a raised voice)* Mr. Ningchu, would you tell me, why you think we need other colors?
Ningchu:	Well, black and blue, as well as dark green and white symbolize pain, harm and bad things in China. The product might be successful in Germany and the States, but it would fail in China. Our suggestion would be a combination of red and yellow. These are seen as sun colors and reflect joy and happiness.
Smith:	*(still a bit angry)* Well, we'll see what we can do.

(Part 4)

Wagner:	At our last meeting, we agreed on "air" as the name of the sports suit. And three weeks ago I sent you 4 different examples for the logo, so you've had time to discuss the design of the logo within your teams. I'm now looking forward to hear about the results. *(He turns towards his Chinese counterpart)* Mr. Ningchu, what has your delegation decided on?
Ningchu:	Yes. *(He opens his binder)* It was not easy to choose only one out of these four. All of them would fit very well as a logo. However, in the end we decided for the third example because it seems to fit best to what we want the suit to represent.
Wagner:	Thank you very much for your contribution. Now, I want to ask you, Mr. Smith! Which logo do you prefer most?
Smith:	Well, we have had an interesting discussion about that. Let me mention here that we have two Muslims in our group and they weren't quite pleased to see example 4.
	(The other participants pay more attention)
	It is the one with the flames. They said the logo looked very similar to the way Muslims spell the name of their god "Allah". Both were very upset about the fact that someone would suggest putting the name of their god on a sports suit. It took us quite some time, explanations and apologies to be able to carry on with the meeting. At the end, we were able to make a decision: Example 2 is, as we think, perfect as a logo.
Wagner:	It is very interesting to hear that the logo caused so much trouble. We had never thought that the logo would be seen as an insult. However, it is good to find out something like that in advance. Just imagine the costs if the sports suit had already been on the market. Anyway, my group decided in favor of the se-

cond example, just like the group in the USA. This seems to be the best solution. Would you all agree that we use example 2?

Smith: I do agree.

Ningchu: If you don't mind, I'll answer that question in our next meeting. Let us find out what our groups think about it.

Wagner: I think I'll have to accept that. As for this meeting we are running out of time. Gentlemen, thank you very much for coming. I hope you will enjoy the rest of your stay and let's hope that we will be able to get a little more done the next time we meet. Have a nice afternoon.

(The managers get up from their seats and say goodbye to each other.)

In: Kolbin/Wormsbächer, Written Assignment – Role Play, Stralsund, 2006 (unpublished), pp. 8ff

---

Interview with Don A. Neuman
Manager and chief pilot of flight inspection for the Federal Aviation Administration in Atlanta:

Students: *In which way were the experiences you have made as a member of an international team helpful for your own personal development?*

Neuman: I learnt a lot; especially it helps me to get a different perspective how to solve problems.

Students: *Before collecting a team, what is necessary for the success of a multicultural team?*

Neuman: Multilingual capabilities are absolutely necessary, especially in our area it is English and Spanish.

In: Projektunterlagen, Bachelor and Master Theses (all unpublished), Stralsund, 2000–2009

8.13   Case Study: Managing diversity at Luxury Island Resort

Patricia Atwell had just accepted a position as a human resource consultant for the Luxury Island Resort in California. The resort's profitability was declining, and Patricia had been hired to evaluate the situation and to make recommendations to the local management and the headquarters management. Feeling a little bit overwhelmed by this task, Patricia pondered where to start.

There had been an extremely high employee turnover rate in the past few years, the quality of the resort's service had declined, and many regular clients were not returning. Patricia decided to start with the clients by interviewing some of them and asking others to fill out a comment slip about the resort. Many clients criticized the poor service from every type of staff member. One regular client said, "This used to be a happy, efficient place. Now I don't even know if I'll come back next year; the atmosphere among the workers seems dismal; nobody ever looks happy."

Patricia began to investigate trends and practices regarding hiring and placement. In reviewing the files, she noticed that the labour pool had become increasingly diverse in the last few years. The majority of the employees at the resort represented a number of racial and ethnic backgrounds, and many were recent immigrants. Many were unskilled and had little schooling, yet there were placed straight into their jobs. The management and office staff was also quite diversified; yet, even with higher education and skill level, there was a considerable turnover.

One day later Patricia decided to get out among the employees – to talk to them and observe them on the job. She started her departmental evaluations in the kitchen, where she found a melange of cultures; the French chef was screaming directions, mostly in French, to his assistants and the waiters, who seemed to be Haitian, Spanish, and Asian. Many seemed confused about what they should do, but did not say anything. After lunch Patricia decided to review the housekeeping department. She observed a new housekeeper who had been hired that day; her name was Sang, and she was a recent immigrant from Taiwan. Sang was given a cleaning cart, an assigned block of rooms, and a key to the rooms; she was told to get to work. That same day there was a customer complaint. Apparently, Sang did not understand the meaning of the sign "Do not disturb" and had interrupted someone taking a shower. Later, she overheard a manager reprimanding another housekeeper, remarking that she was nothing but a "lazy Mexican." Patricia spoke to the young woman and found out that when the manager noticed her leaning against the wall, she was just waiting for the room occupant to come back out, as he had said he was about to do, so that she could clean the room

Patricia interviewed a couple of the housekeepers. She asked a variety of questions: What did they perceive the job duties to be? How should they be performed? What could be done to improve the job? The assortment of answers she received perplexed her; each housekeeper perceived the job differently, and each had valid ideas for improvement based on his or her understanding of the job. Patricia asked one Chinese housekeeper why she did not bring her suggestions to her supervisor. She replied, "Oh, no! I could not do that. He will only think my ideas are stupid." At the end of the week, Patricia was disturbed when she observed two of the Chinese housekeepers throw their ballots in the garbage. When she asked them why they had decided not to vote, they said that they could not make such a difficult decision about their fellow workers.

For the following days, Patricia practiced her "management by walking around", just trying to quietly observe the staff and their interactions. One thing she noticed was that each day the different ethnic groups could be found socializing only among themselves – outsiders were not welcomed. She observed a group of Chinese workers planning a picnic, but as she approached them, they were politely quieted down.

After carefully studying the work processes and interactions in the other resort departments, Patricia decided to interview and evaluate the various managers in the resort, both in the hotel and in the various beach and recreation areas. She started with the restaurants. The manager said that he did not perceive any problems with his staff. When she mentioned some of her observations, he said that he was busy and that he really did not find anything to be concerned about. Next, she approached the manager of housekeeping, Mrs White, who explained that she set the rules and duties and that the only real task was for the staff to follow them; if they did not, she fired them. In consulting with the resort manager, she noticed that he was concerned about declining occupation. However, he explained, he tried not to become involved in employee problems. He said that he hired experienced department managers, and he expected them to be able to handle such problems.

In concluding her evaluation period, Patricia spent a couple of days reviewing her findings. Then she drew up her report and recommendations. Next, she set up two meetings – one with all the managers at resort, and one with the president of the Luxury Island Resorts.

Source: Deresky, H., in: Managing across borders and cultures, New Jersey, 2000, S. 132

Review and Discussion Questions:

1. You are Patricia Atwell. Evaluate the situation and tell us what went wrong.

2. What are your conclusions out of this scenario? Draw up a list of recommendations to the resort management and a list of recommendations to the company president.

3. Assuming your recommendations are accepted, outline your plan for implementing them. What specific steps must be taken, by whom, and when? What results do you anticipate?

9 Intercultural Preparation and Reintegration

9.0 Statement of the problem

> **The cost of failure**
> (Jeremy Williams)
>
> Unfortunately, many Western companies and individuals fail to face the realities of life and work in the Gulf. Many costly mistakes can be made, both financially and personally. Western companies sometimes believe that simply by dispatching highly qualified and intelligent staff to undertake duties in the Gulf all will be well. Foolish companies will presume that professional qualifications is the overriding requirement and give no weight to the wider mental preparation (and selection) of such people and their spouses. Professional competence is the starting point for selection purposes; what is also needed, in the character of those under consideration for Gulf employment, is an intercultural preparation. Without knowing the peculiarities of Arab culture, business practices and the relevant behaviour patterns, which include a comprehensive understanding of Islam, each expatriate will definitely fail.
>
> In: Don't they know it's Friday? 2004, p. 3

9.1 The role of expatriates

International labor mobility is becoming a component in the globalization of industries worldwide. Regions, nations, industries and people are in a permanent state of flux in which geographical mobility plays an important role. Globalization has led to intensified interaction among businesses and their managers from different countries and cultures. It is generally accepted that it is essential for multinational companies to attract, select, train and retain employees who are able to effectively work outside their own national borders (Flyztani & Nijkamp, 2008, pp. 2-3).

This dynamic business environment has introduced the phenomenon of expatriates. They are

"a particular class of foreign workers who are sent on a temporary basis by a parent company located in a given country to live and work in another country, notably as an employee in a subsidiary abroad" (ibid., p.1).

Expatriates have to perform in an unfamiliar work context, and need to handle and adapt to a different way of life and management styles (ibid. p.3).

Windham International and the National Foreign Trade Council, Inc. (NFTC) conducted a study among 180 companies representing small, medium, and large organizations with offices located throughout the world. The companies were mainly headquartered in the Americas (48 %) or the EMEA (49 %) with only few from the Asia-Pacific region (3 %) (Windham & NFTC, 2007, p. 4).

The survey revealed that the majority (56 %) of responding companies deployed more than 100 expatriates (ibid., p. 5). Moreover, 69 % reported an increase in the number of expatriates over the last year, whereas in the 2005-survey, the percentage was just 47 % (ibid., p.6). Only 19 % reported a reduction in their number of international assignments. Prospects regarding the future development were also optimistic, since 65 % of the respondents expected a rising number of expatriates in 2007 (ibid.).

These figures are similar to the survey by Mercer Human Resource Consulting, where 44 % of all multinational corporations questioned had increased the number of their international assignments in 2005 and 2006.

International assignments as career opportunities

Henrick Wegner, Project Director of Netcom Consultants, currently working on the "Tigo Rwanda Project" in Kigali answered questions raised by the students of the University of Applied Sciences Stralsund on 28th May 2010:

Students: *What is your best career advice to somebody who has just graduated from university?*

Wegner: Do seek maximum exposure by specifically pursuing overseas assignments, ideally with a global company that is head-quartered in Central Europe. Do not mind the tough challenges as they will prove to be your best trainer and valuable for future references. The better you manage to cope with unaccustomed working conditions, the more appreciation you would be able to reasonably expect from your organization, thus making the foundation of your professional career ever more solid.

In. Günther/Kerber/Laudahn/Wiese, Written Assignment, 2010, unpublished

---

9.2   Intercultural learning and culture shock

9.2.1   Definition of culture shock

Due to the change of the social and non-social environment, the expatriate is confronted with patterns of perception, thinking, feeling and acting that are different from his/her previous "world of implicitness" (Kühlmann, 1995, p.4). The relativity and culture dependency of of our experience and behavioral patterns becomes obvious (ibid.).

This experience of inappropriateness of one's own behavior in a different culture and the consequent loss of orientation, unstableness and insecurity is often described in literature as the concept of a "culture shock" (Eulenburg, 2001, p. 62).

Oberg introduced the term "culture shock" for the first time to describe the adaption process to an alien environment; from entering the host culture to the successful integration

(Wengert, p. 2). To Oberg, the culture shock is similar to a sickness with a certain cause, symptoms and treatment (1960, p. 7).

> *"Culture shock tends to be an occupational disease of people who have been suddenly transplanted abroad (…). Culture shock is precipitated by the anxiety that results from losing all our familiar signs and symbols of social intercourse" (Oberg, 1960, p. 177).*

Nowadays, the term has a negative connotation, which usually implies that the person experiencing it is not willing to adapt and that certain experiences in the other culture have resulted in a shock (Löwe, 2002, p. 10). Layes (2003, p. 130) agrees that the term "culture shock" is deceptive, because people understand it like a severe shock phenomena, although culture shock also embraces soft irritations and confusion when experiencing the otherness of the new culture, which can lead to alienation and rejection of the host culture.

Wagner concludes that a culture shock is the sum of all intercultural confusions, all the times putting one foot in it (1996, pp. 33–34). He thinks that the cause of culture shock is connected to the norms creating meaning in one's own culture (ibid.).

Kopper and Kiechl (1997, p. 33) clearly state that culture shock is not a illness but a process of adaption after the relocation to another culture, and is associated with the gathering and processing of different behavioral norms and patterns, customs, rites, as well as their own psychological reaction to the unknown. Adler (2002, p. 264) agrees, stating that

> *"Culture shock is not a disease, but rather a natural response to the stress of immersing oneself in a new environment".*

9.2.2   Culture shock models

The cross-cultural research literature features several terms to describe the development of skills that allow foreigners to function adequately in a new culture. Adjustment, adaptation, and acculturation are the ones most often used and they describe the process and resulting change when people move into an unfamiliar cultural environment. (Haslberger & Brewster, 2005)

The best known culture shock model introduced by Oberg (1960) describes the four different stages of adjustment: Honeymoon, Crisis, Recovery, and Adjustment. Moreover, the "U-curve" hypothesis introduced by Lysgaard (1955) has been a researchers' favorite for describing the adjustment process over the last half a century.

The Honeymoon Phase or Euphoria is characterized by fascination and enthusiasm for the new culture having friendly – but superficial – relationships to host country members (Kühlmann, 1995, p. 6). Expatriates enjoy a great deal of excitement when they discover the new culture (Adler, 2002, p. 263).

In the second phase, the actual culture shock sets in. The problems in terms of language, values and symbols create negative emotions, anxiety and frustration (Kühlmann, 1995, p. 6). It is a period of disillusionment and

> *"(…) a result from being bombarded by too many new and uninterpretable cues" (Adler, 2002, p. 263).*

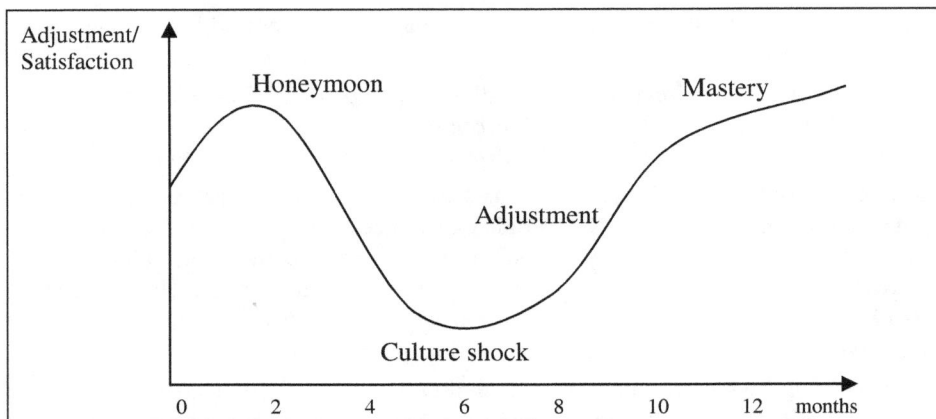

Fig. 9.1:   Adjustment in an international assignment: The "U-Curve Hypothesis A"
Source: Lysgaard (1955), as cited in Stahl, G.K., n.d.

After that, when time goes on, the Recovery or Adjustment Phase begins, when the knowledge about the host country is improving, the foreigner can orientate him/herself within the new culture and the attitude towards the host culture improves (Kühlmann, 1995, p. 6). Thus, after the culture shock phase, expatriates start adapting to the new culture, feeling more positive about their host country, working more effectively and living a more satisfying life (Adler, 2002, p. 263). Finally, the Mastery phase begins; reaching a stable state of well-being, where the habits of the other culture are accepted and and anxiety rarely appears.

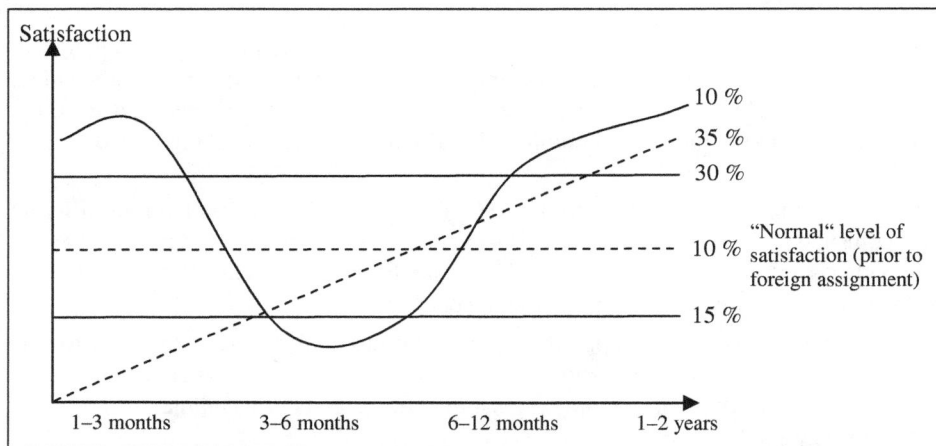

Fig. 9.2:   Adjustment during an international assignment: The "U-Curve Hypothesis B"
Source: Lysgaard (1955), as cited in Stahl, G.K., n.d.

When people are experiencing the culture shock, there are several possible symptoms manifesting themselves in physical conditions, perceptions and behavior. Health impairments can be insomnia, a loss of appetite, digestion problems and high blood pressure (ibid., p. 7; Adler, 2002, p. 265). Moreover, an affected person might also undergo psychological effects like mistrust towards the members of the host culture, the feeling of being constantly deceived and helplessness when confronted with everyday problems. The host culture is blamed for one's own destiny (ibid.). Ultimately, a change of behavior could become apparent, such as a decrease in performance and creativity, a focus on contacts with country fellowmen, the avoidance of members of the other culture, a resistance to speaking the foreign language, and deprecatory statements towards the host country and its habitants.

The culture shock causes similar symptoms like stress. Therefore, it is also recognized as a stress reaction (Kühlmann, 1995, p. 16; Furnham, 1990, p. 281). During the international assignment, the expatriate is confronted with plenty of daily hassles which can cause some, but feasible problems. However, if they seem to accumulate, the expatriate gets the feeling of excessive demand and dissatisfaction of his stay abroad (Kühlmann, 1995, p. 16). Factors that provoke stress are ambiguity, unpredictability, loss of control, sensory overload (ibid.), role conflicts, ambiguity, and adjustment processes (Udris/Frese, 1992, p. 343). Thus, the stress-related culture shock may take many forms, like anger, anxiety, disappointment, embarrassment, frustration, identity confusion or impatience (Adler, 2002, p. 265).

To reduce the culture shock stress for global managers, Adler (2002, pp. 265–266) suggested the creation of personal stability zones, like going to an international club, watching movies in one's native language, or checking into a home-country hotel for the weekend top, to reduce stress. Furthermore, it is recommendable to use stress management mechanisms, like meditation and relaxation techniques, keep a journal, or physical exercise. On the job, the expatriate must recognize that he/her will neither work as efficiently nor as effectively as before and consequently also adjust his/her expectations.

The mentioned culture shock symptoms vary in their number, duration and intensity depending on the person concerned (Kühlmann, 1995, p. 16). Factors that influence this variability can only be speculated. The U-curve model has its defects, since it is not clear if the phases can only proceed in this order, if phases can be left out, how long one phase lasts etc. (ibid.).

In 1985 Grove and Toribiörn developed a newer approach, trying to explain the subjective adaption process with the coherence of three psychological aspects: clarity of the mental frame of reference, applicability of behavior and the subjective level of mere adequacy (Kühlmann, 1995, p.8).

9.2.3 Types of reaction to culture shock

The positive adaption to the host culture has been finalized when the expatriate feels comfortable in his/her new environment and established social contacts to "natives" (social and non-work integration), and executes his/her professional task successfully (work integration). The expatriate, in this case Type A, overcomes the culture shock and reaches his original emotional satisfaction level. He combines his accustomed behavioral patterns with the newly learned ones (Synthesis) (Kühlmann, 1995, p. 17), feeling an attraction to the host culture, but preserving the own cultural norms (Integration) (Berry/Kailin, 1995). The international assignment and the conjoint experiences enrich the expatriate's personality (Eulenburg, 2001, p. 70).

What to expect in China – Dealing with culture shock
(Greg Rodgers)

1.   Remember the language difference
Don't expect everyone whom you encounter to speak English well, why would they? Saying the same thing again only louder makes you look like a newbie traveler and won't help them to understand any better. The same goes for showing others a map or written words; can you read Chinese?

2.   Starting and pointing
All foreign visitors to China, particularly blond or fair-skinned people, receive plenty of attention when in public. People will openly stare at you, expressionless, and sometimes even point you out to friends and family by jabbing a finger in your direction. Pointing is often accompanied with the word laowai which means "old outsider". You will hear the term often, despite the government's efforts to curb its usage.

3.   Spitting and mucus clearing
Spitting in public and clearing the deepest sinus recesses of the head – with sound effects – are common throughout China – even on public transportation and sometimes indoors! Choking pollution in big cities and excessive smoking are good reasons to send a lot of mucus flying.

4.   Personal space is a luxury
Don't be offended if someone stands just a little too close when speaking to you, or people are calmly pressed against you in crowded public transportation. With such an enormous population, the Chinese do not share the same concept of personal buffer space that Westerners monitor. You will rarely receive an "excuse me" when someone bumps into you or squeezes past while knocking you out of the way.

5.   Fight your position
Orderly queues, especially of more than a few people, are generally disregarded in China. As a foreigner, people will blatantly step in front of you, cut line, or push past you to the counter as if you aren't even there. Again, remember that overpopulation plays a big part in this behavior and do your best to keep cool while holding your place in line. Don't be afraid to stick elbows out or to shuffle around defensively to keep people from stepping in front of you.

6.   Watch out for road rage
Crossing the road in busy cities can be a daunting affair. Drivers rarely observe a pedestrian's right of way, even if you have a working walk signal! Be cautious when crossing roads; don't assume that drivers will stop just because they have a red light. You are best off crossing safely as a group with others.

In: http://goasia.about.com/od/Customs-and-Traditions/tp/China-Culture-Shock.htm, accessed: 10/09/2014

However, there are more ways of coping. There is the possibility of "going native", which leads to the highest satisfaction level in the foreign culture, but causes problems when returning home. Type B – also called assimilation type – substitutes his behavioral patterns to the foreign one, absolutely refuses the own culture and loses the own cultural identity (Kühlmann, 1995, p. 17, Thomas/Hagemann, 1992, p. 179, Berry/Kailin, 1995). This coping behavior does not lead to better acceptance in the host culture On the contrary; the expatriate even loses his authenticity (Eulenburg, 2001, p. 70).

In total contrast to this, there is Type C who does not succeed in adapting to the host country's culture, not overcomes the culture shock. This is also known as the the separation type, who just preserves his own culture, but does not feel attraction to the host culture (Berry/Kailin, 1995). This marginalization type refuses the host culture, avoids contact to the host country's habitants and integration does not take place, since this type does not learn new behavioral patterns (Kühlmann, 1995, p. 17). Thomas and Hagemann call this the contrast-type (1992, p.179).

For the last type (D), the culture shock means a crucial crisis, resulting in defense-mechanisms with possibly even severe consequences like alcoholism, because there is a non-attraction felt to the host culture and the own cultural norms do not hold any longer. (Weaver, 1986, p. 112; Berry/Kailin, 1995).

Kühlmann (1995, p. 17) describes two more coping types, the addition type, who is an expatriate capable of using the host culture behavioral patterns, but just doing it selectively. Another rather inefficient type is the creation. In this case, expatriates unite the two cultural behavioral patterns to a new unit, which means a synthesis that is not adequate neither in the own nor in the host culture (ibid.).

9.2.4 Culture Shock: India

When you encounter a new environment, all habits and behaviors that allow you to get around survive at home suddenly no longer work. Things as simple and automatic as getting lunch, saying hello to colleagues, or setting up a meeting become difficult and strange. The rules have changed and no one has told you what the new rules are. Even as far as your understanding of truth is concerned not everybody sees it as binding. In order to get a better understanding what is meant in this context the following example should underline the difficult approach to get familiar with a new culture. There are a lot of things that strike people from other cultures when they interact with Indians for the first time (Messmer, 2009, p. 118–119):

1. *Lack of order and structure*
   Life functions differently in India, everything seems to run in its own rhythm. Following schedules, adherence or existence of rules cannot be taken for granted. Everybody follows their own destination, logic, and rhythm.
2. *Decibel level*
   Indians tend to speak all at the same time and at much louder volumes than necessary. People are used to living and working in overcrowded spaces and it is thought to be important to raise the voice in order to catch attention.

3. *Display of emotions*

Indians control their emotions far less than foreigners do. Uncontrolled outbursts of irritation, overwhelming appreciation, open anxiety, and declaration of loyalty can be a challenge to deal with.

4. *Respect for hierarchy*

Elders in the family enjoy a special superior status because of their seniority. Most organizations have a very steep hierarchy and authority is often not questioned.

5. *Lack of private sphere*

Colleagues at work and also total strangers surprise you with questions about your age, work experience, marital status, number of children - and even your income. All this is not viewed as a violation of personal space in India. Colleagues at work are very much aware on where their peers stand in terms of monetary compensation.

6. *Juggling of appointments and multitasking*

Appointments are not necessarily written in stone, as they are more considered like a tentative reservation that can be cancelled without notice if anything more important comes up. It is very rare that a telephone conference starts at the scheduled time; most Indian participants will dial in five to fifteen minutes later. When in a meeting, Indians will not switch off their cell phones but take each and every call – it might be an important one. This goes as far as telephone calls being answered while visiting the restroom.

7. *Peace over truth*

In cases of conflicts or disputes, the value of peace comes before truth. This means that you will not be told the complete truth or be told an adjusted version of the story in order to allow the Indian to keep face and continue with a harmonic relationship. Facts can be switched and turned, if it serves a good purpose; there is not only one version of truth.

9.2.5   Culture Shock: Saudi Arabia

From 1991 till 1994 I have worked as a Senior Commercial Adviser for the GIZ (Gesellschaft für Internationale Zusammenarbeit) former GTZ. During that time some challenging situations did occur in a completely new environment (Seminarunterlagen, 2012):

"When I came to Saudi Arabia, I was confronted with a Muslim society in which the Qur'an determines the whole life, regardless, if someone is a Muslim or not.

The Muslim day starts very early at about 4.45 am. The exact time depends on the sunrise of this day and is to be found in any newspaper well ahead of the given day. From more than 2,500 mosques the respective loudspeaker informs all people in the area that the time has come to perform the first prayer. There is no escape from receiving this message, especially not from the noise linked to the loudspeakers, because you will find a mosque within a distance of about 200 m. However, after a while, one gets familiar with these circumstances and only those living quite close to a mosque will not find sleep again.

The next time you have to adjust your behavior - now towards your Muslim colleagues - occurs when the second prayer time will take place. At about 11.25 am the colleagues will leave the working place in order to pray. They have two opportunities to perform the praying. Either they go to one of the praying rooms set up at every floor within the building, or they have the possibility to walk to the nearby mosque

outside the working place. The overwhelming majority of all governmental clerks de-
cide to go to the next mosque. Why? I presume, in order to avoid working too long. At
about 12.20 pm or later, you can continue the collaboration with your Muslim col-
leagues.

As far as the third and fourth prayer time is concerned an interesting explanation will
be given to you. Normally, each Muslim has to pray five times a day. The Saudi inter-
pretation of the Qur'an now says that those who have to travel are allowed to pray
only three times. What does that mean in reality? At around 3.25 pm thousands of
cars are moving from their home to the next mall. The same can be observed about
two hours later when the fourth praying time will take place, with the difference that
the cars are now moving home.

The fifth prayer time will take place at about 7.30 pm. If you expect guests from Saudi
Arabia, keep in mind that they will not arrive before 9.00 pm. The heavy traffic causes
a lot of delays and those who want to pray should be given sufficient time to perform
their duties as Muslims."

9.3   Failure of expatriation: costs & causes

Expatriates are a major investment for multinational corporations. It has been estimated that
the first-year costs of sending employees on intenational assignments are at least three times
the base salaries of their domestic counterparts (Wederspahn, 1992).

Still, depending on the respective survey, about 15 to 50 % of the international assignments
fail (Thomas/Hagemann/Stumpf, 2003, p. 242), which costs the company about US$ 250,000
to US$ 1,000,000 per failure (Bhagat/Prien, 1996, p. 217).

The study of Black and Gregersen (1999, p. 53) among 750 US-American, European, and
Japanese companies about expatriates revealed that between 10 to 20 % of the expatriates
have returned early without completing their international assignment, with one third of the
managers not reaching the performance expectations, and one quarter quitting the employment afterwards. About this rougly 30 %-group, Althauser (1996, p. 3) found out that third of
the expatriate managers had to return prematurely due to an insufficient performance, causing costs of about DM 250,000 (≈ EUR 128,000) per assignment.

Based on a study with only American companies, Keller (1998, p. 320) refers to a premature
return rate of expatriates of 15 to 30 %, He estimates the follow-up costs to amoung to three
or four times the managers' annual salaries. Kealy (1996, p. 83) even speaks of early return
rates of American managers ranging between 15 to 40 %. Whereas Kühlmann & Stahl (1998,
p. 44) assume 10 % to be a realistic premature return rate, Cendant found out in 2001 that
44 % of MNCs were reporting failures in the Asia Pacific region, and 63 % in Europe.

Moreover, Black and Gregersen (1999, p. 103) highlighted the selection of inappropriate
personnel, bad preparation, and unreflecting treatment during the repatriation as the main
reasons for failure.

Already in 1982, Tung and also Toribörn recognized the (dis)satisfaction of the expatriates'
spouses and families and their adaption to the new cultural environment as a central determi-
nant for early termination and cultural adjustment of the expatriate. Mendenhall and Oddou

(1998) also showed that the lacking adaption of spouses and partners of the expatriate lead to international assignment failures.

Similar explanations of assignment failures are given by the Zürich-Versicherungs-gesellschaft, which states the missing social contacts and personal relations with the local habitants, communication problems within the teams, and adaption difficulties of the family as the main reasons (Saunders, 1997, p.94).

In a survey by Windham International & NFTC (2006, p. 14), however, 10 % of assignments were not completed because expatriates returned prematurely. The named key factors leading to assignment failure were partner dissatisfaction (57 %), inability to adapt (47 %), family concerns (39 %), and poor candidate selection (39 %) (Windham & NFTC, 2007, p. 14). Spouse dissatisfaction has always been the most frequently cited factor (ibid., p. 50).

However, international failures do not necessarily involve a premature return. Bittner and Reisch (n.d., p. 53) see it as a complex term, which also includes a refusal of contract prolongation, missing the targeted objects, just marking the time, lasting personal problems, massive conflicts etc. That can clearly bring up the percentage of failure to about 25 to 30 %, but those costs are difficult to estimate.

As far as international joint ventures are concerned the failing rate is extremely high. Between 50 to 80 % of those business activities are assumed not to be successful (Kealey, 1996, p. 85).

9.4   The expatriation cycle

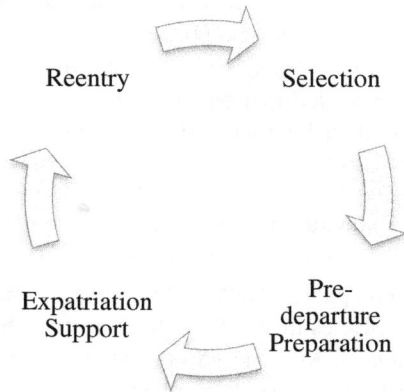

Fig. 9.3:   Expatriation Cycle
Source: Own graph

The transition back into the home country can cause problems just like the new environment and lifestyle when entering another culture (Adler, 2002, p. 274).

While abroad, the expatriate changes, the organization and the country change as well, and during the culture shock phase of adjusting to the host culture, expatriates often idealize their home country, just remembering the good aspects. Then, upon return, the gap between the way it was and the way it is, and the gap between their idealized memories and reality can be a shock (ibid., p. 273).

> *"Successful global companies understand and manage each phase of the expatriate global career cycle" (ibid., p. 262).*

The reintegration process will be looked at more closely in the second part of this chapter.

9.4.1   Aspects of a successful international assignments

In order to make an international assignment successful, the support of the whole family is needed. Thus, their willingness to relocate is a big step towards successful expatriation.

According to McNulty (2005), the factors influencing the willingness to relocate are: standard of education for children (66 %), company funded home-country visits (59 %), transferring spouse's attitude towards relocating (57 %), ability to re-establish a support network (56 %), perceived standard of living in host-country (54 %), and the impact of relocation on trailing spouse's career meaning the dual-career issue (35 %).

Moreover, important factors of organizational support for the success are the assistance to set-up internet and email (94 %), housing assistance (94 %), ongoing organizational support also after relocation (85 %), financial and time support for home-country visits (82 %), and the provision of extended time for the entire family to adjust including expatriate's spouse (82 %). 26 % also listed the pre-departure training for the trailing spouse. For him or her, there is a strong need to establish or improve a direct communication link between the sponsoring organization and the spouse or partner, irrespective of their non-employee status with the organization (ibid.).

Windham International & NFTC (2006) identified major expatriate and family support initiatives:

- Better candidate assessment and selection
- Better assignment preparation
- Career-path planning for better cross-border skills utilization upon return
- Effective communication of assignment objectives
- Mandatory cross-cultural training
- More communications and recognition during an assignment
- Development of company intranet for expatriates
- Mandatory destination-support services

9.4.2   Role of the family

Companies sending their employees on international assignments do not only send one member of the staff but in many cases the family is part of the decision to go abroad. The influence of the family on the job as well as on the wellbeing of all family members was part of many studies. The families' disposition to go, the adaption to and familiarization with the new culture has a great impact on the expatriates' success and well-being (Kühlmann, 1995; Black/Gregersen 1990, Harvey, 1985; Mendenhall/Oddou 1985, Tung, 1981).

To specify the adaption problem for the spouse, there are three characteristics according to Kühlmann (1995, p. 20):

- Firstly, the spouse or partner is often forced to do nothing in the new country, because only the expatriate has been granted a work permit.
- Secondly, the partner experiences the phenomenon of the culture shock more intensively. The expatriate is supported by the familiarity of his work and his colleagues; the spouse has to manage the every-day-life in an alien culture, different habits and language.
- And lastly, compared to the expatriate, the partner normally is not so skilled in the foreign language and has to struggle with communication barriers and additionally has to handle the family's needs.

Hence, the expatriate him/herself has the continuity of work, the children have the continuity of school, but the spouse has to give up his/her entire social life, the family, the friends and also his/her employment, and with that a feeling of usefulness. So the expatriate's spouse is confronted with the greatest burden especially in the beginning phase (Adler, 1991). Although, as mentioned above, the spouse does not possess the language capability like the expatriate, he/she is responsible to build up the new household, doing the necessary phone calls and assuring the medical support etc. (Kühlmann, 1995, p. 41).

Aram et al. (1972) discovered that the positive support of a spouse to go abroad is important to the professional success of the expatriate.

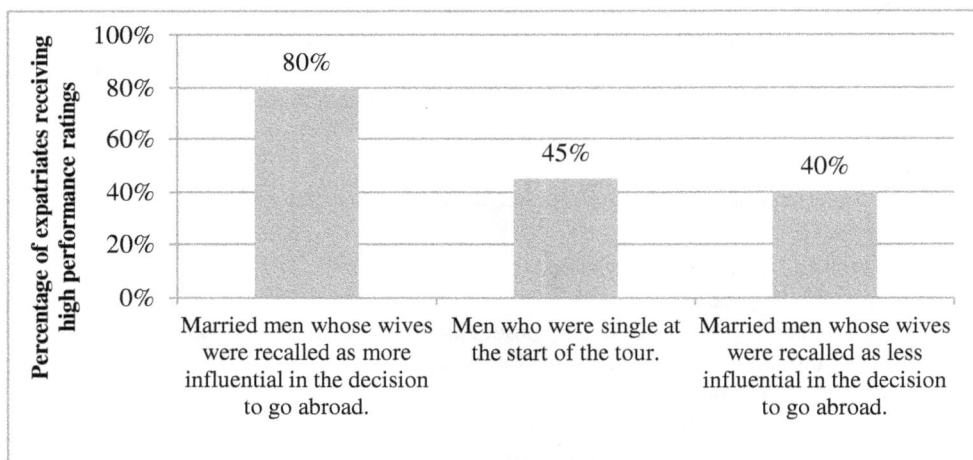

Fig. 9.4:   Performance evaluation of expatriates with or without the influence of their wives
Source: Own graph based on Stoner/Aram/Rubin, 1972, p. 310

Thus, it is not decisive for the acculturation of the expatriate if he/she is married, but if he/she gets emotional support of the family. Therefore, the spouse and children can be an important stress-coping resource, if they are not overstrained themselves with the experience of the alien culture (Fontaine, 1986). Additionally, there is the danger of the "contagion effect" of culture shock, meaning that the adaption difficulties of one family member influences the performance of the other, as it is described by Adelmann (1988, p. 192):

> *"For families that experience severe culture shock, mutual dependency can intensify the stress rather than solidify relational bonds."*

Since the dissatisfaction of the spouse is one of the most frequent reasons for expatriation failure as depicted above, companies relocating their staff should include the potential expatriates' families within the selection and preparation process (Kühlmann, 1995, Tung, 1984). But reality still varies from the theoretical ideas. None of the questioned Spanish companies of the Deloitte and Touche survey (2003, p. 9) included the spouse or partner in the process of the expatriates' selection. In the 2000 Survey of Key Trends in European Expatriate Management (PricewaterhouseCooper, 2000) the five least important criteria for selection of candidates were listed as: intercultural adaptability of the spouse, children's educational needs, emotional resilience, spouse's career (dual career issue), lifestyle suitability. It is interesting that these five least important criteria were also the most common reasons given for assignment failure (McNulty, 2005).

McNulty accentuates the role of the accompanying spouse as well as one of the most critical and important factors influencing international assignment success, since lack of spousal and family adjustment can have a direct impact on an expatriate employee's performance.

In the following, the study of Windham International & NFTC (2006) will be analyzed. The survey revealed that the majority of expatriates were male (80 %), 60 % were married and 54 % had children accompanying them during an assignment (ibid., pp. 22–24). 82 % were accompanied by a partner. Whereby 51% of the partners had lost their employment due to the expatriation and remained unemployed.

Family challenges indicated by the respondents were children's education (14 %), family adjustment (13 %), and partner resistance (13 %) being the most critical issues, followed by location difficulties (12 %), cultural adjustment (11 %), partner career (10 %), and 9 % even mentioned language difficulties (ibid, p. 43).

When asked about how companies assist spouses or partners, 69 % of respondents named language training, 36 % work permits, 30 % education/training assistance and 22 % employee assistance program services (ibid., p. 46).

In contrast to a Spanish company survey, where none of the questioned companies paid for the subscription at a sports or social club (Deloitte & Touche, 2003, p. 13), here 16 % offered a club membership (Windham international & NFTC, 2006, p. 46). However, only 17 % assisted in the job finding in the new country (ibid.), whereas this was offered by 27 % of the participants in the Spanish survey (Deloitte & Touche, 2003, p. 9).

Cultural Shock
(Beniers/Hundt)

Imagine an American visiting Japan. At first sight everything looks like at home: hotels, taxis, neonlights etc. Soon the American is going to find out that there are big differences under the surface: If the Japanese nods his head, this doesn't mean that he agrees. It just means that he understands. When Japanese smile, it doesn't mean that they are delighted. This way the first feeling of well-being can change into a feeling of disorientation and insecurity. Especially people who spend a long time in a foreign country go through this experience. This phenomenon is called cultural shock. The first to use this expression was the Amercian anthropologist Oberg.

In: International Business Communication for Industrial Engineers, 2004, p. 106

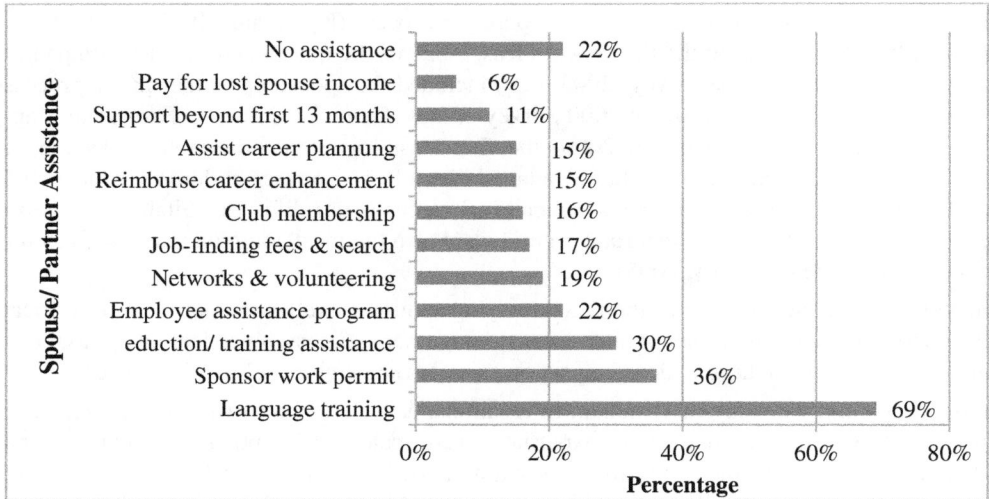

Fig. 9.5: Spouse/Partner Assistance
Source: Own graph based on Windham International & NFTC, 2007, p. 46

McNulty (2005) mentioned five top factors for the success of spousal adjustment: a strong and stable marriage (99 %), access to technology like the internet (96 %), organizational assistance (94 %), degree of intimacy with other expatriates (87 %), and transferring spouse's overall job satisfaction (76 %). 40 % also named children's adjustment as essential.

There are different opinions at what age children should be involved in an intercultural preparation program. IFIM argues that those trainings are only relevant for teenagers from 16 years and older, because younger children lack the capability of mentally preparing for situations that are not immediate (IFIM, 2002/3, p. 3). It is more about responding to their emotions and preparing them for the relocation, and for that there are books helping the parents and the children to deal with the issue (ibid., p. 4). There is also the possibility that parents and their children visit interactive websites like www.ori-and-ricki.net, and web sites that prepare especially children for their adventure, like http://www.ipl.org/youth/cquest/.

A different view has Angelika Plett from mitteconsult Berlin (2009, p. 41) who describes the general situation for the children as:

"They go into a totally different environment, they leave their friends, they leave whatever they know and they are familiar with. They have to dive into a new culture with a new language. And they need support as well. Only a few companies are doing it right now and only a few are doing it with the spouses."

As far as the age of the children is concerned, she says (ibid.):

"Well, school kids and then from a very early stage on: 7, 8, 9 years old, you could do that. But it is more a child appropriate approach like painting things and talking about what is missing and also having a discussion between the child and the parents. So that the parents are aware of what it means for the children to leave everything behind them. It is not their choice. They are kind of the victims of this situation and they feel like this. And so they need support."

In general, the expatriation must be pitched to the children, presenting them advantages of the stay abroad, answering their questions about the school and leisure time activities, giving solutions to their problems. Since often the most urgent issue is the loss of friends, the family can enable their children to communicate via Internet to keep in contact and prepare parties when visiting the home country (ibid., p. 3.).

9.4.3   Pre-departure preparation

To the degree that assignees are able to deal effectively with the challenges of encountering new cultures, their assignments will be successful. Thus, effective preparation, support and training for international assignments need to be based on sound research-supported models of the skills required to meet the challenges of those assignments for the assignees, their families accompanying them, those managing them, and the host with whom they are working. According to Britt (2002, p. 22), the second annual Global Expatriate Study revealed that nearly 40 % of the 709 responding expatriates stated that they were not adequately prepared for the international assignment.

Organizational preparation

Before expatriation, a high amount of organizational tasks has to be solved: obtaining all necessary documents (visa etc.), medical support, finding schooling possibilities for children, finding housing possibilities, making a new car available, etc. (Debrus, 1995a, p. 127)

According to Fitzgerald-Turner (1997, pp. 70–72), MNCs should hire a relocation service in the host country, so that the expatriate can concentrate on the challenges at work. Services provided include obtaining work permits, car and home insurance, locating housing, finding doctors and sorting out health care issues, selecting schools, and helping to assimilate in the new culture.

In Spain, 91 % of the companies pay for the relocation of the family, the same percentage pays the costs linked to accommodation for the first 15 days. All pay for the obtainment of the expatriate's residence permit, and even 91 % cover those costs for the entire family (Deloitte & Touche, 2003, p.13).

Intercultural preparation

Besides the administrational preparation, intercultural orientation help is necessary. MNCs should also provide pre-departure assistance and ongoing consultation for expatriates and their families. It is crucial that, at the very least, basic language skills and cross-cultural training is offered (Fitzgerald-Turner, 1997, p.72). Training can help the manager and spouse to cope with adjustment difficulties; cultural training, language training, and practical training all seem to reduce expatriate failure (Vögel, 2006, p. 7).

The goal is to prepare the expatriate and the families for the new situation, sensitize them for different behavior and beliefs in the host culture, and achieve integration (Debrus, 1995a, p. 124). Pre-departure training programs administered by the parent company can ease the transition of the expatriates and facilitate expatriate adjustment to amenities, general living conditions and social interactions (Yavas/Bodur, 1999). Pre-departure preparations should include the teaching of effective communication styles, providing insight of stress management strategies, teaching expatriates how to work in teams and to manage conflicts, and how to manage relationships across the globe (Koteswari and Bhattacharya, 2007).

In general, intercultural training methods can be differentiated into information-oriented, culture-oriented and interaction-oriented training as it is illustrated in Fig. 9.6. The degree of active participation also greatly differs between the training programmes. Beyond that categorization, some intercultural training methods and measures wil be described in the following.

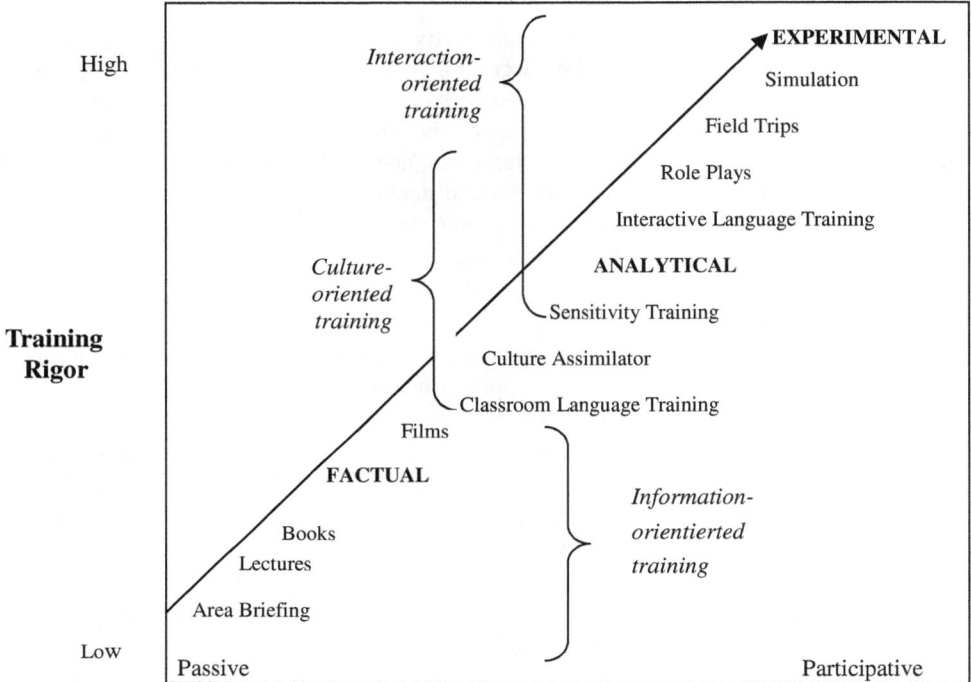

Fig. 9.6:   Intercultural training methods
Source: Own illustration based on Stahl, 1998, p. 248

Linguistic preparation

Sufficient fluency of the host country's language is essential to get integrated into the new culture. The linguistic preparation aims at imparting the language requisites to manage the new job task, but also for the integration in the host culture. The integration of the family in the linguistic preparation is vitally important, since the spouse and children are in more contact with the inhabitants and host culture (Debrus, 1995a, p. 125).

An exclusive reliance on English diminishes an expatriate's ability to interact with the host country nationals, a willingness to communicate in the host country language can help to build rapport with local employees and improve the expatriate's effectiveness (Hill, 2003, p. 617). Williams, associate of Mercer, states that linguistic and intercultural preparation can increase drastically the probability of international assignment success (Paus, 2006). At present about 75 percent of the companies questioned by the Mercer Human Resource Consulting survey offer language courses (ibid.).

Country information

Expatriates have a great interest in information about the host country, its people, habits, and culture. But it is not sufficient to supply tourism information. More important are facts about the living conditions, schools, shopping facilities, transportation possibilities, insurance and judicial questions, and medical support. It has been suggested that expatriates should receive training in the host country's culture, history, politics, economy, religion, and social and business practices (Hill, 2005, p. 629).

Derbus demonstrates the manner how the Henkel KGaA solves the problem. They provide the expatriates with country information maps and more literature for the first meetings and get support by country reports of former expatriates (Debrus, 1995a, p. 126). More and more companies now include spouses in information sessions with relocation managers prior to the transfer (Hill, 2003, p. 616). DuPont, for instance, invites the spouse to attend an orientation session where they can ask specific questions about any aspect of the transfer (Vögel, 2006, p. 3). They feel that the relocation is very much a family dislocation and the extent that the spouse can feel a part of each step is important.

Former expatriate's information

Former expatriates are helpful to support with insider know-how. However, the advice is very subjective and depends on the experience the expatriate and his family had made and could lead to discouragement (Debrus, 1995a, p. 126). Shell International employees simply contact Outpost, a network of 40 information centers set up for Shell expatriates and their families in 30 countries in the world. These Outpost Centers, staffed by the spouses of Shell's expatriate employees, provide a comprehensive and personal briefing service to any-one who is considering or has accepted an international assignment. Moreover, the Outpost centers have structured welcome groups who help new families to get familiar with the new situation after their arrival (Sievers, 1998, pp. 9–10).

Culture Assimilator

During the last years, critical incidents have been modified to better conform to the require-ments of a successful intercultural training. This process resulted in the development of the Culture Assimilator, which consists of several critical incidents that describe "incomprehen-sible" reactions of members of another culture. For each incident several answers are offered. The trainee is requested to decide on one of these possibilities and can read the feedback on his chosen answer. If it is not the right one, the reader has to try it again. When appropriate, the most important pieces of information are summarised at the end of each section. (Bittner, 2006, p. 2) Contents of these descriptions are anxieties, expectations, uncertainties, ambigui-ties, prejudices, attitudes, hierarchies, values and sense of time, just to mention some (Götz/Bleher, 2000, p. 37).

A major benefit of culture assimilators is the existence of both culture-general and culture-specific assimilators. The content is adaptable to a very high degree, because if existing as-similators are not suitable, the trainer can easily create his own assimilator by adjusting it to several factors such as gender, age and aims of the participants. (Landis/Bennett/Bennett, 2004, p. 69)

Role Plays

In role plays, a new situation is created in which the participant has to cope with a problem or task he or she is normally not confronted with, using his recent awareness and knowledge of the foreign culture. (Götz/Bleher, 2000, p. 43) The chosen situations should be relevant to the trainee's job or situation. It is a good possibility for the attendees to try to participate with unfamiliar situations in a safe environment, getting the chance to try it again, and compare their own approach and solution to the other participants' ones.

Furthermore, the future expatriates receive feedback, so that they can recognise their faults and get the opportunity to improve their intercultural skills. Role plays mostly motivate people, but there might still be some who feel uncomfortable with acting in front of others. In that case, the learning effect is inhibited by emotional rejection. (Landis/Bennett/Bennett, 2004, p. 61)

InterCulture 2.0 – The world's first e-intercultural business game

We play the game at four different places of the world. Four teams with 3-4 members each are connected by internet and webcam in a virtual classroom. Each team represents an enterprise that is acting on the world-market for drinking bottles.

The market is highly competitive. Therefore, the teams have to co-operate, i.e. build up alliances or joint ventures. In this context it is necessary to negotiate across cultures and languages, to make decisions with partners from other parts of the world. The game consists of 6 business periods and will take seven weeks. Because of the differences between the time zones team will meet only for one virtual conference a week. The conference takes 3–4 hours and will be supervised by intercultural coaches. The supervising coaches of the four countries will evaluate these "live" sessions and are thus able to give support to their coaches.

During the week the coaches (team member) do their "normal" work. Via the e-platform, they have a lot of opportunities to communicate with each other (via mail, voip, forum, chat) or to learn more about the cultures of their partners of about intercultural competence.

Simulation games

Simulation games are experiential exercises, in which the trainees re-enact situations which illustrate the contrastive features of different culture groups. Values, social behaviour or forms of motivation of culture groups are possible issues dealt with in the simulation. (Götz/Bleher, 2000, p. 39)

One simulation game which has become very famous is called "BaFá BaFá" and was established by Robert Shirts. In this game, two completely different cultures are created. Members of the Alpha culture place a high value on relationships whereas the Beta culture is a rather materialistic trading culture. After the members have learned the rules of their culture, they are exchanged. Possible results like stereotyping and misunderstanding are discussed later in the debriefing phase. (Shirts, 1974, p. 23)

The game is mostly used for people who are going abroad for a longer period, and therefore need the knowledge about communication barriers, value differences, the reduction of prejudices and many more. It is a good opportunity to test and improve your own behaviour within your culture and in exchange with other cultures in a safe environment. Many simulation games take at least three hours, which might be a disadvantage, if the time frame of the whole training is strictly limited. (Landis/Bennett/Bennett, 2004, p. 63)

With the help of these experiential methods the trainees get the impression that cultural differences can influence relationships in a negative manner, which can also have an unfavourable impact on the way of living and working in the host country. On the other hand, trainees have to learn that there are not only disadvantages, but also many positive influences. One must neither suppress his own nor the foreign culture, but gain the positive from the differences. (Puck, 2006, p. 19)

Look-and-see-trip

It is advisable to arrange a short 5–7-day trip before the formal departure. Those short pre-expatriation visits of the expatriate and his or her partner is a possibility for the expatriate to meet the new colleagues and for the accompanying partner to look for accommodation and register the children in schools (Derbus, 1995a, p. 127). This short trip cannot prepare the expatriate for the habits of a culture, but it can shorten the preparation period and encourage the willingness for expatriation.

The study of Deloitte & Touche (2003) shows that the majority of 64 percent of the questioned companies in Spain paid for the look-and-see-trip for the expatriates and the accompanying partner to get familiar with the new destination. 18 percent only paid for the expatriate him-/herself and another 18 percent did not pay a look-and-see-trip at all.

9.4.4 Expatriate support

There are three categories of expatriates' support according to Schröder (1995, p.146): Professional support, administrative support, and psychological support. The professional support provides general information and gives the expatriate some specific information about the job, takes care of a contact person within the organization, or a cultural mediator and so on (ibid.). Administrative support involves all tasks necessary for the relocation, like remuneration calculation, transfer tasks like running errands and finding housing possibilities (ibid). Many companies engage a professional relocation service for that purpose. Normally, much of those tasks had to be fulfilled before the departure, but must be carried on afterwards as well (ibid.). Psychological support is confronted with the challenge of helping the expatriate and his/her family with the adjustment process and settling in, and preventing or alleviating stress situations that in the initial phase tend to be a factor (ibid.).

Black et al. (1991) argued that the degree of cross-cultural adjustment should be treated as a multidimensional concept, rather than a unitary phenomenon as was the dominating view previously. In their proposed model for international adjustment, Black et al. (1991) proposed two major components of the expatriate adjustment process. The first aspect, anticipatory adjustment, includes selection mechanisms and accurate expectations, which are based on training and previous international experience.

However, the proper level of anticipatory adjustment facilitates the second major component, the in-country adjustment. This component consists of four main factors: job (role clarity, discretion, conflict, and novelty), organizational (organizational culture novelty, social support, and logistical help), non-work (culture novelty and spouse adjustment), and individual (self-efficacy, relation skills, and perception skills) factors (Shaffer, Harrison, & Gilley, 1999). Thus, in-country adjustment influences three main dimensions of adjustment:

1. adjustment to work.
2. adjustment to interacting with host nationals.
3. adjustment to the general non-work environment.

This theoretical framework of international adjustment covers socio-cultural aspects of adjustment and it has been supported by a series of empirical studies of U.S. expatriates and their spouses (Selmer, n.d., p. 8).

Nevertheless, there are several deficits when looking at the MNCs performance of expatriation support. The three main shortcomings are the fade-out of family problems, the lack of further on-site training and preparation, and missing help for unpredictable difficulties (Schröder, 1995, p. 149).

It is important to consider that the expatriation support is a social resource, there are several sources (colleagues, mentor, family), but also different manners of social support (ibid., p. 156). Due to that, expatriation support must only be used in short term, but as a support system at all times during the international assignment (ibid.).

Adjustment to the general non-work environment

In order to adjust to the non-work environment, stress coping has to be considered, since it is proved that culture shock shows similar signs to stress.

Psychologists have proposed two approaches to cope with expatriate stress: Symptom-focused strategies and problem-focused strategies (Lazarus & Folkman, 1984). Symptom-focused strategies are used to diminish emotional distress by attending to behavior and expression, physiological disturbance and subjective distress. Problem-focused coping strategies are efforts to take constructive action to change the situation creating the stress and address the problem and minimize the anxiety and distress (Folkman et al., 1986). Expatriates who use the problem-focused coping strategy will be able to cope better with the stress than the symptom-focused coping strategy. Hence expatriates should be trained in using the constructive coping strategy (Koteswari/Bhattacharya, 2007).

Furthermore, practical training is aimed at helping the expatriate manager and family ease themselves into day-to-day life in the host country. The sooner the routine is established, the prospects are better that the expatriate and his/her family will adapt successfully. One critical need is a support network of friends for the expatriate (Vögel, 2006, p. 11). One of the main burdens of expatriates is the breaking up of social relationships (Fontaine, 1986). One solution is the expatriate community, which can be a useful source of support and information, and can be crucial for helping the families adapt to the foreign culture (Hill, 2003, p. 617). The integration into social networks can help to prevent psychological and physical health problems and family crises (Fanning, 1967, Loewenthal/Snedden, 1981).

Moreover, social contacts help with their experience in the foreign culture, for instance how to handle errands etc. They enable the expatriate to deal with the confusing impressions and negative feelings by just sympathetic listening and convey the feeling of appreciation, belonging, and trust (ibid.). Nowadays, the Internet is a potential social contact using expatriate websites like www.expatexchange.com. Social contacts are a cornerstone for the overall success. They enable the expatriate to integrate and handle the new cultural environment (Schröder, 1995, p.154).

Both culture novelty, which is the perceived distance between the host and home cultures, and spouse/family adjustment have been found to be significantly related to expatriate adjustment (Black/Gregersen, 1991). Lower levels of perceived discrepancy between host and home cultures (e.g. less cultural novelty) will facilitate expatriate interaction and general adjustment (Shaffer/Harrison/Gilley, 1999). Therefore, Sievers (1998, p. 9) makes suggestions on how MNCs can support the trailing spouse and families of expatriates while on an international assignment. MNCs should help the spouse to find employment, since the spouse needs the possibility of self-fulfillment (Debrus, 1995b, p. 166). Since, the non-work factors, culture novelty and spouse adjustment, are important direct effects of interaction and general adjustment, cross-cultural training for expatriates and their spouses, whose own adjustment will likely be affected by culture novelty, is vital for the success of international assignments.

To get familiar with the new environment is always a challenge, but insufficient language skills, loneliness, boredom and a sense of meaninglessness are much more challenging (Adler, 2002, p. 312). Expatriates' wifes or the non-working partners feel alone and sometimes misunderstood, which leads to demotivation and frustration. For that purpose, some internet addresses like www.expatwomen.com or www.femmexpat.com can be seen as an additional help. Certainly, this can also apply to husbands or male partners.

The Henkel corporation supports the spouse integration with systematic language courses, including them within pre-departure preparation, trying to find employment possibilities within the company, administrative support for work permits, and the help to find employment opportunities in other companies (Debrus, 1995b, p. 166), since higher levels of logistical support will facilitate expatriate interaction and general adjustment (Shaffer/Harrison/Gilley, 1999).

In the beginning of the assignment, the work load for the expatriate is very high because he or she has to get familiar with a lot of different tasks in a completely new environment. There is less time left to take care of the family and the kids, exactly at a time when the family needs attention and support. Therefore, Van Swol-Ulbrich suggests to invest as much time as possible for the family, when expatriates arrive in a country (2007). It is up to the company to understand these needs. The expatriates should get some additional time, especially at the beginning of his job, to take care of tasks directly or indirectly related to the family, like school transfer, Kindergarten, the distance to the next supermarket, the availability of the car and so on. Van Swol-Ulbrich states that the first three months are like the first 100 days in office of a new government. They are crucial but you can get away with a lot during this time, since the employer will understand that the expatriate might need to take off an afternoon or to come in a little later because of things that had to be done at home (ibid.). If the expatriate does not take advantage of this, the first 100 days will be quickly over and the employer will no longer be so supportive.

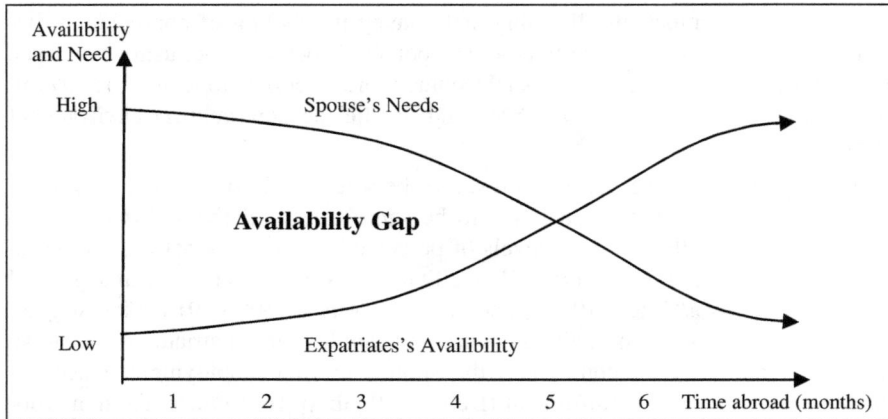

Fig. 9.7:   Need versus Availability Gap
Source: Adler, 2002, p. 316, as cited in Stahl, G.K.

One of the most challenging questions to be raised in this context is the future of the accompanying partner (Adler, 2002, p. 316). The spouses/partners often engage in cultural or charitable tasks, or leisure time activities, although that does not help their career development (ibid., p. 167). Additionally, the possibility to start another academic study is not promoted in many countries due to foreigner quota, or acceptance of foreign diploma (ibid.). At least there is now a chance within the European Union, since restrictions have disappeared. More frequently today the question focus on identifying ways for the spouse to continue a career while living abroad. One solution could be using the internet for dual career possibilities, for instance www.netexpat.com, www.overseasjobs.com, www.partnerjob.com, www.r-e-a.com, www.focus-info.org, www.outpostexpat.nl.

Why Worry?
(Unknown)

There are only two things to worry about;
Either you are well or you are sick.

If you are well, then there is nothing to worry about;
But if you are sick, there are two things to worry about:
Either you will get well, or you will die.

If you get well, there is nothing to worry about.
If you die, there are only two things to worry about;
Either you will go to Heaven or Hell.

If you go to Heaven, there is nothing to worry about;
But if you go to Hell, you'll be so damn busy shaking hands with friends,
You won't have time to worry.

Adjustment to work

According to Yavas and Bodur (1999) job/task characteristics and organizational variables are also believed to affect expatriate adjustment like role ambiguity or role clarity, role discretion (Black, 1988; 1990), role conflict and role novelty (Black, 1988) and organizational culture and size (McEvoy/Parker, 1995). Role clarity and role discretion will facilitate expatriate work adjustment, whereas role novelty and role conflict will inhibit expatriate work adjustment (Shaffer/Harrison/Gilley, 1999). The significance of three job-related factors (i,e., role clarity, role discretion, and role novelty) highlights the importance of job design to the success of international assignments. This suggests that multinational firms should place more emphasis on designing global positions that expatriates have more clearly defined jobs and greater decision-making authority (ibid.). Additionally, greater levels of pre-departure training may be necessary for expatriates expected to experience higher levels of role novelty (ibid.).

Moreover, the quality of work relationships is crucial for the success of any assignment. Relationships between superiors and subordinates who are from different cultures form the significant aspect of multi-national organization effectiveness (Ralston/Terpstra/Cunniff/ Gustafson 1995). Higher levels of social support from supervisors and coworkers will facilitate expatriate work adjustment (Shaffer/Harrison/Gilley, 1999). Companies which are successful in assimilating non-natives into their workforces provide training not only to the expatriates but also to their local supervisors (John/Roberts, 1996).

Beneficial for the challenges at work is the allocation of a tutor or mentor that helps to integrate the expatriate in the new working environment. This mentor is the contact person on-site and has a pate function. The help of a tutor encompasses: personal adviser, giving the expatriate a feeling of security, giving evaluations and feedbacks and be a source of formal and informal social contact, and prevents professional isolation (Debrus, 1995b, p.168; Koteswari & Bhattacharya, 2007). To fulfill the task of a mentor, there is a need for continuous dialogue which is based upon regular meetings and an open exchange of opinions (Schröder, 1995, p. 148, Koteswari/Bhattacharya, 2007).

Negotiating across Cultural Lines
(Claudio Guimaraes)

I was on a three-week trip to Germany from Brazil in order to buy special breeds of cattle from European farmers. One of the strangest things about the Germans was that they didn't give us any special treatment. In Brazil, if someone is seriously interested in buying our product, we give them preferential treatment in order to get the deal done. We spend time making sure they are comfortable and that their needs and wishes are met. The German farmers asked some polite questions aobut our home country, but they did not discuss prices or other business matters. At the end of the trip, they showed us the prices and bid and payment conditions. We made our bid and they said yes or no, but they did not chat about the offer.

In: Global Smarts, 2000, p. 212

Experience has shown that it can have a negative influence if the colleagues are country fellowmen that make the expatriate insecure with negative talking (ibid.). But helpful colleagues and supervisors are a social resource for the expatriate and can reduce stress and prevent stress reactions (Udris, 1982). It is even proven that social support of the spouse and family cannot substitute the social backing of fellow workers (Schröder, 1995, p. 154). This social support has the characteristics of informational support, looking at advices, hints, and information, and the appraisal support, giving the expatriate feedback about his/her behavior and work (Schröder, 1995, pp. 154–155).

Company picnic
(Terpstra/David)

The managers of one American firm retired to export the "company picnic" idea into their Spanish subsidiary. On the day of the picnic, the U.S. executives turned up dressed as cooks and proceeded to serve the food to their Spanish employees. Far from creating a relaxed atmosphere, this merely embarrassed the Spanish workers. Instead of socializing with their superiors, the employees clung together uneasily and whenever an executive approached their table, everyone stood up.

In: The Cultural Environment of International Business, 1991, p. 175

Within the professional area, it is often up to the expatriate if he/ she is accepted by his/her colleagues. Efforts to learn the host language are positively evaluated. Another strong advice is that expatriate among one another should not speak in their home country language, because they separate themselves from the others and create an atmosphere of mistrust (Debrus, 1995b, p. 174).

Adjustment to interacting with host nationals

Previous international experience and fluency in the host-country language have significant, direct effects on expatriate interaction adjustment.

The social integration of the expatriate and his/her family depends a lot on their ability to speak the host country's language, since it is a powerful mean to communicate and interact. Language skills help to adapt to the new environment and to understand the new culture (Debrus, 1995b, p. 175). Despite the prevalence of English, an exclusive reliance on the same diminishes an expatriate manager's ability to interact with host country nationals. Knowledge and fluency in local language enable expatriate to understand and communicate effectively. Expatriate should be definitely trained in the foreign languages in view of the future need (Koteswari/Bhattacharya, 2007).

Moreover, the number, variety and intensity of social contacts that are established during the expatriation with fellow countrymen and members of the host country, are determinants for a successful adaption to the foreign culture (Kühlmann, 1995, p. 20). Those contact persons can support the interpretation of the initially strange experiences in the host country and can serve as a role model for adequate behavior (ibid., p. 21). Thus, when the expatriate is sent on the assignment to the host country, he or she will get better adjusted and will be less frustrated by cultural differences than expatriates who are isolated and have less communication with the host country nationals (Hanvey, 1979; Selmer, 1999).

SIETAR

The Society for Intercultural Education, Training and Research (SIETAR) was established in 1974 in the United States, by a couple of professionals with a specific focus on all kinds of intercultural learning. Originally it was called SITAR, but it became SIETAR to involve the aspect of education. The goal of the organization was to provide a platform where new ideas about intercultural theory and training could be exchanged. The members of SIETAR are professionals from a variety of academic and practical disciplines who share a common concern for intercultural understanding. Their objective is to encourage the development and application of knowledge, values and skills which enable effective intercultural and interethnic actions at the individual, group, organization, and community and national levels.

In: http://sietar.org/about.htm

9.4.5   Training methods and their application in the training practice

In the framework of university projects and assignments, we regularly try to get in contact with companies in order to find out to what extent intercultural training programs are asked for and which methods are applied in the training practice among others.

In a project study conducted in 2008, training institutes were e.g. asked which methods they used and how high those were in demand. Sixteen institutes kindly filled in the questionnaire. In the following, selected results and a consequent analysis can be found.

Tab. 9.1:   Frequency of intercultural training methods used (0 = not offered, 5 = very often)
Source: Warnke/Hanisch, 2008, S. 43

	Mean	Mode	Median
Lectures	3.23	4	3
Written materials	3.36	5	3.5
Films	2.31	3	3
Self-assessment	2.79	3	3
Discussions	4.07	4	4
Case studies	3.86	4	4
Critical incidents	3.93	5	4
Role plays	3.79	4	4
Language training	1.58	0	1
Immersion	0.82	1	1

"The frequency was measured on a scale from zero to five, at which zero means that the method is not offered, and five implies that the method is used very often. The table shows the results of the 16 respondents out of 35 training institutes. For a complex and proper analysis of the data, not only mean, but also mode and median were calculated.

The survey showed that discussions, case studies, critical incidents and role plays are the most frequently used methods. Case studies, critical incidents and role plays are methods which were especially developed and adapted for intercultural training; therefore it seems reasonable that these methods are applied quite often. It might seem astonishing that discussions are as frequent as these intercultural methods. But a discussion is a method which is suitable for combining all other methods, so it is mostly part of intercultural trainings. The same reason applies to written materials. Although they are used less on average, the mode shows that most of the institutions which answered the question indicate text materials as frequently provided.

Lectures and films are considered as moderately used. Reasons for this might be that participants are only observers and do not participate actively which can reduce the learning effect. Surprisingly, films are not provided that often as lectures, although they are said to be more lively and motivating than lectures. An explanation which was given by one training institute is that films are often too time consuming and therefore offered rather seldom. Furthermore, the contents of lectures are more adaptable than those of films. Self-assessment is a method which is approximately used as often as films. One reason for this is the limited time frame, too, which makes it almost impossible for the trainer to evaluate the results in a proper way by getting all group members involved.

Language trainings do not play an important role, indicated by all three statistical measures. The mode even points out that most of the training institutes do not offer language courses at all. However, three of the institutes declared language courses as one of the most important methods. This difference is not difficult to explain: some of the institutes have specialised on language trainings whereas others do rather concentrate on intercultural competence apart from language skills.

Comparing the arithmetic means, it appears that immersion, also called look-and-see-trip, is the least frequently used method in intercultural training. Though the mode states that immersion is more likely to be used than language trainings, it achieved one of the worst results by far. Only one institution acknowledged that immersion is one of the most frequently used methods. Immersion is the most intensive form of experiential learning in terms of intercultural training. But considering the high costs of a trip to the host country, many institutes do not offer the method which at the end has to be decided and paid by the companies."

9.5   Intercultural training institutions – A selection

Working, meeting, dealing, entertaining, negotiating and corresponding with colleagues or clients from different cultures can become a minefield without the support of interculturally trained and experienced experts. Understanding and appreciating intercultural differences will ultimately promote clearer communications, break down barriers, build trust, strengthen relationships, open horizons and yield tangible results in terms of business success. Acknowledging and understanding the intercultural environment is vital in order to be a successful leader in a globalized world. A wide range of institutes provide intercultural training courses on different levels. Only to name a few is hard, because there are so many excellent providers not only in Germany, but all around the world. The choice I have made is based upon experiences and international reputation

9.5.1   Kwintessential

Kwintessential was conceptualised in 2003 by three partners keen to support businesses through the challenges of globalization and internationalization. They foresaw the future demand for language service and solutions as well as culturally and globally savvy insight into business functions. The company started offering language lessons, cultural awareness training, translation and interpreting services. It expanded to encompass further key products such as website design, desktop publishing, conference interpreting and transcription. They started their business in Hounslow before moving to Croydon. From there the business has grown and now operates within the UK from offices in Somerset (HQ), Croydon and Central London. Abroad, the clients are served by local offices in America, South Africa, Switzerland, the UAE and Argentina. They do offer two main areas:

1.   Localisation, Translation and Language
2.   Training and Consultancy

9.5.2   CDC – Carl Duisberg Centren

This institution was first founded under the name "Carl Duisberg Gesellschaft" in 1962 as a non-profit organisation offering accommodations for foreign scholarship receivers. It changed its name into "Carl Duisberg Centren" in 1965. Apart from initiating language programmes in the 1960s and 1970s the CDC began to provide their first training programmes for businessrepresentatives in 1976. Since then they have become an internationally operating training institution with branches from Russia, China and Malaysia to Cameroon and several positions in Germany. The headquarters are located in Cologne.

This organisation defines itself as a non-profit service provider in the education and qualification sector. It focuses not only on foreign language programmes for students but also intercultural competence training with private and business customers as well as public sector clients and international institutions. In order to act under the name of a non-profit organisation it targets projects that contribute to society. Limiting communication problems and encouraging people to gain an understanding of cultural diversity has been its intention for years.

To meet own quality standards the CDC collaborate with business experts who bring invaluable practical experience with them. This practice-orientation has always been a major criterion for their performance. Apart from cultural awareness and culture-specific training a coaching service for managers and an assessment tool of the intercultural competence for personnel is also offered. (CDC Website)

9.5.3   IFIM – Institute for Intercultural Management

Founded in 1990, the "Institute for Intercultural Management" in Königswinter, Germany, rapidly assumed its position as a leading provider of cross-cultural training services. It has further gained reputation for scientific research in the field of practice-orientation through its numerous publications. The long-term research about culture-related society differences in business interactions allows a profound and substantiated training service.

A special emphasis lies on meeting the needs of its customers. Their tasks range from a foreign assignment in leading positions, negotiating across national borders or managing multi-national teams and helping to assume leading roles in joint ventures and product launches which are covered additionally by its experts. Further, IFIM supports projects for companies that plan to go international from the beginning to the final implementation. In order to improve the quality of all offered seminars, the participants are asked to evaluate the benefit of the training even twelve months after leaving the country. Until 2008, the IFIM has covered a wide range of different countries from all over the world.

However, not just training seminars for Germans are offered, but also American and French people can get an insight into the business practices and cultural particularities. Moreover, the institute provides a detailed preparation service homepage filled with recommendations for current and future expatriates. (IFIM Website)

9.5.4   IKUD – Institute for Intercultural Didactics

The registered association "Institute of Intercultural Didactics" was founded in the year 2000. It is the successor of the same-called institution of the German "Georg-August University" of Göttingen. IKUD gained its expertise through long-term research and is experienced in teaching for more than 30 years now.

Developing and implementing new training approaches for culture-specific seminars lies in the focus of its members. They further publish articles in the field of intercultural didactics. Workshops and lectures to provide a comprised way to convey knowledge are part of their work. Usually, their customers come from companies as well as from organisations which IKUD consults on teaching and training methods. Among their activities is also the development and testing of building block systems that help to improve target group specific trainings. These building blocks are for instance culture-contrast experiences or aim at recognizing own cultural patterns. IKUD is also a partner of municipal projects encouraging intercultural awareness and promoting the integration of migrants. (IKUD-Website)

9.5.5   Further training institutes

- Asien-Pazifik Institut für Management in Hamburg
- Gesellschaft für interkulturelle Kommunikation und Auslandsvorbereitung in Hildesheim
- Institut für Auslandsbeziehungen in Stuttgart
- Institut für interkulturelle Kommunikation in Aachen
- ICUnet.AG in various German cities, Vienna and Shanghai

9.6 Intercultural training at Robert Bosch India Limited

The following program descriptions of Robert Bosch India Limited show some of the elements which can be involved in the company's intercultural training programs.

9.6.1 Global Corporate Etiquette

Target group: project managers/project leaders   *Duration:* 1 day

Focus:

Global Etiquette today goes a long way in determining one's acceptance in business interactions. As they say, we don't get a second chance to make a first impression. By ironing out deviations from expected international norms of behavior, we improve our chances of operating successfully in a multinational business environment.

Objectives:

- Understanding the importance of good mannerisms and their importance in the Global Business environment
- Developing professional work habits and corporate pride through appropriate office conduct and discipline
- Developing an understanding of image in business and use of appropriate etiquette for business communication
- Learning the art of conversation, correct dining etiquette and the importance of interacting in a relaxed and confident style

Contents:

- Importance of etiquette excellence
- Professional presence in business meetings and maintaining the office decorum
- Successful encounters in the profession
- Diplomacy and its 3-dimensions
- Specific mannerisms such as exchanging business cards and dining habits in business gatherings

Methodology

- Video presentations/clips
- Simulation
- Games and Group Discussions

In: Robert Bosch India Limited: Enhancing Competencies – Behavioral, Intercultural, CIP and Leadership Programs & Offerings, 2006, p. 18

9.6.2   Intercultural Training: Country-specific

Target group: All for country Training Germany [Essential],
                  others according to customer/business needs4

Duration: 1 day

Focus:
[…] In an increasingly globalized world, it is vital to become more aware of one's own culture and to have a better understanding of other cultural environments. The aim of this program is to increase understanding, tolerance, respect for a specific country and the concerning culture. It enables to communicate appropriately to the specific intercultural situation and to grab business opportunities. Currently we are offering Country specific training for Germany, India, Japan, China, Austria, USA, Switzerland, Korea, Brazil, France, Italy, UK and Netherlands.

Objectives
- Understanding the purpose of intercultural sensitivity
- Reflecting on one's own attitudes, behaviors and cultural patterns
- Training to change perspectives by using different "cultural glasses"
- Gaining data competence on country specific issues
- Developing social and self-competence

Contents
- Cognitive Approach: information on political, historical, economical issues
- Communicative Approach: information on everyday life, forms of communication, ways of working and living
- Intercultural Approach: sensitization for other cultures and understanding of cultural differences
- Empathy and Social Competence

Methodology
- Case Studies/Critical incidents
- Culture-Assimilator-Method
- Role-plays
- Group-Activity/Discussion

In: Robert Bosch India Limited: Enhancing Competencies – Behavioral, Intercultural, CIP and Leadership Programs & Offerings, 2006, p. 16

9.7 Surveys on intercultural preparation

In order to get some relevant information about the importance of an Intercultural training and its handling in companies a lot of studies have been carried out by my students in Stralsund/Germany or in Mulhouse/France during the last decade. Regardless if the focus was on global players or on small and medium seized companies, the following results have been found out:

- a tremendous lack as far as the involvement of families is concerned
- the negligence of a look and see trip
- unused experiences of those who have just returned from an international assignment.

On the one hand, the overwhelming majorities of the companies in Germany or in France underline the importance of being interculturally prepared before the employees are sent abroad and most of the enterprises offer a certain kind of intercultural training. On the other hand the real picture is quite different and questions, for example like the length of such a preparation, the money that is spent for this purpose, the contents of a comprehensive intercultural training are not fully addressed. The following studies try to give an overview about the strength and weaknesses in this context. With this in mind, companies and institutions have now the opportunity to draw the right conclusions out of this scenario.

9.7.1 Intercultural preparation in big companies

In June 2009 Susanne Kluth, Jonas Linke and Hendrik Walter, students of "Baltic Management Studies" in Stralsund, conducted a survey among 21 big international companies, including Aida-Seetours, BBC World Service, BMW, Brose, Daimler, Deere, Deutsche Bank, Hannover Rückversicherung, Hitachi, PricewaterhouseCoopers, Schott, Sear, Shell, Villeroy & Boch.

1. **How would you rate the importance of intercultural preparation?**

Number of answers: 21
From 1 (unimportant) to 6 (very important)

Value matrix	1	2	3	4	5	6	no answer	Ø	1	2	3	4	5	6
importance	-	-	1x	2x	8x	10x	-	5.29						

2. **How many employees do you send abroad each year?**

Number of answers: 20
0–5: 2 (10.00 %)
5–20: 9 (45.00 %)
20–100: 4 (20.00 %)
>100: 5 (25.00 %)

3. **Do your expatriates receive intercultural preparation?**

Number of answers: 21
Yes: 18 (85.7 %)
No: 3 (14.3 %)

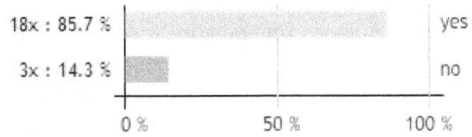

18x : 85.7 %   yes
3x : 14.3 %   no

0 %   50 %   100 %

4. **Is intercultural training offered to their families?**

Number of answers: 21
Yes: 11 (52.4 %)
No: 10 (47.6 %)

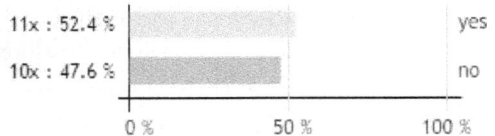

11x : 52.4 %   yes
10x : 47.6 %   no

0 %   50 %   100 %

5. **Do you train your future expatriates in your company or do you hire a special training institute?**

Number of answers: 20
In-company training: 6 (30.00 %)
Training institute: 5 (25.00 %)
Both: 9 (45.00 %)

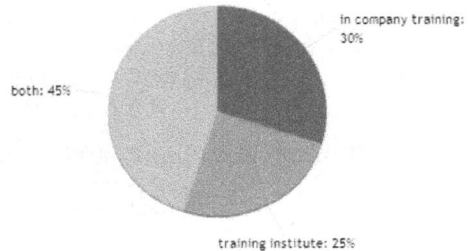

in company training: 30%
both: 45%
training institute: 25%

6. **How long does the training last?**

Number of answers: 19
1 day: 4 (21.05 %)
3 days: 4 (21.05 %)
1 week: 1 (5.26 %)
Weekly seminars: 1 (5.26 %)
Others: 9 (47.37 %)
e.g.:
- sometimes 1 day, but sometimes several months
- depends on the location
- various offerings
- 1 day intercultural, language training is offered permanent (weeks, months...)
- 12 weeks
- varies depending on circumstances
- 2 days to 4 weeks (included in other trainings)

7. **When does the training phase start?**

Number of answers: 19
1 year before: – (0.00 %)
6 months before: 2 (10.53 %)
3 months before: 7 (36.84 %)
< 3 months before: 10 (52.63 %)

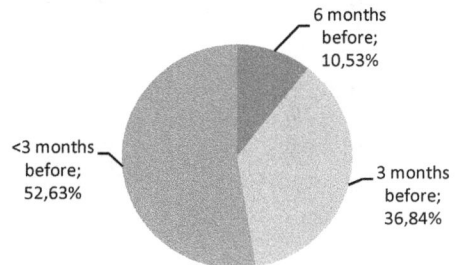

6 months before; 10,53%
3 months before; 36,84%
<3 months before; 52,63%

8. Of which components does the training consist?

Number of answers (several answers possible): 20
Linguistic Preparation: 12 (21.43%)
Intercultural training seminars: 12 (21.43%)
Country information and briefing the culture of the host country: 16 (28.57%)
Expatriate colleagues' information: 8 (14.29%)
Look-and-see-trip: 8 (14.29%)
Others: – (0.00%)

9. Are former expatriates a part of the intercultural training?

Number of answers: 19
Yes: 7 (36.8 %)
No: 12 (63.2 %)

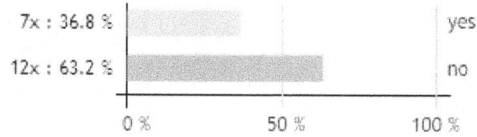

10. Do you think the preparation is sufficient?

Number of answers: 19
Yes: 17 (89.5 %)
No: 2 (10.5 %)

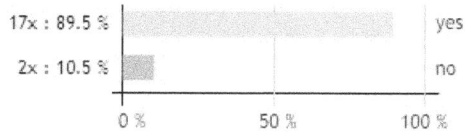

11. How much money do you spend on intercultural preparation per year?

Number of answers: 17
< 500€: 1 (5.88%)
500€–2000€: 2 (11.76 %)
2000€–5000€: 1 (5.88 %)
5000€–10,000€: 4 (23.53 %)
10,000€–50,000€: 4 (23.53 %)
Others: 5 (29.41 %)
e.g.:

– more than 50.000€
– don't know

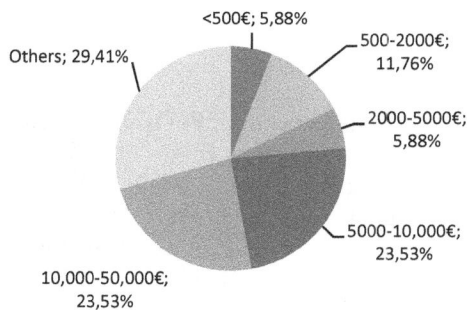

Source: Kluth/Linke/Walter, 2009, p. 45

9.7.2   Intercultural preparation in SME

Four years later, the same questionnaire was sent to 100 small and medium seized companies by the students Hannes Borgwardt, Lasse Frank and Christopher Stubenrauch. The following results (extract) show that the majority of participating SME does not offer intercultural training for their expatriates and if training is offered, it starts rather late in the preparation process and usually is fairly short. Still, the absolute majority of companies considers the preparation of their employees as sufficient. We can conclude that many internationally active SME need to pay more attention to the topic of intercultural preparation.

1. **Do your expatriates receive intercultural preparation?**
Number of answers: 23

Yes: 9 (39.1 %)
No: 14 (60.9 %)

2. **How long does the training last?**
Number of answers: 19

1 day:	5
3 days:	7
1 week:	3
Weekly seminars:	2
Other:	2

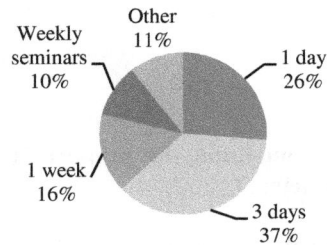

3. **When does the training phase start?**
Number of answers: 18

1 year before	0
6 months before	2
3 months before	5
<3 months before	11

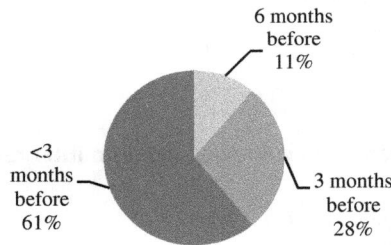

4. **Of which components does the training consist?**
Number of answers: 21 (several answers possible)

Linguistic preparation:	14 (21.9 %)
Intercultural training seminars:	16 (25 %)
Country information and briefing the culture of the host country:	21 (32.8 %)
Expatriate colleagues' information:	10 (15.6 %)
Look-and-see-trip:	3 (4.7 %)
Other:	0 (0 %)

5. **Do you think the preparation is sufficient?**
Number of answers: 23

Yes: 3 (13 %)
No: 20 (87 %)

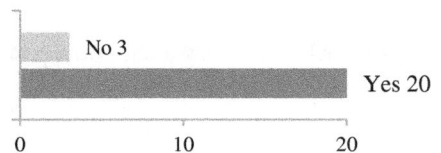

Source: Borgwardt, H./Frank, L./Stubenrauch, C., 2014, pp. 64ff

Living in Germany – Do's and Don'ts
(ohne Verfasser)

As in all countries, also in Germany there are certain norms of behaviour and politeness which you should observe if you do not want to put your foot in it.

Greeting People
People usually greet each other without shaking hands saying "Hallo", "Grüß Dich" or "Servus" (in Bavaria) and leave saying "Tschüß", "Bis bald" (see you soon) etc.

To shake hands or not to shake hands? That is the question
The rule of thumb is: Do not shake hands with fellow students or in public offices. If you attend an interview or go to a professor's office hour, always shake hands. Just wait until the senior person (i.e. the professor or prospective boss) offers you his/her hand to shake.

"Sie" (formal) or "Du" (informal)?
Adults generally address each other in the formal "Sie"-form and with "Herr" or "Frau" plus surname and possibly even a title: "Guten Tag, Frau Dr. Meier". Colleagues often still use the formal "Sie", even after working together for years. Younger people, until roughly the age of 30, address themselves with "Du" in public, even though they do not know each other.

Formal and Informal Address
Germans only abandon their formal attitude and use the informal Du-form with their friends, and even this is only possible after it has been formally offered. However, students usually use the Du-form all the time amongst themselves, so when you address a fellow-student feel free to say Du.

Titles
Titles are very important in Germany. If someone has a doctorate it is usual to address them as Herr Doktor Meier or Frau Doktor Müller. Professors are usually addressed as Professor plus surname. There are doctors and professors who prefer their titles not to be used; they will soon let you know if this is the case.

Punctuality
It cannot be denied that Germans place a lot of emphasis on punctuality. If you have an appointment with your professor there is one thing you should certainly not do – keep him or her waiting! However, amongst students punctuality is taken less seriously. Nevertheless, individual affections towards punctuality have to be considered.

In: www.daad.de

9.8   Reintegration

While the focus is often put on improving the preparation phase, the reintegration phase seems to be still neglected. Literature research points out several problems that appear in the professional, private and sociocultural environment when expatriates return to their home country (DGFP e.V., 2012, p. 123; Weber et al. 2001, pp. 137f). They often do not feel supported and the reintegration process within the company turns out to be difficult. This phase is often accompanied by a second culture shock (Rothlauf 2012, pp. 363ff). Implementing individual and purposeful reintegration support would help the employee to settle more easily. Coping strategies can be learned as well in order to avoid helplessness in the unfamiliar situation in the home country. How those strategies can look like will be further explained later in this chapter. Furthermore, the employee can take advantage of the return situation to broaden his or her own competence spectrum through learning how to integrate foreign cultural elements into the own culture system. This also facilitates the reintegration process in the familiar culture that became unaccustomed to the repatriate during the stay abroad (Götz, 2010, pp. 95f). The point in time when repatriation is addressed varies significantly as the 2012 Survey Report found out:

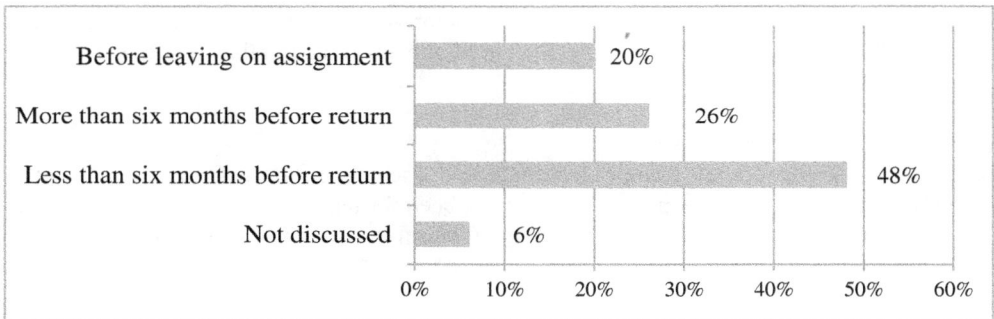

Fig. 9.8   When repatriation is addressed
Source: Own illustration based on Brookfield Global Relocation Services, 2012, p. 61

Almost half of the companies address the repatriation process less than six months before the return. Twenty percent of the responding companies discuss the topic even prior to the expatriates' departure. Only 6 % of them do not offer their employees such meetings. The report also revealed that no more than 16 % of the companies link their repatriation policy to career management and retention. This gives some indication that many companies have not yet seen the benefits from a well-structured reintegration programme.

9.8.1   Definitions

To explain the difficulties upon the return of an employee, several terms are used: re-entry, reintegration or repatriation. All three of them define the process when an employee, who has been abroad for some years, returns to the parent company. (Kühlmann/Stahl 1995, p. 178).

A well organised repatriation is an important key factor in the process of an international assignment (Weber et al. 2001, p. 196). This becomes clear by looking at the various aims of a stay abroad in the eyes of the company. Those can be summarised as follows: 1) The employee goes abroad in terms of a management or control function, e.g. knowledge should be transferred or new technologies and product lines have to be implemented. 2) Another main focus of an international assignment is the personal development of the employee. Benefits from the international experience, the development of intercultural competences and the personal progress in management skills as a leader are important factors in the personal advancement. 3) Finally, companies are sending their employees abroad in order to broaden their international network and to further develop the organisation with the help of the returning employee's knowledge (Klemm/Popp, 2006, p. 191; Mesmer-Magnus/Viswesvaran, 2008, p. 184; Weber et al., 2001, p. 196).

Expatriates have gained experiences which are often very useful to identify measures of improvement in the parent company. This aspect points out how important it is for the company to invest in the successful reintegration of their employees, in order to retain them in the company and to profit from their qualifications in various meanings in the long run. Nevertheless, the practice looks slightly different: The average attrition rate for international assignments was 12 % (BGRS, 2012, p. 24). Among the international assignees who left the company, 24 % left within one year of repatriation (ibid.). Another survey conducted by Deloitte & Touche (2008, pp. 23f) states that 25% of the companies leave their repatriates alone in this last phase of the process. However, initiatives to develop a reintegration programme will lead to improved results. With 30 %, repatriation belongs to the top five priorities in managing mobility that companies want to focus on in the next year (Rodin, 2012).

9.8.2   The repatriation process

The reintegration of the expatriate is the last step of the four-part international assignment process:

Fig. 9.9:   International assignment process
Source: Own illustration

> *"The problems in going over, I expected; the real problems – the ones I didn't expect – were all in coming back"* (Labovitz 1977, pp. 34f).

This statement was made by an executive who returned from his international assignment. A survey conducted by Deloitte & Touche (2008, pp. 23f), who interviewed 200 globally active companies in Germany, points out that only 7 % offer repatriation trainings and 5 % provide a post-processing training after the return to the home country. The extent of scientific literature also leaves to be desired (Kühlmann/Stahl, 1995, p. 177).

The general preception is quite obvious that those who are coming home do not face any substantial difficulties. But the companies do not realize that the once familiar environment has become alien due to a long absence and changes, so the employee often has a feeling of being thrown back (Klemm/Popp, 2006, pp. 201f). A second culture shock is experienced during the settling in period (Rothlauf, 2012, p. 365). The sociocultural problems are thereby seen as most critical (Ladwig/Loose, 1998, pp. 59ff). This has the following background: Firstly, the employee has gained new insights through the contact with a foreign culture. Other ways of life have been recognised and might have led to a conscious or unconscious adaption and a change of the own behaviour. Secondly, the experiences made abroad have changed the perception of the home country. Circumstances in both countries are compared, for example the higher flexibility in the host country on the one hand and the structure at home, which is perceived as complicated and tight, on the other hand (Hirsch, 2003, pp. 418f). This raises the question for the employee, whether to adjust to the situation at home or to decide for another international assignment. Those aspects point out how extensive the return phase is, which situations the repatriate has to deal with and how important it becomes for the company to support this reintegration process. Neglecting the concerns of the employee and leaving him or her alone has far-reaching consequences for the company (Hirsch, 2003, p. 427; Horsch, 1995, pp. 104f).

9.8.3   Major difficulties for employees

To reintegrate the employee in the parent company's structure in terms of offering an appropriate position might cause difficulties for the company as well for the employee. The expectations of the employee to move on with his career, getting promoted to a new more challenging job than the previous one, can cause some problems.

Reintegration problems from the viewpoint of the company
(Dülfer/Joestingmeier)

The difficulties associated with reintegration might prompt certain measures:
- Should it seem improbable that a sensible integration will occur the company will attempt to send the delegate on a subsequent foreign assignment, even if this appears problematic from the specific task assignment. This is only postponing the point at which the problems will inevitably occur.
- For the same reason the foreign assignment can be extended in the host country.
- Another option is working for an important project.
- Top management in the corporate headquarters is often forced to create a pseudo-position in the corporate headquarters in order to accommodate the returning delegate in an appropriate fashion for the interim.
- As a last resort top management in the corporate headquarters might consider dismissing the delegate from the company with a commensurate indemnity package as the only solution to the roblem at hand.

In: International Management in Diverse Cultural Areas, 2011, p. 542–543

Work-related problems

The reasons why employees are highly motivated to go abroad for a couple of years – especially for younger employees – are manigfold. Whereas the younger generation is trying to get in touch which a completely new environment, the older employees rather focus on further job experiences and to escape from everyday-work in the home country (Blom/Meier, 2004, pp. 163f). However, the personal career development remains as one of the main motives for both. During their assignment, they have often had more responsibility than in their job at home and have worked in smaller dimensions. The employee has learned to work in a rather complex environment. Especially the personal and managerial competences were hereby strongly developed (Berthier/Roger, 2013, pp. 158–163). After returning to the home country, the employee wants to apply those experiences.

In addition to his or her expectations, the returning employee might have to deal with the following changes and challenges:

- Technological developments could have the effect that the employee's professional knowledge is outdated.
- Changes in formal and informal operations and information channels of the organisation might lead to adjustment problems – especially if the expatriate and the parent company have had only little contact. The result is a feeling of isolation and the host country becomes an exile.
- A poor repatriation policy leads to dissatisfied repatriates and might result in a high attrition rate. This is especially the case if the employees know that other companies would invest more in their competences.
- "Out of sight, out of mind" syndrome: Companies might forget about their expatriates and their return, so that nothing or only little has been planned for their arrival. This leads to a high degree of frustration of the repatriate (Weber et al., 2001, p. 137f).

Job position
First of all, the employee has to deal with a salary decrease after the return, as the additional allowances are omitted and also with a loss of status (Emrich, 2011, pp. 189f). The position in the host country often offers employees a better social standing, especially if it is the work of a branch manager (Dülfer/Jöstingmeier, 2008, p. 544). If this is the case, the employee holds a social position that can be compared to the one of a member of the diplomatic service. If the subsidiary is even located in the capital of the country, the expatriate might be invited to important national events etc. that are organised by the home country's embassy. There, he or she could get in contact with ministers, high officials and influential representatives of companies in the host country. A discontinuation of those privileges can cause dissatisfaction for the employee. There is no participation in public life anymore, especially on a national level. The social contacts are firstly confined to colleagues, acquaintances or neighbours. Life seems rather provincial (ibid.).

Another major factor is the undervaluation of the international experiences by companies (ibid.). Some employees experience a career setback, as the new job does not offer the opportunity to apply the gained knowledge or the position does not match their expectations. Temporary project work is also a solution offered if there is no vacancy (Hirsch, 2003, p. 418; Kühlmann, 2004, p. 26). According to Mesmer-Magnus and Viswesvaran (2008, pp. 195f), half of the employees feel that the re-entry position is less satisfying than the position they held abroad. They are not pleased with the career planned by the HRM. Also Stahl et al. (2009, p. 91) point out that "although top managers often claim that global mobility and international experience are highly valued assets and a prerequisite for promotion into senior management, the career implications for employees returning from an international assignment are often disappointing." Consequently, they leave the company and look for a position that corresponds to their expectations, as they know that their international experience is a competitive advantage on the job market (Berthier/Roger, 2013, pp. 163f; Hirsch, 2003, p. 418). Nevertheless, many companies try to find an appropriate job that fits to the qualifications of the repatriate (Dülfer/Jöstingmeier, 2008, pp. 543f) Entitlements are in most cases implemented in the company's repatriation policy.

Overall, it is an uncertain situation causing stress for the repatriate. The dissatisfaction of the employees even increases if they realise that former colleagues have got several promotions in the meantime (ibid., p. 546). They get the impression that the international assignment has a negative impact on their own career and that it does not bring the promised effect in the parent company.

Knowledge transfer

Further problems concern the company's disinterest in the employee's acquired knowledge and experiences (Schipper, 2007, p. 111). This seems surprising, as a transfer of knowledge offers the opportunity to create a global mindset within the company. Especially nowadays, this has a significant importance, since the economy becomes increasingly global (Kühlmann/Stahl, 1995, p. 189). The company can benefit, for example, from the repatriate's openness to foreign working methods and lifestyles or the independence in thinking and acting (ibid.) Knowledge transfer also helps future expatriates in their preparation. It is also an advantage for colleagues going abroad to get some useful information about some peculiarities of the host country (Berthier/Roger, 2013, p. 152). Nonetheless, repatriates, who would like to share and apply their skills, often encounter resistance from their surroundings (Kühlmann/Stahl 1995, p. 189).

Hirsch (2003) critically remarks that negative perceptions by colleagues often concern the country in which the assignee stayed. Some of them also have the attitude that repatriates have enjoyed a well-paid holiday overseas and are now learning how to work in Germany again (ibid., p. 422). It is difficult for them to understand how the repatriate has changed and what he or she is talking about. The colleagues cannot find access to the ideas of the repatriate, as they cannot identify themselves with the situations abroad (ibid.). They have got the idea that the returning employee is the one who has to adapt to the circumstances that dominate the home country and not the other way round. Resistance and a lack of understanding by colleagues are therefore the main problems that the employee is confronted with and which cause the feeling of high pressure for the employee itself (Hirsch, 2003, p. 422; Klemm/Popp, 2006, pp. 201f). The chance to benefit from the ideas of the repatriate is not yet seen by most of the companies.

Considering the advantages of collecting the repatriates' knowledge and the insufficient use of this possibility in companies nowadays, Adler (1981, p. 355) points out that it is clearly recognisable that this process has to be reconsidered by the companies' management: "One may wonder whether "effectiveness" means simply fitting back in the home organisation or contributing maximally towards the goals of the organisation and using the skills acquired abroad" (ibid.).

9.8.4   Personal and intercultural problems

Another field where the employee and the accompanying family might have to face challenges is the personal and social area back in their home country. The feeling that can dominate the situation at home is that of a stranger, even if the environment and the culture is
familiar. Repatriates describe this situation as "life in the middle" or a "not yet, not anymore"
feeling (Hirsch, 2003, p. 417f). This re-socialisation process takes time, depending on the
person itself, the overall reintegration situation and the support from others, especially the
company, family and friends (Kühlmann/Stahl, 1995, p. 179).

As mentioned before, two of the main changes are the new financial situation and the lower
social standing in the home country (Schipper, 2007, p. 111; Weber et al. 2001, p. 138).
Those two aspects influence the private environment of the expatriate and the family as well.

In addition, the social environment might have changed as well. The society can be different
due to certain events or technical innovations (Emrich, 2011, p. 189f). Furthermore, the relationship to family, friends and acquaintances can be less intense or even difficult if there has
been only little contact during the time abroad (Schipper, 2007, p. 111). Moreover, it might
be hard to to renew the old contacts as the own personality has changed and therefore the
expatriate and the family now have other attitudes not matching the ones from their former
social network anymore (ibid.). They have experienced challenging and different situations
abroad and have developed a broader intercultural understanding. This results for example in
another way of life which others might not necessarily understand, as they might hold little
interest interested in hearing about it (Weber et al., 2001, p. 138). As a consequence, life back
home

If children have stayed abroad, an adequate school has to be found that supports them in the
transitional phase and which fits to their education level in order to avoid problems
(Kühlmann, 2004, p. 29). This requires a lot of additional work because the old school may
not be the best choice anymore and if the new job is offered in another city, completely new
challenges are waiting for the kids to be solved.

The transition from the foreign culture to the familiar culture does not always happen
smoothly for everyone. The once familiar culture might have become alien due to a long
absence. This effect is even stronger if no home trips were made during the time abroad
(Klemm/Popp, 2006, p. 205). The acculturation phase often includes a second culture shock
(Mesmer-Magnus/Viswesvaran, 2008, pp. 195ff). A reflection of the intercultural experiences
in living and working abroad is also an integral part of this process (Menis, 2009, p. 82).

9.8.5   Phases of reintegration

Coming home from an international assignment causes a lot of problems because the expectations of the employee and his family are not always in line with the real situation he or she
is confronted with. As further pointed out in the study by Stroh et al. (2000, pp. 684ff), it
therefore plays a significant role to what extent the employee's expectations are met, exceed-
ed or whether they remain unfulfilled after the return, as the commitment to the company
depends significantly on this situation (ibid., p. 685). This includes, which feelings and expectations the individual might have, which will be explained with the help of three models.

Reverse culture shock

The reverse culture shock is a pervasive occurrence that repatriates experience in their home country. It was the American anthropologist Oberg who found out that longer stays abroad lead to a mental and physical strain caused by a new work and living environment (Emrich, 2011, p. 88). He defines the culture shock in general as being

> *"precipitated by the anxiety that results from losing all your familiar signs and symbols of social intercourse. These signs or cues include the thousands and one ways in which we orient ourselves to the situation of daily life: [...] how to give orders to servants, how to make purchases [...]. Now these cues, which may be words, gestures, facial expressions, customs, or norms, are acquired by all of us in the course of growing up and are as much a part of our culture as the language we speak or the beliefs we accept. All of us depend for our peace of mind and efficiency on hundreds of these cues, most of which we do not carry on the level of conscious awareness"* (Oberg, 1960, p. 142).

Adler and Adler (2008) have pointed out that the culture shock is a clash of situations and circumstances. The W-curve model developed by Gullahorn and Gullahorn (1963, pp. 33–47) describes the different phases the repatriate has to deal with.

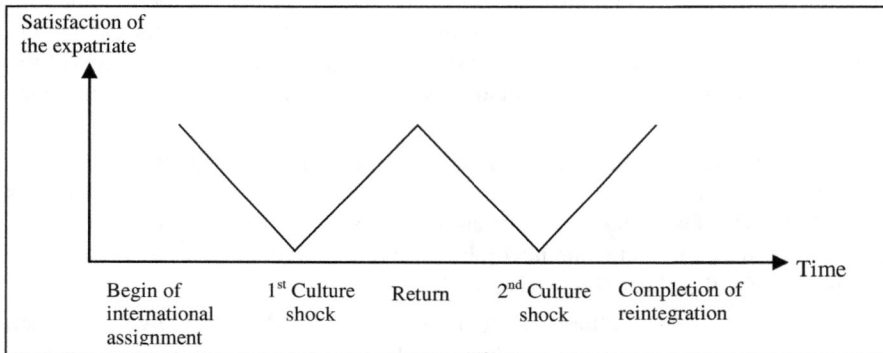

Fig. 9.10:   W-curve hypothesis
Source: Own illustration based on Gullahorn/Gullahorn, 1963, pp. 33–47

At the beginning of the return to the home country, the employee is highly satisfied (Kühlmann/Stahl, 1995, p. 179). There is excitement about seeing family and friends again and to re-adopt old habits and contacts. Furthermore, the employee is proud of the successful termination of the international assignment and has high expectations about the future career development. After a while, the repatriate recognises that the situation at home has changed – as well as their own personality. This demands a readjustment by the employee which was not expected. A reverse culture shock often is the consequence (Hofstede et al., 2010, p. 386). Possible symptoms are e.g. solitude, physical stress reactions and anxiety (ibid.; Emrich, 2011, p. 91). The satisfaction level is very low at this point and it takes time until the employee recovers and finds a way to adapt to the old environment with the acquired competences including the situation at work as well as in the private surrounding (Kühlmann/Stahl, 1995, p. 179). How long the different steps take depends on various aspects, for instance the duration of the international assignment, experiences with former stays abroad, the cultural differences between host and home culture, etc. (ibid., p. 180; Hofstede et al. 2010, p. 385).

Three-phase-model by Fritz

Another model about the employee's reintegration process was developed by Fritz (1982, p. 39), who analyzed the situation before the departure and after the return of the employees. The result is an idealized model that summarizes characteristic behavior patterns during this process, which consists of the following three phases:

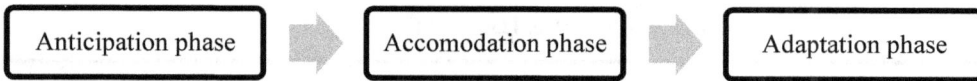

| Anticipation phase | ⇨ | Accomodation phase | ⇨ | Adaptation phase |

Fig. 9.11:   Three-phase model by Fritz
Source: Own illustration based on Fritz, 1982, p. 39

The "anticipation phase" is characterised by the expatriate's imagination of the own return situation based on professional and personal experiences he or she has made. As a result, expectations are usually very high.

The second phase, called "accommodation phase", comprises the confrontation of the imagined situation with reality. Expectations might not be fulfilled and the expatriate tries to explain those circumstances. As a consequence, expectations are adjusted as well as the own behavior based on explanatory models. Furthermore, four possibilities on how to react regarding the social integration are:

- *Adjustment:* Upcoming problems and contradictions are successfully solved through gained competences.
- *Dissociation:* The employee does not reintegrate but instead decides to go on another overseas assignment.
- *Refusal:* The repatriate refuses the home country's culture.
- *Dependency:* The norms and values of the home country or parent company are completely taken over. (ibid., p. 46f)

The last phase, called the "adaption phase", is shaped by the identification with the organization and the home country. This leads to the mutual acceptance and the social integration of the repatriate that means the inclusion of the repatriate on all levels will take place (ibid., p. 48). In contrast to the following model by Hirsch, no information is provided about how long each phase will last.

What is normal?
(John Mattock)

I was running a three-month management training program for entrepreneurs in Nizhni Novgorod – one evening a week. I closed one of the sessions by saying, "Next week we will be working on Time Management. In preparation for that, please will you keep this piece of paper on your desk? I'd like you to spend five minutes a day filling it in as a record of how you are spending your time." There they were the next Tuesday evening, all 35 of them, smiling and ready. How many have completed the form? Not a single one!

In: International Management, 1999, p. 6

Process model by Hirsch

The third model was developed by Hirsch (2003, p. 423). As part of a reintegration seminar, he interviewed repatriates about their integration process. Compared to the model of Fritz, the first phase is based upon the opinions of the repatriates after their return to the home country.

Tab. 9.2:   Process model of reintegration
Source: Own illustration based on Hirsch, 2003, p. 423

Phase A: Naïve integration	Phase B: Reintegration shock	Phase C: Real integration
Characteristics:	Characteristics:	Characteristics:
Friendly; superficial understanding; willingness and openness for new experiences; optimism; euphoria "to be back at home"	First euphoria crumbles; feeling of being not understood by colleagues; circle of friends does not exist anymore; everything changed; falling into resignation, arrogance, anger and dissatisfaction; no feeling of being home	Developing realistic expectations; adjustment without self-abandonment; wide range of behaviour; recognition of old behaviour pattern
Until 6 months after return	Between 6 and 12 months after return	From 12 months after return

Phase A "Naïve integration": In the first phase, the employee is ready to come back home and to reintegrate into the old familiar environment. The phase is characterised by the willingness to readjust and the openness for the local circumstances. This is called the "naïve integration", as it is only a superficial readjustment. It takes up to six months after the return until the more complicated second phase starts (ibid.).

Phase B "Reintegration shock": Little problems, which appeared in the first phase, e.g. the incomprehension by colleagues or difficulties during the workday, gain in importance. This often results in an arrogant attitude of the repatriate towards the social environment including an aggressive prevailing mood. Disappointment and dissatisfaction dominate the feelings and it becomes difficult to lower one's own expectations. Hirsch describes a disinterest for gained experiences from others as a high burden for the employee. The situation resembles the one of an outsider. If more problems arise, for example if the family has difficulties to reintegrate or the working atmosphere is not comfortable, the whole situation will become even worse. One solution is to go abroad again, but this option is rarely chosen according to Hirsch's experiences. Instead, the employee moves on to phase C (ibid.).

Phase C "Real integration": The repatriate has learned to adjust to the old environment and to match his or her own expectations with the real circumstances. Confidence has grown and a new behavioural pattern is recognisable. In general, upcoming difficulties can be handled, but it is also possible that the repatriate is occasionally falling back into phase B. This happens, for example, if a problem appears that is automatically compared to the situation in the host country, which then causes dissatisfaction with the current situation at home (ibid., p. 424). Hirsch underlines that this process model helps repatriates to better understand the whole situation and to identify their current position in the overall process. Difficulties can be overcome through the comprehension of what might happen in each phase and that it is a normal process, which takes time depending on the individual situation (ibid.).

9.8.6   Theoretical reintegration model by Jassawalla, Connolly and Slojkowski

Jassawalla, Connolly and Slojkowski analysed the difficulties during the reintegration process and developed a model of "effective repatriation". The emphasis is on delivering analytical data for HR managers who are interested in finding the best solution for a specific situation. The study is based on literature review and an exploratory field study. However, only a small number of companies and managers was included and consequently, the findings cannot be generalised (Jassawalla et al., 2004, p. 39)

The holistic model focuses on key actions taken prior to departure, during the international assignment and upon repatriation. It is pointed out that companies, which manage the reintegration process successfully, plan most aspects of the employee's return prior to their departure. This provides more certainty for the employee, since the whole international assignment process is often marked by uncertainty and anxiety. The results of the study showed that issues arising during the reintegration phase cannot be separated from the ones arising before the departure and during the stay abroad (ibid., p. 39).

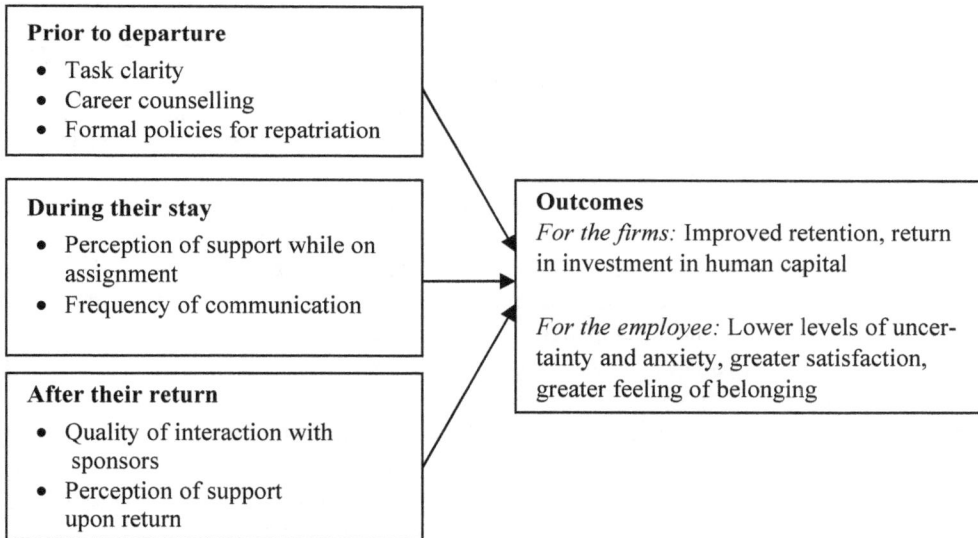

Prior to departure
- Task clarity
- Career counselling
- Formal policies for repatriation

During their stay
- Perception of support while on assignment
- Frequency of communication

After their return
- Quality of interaction with sponsors
- Perception of support upon return

Outcomes
For the firms: Improved retention, return in investment in human capital

For the employee: Lower levels of uncertainty and anxiety, greater satisfaction, greater feeling of belonging

Fig. 9.12:   Model of effective repatriation
Source: Own illustration based on Jassawalla et al., 2004, p. 40

Prior to departure:

Many international assignments are arranged on short notice and are therefore often poorly planned. This lack of planning leads to uncertainty for the employee concerning details about the stay abroad as well as future responsibilities. Furthermore, the link between the international assignment and the own career development is often not clearly understood (ibid.: p. 39).

Thus, three aspects were identified by experienced expatriates for improving the reintegration: *task clarity, career counselling and formal policies for repatriation.* Task clarity means for expatriates to know what to do abroad including time horizons and deadlines – besides what is expected and how it will be evaluated. This provides confidence for the process ahead. The money the company invests in career counselling gives information on the value the firm puts in its human resource capital. A high investment – and therefore a positive linkage between career counselling and the international assignment – is a motivational factor for the employee. Consequently, effective repatriation requires a highly qualitative career counselling including clarity about the reasons for being sent abroad, the benefits for the expatriate him- or herself as well as the company and finally, the career options upon return. If the contrary is the case, the expatriate will experience a high level of stress:

> *"We didn't actually know what we were doing or where we were going until a few weeks before we returned home, which added a huge element of stress" (Jassawalla et al. 2004, p. 41).*

Formal policies for repatriation also seem to contribute to the assurance of the expatriate, as they include guidelines that the expatriate can relate to before, during and after the assignment. False expectations rarely come up as the company's objectives are clarified, including the repatriation process (ibid.).

During their stay:

According to Jassawalla et al., a feeling of isolation and a missing connection to the parent company are two of the main problems expatriates are confronted with during their overseas stay. The following suggestions can help to optimise this situation:

Results of the study showed that the perception of support while on assignment has a high influence on the employees' reintegration. If they felt well supported during their stay abroad, they were willing to reintegrate into the parent company due to their high degree of loyalty. On the contrary, if the expatriate feels only little support and interest in his or her smooth adjustment abroad, feelings of anxiety and diffusion will dominate. Consequently, the expatriate fears to have further problems when reintegrating back home. Therefore, Jassawalla, Connolly and Slojkowski recommend companies to show concern for the well-being of the expatriate and the accompanying family in terms of taking actions (ibid., p. 42).

To reduce the feeling of isolation, frequent communication between the parent company and the expatriate should take place. It is important not to only have contact to one person at home in order to avoid unilateral information. Moreover, maintaining a social network at work is seen as very beneficial as well as frequent visits to the parent company. Communication also demonstrates the importance of the international assignment to the expatriate and the company and therefore increases the motivation and morale. Furthermore, the company shows its intention to keep the expatriate updated about any changes at home and signals that the employee is still a part of the parent company (ibid.).

Upon their return:

When the expatriate returns to the home country after several years, some changes will have taken place in the company and the old environment and the expatriate might not know about them. Receiving support in readjusting to those circumstances contributes to a successful reintegration.

Many former expatriates assess the quality of interactions with sponsors as a very helpful mean in making reintegration a positive experience. In this case, a "sponsor" is defined as a person who has *"more formal authority than the manager, who has a personal stake in the success of the foreign assignment, and who is vested in the career growth of the returning expatriate"* (ibid., p. 43). In detail, further responsibilities include acting confidant and advocate, looking for adequate job positions, keeping the expatriate in the consciousness of key-decision makers in the parent company and making sure that the expatriate's competences can be applied in the company after his or her return. Therefore, the provision of a sponsor for the expatriate is a good opportunity to support the reintegration in terms of a successful termination of the international assignment, the career development and the personal well-being of the expatriate (ibid).

Finally, the perception of support upon return can be strengthened by the company if expatriates are offered a job position signaling them that they are valued in the parent company as much as they were valued while being overseas. As expatriates firstly lose autonomy, attention, monetary benefits etc. when returning home, the company should provide adequate job propositions, where the acquired skills can be applied and which offer the possibility to transfer the gained knowledge. Furthermore, organising trainings, seminars and other measures to help the employee finding the way, are exemplary opportunities to establish a well planned reintegration process (ibid.).

The outcomes of investments in an efficient repatriation process are significant in terms of an

> *"effective utilisation of skills developed overseas, enhancement of human and intellectual capital, improved return on investment in skills and talents, higher retention and loyalty, and enhanced reputation for the firm in general" (ibid.).*

Jassawalla et al. also underline the high satisfaction among expatriates with their career development, a reduced uncertainty and greater loyalty to the company. It cannot be denied that those findings are only based on a small sample of companies and are intended to stimulate further research. Nonetheless, they provide a comprehensive view on the reintegration planning. The following chapter will provide more details concerning specific measures that can be applied before, during and after the international assignment for a successful completion.

9.8.7   Consequences of insufficient reintegration

The priorly discussed problems, which are associated with the employee's return, put emphasis on the fact that solutions have to be developed in order to avoid negative impacts, as the consequences would affect the company the most.

First of all, if expatriates experience difficulties upon their return, they will become dissatisfied and leave the company in the worst case (Berthier/Roger, 2013, pp. 163f; Hirsch, 2003, p. 418). The result is a high loss of return on investment for the former company (Mesmer-Magnus/Viswesvaran, 2008, pp. 195ff). International assignments cost a large sum of money and the consequences are unfavorable if this investment does not bring the expected benefit (Berthier/Roger, 2013, p. 153; Horsch, 1995, pp. 104f). Nevertheless, the average attrition rate for international assignees amounted to 13 % in 2012 (Brookfield Global Relocation Trends Survey, 2012, p. 24). Among those who left, 22 % left while on assignment, 24 % within one year of repatriation, 26 % between the first and second year of repatriation and 28 % more than two years after repatriation (ibid.):

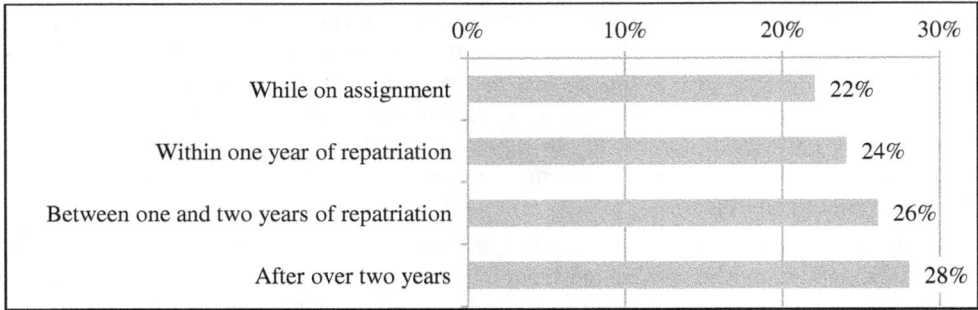

Fig. 9.13:   When international assignees leave the company
Source: Own illustration based on Brookfield Global Relocation Trends Survey, 2012, p. 62

As a result, well qualified managers in the same company hear about those problems and are discouraged to go abroad (Horsch, 1995, pp. 104f). A high level of scepticism spreads and they become "tired" of going abroad (Dülfer/Jöstingmeier, 2008, p. 546). Colleagues who are currently abroad start to worry about their own return and want to extend their stay. Others are interested in a subsequent international assignment to avoid potential problems (Blom/Meier, 2004, pp. 179f).

The disinterest in the acquired competences might result in a "quit-stay", which means that the employee has mentally quit the job but still stays on the job without being productive. This calls the current way of reintegrating expatriates into question: from utilising acquired skills to realising the high ROI (return on investment) in human capital (Jassawalla et al., 2004, p. 38).

9.8.8   Repatriation planning

Regarding the repatriation planning for the employee and the accompanying partner or family, successful actions have to be developed by the human resources department for the private and work-related surroundings (DGFP e.V., 2012, p. 123). The whole process of reintegration should be a dynamic interaction, which means that the company supports the employee in the daily life at work and at home, considers the repatriate's experiences as enrichment and therefore, enables the employee to share and apply newly acquired competences and information (Hirsch, 2003, p. 425; Klemm/Popp 2006, pp. 205f).

These issues have to be initially considered in the context of the superior business strategy (Kühlmann/Stahl, 1995, p. 190). Depending on the strategic orientation of the company, the extent and development of international assignments vary. If the companies are willing to invest money in the repatriation process, in the long run, they can benefit from this investment (Kühlmann/Stahl, 1995, p. 192f).

Most of the successfully conducted reintegrations had been planned before the employee actually left for the international assignment (Weber et al., 2001, p. 138). This is in line with the findings by a study conducted by Deloitte (2008, pp. 23f), which states that 77 % of the participating companies start preparations for the repatriation before the start of the overseas stay. Regular home trips, a mentor from the parent company and an early determination of the return position at home are some aspects that help the employee to build more confidence in the company and to increase his or her motivation (ibid.). In the following, concrete examples will be given.

Support prior to return

To avoid difficulties upon return, several measures can be initiated in the professional environment as well as in private surroundings beforehand:

Mentoring system:

The role of a mentor is usually filled by a manager, who holds a higher position in the company's hierarchy, e.g. from the senior management (Weber et al., 2001, p. 201). The person acts as a link between the parent company and the expatriate. He or she is a contact person who represents the interests of the expatriate during the absence including staffing, informs about important changes in the parent company, observes the performance abroad and finally supports the mentee during the reintegration phase (Blom/Meier, 2004, pp. 179f; Kühlmann/Stahl, 1995, p. 199; Weber et al. 2001, p. 201). 60 % of the companies offer a mentor from the home country according to the study by Deloitte (Deloitte & Touche 2008).

Preparation for potential reintegration difficulties:

If potential reintegration problems are discussed and solutions are offered, the repatriate will get a realistic view about the given circumstances. Moreover, changes in the parent company demand a certain degree of flexibility from the employee. If those issues addressed in an open way, the risks of a premature return will be reduced. (Fritz, 1982, pp. 93ff; Kühlmann/Stahl, 1995, p. 199).

Visits by HR managers in the host country:

Many expatriates are afraid of being forgotten by the parent company during their time abroad (Weber et al., 2001, pp. 137f). Regular visits by the responsible HR managers in the host country are an option to minimize this anxiety. They can use this opportunity to help the expatriate and the partner or family to build up realistic expectations about the repatriation process – including new information about expected changes within the company. A positive side effect is that HR managers get a better insight into the work and living conditions in the host country which might help them in the future to be fully aware of challenges that can be expected in this context (Fröhlich, 1987, p. 458).

Career planning:

How the career path can look like after the successful completion of the international assignment should be discussed beforehand (Kühlmann/Stahl, 1995, pp. 196ff). This includes basic facts about the duration of the stay abroad, the specific tasks, the performance measurement, the line manager's role during the reintegration phase and the job position intended for the expatriate after return (Solomon, 2002, p. 23). If any changes take place during the assignment, e.g. the employee's performance deteriorates abroad or the intended position is not available anymore, it has to be clearly communicated (ibid.; Andresen/Domsch, 2009, p. 462). This provides security for the employee and goes beyond the contractually agreed reintegration guarantee.

Information service:

To inform the expatriate on a regular basis about changes in the parent company and inci-
dences will result in realistic expectations and less negative surprises (Adler/Adler, 1982,
pp. 341–356). It also counteracts the anxiety of isolation and increases the feeling of involvement (Fritz, 1982, p. 184). The information transfer includes e.g. professional journals,
company magazines and company-internal circulars that are sent abroad (Kühlmann/Stahl
1995, p. 202; Weber et al., 2001, p. 138).

Timely search for a return position:

Based on Kühlmann and Stahl, the HR department in the home country should start planning
the reintegration process approximately one year before the end of the international assignment. This is a good time frame to give the expatriate the right information about what is
going to happen after his or her return. At least six months before departure the expatriate
should know which specific position will be offered. (1995, p. 203). This will avoid unnecessary worries by the employee regarding the uncertainty of the future career at home. A one-
to-one conversation between a HR manager and the expatriate is the ideal possibility to discuss further details about the return including the future income and contractual terms (ibid.).

Annual trip home:

Regular trips home, at least once a year, have the benefit that the employee can use this time
to visit the parent cmpany and hence keep personal contact with the former department, the
mentor and other colleagues (Solomon, 2002, p. 23). The trip home also enables the accompanying family to keep contact with their family and friends. This reduces the risk of social
isolation after return (Kühlmann/Stahl 1995, p. 203).

Relocation service:

Keeping the house or flat can ease the reintegration process, since no apartment search is
necessary during the reintegration phase. Companies like Siemens offer here a special relocation service that takes care of all those activities necessary for a new start, including the
search for a house or an apartment. The idea is quite simple: the repatriate and the accompanying family shall get the feeling of still having a "nest" at home, which can also increase the
loyalty towards the company and the likelihood of returning to the parent company after the
completion of the international assignment (Kühlmann/Stahl, 1995, p. 204).

Support during reintegration phase

Following Kühlmann and Stahl (1995, pp. 204f), the subsequent table will give an overview
on several support measures focusing on the assistance during the employee's reintegration
phase in the professional environment.

> *"A nations's well-being, as well as its ability to compete,*
> *is conditioned by a single, pervasive cultural characteristic:*
> *the level of trust inherent in the society".*
>
> (Francis Fukuyama)

Tab. 9.3: Support measures during reintegration phase in professional environment
Source: based on Kühlmann/Stahl, 1995, p. 204

Support measure	Description
Training period	• Emplyoee's alienation from the local circumstances in home country • granting a training period to increase the well-being of employee • step-by-step increase of requirements
Advanced training methods	• providing training opportunities to update the expatriate's knowledge that might be outdated after spending years abroad • training in managerial behavior • on-the-job training to avoid separation from family during reintegration process
Introduction to colleagues	• often little understanding by colleagues for the repatriate's situation • sensitising colleagues for reintegration problems of former expatriate and asking for sympathy
Naming a contact person in parent company	• in addition to a mentor, naming a contact person on the same hierarchy level, e.g. a former colleague functioning as a trainer "on-the-job" and as confidant • reason: mentor might not always be available due to higher position, potential inhibition by expatriate to contact mentor too frequently
Reintegration seminar	• recognising the changes in parent company and of the own personality • exchanging experiences with other repatriates • developing solutions for conflict situations • offering these seminars 1–2 months after return at the earliest

Regarding the private environment of the employee and the family, the following five suggestions have been made by Kühlmann and Stahl (1995, pp. 206f):

Tab. 9.4: Support measures during reintegration phase in private environment
Source: Based on Kühlmann/Stahl, 1995, pp. 206f

Support measure	•	Description
Relocation support		• removal support • relocation support, including house sale, visits to the authorities, house hunting in home country • checklist by parent company including tasks to be done by the employee

Financial help and consulting		• High gap between host and home country income:
		   – financial consulting by parent company
		   – offering non-interest-bearing loans, paying salary in advance for necessary acquisitions

Reintegration seminar		• reintegration seminars for accompanying family • opportunity to discuss family-related reintegration problems
Contact to other repatriates		• mutual support from other returning families • providing address lists of former expatriates who are willing to share their experiences, e.g. "repatriates club"

Support after return

After listing reintegration support measures that can be applied before and during the reintegration phase, there are now a few examples regarding the support after the employee's return to be found in the following:

Tab. 9.5:   Support measures after reintegration phase in the professional and private environment
Source: Based on Kühlmann/Stahl, 1995, pp. 207f

Support measure	Description
Utilising international experiences at the workplace	• applying ability of intercultural communication • being involved in international projects
Implementation of transfer workshops	• repatriates discuss their experiences and develop improvement suggestions concerning technical and organisational operational procedures
Participation in reintegration seminars or becoming a mentor	• recognition of the employee's acquired competences by offering a participation in reintegration seminars for future expatriates • transfer of knowledge (country-specific, general experiences) • repatriates in executive positions: participation in mentoring programmes
Spousal support	• supporting the process of finding a new job position for the partner

Beside the mentioned examples, there are some more studies (Blom/Meier, 2004; Weber, 2001; Martin/Anthony, 2006) that deal with problems and challenges caused by the reintegration process.

On the one hand, the success of those suggestions is not guaranteed due to insufficient research findings. On the other hand, it can be expected that a combination of some of those support measures is more likely to lead to a successful reintegration than only one measure. An important factor also is the timely planning. This is much more sufficient than short-term actions after the employee's return (Kühlmann/Stahl, 1995, p. 209).

Furthermore, it is important to see the responsibility not only on the company's side but also on the employee's side.

9.8.9   The employees' view on reintegration

The success of a reintegration also depends on the employees' efforts. Emrich (2011, p. 190) even sees most of the responsibility on the employees' side. Companies can offer financial, family-oriented, psychological and career-related support, but the biggest contribution to the cultural reintegration has to be made by the employee him- or herself (ibid.). This includes e.g. maintaining contacts at home. Moreover, it is also the responsibility of the expatriate to actively quest for information about the situation in the parent company. Showing a certain flexibility regarding the return position is another positive contribution which will make a successful repatriation easier (Kühlmann/Stahl, 1995, p. 209). In summary, reintegration is also what the repatriate makes of it (Peltonen/Ladwig 2005, p. 342).

Beyond that, three main strategies that are used by repatriates to transition into the old environment can be identified. Those were identified by Adler/Gundersen (2008, pp. 292f) and are based on interviews with 200 Canadian repatriates from companies and state institutions:

Re-socialisation:

The employees think that their knowledge acquired abroad is not applicable at home and, therefore, subject themselves to the requirements of the life in the home country. They try to avoid attention and to behave like colleagues who have not been abroad. This implicates that no organisational and individual learning can take place.

Alienation:

The experienced way of life and working abroad is seen as more positive than the one at home. They have "gone native". Consequently, the employees withdraw and do not apply their competences as they do not see any possibility. A personal isolation is the consequence and hence the company can scarcely profit from the employee's international experiences.

Synthesis:

The employees try to find synergies between the foreign culture and their own culture. It is tried to apply positive experiences gained abroad to the way of life at home in finding new approaches. The proactive employees will bring high benefits for the company, as they are able to combine multiple cultures' way of working, as long as the organisation is open for the employees' ideas and contributions.

According to Kühlmann und Stahl, who criticise this model as not being comprehensive enough, the real return situations and consequently the transition strategies might even be more complex than explained above (1995, pp. 186f). It is difficult to say that repatriates will always choose one of the three strategies and react accordingly. Findings from stress research underline that several attempts are necessary to cope with stress situations and that the first attempt is not always successful (ibid.). Furthermore, the transition strategies are also influenced by the support from superiors, colleagues and friends, the potential offer for another international assignment and the employee's own character (ibid.)

9.8.10 Repatriation checklist

The following timeline advises useful arrangements which should be made one year prior relocation to enable an accurate return to the home nation. This timeline can be arranged into four sections which can be seen below.

1.	9–12 Months before Reassignment
☐	clarify dates of transition
☐	inform friends, colleagues and family members
☐	notify Human Resource Managers about desires concerning e.g. vendors
☐	plan ways for enjoyment and festivity
☐	keep journal of experiences

2.	6–9 Months before Reassignment
☐	arrange interview with host and home-country supervisor
☐	create a financial plan
☐	discuss a date to reduce or stop salary to avoid a loss of money throughout converting
☐	consult a tax supervisor
☐	notify host schools of departure

☐	recover deposits and fees
☐	cancel local club memberships
☐	inform spouse's employer in the host nation

3.	**1–6 Months before Reassignment**
☐	book flight tickets for the return
☐	close down bank accounts
☐	Send word to the home and host supervisor, Human Resource and tax advisor of home-country employment and living or residential details, telephone / fax numbers, and e-mail
☐	say good-bye to workmates and friends
☐	summarize your experiences
☐	collect photos, videos and other souvenirs
☐	consult repatriation services

4.	**Post-Repatriation**
☐	explicit career discussions with your supervisor
☐	continue language studies
☐	share experiences with families and others
☐	establish a service or support group
☐	attend follow-up training
☐	finish expense report
☐	evaluate the company's support, make suggestions for enhancement and highlight best parts

Fig. 9.14:   Repatriation Checklist
Source: Tanski, A., in web

9.9   Role Play: Time for a coffee break

There is a conference at the Tokyo Convention Centre involving business executives from all over the world. Mr. Schmidt from Berlin is one of the attendees, and he is interested in meeting many people from different countries during the coffee break in the conference.

While walking around looking for someone to talk to, he spots two men – one Japanese and one Arab – who are talking together on the other side of the room; Mr. Schmidt approaches them.

Schmidt:	Good morning gentlemen, I'm Peter Schmidt. *(He extends his hand to the Arab man first and then to the Japanese)*. Do you mind if I join you?
Mohamed:	*(As he shakes Schmidt's hand with both of his.)* Welcome, please join us.
Suzuki:	*(He steps backward and bows slightly. He shakes Mr. Schmidt's hand without saying anything, ready to exchange business cards.)*
Mohamed:	Are you enjoying yourself in this wonderful country, Mr. Schmidt?
Schmidt:	Oh, sure, it's very nice here. What do you do Mr....?
Mohamed:	Mohamed Binager. I'm from Egypt and the president of my import company. We are here to look at some of the available products and meet our Japanese friends.
Schmidt:	*(Turning to Suzuki)*. And your name, sir?
Suzuki:	*(He silently hands Schmidt his business card.)*
Schmidt:	*(After looking at it quickly.)* Oh, you're Mr. Suzuki.
Suzuki:	Yes, Sany Corporation.
Schmidt:	I see *(Puts Suzuki's card quickly in his pocket and turns back to Mohamed. Afterwards he hands both of them his business card.)* Do you have a business card, Mohamed?
Mohamed:	*(Smiling.)* No, I don't carry them with me. Everybody knows me. *(Moving closer to Mr. Schmidt to show him his hospitality.)* I'm the president.
Schmidt:	*(Stepping back from Mohamed.)* Oh, I understand.
Suzuki:	Mr. Schmidt, you are from the Siemens Company, aren't you?
Schmidt:	Yes, I'm the marketing director in charge of the European Division.
Mohamed:	Well, should we all go have some coffee and enjoy our break time together?
Schmidt:	I'm sorry, but I have to go to talk to some other people. Maybe we'll get together later on. It was very nice to meet you. Goodbye.

Peter Schmidt walks away in search of more people to make contact with, as Mohamed and Suzuki look at each other, smiling. They overhear him: "Good morning, gentlemen, I'm Peter Schmidt. Do you mind if I join you?"

Review and Discussion Questions:

1. There are many culture clashes present in this scenario. What would you think went wrong with Mr. Schmidt's presentation?

2. In order to avoid such a bad performance what should generally be done by companies preparing managers for intercultural meetings?

9.10   Case Study: Outsourcing Sends U.S. Firms to "Trainer"

When Axcelis Technologies Inc. outsourced some engineering jobs to India last year, the Beverly, Massachusetts, company worried that some of its workers might resent their new Indian colleagues. So Axcelis called in Bidhan Chandra.

Over two days, the Indian born Mr. Chandra taught about 60 Axcelis employees the finer points of how to shake hands with Indians and why not to get frustrated if an Indian worker made no eye contact during a meeting. He got the group to role-play scenarios where one person would pretend to be an Indian and the other his U.S.-based colleague. Indian music throbbed in the background during the breaks.

"At first, I was sceptical and wondered what I'd get out of the class," says Randy Longo, a human resources director at Axcelis, producing tools for manufacturing semiconductors. "But it was enlightening for me. Not everyone operates like we do in America."

Even as the debate about the outsourcing of jobs to India mounts, people like Mr. Chandra are preaching understanding. As one of the country's premier "awareness trainers", the 56-year-old former mechanical engineer travels the U.S. to teach workers how – in essence – to be sensitive to their counterparts abroad.

His business is booming. Mr. Chandra, an international business professor at Empire State College in Saratoga, New York, teaches his sensitivity course once or twice a month, up from once every two months last year. Tech companies such as Axcelis, Advanced Micro Devices Inc. and KLA-Tencor Corp. have hired him. For these companies, Mr. Chandra holds a course dubbed "Working Effectively with Indians," which includes a cultural-sensitivity quiz. And he is now offering "immersion programs", where executives can travel to India with him as a guide.

The knowledge he imparts might be basic, but it can help to avoid business mis-understandings, says Mr. Chandra. For example, he notes that when Indians shake hands, they sometimes do so rather limply. That is not a sign of weakness or dislike; instead, a soft handshake conveys respect, Mr. Chandra says. When an Indian avoids eye contact, he adds, that is also a sign of deference.

At the root of potential problems between U.S and Indian workers is a vast cultural gap, argues Mr. Chandra. India is what he calls a "high context" society, which relies heavily on relationships and moral codes. "When people understand these differences, they are less likely to make mistakes with each other," Mr. Chandra says.

Mr. Chandra began developing his courses four years ago when a company in Singapore approached him to teach an awareness course on India. Over the next few years, he linked up with several U.S. intercultural-training firms, including Meridian Resources Associates, Inc., Change Management Consulting & Training LLC, Cultural Savvy and Intercultural Business

Center Inc., which hired him as their primary trainer for India. These firms provide Mr. Chandra with the bulk of his corporate assignments, for which some of them charge 5,000 U.S. dollar, or about 4,000 Euro a day.

Each of Mr. Chandra's day long courses starts with a quiz to assess how much students already know about India. Then he discusses aspects of India's religious and linguistic diversity and its differences with the U.S., after which he divides the class into groups to analyse case studies of working situations. He follows that up with a tutorial on communication tips, including pointers on shaking hands, business protocol and business attire in India. Sometimes he ends the class with an Indian meal.

Mr. Chandra's clients say his teachings have helped minimising some common problems, such as misunderstandings about commitments made by Indian employees or contractors. Several years ago, for instance, tech firm KLA-Tencor was having communication mix-ups with its Indian partner, leading to some work deadlines being missed, says David Pitts, director of global alliances at KLA-Tencor.

After hiring Mr. Chandra to teach a class, "the most practical thing we learned was to get the individual in India to give feedback to you in a different medium – that is, if you'd spoken to them in a conference call, then get them to write an e-mail and repeat back what you have said," Mr. Pitt says. "We tended to forget that while Indians have good English, they might not be processing the information the same way that we do."

Last month, Mr. Chandra took about 20 executives from Advanced Micro Devices on a two-week "immersion" trip to India. The program required six months of planning, with Mr. Chandra preparing information on security issues they might confront. The group traveled to New Delhi, Bangalore and Bombay, meeting with local government officials and businessmen. As one tip, Mr. Chandra advised the team not to plunge into business talks right away during meetings, but to first chat about current events and other issues. AMD India President Ajay Marathe, an Indian who has worked for years in the company's U.S. operations, says Mr. Chandra helped the group learn how to better interact with Indians. "We know it takes a different kind of business behavior to succeed there," he says.

While few would dispute that, some executives believe cross-cultural training is best handled internally. After PeopleSoft Inc. opened an operation in India last July, Michael Gregoire, executive vice president of the software company, sent an executive team to India to get to know the operation. He also asked his team to take their staffs out for Indian meals. "I wouldn't advocate us taking our corporate culture out to anyone else" for training, Mr. Gregoire says.

Source: Tam, Pui-Wing, Outsourcing Sends U.S. Firms to "Trainer", in: The Wall Street Journal – Arab news, 06/03/2006, p. 20

Review and Discussion Questions:

1. What different forms and methods of intercultural training are mentioned in this article? Please, list them all here.

2. Now put them in an order that starts with more passive forms of intercultural training and continue your scale till the most active form of intercultural training has been reached.

3. The author has pointed to a low and high-context example in this context. Who is the father of this concept? Could you give a brief overview of his model?

4. What did you learn about the right intercultural behavior in doing business with Indian partners? Name all important aspects!

5. What is your position regarding the trainer, respectively training institutes. Should they come from outside the company, would you prefer to have an in-company trainer or do you see another possibility to cross-culturally train the staff for international assignments?

10 Three Global Intercultural Tests

10.1 Siemens AG – Globality Check

10.1.1 Presentation

You have been asked by the Headquarters to give a presentation about a new product to sales representatives from the Siemens region. You know that there will be colleagues from the USA, China, Middle East, South Africa and a number of European countries in your audience. What cultural factors do you think are important for the success of your presentation?

10.1.2 Feedback

You are working in Thailand and some of your staff arrive regularly late to work. You feel you need to talk to them about the issue – how do you approach the problem?

10.1.3 Meetings

In your work at Siemens you spend a lot of time taking part in meetings – many of them include people from a wide range of different countries. What cultural factors should you take into account to make sure that the meetings are effective?

10.1.4 Negotiating

You are involved in a negotiation for Siemens with partners from Japan, North and South America. What cultural factors do you think you need to consider when doing the negotiations?

10.1.5 Socializing

An important part of doing business is getting to know your business partners. In your culture how do people combine business and socializing? What cultural differences are you aware of concerning socializing with business partners?

10.1.6 International Projects

You are part of a team with French, Germans and Indians working on a major IT project. The market is highly competitive and it is essential that everything runs according to schedule.

Communication is mostly virtual as you are based in different countries. What cultural factors do you think will be important in working together?

10.1.7   Delegation

You have been sent by Siemens on a delegation to another country. You expect to stay in your new position for at least three years. How will you make sure that the delegation is a success?

10.1.8   Debriefing

You have now worked through some typical situations that you can expect to experience at the "global network of innovation". What did you learn from the assignment?

Record your ideas and afterwards compare them with our suggested solutions, which can be found later in this chapter!

10.2   An intercultural crossword puzzle

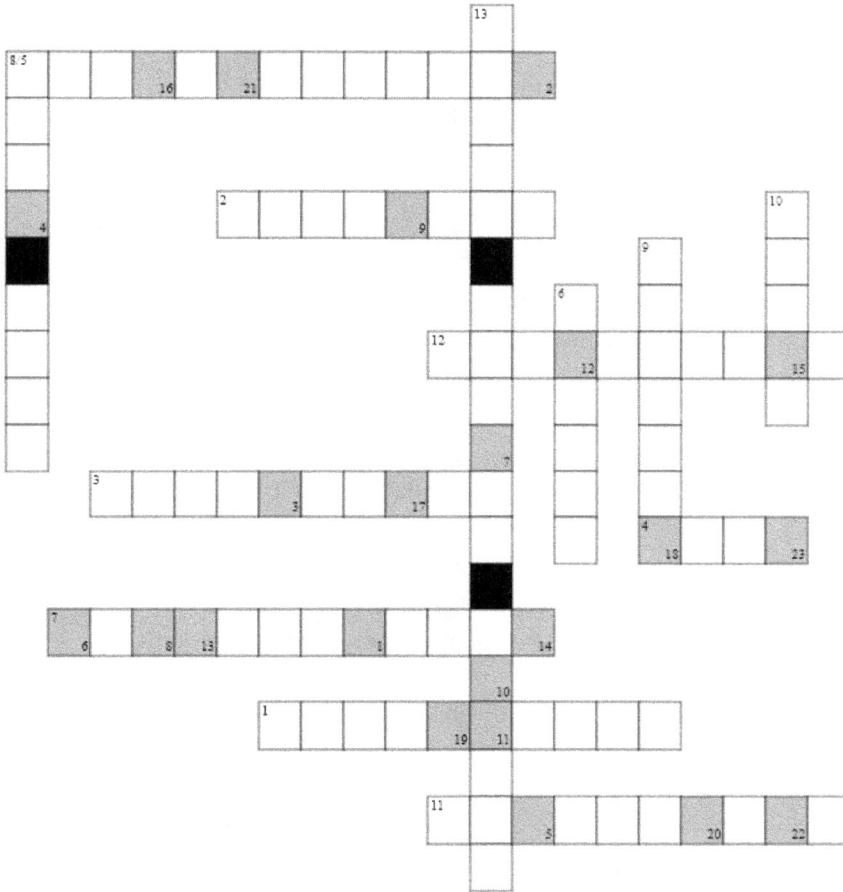

1. A process by which a person influences others to accomplish an objective and directs the organization in a way that makes it more cohesive and coherent.

2. The father of the 5-D model

3. Term used for an employee on an international assignment

4. Sign of appreciation when accepting an invitation to a private home

5. Important tool to practice the right reactions in intercultural business encounters

6. One of the most important values for Asians

7. One of Trompenaars' cultural dimensions (Individualism vs. ...)

8. The ... can be facilitated by regular contact with colleagues, friends and family members in the home country during the assignment abroad.

9. Instrument to explain the term "culture": ...-Model

10. A religion based on five pillars of faith

11. One of Tuckman's stages of team development

12. Intonation, volume and speech tempo are part of the ... communication

13. Global research project on values and beliefs

10.3   A test of global management skills

A) Companies may fail in their globalization efforts because of…

    1. A lack of financial resources.

    2. Government regulations.

    3. Consumer demand for low-cost products.

    4. A lack of multicultural management expertise.

B) During a break for a meeting between you and a group of Omanis, you walk into the men's room to find a few of them washing their feet in the sink. You think:

    1. They must have had smelly feet.

    2. They are simply freshening themselves up.

    3. They are preparing for their prayers.

C) You are making a presentation to a group of American managers on your project. One of them disagrees with the data you are presenting. Will you…

    1. Ignore his remarks and proceed?

    2. Ask him why and then justify your point?

    3. Tell him you can discuss the point with him after the meeting?

    4. Remind him that you do not accept questions during presentations?

D) At the end of your telephone discussion with your Indian friend, you ask him if the price is acceptable. He answers, "Yes, yes," meaning…

    1. He is confirming his acceptance of your price.

    2. He has heard and understood your offer.

    3. You should give a deeper discount.

    4. He is politely saying no.

E) Lucy Chen, in Taiwan, is new on the assembly line and she is still having difficulties putting the units together properly. You want to train her. You should…

    1. Say, "Lucy, you should pay closer attention to what you are doing"

    2. Shout across the room, "Lucy, do you need help?"

    3. Tell her, "Lucy Chen, you are learning very fast", and then show her exactly how the units are put together.

    4. Move her aside and show her how to put the units together.

F) Which three words best sum up Japanese society?

    1. Individualism, Respect and Hinduism.

    2. Altruism, Hierarchy and Confucianism.

3. Materialism, Work and Honor.

4. Directness, Confrontation, Success.

G) Your company has just received confirmation that a high-level delegation from China will visit your office. Since the Chinese have already received a sample of your products, the purpose of their visits is probably to …

1. Sign an agreement to act as your local distributor in China.

2. Establish a firm relationship with the company's management.

3. Visit your country as a reward for their hard work at home.

4. Getting to know some technological advancements.

H) You are conducting a performance appraisal with a Vietnamese member of your group. You ask, "Where would you like to be in two years?" He looks at you in surprise. The reason may be…

1. He expects you, as the manager, to know the answer to that question.

2. He thinks you are suggesting that he will leave the company.

3. He thinks you want him to change the jobs within the company.

4. He thinks you are not giving him a good evaluation.

I) You are the new manager in an Indian office. You ask one of your supervisors to move a desk and place it in another corner of the office. The next day you notice it has not yet been done. Why?

1. The supervisor was offended you asked him/her and refused to do anything about it.

2. The supervisor could not find a laborer to move it and would not do so him/herself.

3. Because things get done slowly in India.

J) Upon being met at the office of a potential Indonesian client you are met with very personal questions about your job, education and salary. Why?

1. These questions are just being part of getting to know you.

2. These questions are meant to establish your rank.

3. These questions are thought to be of importance in your own country, so are being asked out of politeness.

K) In Latin America, managers …

    1. Are most likely to hire members of their own family.

    2. Consider hiring members of their own families to be inappropriate.

    3. Stress the importance of hiring members of minority groups.

    4. Usually hire more people than are actually needed to do a job.

L) When eating in India, it is appropriate to

    1. Take food with your right hand and eat with your left.

    2. Take food with your left hand and eat with your right.

    3. Take food and eat it with your left hand.

    4. Take food and eat it with your right hand.

M) In China, the status of every business negotiation is…

    1. Reported daily in the press.

    2. Private and details are not discussed publicly.

    3. Subjected to scrutiny by a public tribunal on a regular basis.

    4. Directed by the elders of every commune.

N) You are making a presentation to American company executives who are considering appointing you to lead their negotiating team. To impress them, you should emphasize your

    1. Harvard Ph.D. and Stanford MBA.

    2. Managerial style as a motivating leader.

    3. Past accomplishments.

    4. Family background.

O) You have a business discussion with Japanese managers. During a period of silence in that meeting you should

    1. Ask what is wrong.

    2. Break the silence immediately.

    3. Stay silent too.

P) After finishing your visit to an Arab company, the president offers to escort you to your car. He is offering this gesture in order to

    1. Discuss privately the final commissions.

    2. Further express his hospitality.

    3. Show his competitors next door that he has a contract with you.

    4. Give you a last chance to offer that discount he has been seeking.

Q) Your Japanese team achieved its production quota last month. How should you acknowledge their achievement?

    1. Treat them to a sushi dinner where you give a special recognition to the group leader.

    2. Do not mention it, because meeting quotas is their job.

    3. Call the oldest person aside and thank him.

    4. Thank the group at your next meeting and ask them to increase production even more.

R) An Arab businessman offers you a cup of Arabian coffee at his office. You don't drink coffee. You should say

    1. "No, thank you."

    2. "Thank you, but, I don't drink coffee."

    3. "Thank you," and accept the cup of coffee.

    4. "No, thank you. Coffee makes me nervous."

S) True or false?

- Japanese and Chinese can read each other's newspapers.
- Germans like deadlines.
- Arabs expect gifts to be opened in front of the giver.
- Japanese, unlike Chinese, do not mind "losing face".
- When training Thais, use local examples and case studies.
- Indian society is family-oriented and collectivistic, and emphasis is on harmony and conformity.
- In China you should avoid giving clocks as a gift.
- American businessmen dislike written contracts.
- In the Malaysian culture, group achievement is not as important as individual achievement.
- The Chinese prefer white and black wrapping paper colors.
- Gender dynamics are changing fast in India as young, educated women lead the workforce in certain industries and become in some cases the primary financial support for the entire family.
- The senior Thai always greets the junior Thai first.
- Indonesians regard your personal references more than your technical skills.
- For the Chinese a contract is a complete and binding set of specifications.
- When giving or receiving gifts in Japan, you should use both hands.
- Business with Muslims should normally not be done on Friday.
- Asking a Chinese counterpart about his income is taboo.
- Eating with the left hand in Egypt is normal.
- Interruptions in Brazil are considered as rude.
- Handshakes are the accepted form of greeting in China, even among Chinese.
- Koreans prefer a well-documented training manual for post-training study.

- You must remind your Malaysian business partner three times to respond to your proposal.
- In order to work with your Singaporean team, you must first exhibit your technical capability, and then gain their trust.
- If you plan a sit-down meal with your Chinese guests, mark seats with place cards and follow protocol order in seating.
- If you are invited to an Argentinian`s home or office, wait for an invitation to be seated.
- To motivate Malaysian workers you must allow them independence.
- Chinese may make as many as three refusal gestures when they are offered gifts.

10.4   Solutions

10.4.1   Globality Check

The following solutions – a mixture of comments by the Siemens company and my own opinion – should only serve as a platform for further discussions!

Presentations

- Consider the cultures in your audience when preparing your presentation. Avoid taboo topics and restrict your use of humor.
- Think about what the audience expects from your presentation. How much information do they want? How active do they expect you to be? Do they expect to be able to ask questions during the presentation? What sort of structure are they used to? For instance, presentations in Germany often focus on information whereas in the UK and the USA the big picture is commonly presented with more focus on getting the audience interested in the topic.
- Check that the audience understands the language you are using. Do they all speak English? Is some translation necessary? If you use English then keep your language concrete and as simple as possible – avoid complicated sentences or unusual vocabulary.
- Use visual material when possible to emphasize the main points. Make sure the visuals mean the same thing for the different cultures. For instance if you want to show before and after effects remember that in some cultures people read from the left to the right in others it is the other way around.
- During the presentation look at the body language of the audience: Are there signs that people are uninterested or confused? Remember that different cultures have different ways of showing that they do not understand or are not interested. In USA and Europe interest is often shown by asking questions whereas in some Asian countries it is considered polite to listen.
- Provide written summaries of what you have said – if possible in the language of the audience.

Feedback

- In order to keep others from losing face, communication is often non-verbal, so you must closely watch the facial expression and the body language of the other person, when you ask him/her, e.g. for the reasons for regularly coming late to work.
- Reinforce the importance of the agreed-upon deadlines as far as the time management of the whole company is concerned and how their behavior may negatively affect the rest of the organization.
- Keep to agenda, schedules and deadlines. If you do not stick to the point, you will be regarded as devious and at the same time you lose the respect of others.
- If things do not change for the better, the next step is to ask one of your (e.g. Thai) colleagues being more or less in the same rank you are working to play the role of a mediator.

- The result of such an intervention should be that clear goals now have been jointly defined and everybody is fully aware of the consequences if they are not met.

Meetings

- If you like to make jokes, watch out for those that do not fly so well across cultures.
- Face-to-face relationships are a prerequisite for developing trust across cultures. Do not only rely on e-mails.
- Listen, observe and try to understand before judging and evaluating.
- Be patient. Accept the fact that it may take a much longer time to get results.
- Whenever possible, check your assumptions and expectations with your partner.

Negotiating

- Right at the beginning the team should jointly define team rules and regulations that everybody has to obey and to follow.
- Keep in mind that multicultural teams need more time to come to a final result. Therefore allow plenty of time for meetings and interruptions. Especially the team members from Japan need more time to come to a conclusion because they have to get in contact with the headquarter in Tokyo to reassure their position.
- Even if problems occur remain calm and constructive at all times.
- Working with members from a different cultural background demands a comprehensive understanding of verbal, non-verbal, and paraverbal communication. The right interpretation of the body language, or a situation where silence is part of the negotiating process requires that you behave interculturally correctly.
- If the team appears confused, irritated or offended, ask open questions with "who, what, why, where, how" and try to clear up misunderstandings.
- In order to get a better intercultural understanding of each other and to prevent tensions right from the beginning within the team, you should think about some joint sport activities (basketball, hiking, volleyball, walking) or to persuade them that each other should invite the team members to a dinner prepared by him- or herself.

Socializing

- In some cultures it is important not to mix business with socializing - in others it is vital to do this.
- Where does the socializing take place? In some Scandinavian countries business can take place in the sauna. In the UK and the USA negotiations can take place on the golf course.
- Do you invite business people to your home?
- Who pays for the meal when you go out to a restaurant with business partners?
- Do you have to be careful that an invitation is not seen as a bribe to get a deal done?
- What do you talk about? In some cultures it is appropriate to talk business while socializing, in others this is a taboo topic.

International Projects

- Be aware of the time zones and working hours in different countries.
- Allow time for team building at the early stages of the project.
- Check common understanding of project goals.
- Clarify roles.
- Establish clear rules for communication.
- In this specific case, bear in mind that the team members may have different styles of working together. In the real situation, this case was based upon on the Indians not expressing their ideas during video conferences: they preferred face-to-face communication. For the French team members, it was vital to feel included in the decision-making process. The German project leader needed to be sensitive to cultural differences in order to gain the support of the whole team.

Delegation

- Learn the language of the host country, at least some phrases.
- Before you go, prepare yourself and your family for the delegation, e.g. by talking to previous delegates and their family members, informing yourself about the country you are going to and taking part in intercultural training.
- Build up as many relationships with local people and colleagues as you can.
- Get involved in local activities.
- Get support from people in a similar position
- Keep in contact with family and colleagues in your home country.

Debriefing

- Take every opportunity you can to experience and find out more about cultures other than your own.
- Reflect on your own cultural roots.
- Observe behavior carefully before you interpret what it might mean.
- See differences as an opportunity rather than a problem.
- Enjoy exploring cultures.
- Whenever challenged by cultural differences, think about how boring the world would be with a global, uniform culture.

10.4.2   Further solutions

Chapter 10 - A Test of Global Management Skills:

A/4; B/3; C/2; D/2; E/3; F/2; G/2, H/1; I/2; J/2; K/1; L/4; M/2; N/3; O/3; P/2; Q/4; R/3
S (true/false):

1/f; 2/t; 3/f; 4/f; 5/t; 6/t; 7/t; 8/f; 9/f; 10/f; 11/t; 12/f; 13/t; 14/f; 15/t; 16/t; 17/t;
18/f; 19/f; 20/t; 21/t; 22/t; 23/f; 24/t; 25/t; 26/f; 27/t

Crossword puzzle:

10.4.3 Intercultural Exercise (p. 66): Instructions for the "Ulemans"

You are member of a group of Ulemans, whom **a** team of German experts wants to teach the techniques of bridge construction. The culture of Ulemans is in some points significantly different to the German one.

The following **rules** apply:

Ulemans briefly touch when talking to each other. Not touching each other means: I do not like you. If an expert does not touch an Uleman during a conversation, the latter covers his/her ears. When working, the Ulemans also touch each other just like during conversations, though they take care not to disturb the other person's work.

The traditional greeting of Ulemans is a deep bow. Other forms of greeting are seen as an offence. Holding out one's hand towards an Uleman is also regarded as a sign of humiliation and is answered with a loud "Why don't you greet me?"

Ulemans are extremely friendly people and never use the word "no". They also say yes if they mean no. When Ulemans say "yes"and simultaneously shake their head, they actually mean no.

Ulemans know how to use pencils, scissors, ruler, paper and glue. However, in opposite to the experts, Uleman craftsmen are specialists with a high division of labor. No Uleman is therefore able to use more than one tool during the project, meaning that every Uleman has to commit himself/herself to one specific tool. Paper does not count as a tool and can be unrestrictedly used by all Ulemans.

Ulemans speak the experts' language but since their own behaviour is natural to them, they are not able to explain it to foreigners. They answer questions concerning their behaviour with "Why?" or "I don't understand that".

During the construction phase, the experts will try to teach you how to build bridges. Remember that even though you are familiar with the usage of the tools, the construction techniques are unfamiliar and you have to learn them first.

List of References

Abbas, A., Islamic Perspectives on Management and Organization, Cheltenham 2005.

Adair, J. Confucius on Leadership, Oxford 2013.

Adelman, M.B., Cross-cultural adjustment: A theoretical perspective on social support. International Journal of Intercultural Relations, 12, 183–204, 1988.

Adler, N. J., International Dimensions of Organizational Behaviour, 2nd ed., Boston 1991.

Adler, N. J./Gundersen, A., International Dimensions of Organizational Behaviour, 5th ed., 2008.

Adler, N.J., A Typology of Management Studies Involving Culture, in: Journal of International Business Studies, Nr. 6/1983.

Adler, N.J., Global Leaders: A Dialogue with Future History. International Management, 1 (2), 21–33. 1997.

Adler, N.J., Re-entry: Managing cross-cultural transitions, in: Group & Organizations Studies, Nr. 6/1981.

Adler, P. A./Adler, P., Constructions of Deviance: Social Power, Context and Interaction. Stamford 2008.

Alcalá, M.A./Vera, S., La gestión internacional de recursos humanos en España., 2003, in web: www.deloitte.org/dtt/cda/doc/content/Estudio%20Expatriados, accessed 19/02/2008.

Allen, D.S. /Jensen, R., Freeing the First Amendment: Critical Perspectives on Freedom of Expression, New York. 1995

Al-Omari, J., Simple Guide to the Arab Way: Practical tips on Arab culture, 2003.

Althaus et al., Voraussetzungen für erfolgreiche Cross-Border Transaktionen – Handelszeitung, 2004.

Althauser, U., Internationales Personal-Management in den Kinderschuhen?, in: Personalwirtschaft, Nr. 7/1996.

Andreff, W. New Perspectives in Sports Economics: A European View. 8th IASE Conference: "New Perspectives in Sports Economics", Bochum, May 4-,6 2006 (2006a)., in web: http://www.holycross.edu/departments/economics/RePEc/spe/Andreff_NewPerspectives.pdf accessed 11/03/2008.

Andreff, W. Economic Globalization of Sport. The New Theory of Economics and Management in Organizations: International Scientific Conference in the University of Economics in Prague October 20th 2006 (2006b), in web: http://www.rdes.it/RDES_3_08_ANDREFF.pdf, accessed 13/03/2008.

Andresen, M./Domsch, M.E, Der internationale Personaleinsatz. In: von Rosenstiel, L./ Regnet, E./ Domsch, M.E. (ed.) Führung von Mitarbeitern: Handbuch für erfolgreiches Personalmanagement, 6th edition. Stuttgart 2009.

Angwin, D., Mergers and Acquisitions across European Borders: National Perspective on Pre-acquisition Due Diligence and the Use of Professional Advisors, Journal of World Business/ 36(1) /32–57, 2001

Annual IMI Conference-Website, The 16th Annual IMI Conference on Incultural Relations, in web: http://www.american.edu/sis/imi/conference/, accessed 31/07/ 2014

Anthony, W. P. et al., Human Resource Management – A Strategic Approach, Boston 2002.

Arent, R., Bridging the Cross-Cultural Gap: Listening and Speaking Tasks for Developing Fluency in English, Michigan, 2009

Aretz, H.-J., Strukturwandel in der Weltgesellschaft und Diversity Management in Unternehmen, in: Becker, M./Seidel, A., Diversity Management. Unternehmens- und Personalpolitik der Vielfalt, Stuttgart 2006.

Asendorpf, D., Der gefeierte Verräter, in: Die Zeit, Nr. 18, 2004.

Bagozzi, R./Rosa, J./Celly, K./Coronel, F., Marketing-Management, München/Wien 2000.

Balz, U./Arlinghaus, O., Das Praxisbuch Mergers & Acquisitions; 1st edition, Landsberg am Lech 2003.

Bantel, K./ Jackson, S., Top management and innovations in banking: does the competition of the top team make a difference?, in. Strategic Management Journal, Nr. 10, 1989.

Barlett, C.A., Building and Managing the Transnational: The New Organizational Challenge, in: Porter, M.E. (Hrsg.), Competition in Global Industries, Boston 1986.

Barmeyer, C., Interkulturelles Management und Lernstile – Studierende und Führungskräfte in Frankreich, Deutschland and Quebec, Campus 2000.

Basham, A.L., The Concise Encyclopedia of Living Faiths, Boston 1967.

Beamer, L./Varner, I., Intercultural Communication in the Global Workplace, 5th edition, New York 2011.

Beck, U., in: Wallacher, J./Au, C./Karcher, T.(ed.), Ethik in Wirtschaft und Unternehmen in Zeiten der Krise. Stuttgart 2011.

Becker, M., Wissenschaftstheoretische Grundlagen des Diversity Managements, in: Seidel, A./Becker, M., Diversity Management – Unternehmens- und Personalpolitik der Vielfalt, Ulm 2006.

Beekun, R.I/Badawi, J., The leadership process in Islam, The International Institute of Islamic Thought 1999.

Beerman, L./ Stengel, M., Werte im interkulturellen Vergleich, in: Bergemann/ Sourisseaux (Hrsg.), Interkulturelles Management, 2. Aufl. Heidelberg 1996.

Behfar, K./Brett, J./Kern, M.C., Managing Multicultural Teams, Harvard Business Review, November 2006.

Bennet, J.M., Interculutral Competence, Developing Intercultural Competence, AIEA Conference, February 22, 2011

Bennet, M.J., Basic Concepts of Intercultural Communication: Selected Readings, Boston 1998.

Bergemann, N./ Sourisseaux, A. L. J [ed.] (2003) Interkulturelles Management, 3rd edition. Berlin/ Heidelberg 2013.

Berkemeier, K./Scholz, W., Ein Businessknigge für China: 2nd ed., Grevenbroich 2006.

Berner, W., Cultural Due Diligence, in : OrganisationsEntwicklung Nr. 1, 2008.

Berniers, C.J.M./Hundt, I., International Business Communication for Industrial Engineers – Bridging the Cultural Gap, München 2004.

Berry, J. W./Kalin, R., Multicultural and ethnic attitudes in Canada: An overview of the 1991 National Survey. Canadian Journal of Behavioral Sciences, 27, 301–320, 1995.

Bertels, U./de Vries, S., Kulturenwechsel – ein ethnologischer Ansatz zur Vermittlung von Interkultureller Kompetenz, in: http://bpb.de/veranstaltungen/PGT7TG,0,0.

Berthier, P./Roger, A., International Mobility: An Opportunity for Managers to Acquire and Transfer Competencies. In: Mayrhofer, U. [ed.] Management of Multinational Companies – A French Perspective. Chippenham/Eastbourne 2013.

Bhagat, R.S./Prien, K.O., Cross-cultural training in organizational contexts, in Lanis D./Bhagat, R.S. (Eds.), Handbook of intercultural training, 2nd edition., pp. 216–230,. Thousand Oaks 1996.

Birchall, D., The new Flexi-Manager, London 1996.

Bittner, A./Reisch, B., Anforderungen an den Auslandsmanager. Erfolgs- und Misserfolgskriterien beim Auslandseinsatz: Forschungsergebnisse, 2006, in web: www.ifim.de, accessed 30/04/2008.

Bittner, A., Interkulturelle Trainingsmethoden, Königswinter 2006.

Bittner, A., Rückkehr aus Penang, in: Institut für Interkulturelles Management (Hrsg.), Presse-Service 2/2002.

Black, J.S, The Relationship of Personal Characteristics with the Adjustment of Japanese Expatriate Managers. Management International Review, 30(2), 119–134, 1990.

Black, J.S./Gregersen, H.B., Antecedents to cross-cultural adjustment for expatriates in Pacific Rim assignments. Human Relation, 44, 497–515, 1991.

Black, J.S., Work Role Transitions: A Study of American Expatriate Managers in Japan. Journal of International Business Studies, 19(2), 277–294, 1988.

Black, J.S./ Mendenhall, A., Cross-cultural Training Effectiveness: A Review and a Theoretical Framework for Future Research, in: Academy of Management Review, Nr. 15,1990.

Black, J.S./Gregersen, H.B., Auslandseinsätze: Was sie erfolgreich macht., Harvard Business Manager, 21, 103–111, 1999.

Black, J.S/ Mendenhall, M.E./Oddou, G., Toward a comprehensive model of international adjustment: An integration of multiple theoretical perspectives, Academy of Management Review, 16(2), 291–317, 1991.

Blazejewski, S./ Dorow, W., Sieben Ansatzpunkte zur kulturellen Integration, in: Bertelsmann Stiftung (Hrsg.), Unternehmenskultur in globaler Interaktion, Ein Leitfaden für die Praxis, Gütersloh 2005.

Bleicher, K., Unternehmenskultur und strategische Unternehmensführung, in: Hahn, D., Taylor, B. (Hrsg.), Strategische Unternehmensplanung – strategische Unternehmensführung, 6. Aufl., 1992.

Blom, H./Meier, H., Interkulturelles Management: interkulturelle Kommunikation, Internationales Personalmanagement, Diversity-Ansätze im Unternehmen. In: H. Meier (Ed), Internationales Management, Herne/Berlin 2002.

Blom, H./Meier, H. (ed.), Interkulturelles Management, 2nd ed.. Herne/Berlin 2004.

Blume, G., Der mörderische Makel Frau, in: Die Zeit, 15.03.2012

Boden, C./Guth, E./Heinze,N./Lang,S., Results of a study on Intercultural Aspects of M&A, Stralsund 2011 (unpublished).

Boecker, M.C./Jäger, M., Intercultural competence: The key competence in the 21st century?: Theses by the Bertelsmann Stiftung based on the models of intercultural competence by Dr. Darla K. Deardorff. (Thesis, Bertelsmann Stiftung, 2006)., in web: http://www.bertelsmann-stiftung.de/cps/rde/xchg/bst/hs.xsl/prj_6903_19268.htm

Böhme, B., Ohne Englisch geht es nicht, in: FAZ, 16./17.Oktober 2011.

Bolman, L.G./Deal, T.E., Modern Approaches to Understanding and Managing Organizations, San Francisco 1984.

Bolten, J., Intercultural Training via E-Learning, in Poznan School of Banking (Hrsg.), International Conference: Opportunities and Threats for Management and Education in the Multicultural Europe, Poznan 2008.

Bolten, J., Interkulturelle Kompetenz im E-Learning, in: Straub, J., Wiedemann, D., (Hrsg.), Handbuch Interkulturelle Kompetenz, Stuttgart 2007.

Bolten, J., Interkulturelle Personalentwicklungsmaßnahmen. In: Stahl, G.K./Mayrhofer, W./Kühlmann, T.M. [ed.] Internationales Personalmanagement: neue Aufgaben, neue Lösungen. München/Mering 2005.

Bolton, J., Aktuelle Beiträge zur interkulturen Kompetenzforschung, in: Intercultural journal, Ausgabe, 12/2010

Bond, M.H., The Psychology of the Chinese People, Oxford 1986.

Böning, U./Fritschle, B., Herausforderung Fusion – die Integration entscheidet, Frankfurt/M. 2001

Borgwardt, H./Frank, L./Stubenrauch, C., The Importance of Intercultural Preparation for small sized Companies, Written Assignment (unpublished), Stralsund 2013.

Borning, A., Vom Spezialisten zum Generalisten, in: Personalführung, Nr. 4, 1996.

Bosch GmbH Bamberg (Hrsg.), Interkulturelles Managementhandbuch, 2006.0

Brzezinski, N., Values-Based Leadership and Empowering Women: Interview With CEO of IKEA Group, Huffington Post Business Online, 20/12/2013, in web: http://www.huffingtonpost.com/natalia-lopatniuk-brzezinski/valuesbased-leadership-em_b_4479389.html, accessed 30/08/2014.

Britt, J., Expatriates want more support from home. HR Magazine, 47(7), pp. 21–22., 2002.

Bromann, P./ Piwinger, M., Gestaltung der Unternehmenskultur, Stuttgart 1992.

Brookfield Global Relocation Services (2012) Global Relocation Trends: 2012 Survey Report, 2012, in webt: http://knowledge.brookfieldgrs.com/content/insights_ideas-2012_GRTS, accessed 26/04/2013.

Buchanan, D./ Boddy, D., The Expertise of the Change Agent, Hemel Hempstead, 1992.

Buliczak, S./Gottschalk, L./Kontny, K./Strehlke, C., Written Assignment, Stralsund 2012 (unpublished).

Bundesagentur für Arbeit, in: Internet: www.ba-auslandsvermittlung.de.

Burggraaf, W., cited in: Rothlauf, J., Interkulturelles Management – Mit Beispielen aus Vietnam, China, Japan, Russland und den Golfstaaten, 4th ed.. München/Wien, 2012.

Burggraaf, W., Intercultural Management, in: Nyenrode University (ed.), June, 1998

Buschermöhle, U., Ein neuer Expatriate – Typus entsteht, in: Personalwirtschaft, 05/00.

Büschges, G./ Abraham, M./ Funk, W., Grundzüge der Soziologie, 2. Aufl., München 1996.

Business Spotlight (Hrsg.), Intercultural Communication, Interview mit Robert Gibson, Nr. 1/2004.

Buttermann, W., „Manager Gehalt", in Hamburger Abendblatt, 05/2005.

Carte, P./ Fox, C., Bridging the culture gap: a practical guide to international business communication, London 2004.

CDC-Website, in web: http://www.cdc.de/accessed 16/07/08

Chapman, A., Tuckman Forming Storming Norming Performing Model, 2001.

Cherry, K., Leadership Styles, In: myweb.astate.edu/bounds/AP/Leadership/Styles, accessed 20/11/2013.

Chhokar, J.S., India: Diversity and Complexity in Action, New Jersey, 2007.

Chouhan, K., Managig Diversity – Can it offer anyting to the delivery of race equality or is it a distraction?,, in: Jung, R./Schäfer, H. M./Seibel, F. W., Vielfalt gestalten – Managing Diversity, 3rd, revised edition, Frankfurt a. M. 2003.

Chouhan, K., Managing Diversity, big business, the UN and Global markets, in: Managing Diversity – Can it offer anything to the delivery of race equality or is it a distraction? London 2002.

Chung, L.C. /Ting-Toomey, S., Understanding Intercultural Communication, 2nd ed., Oxford 2012.

Cihak, H. E., Leadership Roles for Librarians, Buffalo 2007.

Clark, D., Concepts of Leadership, Big Dog & Little Dog's Performance Juxtaposition, 18/11/2013, in web: http://www.nwlink.com/~donclark/leader/leadcon.html#definition, accessed 24/06/2014.

Clemens, S., Interkulturelles Management, in: Wirtschaft und Weiterbildung, Ausgabe 05/98.

Clement, U., Was ist interkulturelle Kompetenz, in: Internet: ww.uteclement.de, 08.07.2002.

Cohen, R., The Rise of Generation Global, In: New York Times, 22nd February 2010.

Colombo,L./Engel, V./Knopf, L./Torregrossa, G., Interview with Prof. Dr. Geert Hofstede, Velp, 2011.

Cooper, J.C., Der Weg des Tao, 4. Aufl., München 1985.

Cox, T. Jr., Creating the Multicultural Organisation: A strategy for Capturing the Power of Diversity, New York 2001.

Cross, E. Y., Managing Diversity – The Courage to Lead, Westport 2000.

Czajor, J., Rekrutierung japanischer Toptalente, in: Personalwirtschaft Nr.1/2004.

DAAD, Living in Germany, www.daad.de.

Dalton, M., Success for the New Global Manager: How to work across distances, Countries, and Cultures, New York 2002.

Danckwortt, D., Anmerkungen zur theoretischen Fundierung der Analyse interkultureller Begegnungen, in: Thomas, A. (Hrsg.), Interkultureller Austausch als interkulturelles Handeln, Saarbrücken 1985.

Dannenberg, L., Taskforce für interkulturelle Mediation – Konfliktlösung in komplexen Zusammenhängen, in: mitteconsult (Hrsg.), Berlin 2004.

Darlington, G., Culture: a theoretical review, in: Joynt, P./Warner, M., Managing Across Cultures, Issues and Perspectives, International Thomson Business Press, London, Boston, 1996.

Darmer/Geigle/Persidska/Sikinger, Written Assignement, Stralsund 2013 (unpublished)

Deardorff, D.K., The Identification and Assessment of Intercultural Competence as a Student Outcome of Internationalization at Institutions of Higher Education in the United States. Journal of Studies in International Education, 10, 241–266, 2006.

Debrus, C., Die Betreuung von Mitarbeitern während des Auslandseinsatzes: Aus der Praxis der Henkel KGaA. 1995b, in Kühlmann, T.M. (Ed.), Mitarbeiterentsendung ins Ausland (pp. 119–141), Göttingen 1995.

Debrus, C., Die Vorbereitung von Mitarbeitern auf einen Auslandseinsatz: Aus der Praxis der Henkel KGaA., 1995a, in Kühlmann, T.M. (Ed.), Mitarbeiterentsendung ins Ausland (pp. 119–141), Göttingen 1995.

Definitions, in web: http://www.definitions.net/definition/chronemics, s.v. "Chronemics", accessed 15/07/2013.

Deloitte & Touche GmbH Wirtschaftsprüfungsgesellschaf, Entsendungsmanagement im Wandel, 2008, in web: http://www.deloittehumancapital.at/wp-content/7-1-global-employer-services_ entsendungs-management-im-wandel.pdf, accessed 19/04/2013.

Der Tagesspiegel (Hrsg.), Ausbildung zum Trainer und Coach für Interkulturelle Kompetenzen 02.04.2006.

Deresky, H., International Management, 3rd ed., New Jersey 2000.

Deresky, H., Managing Across Borders and Cultures, Upper Saddle River 2000.

Deutscher Industrie- und Handelstag (DIHT), Direktinvestitionen in China, ein Handbuch für den Mittelstand, Shanghai 1997.

DGFP e.V., Megatrends: Zukunftsthemen im Personalmanagement analysieren und bewerten, DGFP-PraxisEdition Band 100. Bielefeld 2012.

Dictionary.com, s.v. "Nonverbal communication", in web: http://dictionary.reference.com/browse/nonverbal_communication, accessed 18/07/2013.

Dictionary.com, s.v. "Nonverbal communication", in web: http://dictionary.reference.com/browse/nonverbal_communication, accessed 18/07/2013

Diebel, P., Rollenspiele im Training: Alles andere als Theater, in: managerSeminare, Nr. 74/2004.

Dielmann, K., Fusionen aus personalwirtschaftlicher Sicht, in: Personal Nr. 9/2000.

Dignen, B., Germans are often more direct, Interview with Peter Wollmann, in: Business Spotlight, Nr.4/2001.

Dill, P./Hügler, G., Unternehmenskultur und Führung betriebswirtschaftlicher Organisationen – Ansatzpunkte für ein kulturbewusstes Management, in: Heinen, E., Fank, M. (Hrsg.), Unternehmenskultur, 2nd ed.., 1997.

Dinslaken, M., CampusAnzeiger Berlin, Vol. 14, April/Mai 2006.

DiversityInc., in web: http://diversityinc.com/topic/diversity-management/page/3/, accessed 15/09/2011.

Dometeit, G., Fernsehkonsum nach westlichem Muster, in: Focus, Nr. 21/2006.

Dönhoff, M., Gier nach Beute, Das Streben nach Gewinnmaximierung zerstört die Solidarität, in: Die Zeit, Nr.48/1995.

Dormann, J., Wertemanagement, in: Wieland, J. (Hrsg.), Handbuch Wertemanagement, Hamburg 2004.

Dreblow, J. /Kessler, A., Der neue Atlas der Körpercodes: Wie ich jeden Menschen lesen kann, Welt der Wunder 07/2013.

Drozdova, A./Fritzsche, A./Neubert, J./Korkach, T./Steinfeldt, M., Projektarbeit „Intercultural Training", Stralsund 2007 (unveröffentlicht).

Dülfer, E., Die spezifischen Personal- und Kommunikationsprobleme international tätiger Unternehmen – eine Einführung, Berlin 1983.

Dülfer, E., Internationales Management in unterschiedlichen Kulturbereichen, München 1991.

Dülfer, E., Internationales Management, 2nd ed., München 1992.

Dülfer, E., Internationales Management in unterschiedlichen Kulturbereichen, 3rd ed.., Stuttgart 1996.

Dülfer, E., Zum Problem der Umweltberücksichtigung im „Internationalen Management, in: Pausenberger (Hrsg.),Internationales Management, Stuttgart 1981.

Dülfer, E./Jöstingmeier, B., Internationales Management in unterschiedlichen Kulturbereichen, 7th edition. München/Wien 2008.

Duneka,D.,Ein frohes Jahr 2554!, in: DIE ZEIT, 30.12.2010

Dünnebier, A./Hoffmann, M., Written Assignment, Stralsund, 2012 (unpublished)

ECA International, ECA International veröffentlicht Studie „Managing Mobility 2012" zu Auslands-entsendungen von Arbeitskräften: Gesamtmenge steigt, Frauenanteil wächst, 2012, in web: http://www.eca-international.com/news/press_releases/77 27/?HighlightText=Managing+Mobility +2012#.UXEYUEpqPE0, accessed 30/04/2013.

Eckert, D./ Zschäpitz, H., M&A-Welle erfasst Deutschland, in: Die Welt, 30.03.2004.

Edward, H., Expatriate Managers Learning to go the Distance. Director, December Issue, 2000.

Eisenhardt, K./ Schoonhoven, C., Organizational growth: linking founding team, strategy, environment, and growth among U.S. semiconductor ventures, 1978-1988, in: Administrative Science Quarterly, Nr. 35, 1990.

El Kahal, S., Introduction to International Business, London/New York 1994.

El Mansouri,A./Prestel, L./Samouh, N./Wang, Y., Results of a study on Intercultural Mangement in the Framework of Mergers and Acquisitions, Mulhouse, 2011 (unveröffentlicht).

Elashmawi F./ Harris, P.R., Multicultural Management, New Skills for Global Success, Houston 1993.

Elashmawi, F./ Harris, P., Multicultural Team Building, in: Multicultural Management 2000, Houston 1998.

El-Hidaoui, A/ Fehrenbacher, M./ Kempf, Y./Koegler, M., International Teams – Practical application regarding to the teamwork of OCCAR, Mulhouse, 2008, (unpublished).

Elston, B./ Nguyen Thi Hong Hoa, Vietnamese Sayings, in: Destination Vietnam, July/ August, San Francisico 1997.

Ely, R./Thomas, D., Cultural diversity at work: The moderating effects of work group perspectives on diversity, in: Administrative Science Quarterly, 46, 2001.

Emrich, C., Interkulturelles Management. Stuttgart 2011.

Engelmeyer, E., Identitätsorientierte interkulturelle Personalführung aus gesellschaftstheoretischer Sicht, in: Schoppe, S.G. (Hrsg.), Kompendium der Internationalen Betriebswirtschaftslehre, München 1991.

England, G.W./ Lee, R., The Relationship between Managerial Values and Managerial Success in the US, Japan, India and Australia, in: Journal of Applied Psychology,1978.

Erben, G.S., The relationship between paternalistic and organizational commitment, in: Journal of Business Ethics, Nov. 2008.

Erbert, L. A./Perez, F. G./Gareis, E., Turning points and dialectical interpretations of immigrant experi-ences in the United States, in: Western Journal of Communication, 2003.

Ernst & Young, Global Mobility: Auslandsentsendungen gut geplant. Stuttgart/Frankfurt a.M. 2012.

Ethnologue.com, in web: http://www.ethnologue.com/ethno_docs/distribution.asp?by=size#2, accessed 17/05/2014.

Eubel-Kasper, K., Interkulturelle Kompetenz als strategischer Erfolgsfaktor: Erläutert am Beispiel des Förderkreises, in: Kopper/Kiechl (Hrsg.), Globalisierung – Von der Vision zur Praxis, Zürich 1997.

Eulenburg, N., Die Nachwuchsgeneration der deutschen Industrie zwischen   Karriere, Kulturen und Bildung : eine qualitative Studie zu Karriereverhalten und Auslandsentsendung untersucht am Beispiel des Rückkehr- und Wiedereingliederungsverhaltens unter Berücksichtigung generationsspezifischer Merkmale. (Doctoral dissertation, University Carl von Ossietzky, 2001).
In web: http://docserver.bis.uni-oldenburg.de/publikationen/dissertation/2001/eulnac01/inhalt.html

European Communities (Hrsg.), Decision No 1983/2006/EC, in: Official Journal of the European Un-ion, 30.12.2006.

European Communities (Hrsg.), http://www.interculturaldialogue2008.eu/406.0.html.

Fagan, G., The Emerging Paradigm, in
web:http://arts.brighton.ac.uk/__data/assets/pdf_file/0018/6246/The-Emerging-Paradigm.pdf, accessed 15/09/2011.

Falk, H./ Weiß, J., Die Zukunft der Akademiker, Institut der deutschen Wirtschaft (Hrsg.), Köln 1993.

Fank, M., Ansatzpunkte für eine Abgrenzung des Begriffs Unternehmenskultur anhand der Betrachtung verschiedener Kulturebenen und Konzepte der Organisationstheorie, in: Heinen, E./ Fank, M. (Hrsg.), Unternehmenskultur, 2. Aufl., 1997.

Fanning, D.M., Families in flats. British Medical Journal, 4, pp. 382–386, 1967.

Fay, C., Interkulturelle Kompetenz und Auslandserfahrung, in: Stiftung der Deutschen Wirtschaft (Hrsg.), Jahresbericht 2006.

Fayerweather, J., Begriff der Internationalen Unternehmung, in: Macharzina/Welge (Hrsg.), Handwörterbuch Export und Internationale Unternehmung, Stuttgart 1989.

Festing, M., Strategisches internationales Personalmanagement – Vision oder Realität?, in: Personalwirtschaft, Nr. 2/1997.

Finch H., MERGERS AND ACQUISITIONS, Reference for Business – Encyclopedia of Business, 2nd ed, in web: http://www.referenceforbusiness.com/management/Mar-No/Mergers-and-Acquisitions.html, accessed 25/06/2011.

Finke, M., Diversity Management – Förderung und Nutzung personeller Vielfalt in Unternehmen, 2nd edition, Hampp 2006.

Fischer, H./ Steffens-Duch, S., Wegbereiter einer gelungenen Fusion, in: Personalwirtschaft Nr. 9/2001.

Fischer, M., Es gibt keinen globalen Lifestyle, in: Welt am Sonntag, 2003.

Fischer, M., Ghosn und Nissan: Ein internationales Schulbeispiel, in: Welt am Sonntag, 14.12.2003.

Fisher, C./Lovell, A., Business Ethics and Values, Harlow 2003.

Fitschen, A./Liesching, F., Projektarbeit "The Role and Importance of Expatriates", Stralsund 2004 (unveröffentlicht).

Fitzgerald-Turner, B., Myths of expatriate life. HR Magazine, 42(6), 65–74, 1997.

Flechsig, Interkulturelles und kulturelles Lernen, http://www.gwdg.de/~kflechs/iikdiaps1-97.htm, 11/2001.

Flytzani, S. /Nijkamp, P., Locus of control and cross-cultural adjustment of expatriate managers, 2007, in web: ftp://zappa.ubvu.vu.nl/20070007.pdf, accessed 13/03/2008.

Föhlisch, K./Vieweger, C., Projektarbeit „Intercultural Training", Stralsund 2007 (unveröffentlicht).

Follath, E., „Tigerstaaten": Modell oder Menetekel, in Spiegel „special", Nr. 4/1998.

Fong, R./Furuto, S. (Eds.), Culturally competent social work practice: Skills, interventions and evaluation. Boston 2001.

Fontaine, G., Roles of social support systems in overseas relocation: Implications for intercultural training. International Journal of Intercultural Relations, 10, pp. 361–378, 1986.

Ford, in web: http://www.ford.de/UeberFord/FordinDeutschland/Unternehmenspolitik/Diversity, accessed 17/07/2012

Ford-Werke AG, „Diversity – Vielfalt als Stärke", Brochure, 1st edition 2008.

Friedman, M., Kaddisch vor dem Morgengrauen, Aufbau Verlagsgruppe, Berlin 2007.

Friedrich, R., Managementgrundsätze und das Problem der Kulturenverschiedenheit, in: Der Karriereberater, Nr. 6/1997.

Fritz, J. W iedereingliederung höherer Führungskräfte nach einem Auslandseinsatz. Dissertation, Forschungsstelle für Betriebswirtschaft und Sozialpraxis, Universität Mannheim. Mannheim, 1982.

Fröhlich, W., Auslandseinsatz in Problemländern. Personalführung, 7, 454–458, 1987.

Furkel, D., Hype-Themen haben keinen Platz, in: Personalmagazin, November 2008.

Furkel, D., Vielfältiger, toleranter und ökonomisch erfolgreicher, in: Personalmagazin 07/2008.

Furnham, A., Expatriate Stress: The Problems of living abroad. in Fisher, S./Cooper, C.L. (Eds.), On the move: the psychology of change and transition (pp.275–301), 1990.

Gabler, Wirtschaftslexikon, Wiesbaden 1993.

Gancel, C./ Rodgers, I./ Raynaud, M., Successful Mergers, Acquisitions and Strategic Alliances: How to bridge corporate cultures, New York 2002.

Gardenswartz, L./Rowe, A., Managing Diversity – a Complete Desk Reference and Planning Guide, New York 1998.

Gasser, T.P., Nutzung interner Stärken im Wettbewerb, in: Management Zeitschrift in, 61 Jg., Heft 2, 1992.

Gaugler, E., Repatriierung von Stammhausdelegierten, in: Macharzina/Welge (Hrsg.), Handwörterbuch Export und internationale Unternehmung, Stuttgart 1989.

Gebhard, C., Sprachtempo im Sprachvergleich: Eine Untersuchung phonologiscer und kultureller Aspekte anhand von Nachrichtensendungen, 2012, in web: http://edoc.hu-berlin.de/dissertationen/gebhard-christian-2012-07-18/PDF/gebhard.pdf, accessed 22/07/2013.

Geringer, J.-M., Partner selection criteria for developed country joint venture, in: Business Quarterly, Nr. 53/2.

Gerlitz, P., Die Ethik des Buddha, in: Ratschow, C.H. (Hrsg.), Ethik der Religionen, Stuttgart 1980.

Gertsen, M.C., in: Bolten, J., Interkulturelle Personalentwicklungsmaßnahmen. In: Stahl, G.K./ Mayrhofer, W./ Kühlmann, T.M. [ed.] Internationales Personalmanagement: neue Aufgaben, neue Lösungen. München/Mering 2005.

Gertsen, M.C., in: Festing, M., State of the Art: International Human Resource Management and Cultural Learning. In: Gertsen, M.C.[ed.]/ Søderberg, A.-M.[ed.]/ Zølner, M. [ed.] Global Collaboration: Intercultural Experiences and Learning. Chippenham/Eastbourne, 2012.

Gertsen, M.C., Intercultural Competence and expatriates, in: International Journal of Human Resource Management, 3/1990.

Gertsen, M.C./Søderberg, A.-M. , Expatriation: Stories of Intercultural Face-Work. In: Gertsen, M.C.[ed.]/ Søderberg, A.-M.[ed.]/ Zølner, M. [ed.] Global Collaboration: Intercultural Experiences and Learning. Chippenham/Eastbourne, 2012.

Gesteland, R.R., Cross-Cultural Business Behavior: Marketing, Negotiating, Sourcing and Managing Across Cultures, 3rd edition, Copenhagen 2002.

Gibson, R. Intercultural Business Communication. Oxford 2002.

Gibson, R., Chinese and Germans see time and quality in very different ways, in: Business Spotlight, Nr. 4/2001

Gibson, R., in: Rothlauf, J. Interkulturelles Management – Mit Beispielen aus Vietnam, China, Japan, Russland und den Golfstaaten, 4th ed., München 2012.

Gibson, R./ Tang, Z., Aufbau interkultureller Geschäftskompetenz, in: Rosenstiel, L., Pieler, D., Glas, P. (Hrsg.), Strategisches Kompetenzmanagement: Von der Strategie zur Kompetenzentwicklung in der Praxis, Wiesbaden 2004.

Giddens, A., in: Wallacher, J./Au, C./Karcher, T.(ed.), Ethik in Wirtschaft und Unternehmen in Zeiten der Krise. Stuttgart 2011.

Gillies, J. M., Lektionen in Demut, Business Manager, Lufthansa Exclusive, Nr. 11/2006.

Glasenapp von, H., Die fünf Weltreligionen, München 1996.

Goerdel, H. T., Taking initiative: Proactive management and organizational performance in networked environments, in: Journal of Public Administration Research and Theory, No.16, 2006.

Goldman-Eisler, F., A Comparative Study of two Hesitation Phenomena, 27/05/13, in web: http://www.ipersonic.com/blog_files/Understanding-Paraverbal-Communication.html, accessed 22/07/2013.

Golz, J./Kerwin, S./Rimaite, M., Written Assignment, Stralsund 2013 (unpublished)

Götz, K. (ed.), Managementkonzepte Band 8 – Interkulturelles Lernen/ InterkulturellesTraining, 3rd edition, Munich 2000.

Götz, K. (ed.). Interkulturelles Lernen / Interkulturelles Training, 7th edition. München/Mering 2010.

Greenberg, J., Diversity in the Workplace: Benefits, Challenges and Solutions, 2004, Alpha Measure Inc., in web: http://www.multiculturaladvantage.com/recruit/diversity/Diversity-in-the-Workplace-Benefits-Challenges-Solutions.asp, accessed 15/09/2011.

Greene, S., Ikea sets big Russia presence, in: The Russian Journal, 12.10.2000.

Greipel, P., Strategie und Kultur – Grundlagen und mögliche Handlungsfelder kulturbewußten strategischen Managements, Bern 1988.

Grovewell (Hrsg.), Worldwide Differences in Business Values and Practices: Overview of GLOBE Research Findings, http://www.grovewell.com/pub-GLOBE-dimensions.html, 2005.

Gudykunst, W., Bridging differences: Effectice intergroup communication, Newbary Park, CA. 1991.

Gullahorn, J.T./ Gullahorn, J.E. (1963) An extension of the U-curve hypothesis. Journal of Social Issues, 19, 33–47.

Guimaraes, C., Global Smarts, 2000.

Günther, D./Kerber, A./Laudahn, F./ Wiese, J., Written Assignment, Stralsund, 2010 (unpublished)

Gussmann, B./ Breit, C., Ansatzpunkte für eine Theorie der Unternehmenskultur, in: Heinen, E./ Fank, M. (Hrsg.), Unternehmenskultur, 2nd ed.., München 1997.

Hackmann, S., Organisatorische Gestaltung in der Post Merger Integration – Eine organisatorisch theoretische Betrachtung unterschiedlicher Integrationsansätze. Wiesbaden 2011.

Hall, E.T., Beyond Culture, Anchor Books, New York, 1976.

Hall, E.T., The Silent Language, Westport/Conn. 1959.

Hall, E.T./ Hall, M.R., Understanding Cultural Differences, Intercultural Press, Yarmouth 1990.

Hambrick, D./Davidson, S./Snell, S./Snow, Ch., When Groups Consist of Multiple Nationalities: Towards a New Understanding of the Implications, in: Organization Studies, Issue 2/19, 1998.

Hambrick, D.C./Snow, C.C., Strategic Reward Systems, in: Snow (Hrsg.), Strategy, Organization Design and Human Resource Management, Greenwich 1989.

Hammer, K./Hinterhuber, H., Strategisches Management global, Wiesbaden 1993.

Hanisch, A./Warnke, C., Projektarbeit „Intercultural Training", Stralsund 2008 (unveröffentlicht).

Hann, U., Asienkompetenz – Türöffner für den wachstumsstärksten Markt der Welt, in: Scholz, J. (Hrsg.), Internationales Chance-Management, Stuttgart 1995.

Hanoi International Women's Club (HIWC), Hanoi Guide 2nd. ed., Hanoi 1998.

Haritz, J./ Breuer, K., Computersimulierte und dynamische Entscheidungssituationen als Element der multikulturellen Personalentwicklung, in: Scholz, J. (Hrsg.), Internationales Chance-Management, Stuttgart 1995.

Harold, E./Tobin, S./Birdwhistell, R., in web: http://www.culturalequity.org/alanlomax/ce_alanlomax_profile_birdwhistell.php, accessed 16/07/2013

Harper Collins Publishers: Collins English Dictionary: Complete & Unabridged 10th Edition, New York 2009.

Harris, P.R./ Moran, R.T., Managing Cultural Differences, 3rd ed., Houston Gulf Publishing 1991.

Hart, W. B., Three Levels of Cultural Studies, in: The E-Journal of Intercultural Relations, Nr. 6, 1998.

Harvey, M.G., Repatriation of corporate executives: An empirical study, in: Journal of International Business Studies, Nr. 20/1989.

Harvey, M.G., The executive family: An overlooked variable in international assignments. Columbia Journal of World business, 20, 84–92, 1985.

Hasenstab, M., Interkulturelles Management: Bestandsaufnahme und Perspektiven. Sternenfels/Berlin 1999.

Haslberger, A./Brewster, C. , Towards a taxonomy of expatriate adjustment. , 2005, in web: http://www.ashridge.org.uk/Website/IC.nsf/wFARATT/Towards%20a%20taxonomy%20of%20Expatriate%20adjustment/$file/TaxonomyofExpatAdjustment.pdf, accessed 06/05/2008.

Hauch-Fleck, M., Das asiatische Rätsel, in: Die Zeit, Nr. 27/1998.

Heidemann, K./Steckhan, H./ Rietz, C., Erfolgsfaktor Expatriates, in: Personalwirtschaft, Nr. 1/2004

Heidemann, K./Steckhan, H./ Rietz, C., Kriterien für einen erfolgreichen Auslandsaufenthalt, in: Personalwirtschaft, Nr. 11/2004.

Heinen, E., Unternehmenskultur als Gegenstand der Betriebswirtschaftslehre, in: Heinen/Fank (Hrsg.), Unternehmenskultur, 2. Aufl., München 1997.

Hermann, N., BMW mit Riesenschritten zum „Global Player ", in: Scholz, J. (Hrsg.), Internationales Chance Management, Stuttgart 1995.

Hermann, S., Intercultural Aspects of Mergers and Acquisition in Consideration of the Chinese Market. Norderstedt 2008.

Hermes, L., Individuelle Verschiedenheit, in: karriereführer, Nr. 1, 2006.

Hersey, P., Blanchard, K.H., Management of organizational behaviour, 3rd ed., New York 1977.

Heyne, F., Understanding Paraverbal Communication, in web: http://www.directionservice.org/cadre/section4.cfm#Paraverbal Messages, accessed 22(07/2013.

Hilb, M., Der Weg zum Globalpreneur, in: Personalwirtschaft, Nr. 2/1998.

Hill, C.W. L., . International business: Competing in the global marketplace, 5th ed., New York 2005.

Hillstrom, K., Intercultural Communication Law & Legal Definition, in web: http://definitions.uslegal.com/i/intercultural-communication/, accessed 17/05/2014.

Hirsch, K., Reintegration von Auslandsmitarbeitern. In: Bergemann, N./ Sourisseaux, A. [ed.] Interkulturelles Management, 3rd edition. Berlin/Heidelberg 2003.

Hodge, S., Colors in Asian Culture, Global Smarts: The art of communicating and deal making anywhere in the world, 2000.

Hodgetts, R.M., Modern Human Relations at Work, 8th ed. Houghton, 2002.

Hodgetts, R.M./Luthans, F., International Management, 3rd ed., New York 1997.

Hodgetts, R.M./Luthans, F., International Management, 5th ed., New York 2003.

Hodgetts, R.M. Luthans, F., International Management, 6th ed., New York 2006.

Hodgetts,R.M,/Luthhans, F/Doh, J.P., International Management Culture, Strategy, and Behavior, New York 2006.

Hoecklin, L., Managing Cultural Differences: Strategies for Competitive Advantage, Wokingham 1998.

Hoffmann, L.R./ Maier, N., Quality and acceptance of problem solutions by members of homogeneous and heterogeneous groups, in: Journal of Abnormaland Social Psycholgy, Nr. 62, 1961.

Hofstede, G., Culture's Consequences – International Differences in Work-Related Values, Beverly Hills 1980.

Hofstede, G., Cultures and Organizations, Software of the mind, Intercultural Cooperation and its Importance for Survival, IRIC Institute for Research on Intercultural Cooperation, University of Limburg at Maastricht, NL, McGraw-Hill Companies, New York, London et al., 1997.

Hofstede, G., Cultures and Organizations: Software of the Mind, London 1991.

Hofstede, G., Dimensions of national cultures in fifty countries and three regions, in Deregowski/Dziurawiec/Anis (Hrsg.), Expiscations in Cross-Culture Psychology, Lisse 1983.

Hofstede, G., Interkulturelle Zusammenarbeit – Kulturen, Organisationen, Management, Wiesbaden 1993.

Hofstede, G., Riding the waves of commerce: A test of Trompenaars Model of national culture differences, in: International Journal of intercultural relations, Vol.20, No 2., 96.

Hofstede, G./Hofstede, G.J./Minkov, M., Cultures and organizations: software of the mind: intercultural cooperation and its importance for survival, 3rd edition. 2010.

Holzmüller, H.H., Bedeutung und Instrumente zur Handhabung der kulturellen Heterogenität im internationalen Unternehmensverbund, in: Macharzina/Oesterle (Hrsg.), Handbuch Internationales Management, Wiesbaden 1997.

Holzmüller, H.H., Interkulturelle Konsumentenforschung, in: Macharzina/Welge (Hrsg,.): Handwörterbuch Export und Internationale Unternehmung, Stuttgart 1989.

Hoppe, R., The Global Toothbrush, in: Spiegel Special – International Edition, Nr. 7/2005.

Horsch, J., Auslandseinsatz von Stammhaus-Mitarbeitern: Eine Analyse ausgewählter personalwirtschaftlicher Problemfelder multinationaler Unternehmen mit Stammsitz in der Bundesrepublik Deutschland. Dissertation, Universität Bremen. Bremen 1995.

Horsch, J., Reif fürs Ausland?, in: Personalwirtschaft, Nr. 7/1996.

Hoskisson/Hitt/Ireland, Competing for Advantage, 2004.

House, R.J./ Hanges, P.J./ Javidan, M./ Dorfman, P.W./ Gupt, V. (Hrsg.), Culture, Leadership, and Organizations: The GLOBE Study of 62 Societies, 2004.

Hummel, T. R./Jochmann, W., Beurteilungs- und Erfolgskriterien des Personaleinsatzes im internationalen Personalmanagement, in: Kumar, B. N./Wagner, D., Handbuch des Internationalen Personalmanagements, Verlag C.H. Beck, München 1998.

Hummel, T.R./Zander, E., Schriften zum Internationalen Management: Interkulturelles Management. München/Mering 2005.

Huntington, S. P., Kampf der Kulturen. Die Neugestaltung der Weltpolitik im 21. Jahrhundert, Wien 1996.

Hunziker, R., Die Entwicklung eines integralen und globalen Human Resource Ansatzes in einem neu geschaffenen multikulturellen Konzern (Ascom AG), in: Scholz, J.M. (Hrsg.), Internationales Change-Management, Stuttgart 1995.

Ibrahim, F.A. Effective cross-cultural counseling and psychotherapy: A framework. The Counseling Psychologist, 13, 625–638, 1985..

IFIM-Website, in web: http://www.ifim.de/index.htm, accessed 16/07/08

IKUD-Website,in web: http://www.ikud.de/, 16/07/08

imb Augsburg, Erhebungsmethoden: Interview – Vor- und Nachteile. 2013, in web: http://qsf.e-learning.imb-uni-augsburg.de/node/560, accessed 04/06/2013.

Indrová, T., Spoken, Written and Computer-Mediated Communication: The Language of Online Discussion Forums, in web: http://www.is.muni.cz/th/331015/ff_b/Indrova_Tereza-Spoken_Written _and_Computer-Mediated_Communication.pdf, 2011, accessed 22/07/2013.

INSIGHT Into Diversity, Recruiting Magazine for EOE Employment, in web: http://www.insightintodiversity.com/diversity-issues/599-challenges-of-diversity-in-the-workplace- .html, viewed 15/09/2011.

Institut für Interkulturelles Management, Presse Service: Kinder aufs Ausland vorbereiten Eltern unter-stützen oder Kinder trainieren?2003/3, in web: http://www.ifim.de, accessed 22/02/2008.

Institut für Interkulturelles Management, Presse- Service: Verwirrende Vielfalt: Typen interkultureller Training, 2003/3, in web: http://www.ifim.de, accessed 22/02/2008.

Institut für Interkulturelles Management, Presseberichte Nr. 2/2002.

Institut für Interkulturelles Management, www.ifim.de.

Institut für Personalmanagement, Mit Bachelor und Master nach Europa, Berlin 2004.

Intercultural Management Institute – 5th Annual Conference 2004, in: American University, Washing-ton, DC (ed.), Conference Brochure, March 11&12, 2004.

Irving, T. B./ Ahmad, K./ Ahsan, M.M., The Qur'an. Basic Teachings, Leicester 1979.

Isaacson, W., Steve Jobs, New York 2011

Jablonski, H. W., Die Organisation des Diversity Managements: Aufgabeneines Diversity-Managers, in: Becker, M./Seidel, A., Diversity Management. Unternehmens- und Personalpolitik de Vielfalt, Stuttgart 2006.

Jack, A., Russian giant looks westward for leadership, in: Financial Times, 11.02.2004.

Jacob, N., Intercultural Management, 1st ed., London 2003.

Jahns, C., Arbeitsbuch Mergers & Acquisitions, Verlag Wissenschaft und Praxis, 2003.

Jahrmarkt, M., Das TAO Management, Freiburg 1991.

Jandt, F.E., An Introduction to Intercultural Communication: Identities in a Global Community, 6th edition, Thousand Oaks 2013.

Jassawalla, A./ Connolly, T./ Slojkowski, L., Issues of Effective Repatriation: A Model and Managerial Implications. SAM Advanced Management Journal, 69 (2), 38–46, 2004.

Jedrzejczyk, P., Multikulturelle Teams in Organisationen: eine experimentelle

Jehn, K.A., Rispens, S., ,"Conflicts in Workgroups", in The SAGE Handbook of Organizational Behavior: Volume One: Micro Approaches, Barling/Cooper 2008.

Jochmann, W., Unternehmenskultur und Internationalität, in: Scholz, J.M. (Hrsg.), Internationales Change-Management, Stuttgart 1995.

John, M.T./Roberts, D.G. Cultural Adaptation in the Workplace. New York, 1996.

Joseph, C., Advantages of an Autocratic Leadership Style, Houston Chronical Online, in web: http://smallbusiness.chron.com/advantages-autocratic-leadership-style-2980.html, accessed 25/06/2014.

Jung, R. H.,: Vielfalt gestalten – Managing Diversity, Koblenz 2003.

Jung, R. H.: Diversity Managemet – Der Umgang mit Vielfalt als Managementaufgabe, in: Jung, R. H./ Schäfer, H. M/Seibel, F. W.,Vielfalt gestalten – Managing Diversity, 3rd, revised edition, Frankfurt a. M. 2003.

Kakar, S., et al.: Leadership in Indian Organizations from a Comparative Perspective,in: International Journal of Cross Cultural Management, Vol. 2, 2002.

Kals, U., Besuch-Anordung-Entsendung, in: FAZ, 11.11.2002.

Kals, U., Schnuppertage minimieren das Risiko, in: FAZ, 11.11.2002.

Kaminura, K., Kulturelle Unterschiede und Chancengleichheit, in: Personalführung, Nr. 8/1995.

Kandola, R., Managing Diversity: New Broomor Old Hat?, in: International Review of Industrial and Organizational Psychology, Vol.10, 1995.

Kandola, R./ Fullerton, J., Diversity in Action: Managing the Mosaic, 2nd ed., London 1998.

Kandola, R./Fullerton, J., Managing the Mosaic. Diversity in Action, London 1994.

Kasper, H., Organisationskultur: über den Stand der Forschung, Wien 1987.

Kealey, D., The challenge of international personnel selection, in Landis D./Bhagat, R. (Eds.), Handbook of intercultural training (2nd ed., pp.81–105), Thousand Oaks 1996.

Kealey, D.J./ Ruben, B.D., Cross-cultural personnel selection: Criteria, issues and methods, in: Landis/Brislin (Hrsg.), Handbook of intercultural training, New York 1983.

Keller, E., Management in fremden Kulturen – Ziele Ergebnisse und methodische Probleme der kultur-vergleichenden Managementforschung, Bern 1982.

Keller, H-J., Systematische Personalauswahl, Vorbereitung, Betreuung und Reintegration bei der Mit-arbeiterentsendung ins Ausland. NORD-SÜD aktuell, 2, 320–330, 1998.

Kelly, J., Merger & Acquisition Integration – A KPMG Business Guide, London 2003.

Kelly, J., Mergers & Acquisitions: Global Research Report, London 1999.

Kenter, M.E./ Welge, M.K., Die Reintegration von Stammhausdelegierten. Ergebnisse einer explorati-ven empirischen Untersuchung, in: Dülfer (Hrsg.), Personelle Aspekte im internationalen Management, Berlin 1983.

Kiechl, R., Ethnokultur und Unternehmenskultur, in: Lattmann, C. (Hrsg.), Die Unternehmenskultur: ihre Grundlagen und ihre Bedeutung für die Führung der Unternehmung, Heidelberg 1990.

Kiechl, R., Interkulturelle Kompetenz, in: Kopper/Kiechl (Hrsg.), Globalisierung: Von der Vision zur Praxis, Zürich 1997.

Kifayat, A., 6th Silk Road International Conference "Globalization and Security in Black and Caspian Seas Region": Intercultural Nonverbal Communication, 2011, in web: http://silkroad.ibsu.edu.ge/previous/sixth/7_05.pdf, accessed 18/07/2013

Kippenberger, T., Leadership Styles, Oxford 2002

Kirton, G., The costs and opportunities of doing iversity work in mainstream organizations, in: Human Resource Management Journal, Vol. 19, No. 2, 2009.

Klemm, M. Popp, M., „…Ich hatte n heftigen Kulturschock, als ich zurückkam": Wissensvermittlung und Kulturbegegnung im internationalen Führungskräfteeinsatz. In: Pries, L./Bosowski, C. (ed.) Europäische Automobilindustrie am Scheideweg: Harte globale Herausforderungen und weiche lokale Erfolgsfaktoren. München/Mering 2006.

Kluckhohn, C., The study of culture, in: Lerner/Larswell, The Policy Studies, Stanford 1951.

Kluckhohn, F./Strodtbeck, F.L., Variations in Value Orientations, Evanston/IL. 1961.

Kluth,S./Linke, J/Walter, H., Assignment on "Intercultural Training – Focussing on Intercultural Preparation", Stralsund, 2009 (unveröffentlicht)

Koall, I., Managing Diversity: Ansätze und Zumutungen zum Umgang mit Vielfalt in der Organisation, Munich 2004.

Koch, E., Interkulturelles Management. Konstanz/München 2012.

Koester, J./Wiseman, R.C./Sanders, J.A., Multiple Perspectives of Intracultural Communication Competence, in: Wiseman/Koester (Hrsg.), International Communication Competence, Newburg Park, C.A. 1993.

Koh, J., Diversity in our Workforce, in: Siemens AG – Corporate Values, 2006.

Kolbin, C./ Wormsbächer, J., Written Assignment – Role Play, Stralsund, 2006 (unpublished),

Kopper, E., Multicultural Workgroups and Project Teams, in: Bergeman, N. (Hrsg.), Interkulturelles Management, Heidelberg 1992.

Kopper, E., Was ist Kulturschock und wie gehe ich damit um? In Kopper, E./Kiechl, R. (Ed.), Globalisierung- Von der Vision zur Praxis: Methoden und Ansätze zur Entwicklung interkultureller Kompetenz (pp. 32–43). Zürich 1997.

Korth, L.-M./Schlabritz, C./Segger, J./Wegner, G., Leading across different countries – with examples form Russia, China, Japan, Germany, USA, India and the UAE" (unpublished assignment) , Stralsund, 2014

Koteswari, V.B./Bhattacharya, M.S., Managing Expatriate Stress. Delhi Business Review, 8(1), pp. 89–98., 2007

Kothari, V./Helling, A., Internationales Management Training der Henkel-Gruppe – Geschichte, Erfahrungen und Visionen, in: Scholz, J.M. (Hrsg.), Internationales Change-Management, Stuttgart 1995.

Kotler, P., Globalization – Realities and Strategies, in: Die Unternehmung, 44 Jg., Nr. 2, Bern 1990.

Kovacova, M., Komparative Evaluation kulturspezifischer didaktischer und erfahrungsorientierter interkulturellen Trainings, Europäische Hochschulschriften (Hrsg.), Frankfurt/M 2010

Krell, G., Chancengleichheit durch Personalpolitik – Gleichstellung von Frauen und Männern in Unternehmen und Verwaltungen, Rechtliche Regelungen – Problemanalysen – Lösungen, Wiesbaden 1998.

Kroeber, A. L./ Kluckhohn, L., Culture. A Critical Review of Concepts and Definitions, Cambridge, Mass. 1952.

Kroeber-Riehl, W., Konsumentenverhalten, München 1996.

Krulis-Randa, J., Globalisierung, in: Die Unternehmung, 44 Jg., Nr. 2, Bern 1990.

Krystek , U., Unternehmenskultur und Akquisition, in: Zeitschrift für Betriebswirtschaft, Heft 5/1992.

Krystek, U./Zur, E., Unternehmenskultur, Strategie und Akquisition, in: Krystek/Zur (Hrsg.), Internationalisierung. Eine Herausforderung für die Unternehmung, Heidelberg 1997.

Kühlmann, T. M., Auslandseinsatz von Mitarbeitern. Göttingen 2004.

Kühlmann, T.M., Internationales Personalmanagement: neue Aufgaben, neue Lösungen. München/Mering 2005.

Kühlmann, T.M., Mitarbeiterentsendung ins Ausland: Auswahl, Vorbereitung, Betreuung und Wiedereingliederung. Göttingen 1995.

Kühlmann, T.M./Stahl, G.K., Die Wiedereingliederung von Mitarbeitern nach einem Auslandseinsatz: Wissenschaftliche Grundlagen, in: Kühlmann (Hrsg.), Mitarbeiterentsendung ins Ausland, Göttingen 1995.

Kühlmann, T.M./Stahl, G., Anforderungen an Mitarbeiter in internationalen Tätigkeitsfeldern. DGFP Personalführung, 11, 44–55., 1998.

Kühlmann, T.M/Stahl, G.K., Diagnose interkultureller Kompetenz und Examinierung eines Assessment Centers, in: Barmeyer/Bolten (Hrsg.), Interkulturelle Personalorganisation, Berlin 1998.

Kumar, B. N., Konzeptioneller Rahmen, in: Kumar, B. N./Wagner, D., Handbuch des Internationalen Personalmanagements, Verlag C.H. Beck, München 1998.

Kumar, B.N., Interkulturelle Managementforschung. Ein Überblick über Ansätze und Probleme, in: Wirtschaftswissenschaftliches Studium, Nr. 17, 1988.

Kumar, R., Essays on Ancient India, New Delhi 2003.

Kumbruck,C./Derboven,W., Interkulturelles Training, Heidelberg 2005.

Kutschker, M., Internationalisierung der Unternehmensentwicklung, in: Macharzina/Oesterle (Hrsg.) Handbuch Internationales Management Wiesbaden 1997.

Kutschker, M/Schmid, S., Internationales Management, 6th ed.., München 2008.

Kutschker, M/Schmid, S., Internationales Management, München 2002.

Kwintessential Ldt., Intercultural Team Building,in web: http://www.kwintessential.co.uk/culturalservices/ articles/intercultural-teambuilding.html, accessed 14./5/2012.

Kwintessential, China – Language, Culture, Customs and Etiquette, in web: http://www.kwintessential.co.uk/resources/global-etiquette/china-country-profile.html, accessed 22/07/2013.

Kwintessential, http://kwintessential.couk/cultural-services.html.

Kwintessential, www.kwintessential.co.uk.

Labovitz, G.H., Managing the personal side of the personnel move abroad. SAM Advanced Management Journal, 42 (3), 26–39, 1977.

Ladwig, D.H./ Loose, K., Bestimmungsfaktoren und Lösungsansätze der Reintegrationsproblematik von Mitarbeitern nach einem Aufenthalt im arabischen Ausland, Institut für Personalwesen und Internationales Management (Hrsg.), Forschungsbericht der Universität der Bundeswehr Hamburg, Nr. 21/1998.

Landis, D./Bennett, J./Bennett, M., Handbook of Intercultural Training, 2rd ed., Thousand Oaks 2004.

Lane, H.W./ DiStefano, J.J., International Behavior. From Policy to Practice, Scarborough/Ontario 1988.

Laurent, A., The cultural diversity of western conceptions of management, in: International Studies of Management and Organization, 13/1-2, 1983.

Layes, G., Interkulturelles Lernen und Akkulturation, in: Thomas, A./Kinast/E.U./Schroll-Machl, S. (Eds.), Handbuch Interkulturelle Kommunikation und Kooperation (vol.1, pp. 126–137.). Göttingen 2003.

Lazarus, R.S./Folkman, S., Stress, Appraisal and Coping. New York 1984.

Lee Chang-sup, Konfucian Management at Hyundai, in: Korea Times, 28.03.2001.

Lehmann, R., Verschieden sind wir stark, in: Handelsblatt, 05.11.2006.

Leonard, J./Levine, D., The Effect of Diversity on Turnover: A large Case Study, in: Industrial and Labour Relations Review, Vol. 59, No.4, 2006.

Levitt, T., The globalization of markets, in: Harvard Business Review, 61 Bd., May/June, Boston 1983.

Lewis, R., When cultures collide: Leading across cultures, 3rd ed., London/Boston 2006.

Lindecke, C., Frauen und andere Minderheiten. Zur Entstehung und Konkretisierung der US-amerikanischen Gleichstellungsregelungen zugunsten von Frauen und zur Frage eines möglichen Transfers auf die BRD, Munich 1995.

Linzer, U., Stimmt so!, in: Die Zeit, 17.12.2008.

Lippisch, S./Köppel, P., Key to Company's competitiveness: The Ability to Innovate and Cooperate on a Global Level, in: Bertelsmann Stiftung (Hrsg.), Globalization and Change, Gütersloh 2007.

Lippisch, S./Spilker, M., Globalisierung, in: Bertelsmann Stiftung (Hrsg.), Unternehmenskultur in globaler Interaktion, Ein Leitfaden für die Praxis, Gütersloh 2005.

Llopis, G., Diversity Management is the Key to Growth: Make It Authentic. Forbes Online, in web: http://www.forbes.com/sites/glennllopis/2011/06/13/diversity-management-is-the-key-to-growth-make-it-authentic/, accessed 13/11/2011.

Loewenthal, N.P./Snedden, N.L., Managing the overseas assignment process. The bridge, pp. 41–43, 14-15, 1981.

Löwe, B., Kulturschock Russland, Bielefeld 2002.

Luthans, F., Value Differences and Similarities across Cultures, in: Luthans/Hodgetts (Hrsg.), International Management, 3. Aufl., New York, 1997.

Lynch, E.W./Hanson, M.J. , Developing cross-cultural competence: A guide for working with children and families. Pacific Grove 1998..

Lynn, L. E. et al., Improving governance. A new logic for empirical research, Washington, 2001.

Macharzina, K., Internationalisierung und Organisation, in: Zeitschrift für Organisation und Führung, 1992.

Macharzina, K./ Oesterle, M.-J., Das Konzept der Internationalisierung im Spannungsfeld zwischen praktischer Relevanz und theoretischer Unschärfe, in: Macharzina/Oesterle (Hrsg.), Handbuch Internationales Management, Wiesbaden 1997.

Maisch, M., Lloyds TSB übernimmt HBOS, in: http://www.handelsblatt.com/unternehmen/ banken-versicherungen/lloyds-tsb-uebernimmt-hbos;2041788, 18.09.2008.

managerSeminare.de, Petersberger Trainerstage 2012: Life Achievement Award, unter: http://www.managerseminare.de/Petersberger_Trainertage/Programm?subKatID=12083&kat=12078, 2012.

Manusov, V., The Sourcebook of Nonerbal Measures: Going Beyond Words, Taylor & Francis e-Library, 2009

Martin, D.C./Anthony, J.J., The Repatriation and Retention of Employees: factors leading to Successful Programs. International Journal of Management, 23 (3), 620–631, 2006.

Martin, J.N./Nakayama, T.K., Intercultural Communication in Contexts, 5th ed. New York 2010.

Marurano, A., Leadership: The Key Concept, New York 2008.

Matthews, S., Trends in Managing Mobility, in: Personalwirtschaft, 07/2007.

Maucher, H.O., Anforderungen an eine Führungskraft, in: Rothlauf, J., Total Quality Management, 2. Aufl., 2004.

Mauritz, H., Interkulturelle Geschäftsbeziehungen: Eine interkulturelle Perspektive für das Marketing, Wiesbaden 1996.

Mawdudi, A.A., Towards Understanding Islam, Lahore 1960.

Mayer, B. Innovation und Unternehmenskultur. Die Hilti AG fördert weltweit Kommunikation und Teamfähigkeit, in: Personalwirtschaft, Nr. 2/1998.

McEvoy, G.M./Parker, B., Expatriate Adjustment: Causes and Consequences. In Selmer, J. (Ed.), Expatriate Management: New Ideas for International Business (pp.97–114). Westport 1995.

McEwan, T., Managing Values and Beliefs in Organisations, Harlow 2001.

McGrath, J.E./Altman, I., Small Group Research, New York 1966.

McGregor, D., The Human Side of Enterprise, New York 1960.

McNulty, Y., The Trailing Spouse: Barrier to Mobility or International Asset? Seminar presentation at the City University of New York, USA, 16/02/ 2005. in web: http://webusers.anet-chi.com/~smcnulty/docs/Trailing%20Spouse%20Presentation%20-%20FIGT%20March%202004.pdf, accessed 19/02/2008.

Meenakshi, Short Essay on Leadership, in web: http://www.preservearticles.com/2012021323091/short-essay-on-leadership.html, accessed 24/06/2014.

Meffert, K., Implementierungsprobleme globaler Strategien, in: Welge, M.K.: Globales Management, Stuttgart 1990.

Mehrabrian, Elements of Communication, 1976.

Meier, H./Roehr, S., Einführung in das internationale Management, Herne/Berlin 2004.

Meier, K. J./O'Toole, L. J., Managerial strategies and behavior in networks: A model with evidence from U.S. public education, in: Journal of Public Administration Research and Theory, No. 11, 2001.

Meier-Dörzenbach, C., Die erfolgreiche Reintegration von Expatriates: Motivationale und organisationale Einflussfaktoren. Hamburg 2008.

Mendenhall, M.E./Oddou, G.R., The overseas assignment: A practical look, Business Horizons, 31, 78–84, 1999.

Menis, F, Der Auslandseinsatz als interkulturelle Personalentwicklungsmaßnahme. Göttingen 2009.

Merkens, H., Branchentypische und firmentypische Wertvorstellungen in Unternehmenskulturen, in: Dürr, W. (Hrsg.), Stuttgart 1989.

Merrill Lynch, Bank of America Buys Merrill Lynch, Creating Unique Financial Services Firm, in: Press Release, 15.09.2008, http://www.ml.com/index.asp?id=7695_7696_8149_88278_106886_108117&WT.ac=US_bankofamerica_ml_200809.

Mesmer-Magnus, J.R./Viswesvaran, C., Expatriate Management: A Review and Directions for Research in Expatriate Selection, Training, and Repatriation. In: Harris, M. M. [ed.] Handbook of Research in International Human Resource Management. New York 2008.

Messmer, W., Working with India, Heidelberg 2009

Metro Group, METRO Group verkauft Extra, in: Pressemitteilung, 17.01.2008, http://www.metrogroup.de/servlet/PB/menu/1150610_ll/index.htm.

Michahelles, R., So sollten Führungs- und Nachwuchsführungskräfte, Unternehmer und Chefs auf den Auslandseinsatz vorbereitet werden, in: Der Karriereberater, Nr. 6/1997.

Michel, L., Digitales Lernen. Forschung – Praxis –Märkte, Berlin 2006.

Mind Tools, Cross-Culture Communication, in web: http://www.mindtools.com/CommSkll/Cross-Cultural-communication.htm, accessed 20/07/2013.

Mirow, M., Entwicklung internationaler Führungsstrukturen, in: Macharzina/Oesterle (Hrsg.), Handbuch Internationales Management, Wiesbaden 1997.

Mobley, W.H./Wang, L./Fang, K., Organizational Culture. Measuring and developing it and your organization, in: Harvard Business Review, Nr. 3/2005.

Mohn, L., Internationalisierung, in: Bertelsmann Stiftung (Hrsg.), Unternehmenskultur in globaler Interaktion, Ein Leitfaden für die Praxis, Gütersloh 2005.

Mohn, R., Werte, in: Bertelsmann Stiftung (Hrsg.), Change, 3/2008.

Mor Barak, M. E., Managing Diversity. Toward a Globally Inclusive Workplace, Thousand Oaks 2005.

Morrison, T.,/Conaway, W. A./Borden, G. A., Kiss, Bow and Shake Hands – How to Do Business in Sixty Countries, Holbrook, 1994.

Mruk-Badiane, A., Kommunikationstraining: Grundlagen der Kommunikation, in web: http://files.schulbuchzentrum-online.de/onlineanhaenge/files/45070100_kommunikation.pdf, 1/ 2007, accessed 22/07/2013.

Munro, D./Schumaker, J. F./Carr, S. C., Motivation and Culture, Routledge 1997.

myBusinessProcess-Website, 04/02/2012, in web: http://www.mybusinessprocess.net/the-communication-process, accessed 17/05/2014.

Nardon, L. / Sanchez-Runde, C.J. / Steers, R.M., Management Across Cultures: Challenges and Strategies, New York 2010

National Association of Independent Schools. Diversity and Multiculturalism: http://www.nais.org/Articles/Pages/Diversity-and-Multiculturalism-147595.aspx, accessed 15/09/2011.

o. V., Karriere ist Hauptmotiv für Umzug ins Ausland, in: Beruf und Karriere, Süddeutsche Zeitung, 26./27.07.2008.

o.V., Auszug von einem Interview mit G. Cromme,dem Aufsichtsratvorsitzenden von Siemens, in: FAZ, 27.05.2007.

o.V., Fremde Fahrräder, in: Die Welt, 18.07.2007.

o.V., The Economist, "Love is in the air", February 5th – 11th, 2005.

o.V., Vorbereitungsmaßnahmen im Hinblick auf einen Auslandseinsatz, in: Personalwirtschaft 7/2002.

Obama, B., Values, in: The Audacity of Hope, New York 2006.

Oberg, K., Culture shock: Adjustment to new cultural environments. Practical Anthropologist, 7, 177–182, 1960.

Odrakiewicz, P.P./Zator-Peljan, H., Innovative Methods of Cultural, Intercultural and Managerial Competences Acquisition for the Constantly Changing Global Econmy in a New Paradigm Shift. Global Management Journal, 1 (2), 127–137, 2012.

Owens, M., In: Bloomberg Businessweek, October 4 – October 10, 2010

Oxford Dictionaries, s.v. "Haptic", in web, accessed 11/07/2013

Oxford Dictionaries, s.v. "Kinesics", in web, accessed 11/07/2013

Oxford Dictionaries, s.v. "Posture", in web, accessed 17/07/2013

Oxford Dictionaries, s.v. "Proxemics", in web, accessed 11/07/2013.

Page, S., Making the Difference: Applying a Logic of Diversity, in: Academy of Management Perspectives, November 2007, p.6 – 20.;

Pascale, R.T./ Athos, A.G., The art of Japanes Management, Harmondsworth 1981.

Paus, B., Studie von Mercer Human Resource Consulting zeigt: Auslandsentsendungen nehmen zu, 2006, in web: http://www.mercer.de/summary.jhtml?idContent=1240040, accessed 11/02/2008.

Pausenberger, E., Unternehmensakquisitionen und strategische Allianzen, in : Fischer, G. (Hrsg.), Marketing, Loseblatt-Ausgabe, Nr. 6; Landsberg 1992.

Pavkovic, G., Interkulturelle Teamarbeit – Wozu multikulturell zusammengesetze Teams?, in web: http://ww.bqnet.de/content/0/1060/1072/2859/2869/649_Pavkovic_InterkulturelleTeamarbeit.pdf, accessed 11/05/ 2012.

Pease, A. /Pease, B., The Definitive Book of Body Language, New York/Bantam 2004.

Peltonen, T./Ladwig, D. (2005) Repatriierung und Identitätsbildung. In: Stahl, G.K./ Mayrho-fer, W./

Perlitz, M., Internationales Management, 2nd edition. Stuttgart 1995.

Perlmutter, H., L'Enterprise International. Trois Conceptions, in: Revue Economique Sociale, 23 Jg., Nr. 2/1965.

Personalwirtschaft (Hrsg.), Neues Tool prüft die interkulturelle Kompetenz, Heft 8, 2003.

Peters, T.J./Waterman, R.H., In search of excellence, New York 1982.

Phatak, A., International Management. Concepts and Cases, Cincinnati, Ohio 1997.

Pinzler, P., Moral statt Markt, in: Die Zeit, Nr. 49/1994.

Pitts, D. W. et al., What drives the implementation of Diversity Management Programs? Evidence from Public Organizations, in: Journal of Public Administration Research and Theory, Vol. 20, 2010.

Plett, A., Einbeziehung von Kindern in die interkulturelle Vorbereitung, in: Rothlauf, J. (Hrsg.), 14th International Baltic Sea Forum: A Global View on Intercultural Management, Stralsund 2009.

Plett, A./ Franz, L., Cross-Cultural Team-Building Scale, in: mitte consult, Berlin 2004.

Pollack, A., Roche Agrees to Buy Genentech for $46.8 Billion, in: http://www.nytimes.com/2009/03/13/business/worldbusiness/13drugs.html?em, 12.03.2009.

Porter, M.E., Wettbewerbsstrategie, Frankfurt/M. 1992.

Posth, M., 1000 Tage in Shanghai, München 2006.

Pounds, S., Great Wall? Firm eyes great bridge, in: The Herald, Miami, 01/03/2004.

Preuss, S., Der Geradlinige – Bosch-Geschäftsführer Bernd Bohr ist ein harter, aber zuverlässiger Verhandlungspartner, in: FAZ, 21.07.2006.

PricewaterhouseCooper, Survey of Key Trends in European Expatriate Management, 2000, in web: www.pwc.com, accessed 15/05/2008.

Pride, W.M./ Hughes, R.J., Kapoor, J.R., Business, 7th ed., Boston 2002.

PROFIO-Forschungsteam (Hrsg.), Kompetenzen, die bei internationalen Organisationen notwendig sind, in: Professionelle Ausbildung für internationale Organisationen – Abschlusskonferenz im Auswärtigen Amt Berlin, 22/23.06.2006.

Prove Unternehmensberatung GmbH: Neue Blickwinkel, in web: http://www.diversityworks.at/neue-blickwinkel/, accessed 17/08/2011.

Pruzan, P., Rational, Ethical and Spiritual Perspectives on Leadership, Bern 2009.

Puck, J. F., Kulturelles Training für Teams. In: Personal Heft 11/2006, pp. 18–20, 2006.

Pugh, D. S./ Hickson, D.J., Writers on Organizations, 4[th]ed. Nembury Park 1989.

Rabinowitz, P., Leadership and Management: Chapter 13. Orienting Ideas in Leadership: Section 6. Recognizing the Challenges of Leadership, in web: The Community Tool Box, http://ctb.ku.edu/en/table-of-contents/leadership/leadership-ideas/leadership-challenges/main, accessed 29/06/2014

Ralston, D.A./Terpstra, R.H./Cunniff, M.K./Gustafson, D.A., Do Expatriate Managers Change their Behaviors to Fit a Foreign Culture?: A study of American Expatriates' Strategies of Upward Influence. Management International Review, 35, 109–122, 1995.

Rampersad, A., Culture as a Mitigating Factor in the Perception of Path-goal Leadership Styles and Workgroup Effectiveness, Ann Arbor 2009.

Rapaille, C., Der Kultur Code, München 2006.

Rapp, T., Interkulturelles Management: Zwischen Anpassung an fremde Kulturen und Standardisierung. In: Künzel, H.[ed.] Handbuch Kundenzufriedenheit – Strategie und Umsetzung in der Praxis. Berlin/Heidelberg 2005.

Ratiu, I., International Consulting News, in: Managing Cultural Differences, 3rd ed. Houston, 1991.

Reardon, M., Verizon completes Alltel purchase, in: http://news.cnet.com/verizon-completes-alltel-purchase/, 09.01.2009.

Reineke, R./Fussinger, C., Interkulturelles Management – Konzeption – Beratung – Training, Wiesbaden, 2001.

Reineke, R., Akkulturation von Auslandsakquisitionen. Eine Untersuchung zur unternehmenskulturellen Anpassung, Wiesbaden 1989.

Renard, J., The Handy Religion Answer Book, New York 2002.

Reuters, Jung, Frau, Asiatin, in: FAZ, 08./09.11.2008.

Richmond, Y., From Nyet to Da: Understanding the Russians, Yarmouth 1992.

Riggio, R.E, Cutting-Edge Leadership, in: Psychology Today, October 7, 2012.

Robert Bosch India Limited, Behaviour, Intercultural, CIP and Leadership Programs & Offerings – Enhancing Competencies, 2006.

Rocher, G., Introduction à la sociologie générale, Montréal 1969.

Rodgers, G., What to Expect in China – Dealing with Culture Shock, in web: http://goasia.about.com/od/Customs-and-Traditions/tp/China-Culture-Shock.htm, accessed 10/09/2014.

Rodin, B., Managing the complex world of mobility, 2012, in web: http://www.eca-international.com/news/articles/7718/Managing_the_complex_world_of_mobility?HighlightText=Managing+Mobility+2012#.UXE8c0pqPE1, accessed 19/04/2013.

Roetzel, B., Stil zeigen bis ins Detail, in: Capital, Nr. 20/2003.

Rokeach, M., The Nature of Human Values, New York 1973.

Ronen, S./ Kraut, E., Similarities among Countries, New York 1977.

Ronin, K., How to exchange Business cards in Japan and China, 28/02/2013, in web: http://executive-impressions.com/blog/?p=154, accessed 22/07/2013.

Root III, G.N., The Advantages of Participative Leadership, Houston Chronicle Online, in web: smallbusiness.chron.com/advantages-participative-leadership-17629.html, accessed 25/06/2014

Rosken, A., "Diversity erfolgreich implementieren", in: Personalmagazin, January 2011.

Rosken, A., Diversity und Profession, Wiesbaden 2009.

Rothlauf, J., Seminarunterlagen, 2005

Rothlauf, J. ,(Hrsg.), 14th International Baltic Sea Forum: A Global View on Intercultural Management, Stralsund 2009.

Rothlauf, J., Interkulturelles Management, 2. Aufl., München 2006.

Rothlauf, J., Allah sieht alles, in: Personalwirtschaft Nr. 5/1995.

Rothlauf, J., Das Wettrudern, in: Seminarunterlagen, Stralsund 2005.

Rothlauf, J., Geschäftsfreunde auf der arabischen Halbinsel: Wie man sie gewinnt und behält, in: Karriereberater Nr. 6/1997.

Rothlauf, J., Intercultural Management at German Universities, Stralsund, 2007.

Rothlauf, J., Interkulturelle Personalführung im religiösen Kontext: Eine Herausforderung für den Auslandsmanager, in: Fachhochschule Mainz (Hrsg.), Update 7 WS 08/09, Mainz 2008.

Rothlauf, J., Interkulturelles Management, München 1999.

Rothlauf, J., Interkulturelles Management, 4th edition, München 2012.

Rothlauf, J., Interview am 11.04.2008 mit Rüdiger Baumann von BR-alpha zu Fragen des Interkulturellen Managements, in: www.br-online.de/br-alpha/alpha-forum.

Rothlauf, J., Multicultural Management Insights with a specific focus on Multicultural Teams, Pau, 2009.

Rothlauf, J., Multicultural Management Insights, in: Kloss, I. (Hrsg.), More Advertising Worldwide, Berlin 2002.

Rothlauf, J., Projektunterlagen, Stralsund, 2007.

Rothlauf, J., Qualifizierte Nachwuchskräfte für das Auslandsgeschäft, in: WIR, hrsg. v. der IHK Rostock, Nr. 6/1996.

Rothlauf, J., Seminarunterlagen, 2013

Rothlauf, J., Total Quality Management, 2nd ed,. München 2004.

Rothlauf, J., Vortrag bei der ITB, Berlin 2003.

Rühl, I., Ein Benimm-Guide für die wichtigsten Handelspartner Deutschlands, in: Der Karriereberater, Nr. 6/1997.

Rühl, M., Chancengleichheit managen – Basis moderner Personalpolitik, Frankfurt 2001.

Rummelhagen, M./Schüttauf, K., Assignment "Intercultural Leadership", Stralsund 2007 (unpublished).

Sackmann, S., Toyota's guiding Principles, in: Bertelsmann Stiftung (Hrsg.), Toyota Motor Corporation: Eine Fallstudie aus unternehmenskultureller Perspektive, 2007.

Salacuse, J., Intercultural Negotiation in International Business, in: Group Decision and Negotiation, Vol. 8, No.3, 1999.

Samovar, L. A./Porter, R. E./McDaniel, E. R., Communication Between Cultures, Hampshire 2009.

Saunders, M., Working Together in a Multinational Organization: Erfahrungen mit einem interkulturellem Seminar, in: Kopper/Kiechl (Hrsg.), Globalisierung: Von der Vision zur Praxis, Zürich 1997.

Sautter, H., Japan im Aufbruch – Wandel der Zeit, in: Spiegel „special", Nr. 4/1998.

Schein, E.H., Coming to a new awareness of organizational culture, in: Sloan Management Review 25, Nr. 2, 1984.

Scherm, E., Internationales Personalmanagement, Oldenbourg Verlag, München, Wien 1995.

Schipper, K., Interkulturelles Management – Ein Konzept zur Gestaltung von Entsen-dungsprozessen für den internationalen Einsatz von Fach- und Führungskräften. Berlin 2007.

Schmid, S./ Daniel, A., Die Internationalität der Vorstände und Aufsichtsräte in Deutschland, in: Bertelsmann Stiftung (Hrsg.), Gütersloh 2007.

Schmusch, M., Unternehmensakquisitionen und Shareholder Value, Wiesbaden 1998.

Schneck, O. /Zimmer, A., Handbuch Mergers and Acquisition Management (Wirtz B. W.) 1st edition, Wiesbaden 2006.

Schneider, P., Sieg der Sterne, in: Die Zeit, 30.08.2001.

Schneider, S. C./Barsoux, J., Managing Across Cultures, 2nd ed., Harlow 2003.

Schneider, U./Hirt, C. , Multikulturelles Management. München/Wien 2007.

Scholl, R.F., Internationalisierungsstrategien, in: Macharzina/Welge (Hrsg.), Handwörterbuch Export und Internationale Unternehmung, Stuttgart 1989.

Scholz, J.M., Internationales und interkulturelles Change-Management – Deutungen und Bedeutungen einer Begriffswelt in Gesellschaft, Management und Unternehmerpraxis, in: Scholz, J.M. (Hrsg.), Internationales Change-Management, Stuttgart 1995.

Schrempp, J., DaimlerChrysler bleibt auch eine Mensch AG, in: Die Welt, 19.09.1998.

Schröder, A., Aktuelle Trends im interkulturellen und internationalen Personalmana-gement in Deutschland, 2005, in web:t: http://www.interculture-journal.com/index.php/icj/ article/view/37/41, accessed 15/04/2013.

Schröder, A., Die Betreuung von Mitarbeitern während eines Auslandseinsatze, in: Kühlmann, T.M. (Ed.), Mitarbeiterentsendung ins Ausland, pp.143–160, Göttingen 1995.

Schroll, S., „Kulturschock", in: FAZ, 22.07.2006.

Schroll-Machl, S., Die Zusammenarbeit in internationalen Teams – Eine interkulturelle Herausforderung dargestellt am Beispiel USA – Deutschland, in: Scholz, J.M.(Hrsg.), Internationales Change-Management, Stuttgart 1995.

Schwartz, S. H., Beyond individualism/collectivism. New cultural dimensions of values, in: Kim, U./ Triandis, H.C./ Kagitcibasi, C./ Choi, S./ Yoon, G. (Hrsg.), Individualism and collectivism, theory, method and applications, Thousand Oaks 1994.

Schwartz, S. H., Mapping and interpreting cultural differences around the world, in: Vinken/ Soeters/ Ester (Hrsg.), Comparing cultures, Dimensions of culture in a comparative perspective, 2004.

Schwarz, G., Unternehmenskultur als Element des Strategischen Managements, Berlin 1989.

Schwendter, R., Zur Theorie der Subkultur, in: Gessner/Hassemer (Hrsg.), Frankfurt 1985.

Segler, K., Basisstrategien im internationalen Marketing, Frankfurt/M. 1986.

Seidel, A., Kundenorientierung und Diversity Management, in: Becker, M./Seidel, A., Diversity Management. Unternehmens- und Personalpolitik der Vielfalt, Stuttgart 2006.

Seligman, S.D., Chinese business etiquette: a guide to protocol, manners and culture in the People's Republic of China, New York 1999.

Selmer, J., International Adjustment of business Expatriates: The impact of Age, Gender and Marital Status., in web: http://net2.hkbu.edu.hk/~brc/CCMP200008.pdf, accessed 13/03/2008.

Serdyuk, J., Globalization and Business issues, In: Cross-Cultural Blog: management style and globalization, 22/02/2009, http://web.stanford.edu/group/ccr/blog/2009/02/globalization_and_business_iss.html, accessed 23/06/2014

Sess van, J., Bruner-Traut (Hrsg.), Islam, in: Die fünf großen Weltreligionen, Freiburg 1974.

Shaffer, M.A./Harrison, D.A.,/Gilley, K.M., Dimensions, Determinants, and Differences in the Expatriate Adjustment Process. Journal of International Business Studies, 30(3), 557–581, 1999.

Sharma, A., Innenansichten der großen Religionen, Frankfurt/M 1997.

Shay, J.,/Tracey, J.B. Expatriate managers: Reasons for failure and implications for training. Cornell Hotel and Restaurant Administration, Quarterly, February, pp. 30–35, 1997.

Shell, R., Aufbau eines Joint-Ventures in China, in: Zusammenfassung des Vortrages vom 12.04.1995 an der John-F.-Kennedy Schule in Esslingen

Shen, J. et al., Managing diversity through human resource management: an international perspective and conceptual framework, in: Int. J. of Human Resource Management, February 2009.

Shim, Y.-J./Kim, M.-S./Martin, J. N., Changing Korea: Understanding Culture and Communication, New York 2008.

Shirts, R.G., Bafá Bafá: A Cross-Cultural Simulation, Del Mar 1974.

Shujl, H., Silence, in: Culture and Management in Japan, Tokyo, 1991, S. 113

Siedenbiedel, G., Internationales Management. Elemente der Führung grenzüberschreitend agierender Unternehmen, Köln 1997.

SIETAR (Hrsg.), Keynote-Speech, Kongress 2000, Ludwigshafen.

Sievers, C., Work/family: Key to successful assignment. HR Focus, 75(3), pp. 9–10, 1998.

Simon, H., Die rigorose Globalisierung ist der einzige Weg, in: Welt am Sonntag, Nr. 29/27.07.1996.

Simon, H., Unternehmenskultur – Modeerscheinung oder mehr?, in: Simon, H. (Hrsg.), Herausforderung Unternehmenskultur. USW Schriften für Führungskräfte, Bd. 17, Stuttgart 1990.

Singh, K., Dehli: A Novel, New Delhi 1990.

Singh, K., Gods and Godmen of India, New Delhi 2003.

SkillsYouNeed, Effective Speaking, in web: http://www.skillsyouneed.com/ips/effective-speaking.html, accessed July 22, 2013

SkillsYouNeed, Effective Speaking, in web: http://www.skillsyouneed.com/ips/effective-speaking.html, accessed 22/07/2013.

Slackman, M., A vision of a modern Arab world, in: International Herald Tribune, 23.9.2008

Smith, J. M. H., Teamentwicklung eines multikulturellen und interdisziplinären Projektteams, in: Kopper/Kiechl (Hrsg.), Globalisierung: Von der Vision zur Praxis, Zürich 1997.

Smith, K./ Berg, D., Cross-cultural Groups at Work, in: European Management Journal, Vol. 15, No. 1, Febr. 1997.

Solomon, C.M., Global HR: Repatriation Planning. Workforce, 2002.

Sommer, T., Die asiatische Krankheit, in: Die Zeit, Nr. 28/1998.

Song, S. S., Encyclopedia of Philosophy, in web: http://plato.stanford.edu/entries/multiculturalism/, 24/09/2010, accessed 15/09/2011.

Spitzberg, B.H., Issues in the development of a theory of interpersonal competence in the intercultural context, in: International Journal of Intercultural Relations, 13/1989.

Staehle, W., Management, München, 1991.

Staffelbach, B., Moral Leadership, Daimler-Benz Forum: Verantwortung in Management, Stuttgart 1995.

Stahl, G., Internationaler Einsatz von Führungskräften. München 1998.

Stahl, G.K., Challenges in an International Assignment. Lecture presentation at the University INSEAD, in web: http://faculty.insead.edu/stahl/new/ExpatriateChallenges.pdf, accessed 07/05/2008.

Stahl, G.K., Die Auswahl von Mitarbeitern für den Auslandseinsatz: Wissenschaftliche Grundlagen, in: Kühlmann, T.M (Hrsg.), Mitarbeiterentsendung ins Ausland: Auswahl, Vorbereitung, Betreuung und Wiedereingliederung, Göttingen 1995.

Stahl, G.K./Chua, C.H./Caligiuri, P./Cerdin, J.L./ Taniguchi, M. (2009) Predictors of turnover intentions in learning-driven and demand-driven international assignment: the role of repatriation concern, satisfaction, and perceived career advancement opportunities. Human Resource Management, 48 (1), 89–109.

Steger, M.B, James, P., Ideologies of Globalism, in: Globalization and Culture: Vol. 4, London, 2010

Steger, U., Globalisierung der Wirtschaft. Konsequenzen für Arbeit, Technik und Umwelt, Berlin 1996.

Steger, U., Globalisierung verstehen und gestalten, in: Globalisierung der Wirtschaft Konsequenzen für Arbeit, Technik und Umwelt, Berlin 1996.

Steinle, C./Eichenberg, T./Weber-Rymkovska, J., in: Müller-Stewens, G./Kunisch, S./Binder, Mergers & Acquisitions, Analysen, Trends und Best Practices A., Stuttgart 2010.

Steinmann, H./ Kumar, B.N., Personalpolitische Aspekte von im Ausland tätigen Unternehmen, in Dicht/Issing (Hrsg.), Exporte als Herausforderung für die deutsche Wirtschaft, Köln 1984.

Stern, N., The Economics of Climate Change: The Stern Review, March 2008.

Stickling, E., Kulturelle Unterschiede werden unterschätzt, in: Personalwirtschaft, 07/2007.

Stolte, M., Mit Laptop und Lederhose, in: Rheinischer Merkur, Nr. 20/2006.

Stoner, J.A.F./Aram, J.D./Rubin, J., Factors associated with effective performance in overseas work assignments, Personnel Psychology, 25, 303–318, 1972.

Storti, C., Americans at Work – A Guide to the Can-do People. Intercultural Press 2004, übersetzt in: Globalisierung hautnah, hrsg. v. Andrea Beyer und Rüdiger Nagel, Mainz 2010.

Straksiené, M., Analysis of Idiom Translation Strategies from English into Latvian, in web: http://www.kalbos.lt/zurnalai/14_numeris/03.pdf, accessed 18/07/2013.

Stroh, L.K./Gregersen, H.B./Black, J.S. (2000) Triumphs and tragedies: expectations and commitments upon repatriation. International Journal of Human Resource Management, 11 (4), 681–697.

Sue, D.W./Sue, D., Counseling the culturally different: Theory and practice. New York 1990.

Süß, S./Kleiner, M., Diversity Management in Germany: dissemination and design of the concept, in: Int. J. of Human Resource Management, November 2007.

Tam, P. Outsourcing Sends U.S. Firms to "Trainer", in: The Wall Street Journal – Arab news, 06/03/2006

Tanski, A., Repartiation Checklist, in web: http://www.expatexchange.com/lib.cfm?articleID=273, accessed 24/04/09

Tatli, A., Discourses and Practices of Diversity Management in the UK, in: Klarsfeld, Alain (ed.): International Handbook on Diversity Management at Work: Country Perspectives on Diversity and Equal Treatment, Toulouse 2010.

Teagarden, M.B./ Glinow von, M.A., Human Resource Management in Cross-Cultural Contexts, in: Management International Review, 1/1997.

Teagarden, M.B./ Gordon, G.G., Global Human Resource Management: Corporate Selection Strategies and the Success of International Managers, in Selmer (Hrsg.), Expatriate Management: New Ideas for Business, New York 1994.

Terpsta, V./David, K., The Cultural Environment of International Business, 3rd ed., Cincinnati 1991.

The Hebrew University of Jerusalem. Hebrew U. Prof. Shalom Schwartz awarded 2007 Israel Prize in psychology, Press Release (28.02.2007), in: http://www.huji.ac.il/cgi-bin/dovrut/dovrut_search_eng.pl.

The Scout Association, Valuing Diversity, in web: www.scoutbase.org.uk/library/hqdocs/facts/pdfs/fs185089.pdf, 2005.

Thielen, G., Globalisierung braucht Integration, in: Bertelsmann Stiftung (ed..), Change, Nr. 2/2008.

Thomas, A., Interkulturelle Kompetenz im internationalen Management, in: VolkswagenStiftung (ed.) Wir stiften Wissen, Tagungsband, Dresden 2006.

Thomas, A., Psychologie interkulturellen Lernens und Handelns, in: Thomas (Hrsg.), Kulturvergleichende Psychologie: Eine Einführung, Göttingen 1993.

Thomas, A., Psychologische Bedingungen und Wirkungen internationalen Managements – analysiert am Beispiel deutsch-chinesischer Zusammenarbeit, in: Engelhard, J., Interkulturelles Management, Theoretische Fundierung und funktionsbereichsspezifische Konzepte, Wiesbaden 1997.

Thomas, A./Hagemann, K./Stumpf, S., Training interkultureller Kompetenz. in Bergemann, N./Sourisseaux, A.L.J. (Eds.), Interkulturelles Management, 3rd ed., pp. 237–270, Berlin/Heidelberg/New York 2003.

Thomas, A./ Hagemann, K., Training interkultureller Kompetenz, in: Bergemann, N./ Sourisseaux, A. L.J., Interkulturelles Management, 2., überarbeitete Auflage, Physica Verlag, Heidelberg 1996.

Thomas, A,, Handbook of Intercultural Communication and Cooperation: Basics and Areas of Application, Göttingen 2010.

Thomas, D./Ely, R., Making differences matter: a new paradigm for managing diversity, in: Harvard Business Review, September–October 1996.

Thomas, R. R., Unleashing the power of your total work force by managing diversity, New York 1992.

Thompson, N., Anti Discriminatory Practice, London 1998.

Tiessen, M., Die Rückkehr planen, in: uni 2/2006.

Ting, M., Leadership is not "One Size Fits All" at National Income Life, My Life at NILICO, in web: http://www.mylifeatnilico.com/leadership/leadership-is-not-one-size-fits-all-at-national-income-life/, accessed 25/06/2014

Töpfer, A., Der lange Weg zum Global Player, in: Uni – Special, Internationale Unternehmen, Nr. 3/1995.

Tosi, H.L./Rizzo J. R./Caroll, S.J., Managing Organizational Behaviour, Cambridge 1986.

Travis, E., Advantages & Drawbacks of the Autocratic Leadership Style, Houston Chronicle Online, in web: http://smallbusiness.chron.com/advantages-drawbacks-autocratic-leadership-style-16616.html, accessed 25/06/2014.

Trompenaars, F., Hampden-Turner, Ch., Riding the Waves of Culture, New York 1998.

Trompenaars, F., Riding the waves of culture – understanding cultural diversity in Business, New York 1993.

Tudor, P., Adding Value with Diversity: What Business Leaders Need to Know from Workplace Diversity, Conflict and Productivity, in: Managing in the 21st Century, Volume 1, 2001.

Tung, R.L., Selection and Training of Personnel for Overseas Assignments, in: Columbia Journal of World Business, Nr. 16/1981.

Tung, R.L., Selection and training procedures of US, European and Japanese multinationals. California Management Review, 25, 57–71, 1982.

Tung, R.L., Strategic management of human resources in the multinational enterprise. Human Resource Management, 23, 129–143, 1984.

TÜV SÜD, Make friends, do business; TÜV SÜD Journal, 2nd quarter 2011

Tylor, E.B., Primitive Culture, Band 1, New York 1871.

Udris, I./Frese, M., Belastung, Stress, Beanspruchung und ihre Folgen, in Frey D./ Hoyos, C.G./Stahlberg, D. (Eds.), Angewandte Psychologie: Ein Lehrbuch (pp. 427–447). Weihnheim 1992.

Ulrich, A., The importance of intercultural knowledge for the future, in: BSN, Nr. 16, 2004.

Unger, K.R., Internationale Kommunikationspolitik, in: Krystek/Zur (Hrsg.), Internationalisierung – Eine Herausforderung für die Unternehmensführung, Berlin 1997.

Universität Wien, Diversity – 4 Dimensions of Diversity, in web: http://www.univie.ac.at/diversity/graphics, accessed 23/06/2014

Universität Wien, Vielfalt: Dimensionen, in web: http://www.univie.ac.at/diversity/dimensionen.html, accessed 15/09/2011.

Van der Zee, K.I./Van Oudenhoven, J.P. The Multicultural Personality Questionnaire: Reliability and Validity of Self- and Other Ratings of Multicultural Effectiveness. Journal of Research in Personality, 35(3), 278–288, 2001.

Van Gerven, D., The cross-border directive in Europe. New York: 2010.

Van Swol-Ulbirch, H., Global Nomads: At home in the world. Business-Spotlight, 6, 36–41, 2007.

Varner. I./Beamer, L., Intercultural Communication in the Global Workplace, 5th ed., New York 2011.

Vögel, A.J., Guidelines for the preparation of expatriates on international assignments in South African multinational enterprises, Doctoral dissertation, University of Pretoria, 2006, in web http://upetd.up.ac.za/thesis/available/etd-06282006-164959/.

Volvo Car Corporation (Hrsg.), Discrimination is everyone's business, 2000.

Wagner, W., Kulturschock Deutschland. Hamburg 1996.

Wahren, H-K., Zwischenmenschliche Kommunikation und Interaktion in Unternehmen, Berlin 1987.

Wallacher, J./Au, C./Karcher, T.[ed.] (2011) Ethik in Wirtschaft und Unternehmen in Zeiten der Krise. Stuttgart, W. Kohlhammer Verlag.

Warren, S./Windle, R., Communication Skills, in web: http://www.directionservice.org/cadre/section4.cfm#Paraverbal Messages, accessed 22/07/2013.

Watzlawick, P./Beavin, J.H., Menschliche Kommunikation: Formen, Störungen, Paradoxien. Bern 1969.

Weaver, G.R., Understanding and coping with cross-cultural adjustment stress. In Paige, R.M. (Ed.), Cross-cultural orientation: New conceptualizations and applications (pp. 111–145). Lanham 1986.

Weaver, G.,R., Connecting Intercultural Communication and Management, in: Intercultural Management Institute, Washington, DC, Nr. 9/2001.

Weber, W./Festing, M./ Dowling, P.J./Schuler, Internationales Personalmanagement, 2nd ed., Wiesbaden 2001.

Weber, W./Festing, M./Dowling, P. J./Schuler, R. S., Internationales Personalmanagement, Wiesbaden 1998.

Wederspahn, G.M., Costing failures in expatriate human resources management. Human Resource Planning, 15, 27–35, 2002.

Weidmann, W.F., Interkulturelle Kommunikation und nationale Kulturunterschiede in der Managementpraxis, in: Scholz, J.M. (Hrsg.), Internationales Change-Management, Stuttgart 1995.

Weiss, S., Globale Interaktion, In: Bertelsmann Stiftung (Hrsg.), Jahresbericht 2006.

Welge, M./Al-Laham, A., Strategisches Management: Grundlagen – Prozess – Implementierung, 5th ed., 2008.

Welge, M./Holtbrügge, D., Internationales Management, Landsberg/Lech 1998.

Welt Online, Mars und Warren Buffett übernehmen Wrigley, in: http://www.welt.de/wirtschaft/article1944557/Mars_und_Warren_Buffett_uebernehmen_Wrigley.html, 18.04.2008.

Wengert, V. Kulturschock-Phänomene im Erleben deutschsprachiger temporärer Arbeitsmigranten in Russland, in web: http://soemz.euv-frankfurt-o.de/mik/inhalt.htm, accessed 28/02/2008.

Westcombe, J., Boye, S., Mind the gap: Culture in pictures, in: Spotlight, 5/2012.

Wickel-Kirsch, S., Fehlende Reintegrationsplanung, in: Die Personalwirtschaft, Nr. 2/2004.

Wickel-Kirsch, S./ Schütz, M./ Berlich, I., Stolpersteine auf dem Weg zum Weltmarkt, in: Personalwirtschaft Nr. 10/2005.

Wiesenthal, H., Unsicherheit und Multiple-Self-Identität. Eine Spekulation über die Voraussetzungen strategischen Handelns, Köln 1990.

Williams, J., Don't they know it's Friday, Cross-Cultural Considerations for Business and Life in the Gulf, Ajman 2004.

Wilson, D./Donaldson, L., Russian Etiquette & Business Ethics in Business, (Lincolwood) Chicago, 1996.

Windham International,Global Relocation Trends, New York 1998.

Windham International/National Foreign Trade Council, Global Relocation, 2006.

Windham International, & National Foreign Trade Council., Global Relocation Trends Survey, 2006, in web: http://www.gmacglobalrelocation.com/insight_support/grts.asp, accessed 29/04/2008.

Workpapers Mitte Consult, Four Layers of Diversity, in: Managing Diversity – A business tool, 2004.

World Values Survey Association, The World Values Survey: Questionnaires of 2005, 2000, 1995, unter: http://www.worldvaluessurvey.org/index _surveys, 2012.

World Values Survey, Values Change the World, unter: http://www.worldvalues survey.org/wvs/articles/folder_published/article_base_110/files/WVSbrochure6-2008_ 11.pdf, 2008.

WorldBusinessCulture.com, Business Culture in China: Chinese Management Style, in web: http://www.worldbusinessculture.com/Chinese-Management-Style.html, accessed 29/06/2014.

Wunderer, R., Vom bayerischen Kirchturm zur europäischen Kathedrale?, in: SZ, Nr. 243, (S. 117), 01.10.1992.

Yavas, U./Bodur, M., Correlates of Adjustment: A Study of Expatriate Managers in an Emerging Country. Management Decision, 37(3), pp. 267–278, 1999.

Yershova, Y./DeJeagbere, J.,/Mestenhauser, J., Thinking not as usual: Adding the intercultural perspective. Journal of Studies in International Education, 4 (1), 59–78, 2000.

Zeck, M., Andere Kulturen haben eine eigene Logik – Interview mit Susanne Hoppe, FAZ, 10/11.03.2012.

Zubko, K.C./Sahay R.R., Inside the Indian Business Mind, Jaico Publishing House, Mumbai 2011

Zwierlein, E., Moral Leadership?, Das Plädoyer des advocatus diaboli, Daimler-Benz Forum: Verantwortung in Management, Stuttgart 1995.

Index

www.ingramcontent.com/pod-product-compliance
Lightning Source LLC
Chambersburg PA
CBHW081048220326
41598CB00038B/7026